22826

D1427225

James, Brother of Jesus

Pierre-Antoine Bernheim

SCM PRESS LTD

Translated by John Bowden from the French,
Jacques, Frère de Jésus, published 1996
by Éditions Noêsis, 12 rue de Savoie, Paris VIe

0 334 02695 4

First published 1997 by
SCM Press Ltd
9–17 St Albans Place London N1 0NX

Typeset by Regent Typesetting, London
and printed in Great Britain by
Biddles Ltd, Guildford and King's Lynn

Contents

Acknowledgments

I am most grateful to Professors Maurice-Ruben Hayoun, Francis Kaplan, Hedwige Rouillard-Bonraisin, Etienne Trocmé, to Dr Markus Bockmuehl, and to the Revd Dr John Bowden and Monsieur Jacques Duquesne for their encouragement, suggestions and criticisms. I am grateful to Dr William Horbury for having allowed me to present my ideas to his seminar at the University of Cambridge.

To Sandra
and Cynthia

Introduction

Thanks to the Jewish historian Joseph ben Mattathias (37–c.100), better known under the name of Flavius Josephus, we are relatively well informed about the history of Palestine in the time of Jesus and the first Christians. However, without the interest that the church fathers showed in him, beyond question his works would never have reached us. For them, the testimony of Flavius Josephus was of inestimable value because it mentioned Jesus twice. The first reference appears in Book 18 of the *Jewish Antiquities*. This is the famous and very controversial *Testimonium Flavianum*:

> About this time there lived Jesus, a wise man, if indeed one ought to call him a man. For he was one who wrought surprising feats and was a leader of such people as accept the truth gladly. He won over many Jews and many of the Greeks. He was the Christ [the Messiah]. When Pilate, upon hearing him accused by men of the highest standing among us, had condemned him to be crucified, those who had in the first place come to love him did not give up their affection for him. On the third day he appeared to them restored to life, for the prophets of God had prophesied these and countless other marvellous things about him. And the tribe of the Christians, so-called after him, has still to this day not disappeared.[1]

There is hardly any doubt that this apologetic text, steeped in Christian conceptions, could not have been composed by Josephus, who, according to the testimony of Origen (c.185–254), did not believe in Jesus. For some scholars it is simply a gross forgery done by some clumsy and unscrupulous copyist. Nevertheless, the majority of experts think that the copyist contented himself with revising an original text of Josephus in a Christian direction. To support their thesis they cite the second mention of Jesus, this time an indirect one, in Book 20 of the same work. The event related can be dated to the year 62 of our era. Shortly after the death of Festus, the procurator of Judaea, the emperor Nero sent Albinus to replace him. At almost the same moment Agrippa II, king of Galilee and Peraea, made Hanan high priest:

Hanan the younger . . . had a proud character and remarkable courage: he followed the teaching of the Sadducees, who are unbending in their views compared with other Jews . . . He thought he had now a proper opportunity. Festus was now dead, and Albinus was but upon the road. So he assembled the Sanhedrin of judges, and brought before them the brother of Jesus who was called Christ, whose name was James, and some others. And when he had formed an accusation against them as breakers of the law, he delivered them to be stoned. But those who seemed the most equitable of the citizens, and accurate in legal matters, disliked what was done. They also sent to King Agrippa, desiring him to send to Hanan that he should act so no more; for what he had already done was not to be justified. Indeed, some of them went also to meet Albinus, as he was upon his journey from Alexandria, and informed him that it was not lawful for Hanan to assemble a Sanhedrin without his consent. Albinus was persuaded by what they said, and wrote in anger to Hanan, and threatened that he would bring him to punishment for what he had done. On which account King Agrippa took the high priesthood from him when he had ruled only three months, and made Jesus the son of Damneus high priest.[2]

This passage is generally considered authentic.[3] A Christian interpolator would surely not have spoken of Jesus and of the martyrdom of James in so neutral a way. Moreover it would be very difficult to understand what could have motivated a possible forgery. This passage contains the only mention in the works of Josephus of an event involving the primitive church. Nowhere in either the *Jewish War* or the *Jewish Antiquities* is there mention of Peter, Paul, Stephen or James the son of Zebedee. John Dominic Crossan, one of the leading experts on Jesus and the New Testament, recently investigated this disconcerting text.[4] How could the death of James have prompted the dismissal of so powerful a man as Hanan, a member of a family which had produced eight high priests in sixty years? Was James an important figure with powerful allies in Jerusalem?

In his treatise *Against Celsus*,[5] the great theologian Origen explains that according to Josephus the punishment inflicted on the Jews for the murder of James was the destruction of Jerusalem in 70. Eusebius of Caesarea[6] (died 340) and Jerome[7] (c.347–420) also express this opinion, though curiously it does not appear in the manuscripts of the *Jewish Antiquities* that we have. Whether or not it comes from Josephus, this interpretation of the fall of Jerusalem must have enjoyed some popularity in various Christian circles.

The existence of a brother of Jesus called James is confirmed by several writings of the New Testament. We learn in the Gospels of Matthew (13.55) and Mark (6.3) that Jesus had four brothers, one of whom was called James. There is no reason to suppose that this James was not the person put to death by Hanan. Written during the 50s, the letters of Paul, probably the earliest New Testament texts, present James, the brother of Jesus, as one of the leaders of the primitive church. In his letter to the Galatians (1.18–19), Paul relates that during his stay in Jerusalem three years after his conversion he saw only Peter, whom he had come to visit, and 'James the brother of the Lord'. Without again being described as brother of the Lord, James is mentioned twice more in the letter to the Galatians (2.9; 2.12). Thus Paul tells us that at the time of his second visit to Jerusalem, fourteen years after the first, i.e. around 50, he met James, Peter and John, who are described as 'pillars' of the church. We should note that James is mentioned first. This important meeting, somewhat pompously called the 'Council of Jerusalem', made a decision on a key question: could pagans become Christians without having to be converted to Judaism? A little later, at the time of the incident in Antioch, to which we shall be returning often, people sent by James led Peter to modify his behaviour towards Christians of pagan origin. In his first letter to the Corinthians (15.7), Paul indicates that Jesus appeared to James. There is hardly any doubt that he is referring to the person whom he calls the brother of the Lord in Galatians 1.19.

The Acts of the Apostles refers three times (12.17; 15.13; 21.18) to a James who seems to be very important. The author of Acts, traditionally called Luke,[8] is not specific about his identity. However, it is generally thought that this is James whom Paul calls the brother of the Lord. In the version of the Council of Jerusalem given in the Acts of the Apostles, James presides over the meeting and takes the final decision (15.6–29). The last mention of James is at the time of Paul's visit to Jerusalem, around 56 or 57, which leads to his arrest. James again appears as the head of the Jerusalem church. His killing, which is not mentioned in the New Testament, thus took place five or six years after Paul's arrest.

So the New Testament, corroborating Josephus' account, reveals to us the existence of a James, described as brother of Jesus, who was one of the key figures of the primitive church and seems to have been head of the Christian movement around the 50s.

During the first two or three centuries of the Christian church, James enjoyed a considerable, almost mythical, reputation.[9] The veneration of which he was the object was particularly strong in so-called Jewish-Christian circles. The definition of the term 'Jewish-Christian' has led to many discussions. Some scholars, like Jean Daniélou, emphasize the use of concepts and structures of Jewish thought.[10] Others, who are more numerous, like Marcel Simon, put observance of the Mosaic law first.[11] Adopting this latter approach, I shall call Jewish Christians those Jews by birth or conversion who observed all or the greater part of the precepts of the Mosaic law while believing that Jesus was the Messiah, a prophet like Moses or another exalted figure. During the three or four decades following the death of Christ, the vast majority of Christians were in fact Jewish Christians. They would certainly have been surprised had they been told that they were no longer Jews. With the success of the missions among the Gentiles, they saw their influence progressively diminish until it became very marginal; indeed by the third century they found themselves being called heretics. In the Gospel of the Hebrews (see p.98), an apocryphal text[12] which was popular in the Jewish-Christian tradition, the risen Christ gives James the privilege of witnessing his first appearance. The so-called Pseudo-Clementine literature,[13] composed in the fourth century but incorporating Jewish-Christian sources dating from the second, puts the primacy of James at the forefront: he is described as bishop of bishops; in other words, the anachronism apart, the first pope.

James also enjoyed great prestige in the catholic church during the first centuries of our era. Hegesippus,[14] a Christian perhaps of Jewish origin, who lived during the second half of the second century, collected various traditions about him in his memoirs. Fragments of this text are known to us principally through Eusebius of Caesarea, who quotes them in his *Church History*. The traditions handed down by Hegesippus emphasize the very great piety of James and his pre-eminence in the primitive church.

> James, the brother of the Lord, received [the administration of] the church with the apostles. From the time of the Lord to our own, all call him the Just, because many bore the name of James. This man was sanctified from his mother's womb.[15]

There follows an almost legendary evocation of the immense piety of James and a long and imaginative description of his martyrdom which would be taken up many times in Christian hagiography (see pp.253–4).

Clement of Alexandria in his *Hypotyposes*, composed around 200, presents James as the first head of the Jerusalem church.[16] Clement doubtless considered James the supreme authority of the church after the death of Christ (see pp.219–21).

Origen[17] and Eusebius[18] emphasize how eminent James was. However, they tend to reduce his role, subordinating it to that of the twelve apostles. Epiphanius of Salamis (c.315–403), in his treatise on the heresies (*Panarion*), indicates that James was the first bishop of Jerusalem.[19] Jerome mentions him numerous times in his voluminous work. He describes him second, after Peter, in his collection of accounts of the great men of the church (*De viris illustribus*). The notice on James is the longest after that on Paul. Jerome is also the author of a major innovation which considerably influenced the posthumous career of James in the catholic church. Until then James was considered the brother or half-brother of Jesus. Moreover he was not generally included among the Twelve. By means of a highly subtle demonstration, Jerome tried to prove that James, the brother of the Lord, had to be identified with James son of Alphaeus, one of the Twelve, and with James the Little, or the Less, mentioned in Mark 15.40.[20] The identification proposed by Jerome was accepted by the Roman Catholic Church. Although it is rejected today by all serious exegetes, it is still maintained in popular and devotional works. The Orthodox churches distinguish the two Jameses and celebrate them separately.

Several texts with a Gnostic tendency which appear among the manuscripts found at Nag Hammadi[21] give James a pre-eminent position in the primitive church. He is presented as the main beneficiary of the teaching of Jesus. In the Gospel of Thomas, a text which is at least sometimes Gnosticizing, if not Gnostic (see p.99), Jesus designates James the Just as the one whom his disciples are to follow after his own departure (Logion 12). In the Apocryphal Letter of James,[22] a text from the beginning of the second century with Gnostic features, Jesus reveals his teaching to James and Peter, the pre-eminence of James being suggested several times (15.5–9; 16.5–9). In the two Apocalypses of James[23] in Nag Hammadi Codex V, Jesus hands on to James a secret teaching of an entirely Gnostic nature.

The pre-eminence accorded to James in many Jewish-Christian, Catholic and Gnostic traditions is quite remarkable. These traditions have passed on the lofty image which James enjoyed in the primitive Jerusalem church and in the other communities which had a majority of Jewish Christians.

Christian movements with very different and often opposing ideas resorted to the authority and the prestige of James to guarantee the antiquity and orthodoxy of their conceptions.

However, James the brother of the Lord remains largely unknown to most Christians. The equal, not to say the superior, of Peter and Paul right at the beginning of the church, today he has been doubly eclipsed by the former, whom Catholics consider to be the first pope, and the latter, who is unanimously described as the *prince* of theologians. Called James the Less, he is even clearly outstripped in popular devotion by his namesake, the son of Zebedee, who, elevated by the title 'the Great', is celebrated at Santiago di Compostela. The extreme poverty of his iconography is the best indication of the oblivion into which James has fallen. B. H. Streeter, one of the greatest English exegetes at the beginning of the century, taking up a reflection by the famous Anglican bishop and scholar J. B. Lightfoot, emphasized how unjust posterity had been to the brother of Jesus:

> It becomes clear that James of Jerusalem ranks with Peter and Paul as one of the three outstanding individuals by whose personal gifts and influence was determined, humanly speaking, the future development of the Primitive Church. It is one of the ironies of history that his name does not appear in the Calendar of Saints in the Western Church – he having been wrongly identified with James the Less, the son of Alphaeus, one of the inconspicuous members of the Twelve.[24]

Unknown to the wider public, sometimes confused with the son of Zebedee, the brother of the Lord has certainly not been ignored by exegetes and church historians. For around thirty years, academic circles have become increasingly infatuated with James and the Jewish Christians. This revival of interest is part of a new orientation aimed at integrating Jesus and the primitive church better into the Judaism of their time. The majority of impartial experts accept the central place of James, at any rate from the 40s. In his book on the earliest church, Cardinal Daniélou does not hesitate to write that 'it was the party of James and the Jewish Christian church of Jerusalem that exercised the dominant influence during the first decades of the church'.[25]

Despite his pre-eminent position in the primitive church, James remains an enigmatic figure who is not at all well known. The Gospels show hardly any interest in him. They include him among the brothers of Jesus, who are mentioned above all for their lack of belief, but without singling him out. The Acts of the Apostles and the letters of Paul give us hardly any specific information about him, although they present him as a key figure, at the centre of fundamental conflicts. What they do is to show us more of a presence, a kind of Commendatore's statue, rather than a being of flesh and blood. The letter which bears his name cannot be attributed to him with any certainty. But, even accepting that this text is authentic or could reflect his theological views, it tells us very little about his life. Later Christian literature, which is more prolix, cheerfully mixes history and legend. So there could be no question of retracing James's life, as one might do, with courage and imagination, in the case of Paul. That is why I see James above all as the symbol and the most eminent representative of a primitive church firmly anchored in the Judaism of its time and faithful to the Mosaic law. Through him, it is that church which we shall be investigating.

That having been said, answers must be attempted to the questions that everyone asks. What relation was James to Jesus? Was he his brother, as a literal interpretation of the New Testament suggests; his cousin, as is supposed by the Catholic tradition since Jerome; or his half-brother, as numerous church fathers thought? To what degree did his kinship with Jesus favour his rise to become head of the church?

But these questions, which one might describe as biographical, raise a host of others. How did James who, according to the Gospels, did not believe in Jesus, become the chief authority in the Christian movement? Should we not reconsider the nature of the relations between Jesus and his brothers? And similarly, what was the nature of the relations between Peter and James? Why is it the latter, and not the former, who appears as the most influential figure in the church at the time of the Council of Jerusalem?

In another area, one has also to ask why James continued faithfully to respect the law, whereas, according to many exegetes, Jesus is said to have raised radical questions about it. Did James betray the meaning of the activity and the message of Jesus? Did he support Paul's missionary activity, as is suggested by the Acts of the Apostles, or did he have far more reservations? Was he even hostile, as some letters of Paul and Jewish-Christian traditions suggest? Why did the killing of James by the high priest Hanan provoke the protests of the Pharisees and the dismissal of the high priest? What happened to the Jewish Christians after the death of James? Finally, and perhaps above all, how can we explain the oblivion into which James has fallen in Christian tradition?

In an attempt to answer such very different questions we shall first investigate the nature of Judaism at the time of the birth of Christ, and the person and message of Jesus. Then we shall tackle the history of the early church, not from the perspective of the groups and ideologies which were to triumph later, but from that of the groups and ideologies whom history did not favour, although they were dominant at the time. In setting out in search of James, this vision of the forgotten and the defeated is the one that I shall try to reconstruct.

I

Brother of Jesus?

Was James, who is described as the brother of Jesus in the Gospels, the Letter to the Galatians and the Acts of the Apostles, a son of Mary and Joseph, born after Jesus? In a recent book, the Catholic exegete Philippe Rolland is indignant that anyone could reply in the affirmative: 'It may be repeated in good faith . . . that Jesus had brothers and sisters, born of Mary and Joseph. But anyone who claims to have studied all aspects of the question and to have been compelled to come to this conclusion is displaying notorious incompetence, even if he benefits from the attention of the media.'[1] On the other hand, for Maurice Goguel, the great Protestant historian of Jesus and the primitive church, 'from the historical point of view the question of the brothers of Jesus is not a problem; it is a problem in Catholic dogma only'.[2]

We can see that this is a delicate subject. This has recently become clear once again, on the publication of two books about Jesus defending the notion of biological brothers.[3] Doesn't the existence of brothers and sisters contradict a fundamental belief of the Roman Catholic Church, namely the perpetual virginity of Mary?[4] The first official mention of Mary's perpetual virginity appeared in 374, in the creed of Epiphanius which developed the Nicene Creed. This notion, affirmed by the Second Council of Constantinople (553) and the Lateran Council (649), is one of the most constantly recurring teachings of the Catholic Church, even if it has never been the object of an extraordinary, infallible declaration by that church.

Before beginning to answer this question, let us first look at the passages in the New Testament in which the brothers and sisters of Jesus are mentioned.

Scriptural evidence

The evidence in Paul can be found in two texts, the authenticity of which is indisputable, the First Letter to the Corinthians and the Letter to the Galatians, both of which can be dated at the beginning of the 50s of our era. Paul is certainly a witness of prime importance in that he knew James personally. Though Paul mentions James three times in Galatians, only the first reference describes him as brother of the Lord. When Paul went to Jerusalem three years after his 'conversion' to pay a visit to Cephas (Peter), he did not see 'other apostles, but only James, the brother of the Lord' (Gal. 1.19). It is important to note here that the end of the phrase could also be translated 'other than/ except for James, the brother of the Lord'.

In I Corinthians, Paul refers to the brothers of the Lord without mentioning their names:

> Do we not have the right to our food and drink? Do we not have the right to be accompanied by a wife, as the other apostles and the brothers of the Lord and Cephas? (9.4–5).

It is quite clear that Paul describes only a few specific individuals as 'brother of the Lord'. The term is certainly not a synonym for disciple. Moreover Paul never describes Peter, John or Barnabas as a brother of the Lord.

The Gospels refer to the brothers and sometimes also the sisters[5] of Jesus several times. The so-called Synoptic[6] Gospels, attributed to Matthew, Mark and Luke, mention the brothers (and sisters) of Jesus in connection with two episodes. In the first, the mother and the brothers of Jesus try to see him (Matt. 12.46–50/Mark 3.31–35/Luke 8.19–21). Here is the Markan version, which I have extracted from a longer account (see pp. 77f. below).

> And his mother and his brothers came; and standing outside they sent to him and called him. And a crowd was sitting about him; and they said to him, 'Your mother and your brothers are outside, asking for you.' And he replied, 'Who are my mother and my brothers?' And looking around on

those who sat about him, he said, 'Here are my mother and my brothers! Whoever does the will of God is my brother, and sister, and mother.'

The second reference to the brothers of Jesus (Matt. 13.53–58/Mark 6.1–6), which is absent from Luke, occurs in the account of the rejection of Jesus at Nazareth. This is how it reads in Mark 6.3:

Is not this the carpenter, the son of Mary and brother of James and Joses and Judas and Simon, and are not his sisters here with us?

Matthew changes the order of the names and replaces the diminutive Joses with Joseph (13.55). Mark 6.3 and Matthew 13.55 are the only passages in the New Testament in which the number of the brothers of Jesus is given as well as their names. The number of sisters and their names are not indicated anywhere in the New Testament. According to later traditions, to be treated with caution, Jesus had two sisters called Miriam and Salome.

The brothers of Jesus appear twice in the Gospel of John without their names being mentioned. After the episode of the marriage at Cana, Jesus 'went down to Capernaum, with his mother and his brothers and his disciples' (John 2.12). Shortly afterwards, his brothers advise Jesus to go to Judaea to show the wonders of which he is capable (John 7.3–4). This request is followed by a phrase in which the author of the Gospel expresses the unbelief of Jesus' brothers: 'For even his brothers did not believe in him' (John 7.5).

As I have already indicated, the Acts of the Apostles contains three references to James, in which he is never described as brother of the Lord. On the other hand, the author refers to the brothers of Jesus when he describes the activity of the disciples just after the ascension: 'All [the apostles] with one accord devoted themselves to prayer, together with the women and Mary the mother of Jesus, and with his brothers' (Acts 1.14).

Two preliminary conclusions could be drawn from this first group of texts. First, it seems clear that contrary to a notion widespread among many believers, the word 'brother' cannot have the figurative sense of companion or fellow-believer, because in certain passages the brothers of Jesus are explicitly contrasted with his disciples, i.e. his spiritual family. Secondly, in most of the references in the Gospels and the Acts of the Apostles, the brothers of Jesus are associated with Mary, his mother.

Opposing theories

The kinship between Jesus and his 'brothers' does not seems to have provoked debates in the church before the middle of the second century. This question probably did not arise because up to that point the doctrine of the perpetual virginity of Mary did not yet exist. From then on the expression 'brothers and sisters' of Jesus has been understood in three different ways.[7]

According to the first and most natural view, the brothers and sisters of Jesus would simply be the children of Joseph and Mary born after Jesus. So they would be the biological brothers of Jesus or, for those who believe in his virgin birth, only his half-brothers (and sisters). This theory is generally called Helvidian in scholarly circles, after Helvidius, one of its defenders at the end of the fourth century. Apart from Helvidius himself, who is quite an obscure figure, it was supported by Hegesippus,[8] Tertullian[9] (died c.225) and Bonosius (died 400) in the early church.[10] From the fifth century, when it became heretical, this theory received hardly any further backing until the appearance of critical studies on the New Testament two centuries ago. In our day it is accepted by the majority of Protestant exegetes and a number of eminent Catholic exegetes whose scholarly probity is stronger than their dogmatic alignment. Thus in his outstanding commentary on Mark,[11] the German exegete R. Pesch has supported the Helvidian theory. Although his position provoked torrents of protest from German Catholics, Pesch has not yet been excommunicated. More recently, in his big book on Jesus, J. P. Meier, professor at the Catholic University of America and one of the foremost New Testament scholars of our day, has argued that 'from a purely philological and historical point of view, the most probable opinion is that the brothers and sisters of Jesus were his siblings.'[12] The Dominican François Refoulé, former director of the École Biblique in Jerusalem, largely agrees with Meier's conclusions: 'For the exegete and the historian, the brothers and sisters of Jesus are in all probability his blood brothers and sisters.'[13]

According to the second interpretation, James and his brothers would come from a first marriage of Joseph's. This theory is called Epiphanian, after Epiphanius, bishop of Salamis, who was among its famous supporters. It appears for the first time in the Protevangelium of James, an apocryphal work dating from the middle of the second century, and quickly became established in the early church because it did not contradict the increasingly widespread belief in the perpetual virginity of Mary. In addition to Epiphanius, Clement of Alexandria, Origen, Eusebius and many other church fathers adopted it. It is still the dominant position within the Orthodox churches. However, in the Roman Catholic Church it has been eclipsed by the third interpretation, which is due to the ingenuity of Jerome. Nowadays there is hardly any support for the Epiphanian theory. Its last famous defender was J. B. Lightfoot, the great nineteenth-century exegete. We may note that Richard Bauckham, professor at the University of St Andrews, has recently tried to rehabilitate it.[14]

According to the third theory, called Hieronymian after Jerome, who invented it, the brothers would have been first cousins of Jesus. There are several variants of this interpretation, but in Jerome's original version these cousins of Christ were the sons of a sister of Mary called Mary of Clopas. This argument appeared for the first time in the treatise *Against Helvidius*, published around 383 by Jerome in order to refute the theory, recently made fashionable by Helvidius, that the brothers were biological brothers. As we saw earlier, Jerome introduced another original idea which gained ground. He suggested that James the brother of the Lord was none other than James son of Alphaeus, one of the twelve apostles. This suggestion rapidly became established in the Roman Catholic Church, which decided to identify the two Jameses and to devote a single festival, 3 May, to them. In the Catholic tradition,

James the brother of the Lord/James son of Alphaeus is known above all under the name of St James the Less, as opposed to St James the Great, son of Zebedee.

Let us now look at these theories more closely.

The Helvidian theory

We may recall that according to this interpretation James and his brothers will have been the children of Mary and Joseph born after Jesus. This is the most natural interpretation of the New Testament texts. A 'Persian' reader, impartial and ignorant of dogmas and doctrinal controversies, would certainly come to this conclusion. The Greek word which appears in all the key passages is *adelphos*, which, when it is not used in a figurative sense, always refers to brothers born of the same parents or at least to the same mother. Now we have seen that a figurative sense is ruled out. We can also note that the Gospels mention two groups of brothers among the apostles: Peter and Andrew, James and John. To my knowledge no one has supposed that these were not biological brothers.[15] Similarly, we have seen that the brothers of Jesus almost always appear in the company of Mary, which allows us to suppose that she was their mother. Furthermore John's remark (7.5), 'For even his brothers did not believe in him' would lose much of its force if these were not the true brothers of Jesus.

The evidence mentioned earlier from Josephus, who was one of the temple priests at the time of the execution of James, and who calls him the brother of Jesus, should also be emphasized.

We must now ask whether there are other passages in the New Testament which allow us to dismiss or confirm this interpretation.

The opponents of the Helvidian theory usually stress the words which, according to the Gospel of John (19.26–27), Jesus on the cross is said to have addressed to his mother before his death:

When Jesus saw his mother, and the disciple whom he loved standing by, he said to his mother, 'Woman, behold, your son!' Then he said to the disciple, 'Behold, your mother!' And from that hour the disciple took her to his own home.

Following Epiphanius, Hilary of Poitiers (c.315–367) and Jerome, they put forward the following argument. Had Mary had other children living at the time of the crucifixion, these would certainly have taken her in, and the beloved disciple would not have been required to treat her as his own mother. However, this argument has been almost completely dropped by modern commentators. First of all, the authenticity of this dialogue is suspect, since it is not reported in the Synoptic Gospels, which moreover seem to rule it out, since according to them neither the mother of Jesus nor any disciples were near the cross. Furthermore, be this as it may, all present-day scholars see these words of Jesus as something other than a mark of filial piety. In a text steeped in theological considerations, it would be amazing for the last significant words of Jesus to be devoted to the well-being of his mother, about whom he did not seem to be very concerned up to that point.[16] So these words certainly bear an important message, even if the interpretation of them has given rise to much speculation.[17] However, it is probably best to rule out too far-fetched symbolic explanations and suppose simply that Jesus, in affirming the primacy of the beloved disciple, is making him his brother and his successor.[18] One could also accept that in this way Jesus was designating the disciple whom he loved and his community as his true family, placed under the spiritual motherhood of Mary.

Another argument which is at the foundation of the Hieronymian theory is based on the identification of James and Joses mentioned in Mark 6.3 and Matthew 13.55 with James the Less and Joses in Mark 15.40 and Matthew 27.56. But we shall have occasion to discuss this question in detail later.

For the great majority of Catholics, the existence of half-brothers of Jesus is *a priori* unacceptable since it contradicts the dogma of the perpetual virginity of Mary. But such a belief cannot seriously be based on the New Testament texts. First we must note that the virgin birth of Jesus is attested indisputably only in the Gospels of Matthew and Luke.[19] Mary's perpetual virginity (*post partum,* in the jargon of theologians) is not

affirmed anywhere in the New Testament. About fifteen years
ago an inter-confessional group of twelve distinguished exegetes
published an important work on *Mary in the New Testament*.
They agreed on the following points:[20]

– the question of the virginity of Mary after the birth of Jesus is
  not directly raised in the New Testament;
– it was this question which, once it was raised at a later period
  of church history, called attention to the precise nature of the
  kinship between Jesus and his brothers.

That did not prevent one of the collaborators in the very
Catholic *Jerusalem Bible* from writing in a note that Mary's perpetual virginity is, if not affirmed, at least supposed in the New
Testament.[21] Quite apart from the fact that the brothers and
sisters of Jesus are mentioned without any additional qualification, two further passages seem to contradict the notion of perpetual virginity.

According to Luke 2.7, Mary gave birth to 'her firstborn
son'.[22] The author of the Gospel of Luke wants above all to
emphasize the privileges granted to Jesus as the firstborn of a
family of the Davidic line. However, while the expression does
not necessarily imply the existence of later children, it does
suggest it. The Gospel of Matthew mentions that Joseph 'took
his wife, but knew her not until she had borne a son' (1.24–25).
The verb 'know' certainly bears the biblical meaning of having
sexual intercourse. The author wants above all to emphasize
that the birth of Jesus cannot in any way be imputed to Joseph's
action. The nature of relations between Joseph and his wife
after the birth of Jesus clearly does not interest him. Nevertheless, the expression used suggests that they they had normal
conjugal relations. The evangelist would certainly not have used
such an ambiguous expression had he believed in the perpetual
virginity of Mary, above all since later he several times mentions
the existence of brothers and sisters of Jesus.

Granted, neither of the two passages we have looked at so
far is in itself decisive proof of the existence of biological
brothers of Jesus. However, if we consider them in the context
of the repeated use of the word 'brothers' and the constant
association of these last with the mother of Jesus, we can see

clearly that the authors of Matthew and Luke made no attempt to dissuade their readers from believing in the existence of brothers of Jesus. The burden of proof is in fact on the side of those who deny the natural interpretation of the texts. So let us study the arguments put forward by the supporters of other interpretations.

The Epiphanian theory

There is little to say about this reading, according to which the brothers and sisters of Jesus will have come from a first marriage of Joseph. While no passage in the New Testament suggests this, none allows us to reject it. It is not incompatible either with the use of the word *adelphos* or with the association of the brothers of Jesus with Mary. However, it makes it difficult to understand Luke's emphasis (2.7; 2.22–24) on the primogeniture of Jesus,[23] for if Joseph had had other older sons, the fact that Jesus had been the first son of Mary would not have given him any family pre-eminence in inheriting the kingdom of David.

The vast majority of present-day exegetes regard the Epiphanian theory with scepticism.[24] The fact that it appears for the first time in the Protevangelium of James does not give it much credibility. This work, which betrays a flagrant lack of knowledge of the geography of Palestine and Jewish customs,[25] contains numerous legendary elements. The Protevangelium of James deals above all with the miraculous conception of Mary and her childhood. Several times the priests predict an exceptional destiny for the young girl. At the age of twelve, on a sign from the Lord, she is entrusted to the care of Joseph, an old widower. Joseph first of all expresses reluctance: 'I have sons and am old, but she is a girl. I fear lest I should become a laughing-stock to the children of Israel.'[26] Then he yields to the pressing demands of the priests. The end of the Protevangelium, which then draws on Luke and Matthew, is devoted to the virgin birth of Jesus.

To give credibility to his account, the author presents himself as James. He mentions that he wrote this account shortly after the death of Herod. Naturally identified with one of the sons born of Joseph's first marriage, James then seems to the reader to have been an adult at the time of the birth of Jesus.

The Protevangelium of James is the first Christian work to the glory of the Virgin.[27] In addition to defending the virgin birth of Jesus, it suggests the perpetual virginity of Mary. Joseph is presented here as an old man, which makes any sexual relations with his young wife after the birth of Jesus improbable. Later texts were to develop this idea. Thus Epiphanius's *Panarion*, written around 370, tells us that Joseph was aged at least eighty when he took Mary as his spouse.

The Epiphanian theory became very popular because of the increasing importance attached to chastity in Christian piety. As Origen, one of its famous supporters, admits, its success was due more to ideological considerations than to solid historical traditions:

> Those who profess this [Epiphanian] opinion desire to pre-serve the honour of Mary as concerns her virginity . . . And I think that it is reasonable that, just as Jesus gave the first example of chastity among men, Mary should have done so among women. It would not be appropriate to attribute it to another woman.[28]

Richard Bauckham has recently produced several new arguments to support this view. However, they are not enough to make it completely credible.

The Hieronymian theory and its variants

Around 380 in Rome, a certain Helvidius published a work in which he argued with the support of scriptural proofs for the old view that James and his brothers were sons of Joseph and Mary born after Jesus. Some years later, Jerome wrote a short treatise to refute this interpretation, which had regained popularity. Jerome also attacked the Epiphanian theory, which scandalized him almost as much. Christ, who had come to teach virginity, could only have been brought up by virgins. Jerome went on to put forward a new theory which also preserved the virginity of Joseph, making James and his brothers first cousins of Jesus. Jerome's demonstration and his refutation are hard going, so readers in a hurry can happily move on to the last two paragraphs of this chapter.

To understand the theory developed by Jerome, we must remember that the New Testament texts mention several Jameses (Jacobs) and Marys (Miriams). There is nothing surprising about that, since Jacob, and above all Miriam, was a very common name in Palestine at the time of Jesus. The New Testament refers to seven persons, not necessarily all different, who bear the name of James:

1. James, son of Zebedee, one of the twelve apostles. He appears often in the New Testament.
2. James, son of Alphaeus, also one of the Twelve (Matt. 10.3; Mark 3.18; Luke 6.15; Acts 1.13).
3. James, the brother of the Lord (Mark 6.3/ Matt. 13.55; Acts 12.17; 15.13; 21.18; Gal. 1.19; 2.9 and 12; I Cor. 15.7).
4. James the Less or the Little (*mikros*), mentioned in the accounts of the passion (Mark 15.40/Matt. 27.56; Mark 16.1/Luke 24.10).
5. James, the father or less probably the brother of one of the Twelve, called Judas (Luke 6.16; Acts 1.13).
6. The person who presents himself as the author of the Letter of James (1.1).
7. The brother of the presumed author of the Letter of Jude (1.1).

Several women called Mary appear in the passion narratives. For the needs of our enquiry it is enough to mention those who, according to Mark and John, were present at the crucifixion of Jesus.[29] Their number and their identity differ depending on the manuscripts and the translations. Here is the version most generally accepted. For John 19.25, I offer two possible translations:

> Mary Magdalene
>
> Mark 15.40: Mary (mother) of James the Less and Joses
>
> Salome

	The mother of Jesus	The mother of Jesus
John 19.25:	His mother's sister	His mother's sister
	Mary of Clopas *or*	
		Mary of Clopas
	Mary Magdalene	Mary Magdalene

It is difficult to determine whether John is referring to three or four persons. We should note that in John the women are at the foot of the cross, whereas in Mark they keep their distance.

Now that the main figures have been introduced, let us move on to a summary and simplified version of Jerome's demonstration. First of all he establishes that James, the brother of the Lord, was one of the twelve apostles. In fact, in Galatians 1.19 Paul tells us that on his first visit to Jerusalem he saw no other apostles than Peter, but with the exception of James. Now two of the twelve apostles were called James, the son of Zebedee and the son of Alphaeus. The brother of the Lord cannot be identified with the son of Zebedee, since he took part in the Council of Jerusalem, which happened after the latter's death. Thus, Jerome thinks, the brother of the Lord can only be the son of Alphaeus, which excludes any filial relationship to Joseph. Finally, to put paid to rival theories, it only remained to explain why James, Joses, Simon and Jude were described as brothers of Jesus.

Jerome then proposes a novel and ingenious solution. We saw earlier that according to Mark (15.40), who is taken up by Matthew (27.56), a certain Mary, mother of James the Less and Joses, was present at the crucifixion of the Lord. For Jerome, James the Less and Joses must be identified with the James and Joses mentioned among the four brothers of Jesus (Mark 6.3 parr.). If we refer to the list of Jameses above, Jerome thinks that the second, third and fourth are the same person. Mary, the mother of James and Joses (Mark 15.40), being the spouse of the aforesaid Alphaeus, could not be Mary the mother of Jesus and wife of Joseph. Jerome then compares the lists of women present at the crucifixion as given in Mark 15.40 and John 19.25. He concludes from them that Mary, the mother of James the Less and Joses, can only be Mary of Clopas, the sister of the mother of Jesus. Thus James and Joses were first cousins of

Jesus. Jerome is well aware of an obvious objection: if James was only the cousin of Jesus, why was he constantly called his brother? However, he thinks that he can resolve this difficulty by showing that in the holy scriptures in Hebrew the word 'brother' is sometimes used for cousins or nephews. The term 'brother of the Lord' will simply reflect this usage.

Jerome recognizes another less serious problem. He cannot explain why Mary the wife of Alphaeus is called Mary of Clopas. He suggests that Clopas could be the name of her father or her clan. Later exegetes thought that they had found the solution by supposing that Alphaeus and Clopas represented two possible Greek translations of the original Aramaic *Khalphaï*.

However, we should note that in his treatise against Helvidius Jerome does not defend the identification of Mary of Clopas with Mary the mother of James and Joses with any passion. The important thing for him is to distinguish this Mary from the mother of Jesus. Furthermore, in his letter to Hedibia, written thirty years later, Jerome accepts that Mary of Clopas and the mother of James and Joses are two different persons, although, he writes, there are those who identify them. Moreover, he goes on to express certain doubts about the identification of James the brother of the Lord with James of Alphaeus. He attributes the designation 'brother of the Lord' more to his exceptional merits than to an ill-defined kinship to Jesus:

> Suffice it now to say that James was called the Lord's brother on account of his high character, his incomparable faith, and extraordinary wisdom: the other Apostles are also called brothers (John 20.17), but he preeminently so, to whom the Lord at His departure had committed the sons of His mother (i.e. the members of the Church of Jerusalem).[30]

Jerome's doubts hardly crossed the minds of later exegetes who enthusiastically adopted his interpretation, too content to find an apparent solution to a thorny problem. In order to resolve certain difficulties, scholars have proposed modifications to Jerome's view. These variants relate to the basis of the first theory, namely that James and his brothers were really cousins of Jesus. However, they do not agree on the exact nature of this kinship. Moreover, many authors have abandoned the identification of James of Alphaeus with the brother of the Lord.

The Hieronymian theory suffers from serious defects. First of all, as Bishop Lightfoot showed after exhaustive research, it is not attested in any text earlier that the treatise *Against Helvidius*. Moreover, Jerome's doubts about his interpretation clearly emphasize the absence of oral traditions. That is why one feels puzzled when the Catholic exegete Jean Cantinat, in his very serious and learned commentary on the Letter of James, asserts that 'according to the New Testament, James the brother of the Lord is the son of Mary wife of Clopas'.[31] If the New Testament showed that so clearly, it is hard to understand why it should have taken three centuries of intense reflection for someone to be able finally to see it.

A particularly weak link in Jerome's theory is the identification of the brother of the Lord with James of Alphaeus.[32] Jerome and the other defenders of this view base themselves on a very ambiguous passage in the Letter to the Galatians (1.19). According to them, Paul will have met no apostle except James. Now the text can be understood differently, as the Jerusalem Bible translation shows: 'I did not see other apostles, but only James . . . ' This translation, contrary to that of Jerome, excludes James from the group of Twelve. However, even if it were correct, Jerome's interpretation would not necessarily imply that James was one of the Twelve, since in his letters Paul does not reserve the title apostle for the Twelve. The list of the appearances of Christ given by Paul in I Corinthians 15.5–7 reflects this enlarged conception of the apostolate and seems to rule out the possibility that James was one of the Twelve:

> . . . that he [the Christ] appeared to Cephas, then to the Twelve. Then he appeared to more than five hundred brothers at one time . . . then he appeared to James, then to all the apostles.

We shall have occasion to return to this very complex text. But it shows that for Paul the term apostle was not limited to the Twelve, and that James is not to be counted among the

Twelve. A passage in the Acts of the Apostles (1.13–14 – already quoted, see above, p.13) confirms this last point. We should remember that the author of Acts indicates here that after the ascension the Twelve, along with some women and the brothers of Jesus, were assiduous in prayer.

Moreover, the Gospels distinguish the brothers of Jesus, who are sceptical, not to say hostile, from the immediate circle of disciples. Lastly, if James the Less mentioned in Mark 15.40 was James son of Alphaeus, it would be difficult to understand why Mark should not have described him as such. The identification of James son of Alphaeus with James the brother of the Lord thus seems unfounded. Moreover it has virtually ceased to be defended by Catholic exegetes. Even the very cautious *Jerusalem Bible* concedes that 'it seems that James son of Alphaeus should no longer be identified with James brother of the Lord'.[33] The great Catholic exegete Joseph Fitzmyer is more affirmative when he writes that James the son of Alphaeus 'is not to be identified with "James the Little" (Mark 15.40) or with "James, the brother of the Lord"'.[34] Nevertheless, despite the conviction of experts, most of the works of popular piety and some dictionaries of saints continue to maintain this identification.

According to Jerome's theory and its variants, James and his brothers were close relations of Jesus, but without being either his blood brothers or his half-brothers. In identifying James the brother of the Lord with the apostle James of Alphaeus, Jerome refuted the Helvidian and Epiphanian theories, thus making his view very probable, if not irrefutable. That is why this identification has been maintained so long, although it has no serious foundation: since James the brother of the Lord is the son of Alphaeus, he could not be the son of Joseph. Without this identification, the edifice constructed by Jerome and some others becomes much more fragile, indeed may even collapse. To sustain it, it is necessary to demonstrate the four following hypotheses:

1. James the Less and Joses, mentioned in Mark 15.40, are identical with the James and Joses described as brothers of Jesus, also in Mark (6.3).

2. Mary, their mother, is not the mother of Jesus.
3. Mary, their mother, is a close relation of Jesus.
4. Cousins can be described as brothers.

It is instructive to pause over a paradoxical aspect of this theory. We have seen the importance that it attaches to the identity of the women present at the crucifixion and to the comparison of them. Now the Gospel of John emphasizes the presence of Mary the mother of Jesus. She plays a role of prime importance in the scene of the passion, since Jesus addresses her shortly before he dies. Mark and Matthew mention the name of three women present at the execution, this time at a distance. These two Gospels mention Mary Magdalene and Mary the mother of James (the Less) and Joses. The third woman, in Matthew, is the mother of the son of Zebedee, whereas in Mark she is Salome. From this many exegetes conclude, rightly or wrongly, that Salome was the name of the mother of the sons of Zebedee. A comparison of the list of the women in John with those in Mark and Matthew suggests that if the mother of Jesus was truly present, as John indicates, she must be identified with Mary, the mother of James (the Less) and Joses. It is hard to conceive how Mary could have been present at the crucifixion without her presence being mentioned in Mark and Matthew. Thus in his recent and important commentary on Mark,[35] Robert Gundry defends this identity in order to avoid Mark and Matthew contradicting John. He thinks that Mark and Matthew wanted to designate Mary not as the mother of Jesus but as the mother of two other of her sons so as not to trivialize the words of the centurion ('Truly this man was son of God!', Mark 15.39; Matt. 27.54). This interpretation would confirm the Helvidian theory. However, most exegetes think it doubtful that the mother of Jesus could have been called the mother of James and Joses. So in their view the mother of Jesus was not present at the crucifixion. Consequently, for most scholars, the Gospel of John on the one hand and Mark and Matthew on the other disagree on a basic point: the presence of Mary at the crucifixion of her son. This disagreement should raise the utmost doubts about the historicity of the lists of women and show how rash it is for supporters of the Hieronymian theory to base their conclusions on a comparison of these lists. Therefore to accept the truth of the second hypothesis presupposes that the lists of Mark and John contradict each other, which makes the Hieronymian theory rest on extremely fragile foundations. Let us look more closely at the first hypothesis, which is essential to this theory.

In speaking so far of 'Mary the mother of James the Less and Joses', I have been using the most common translation of Mark 15.40. But the text is ambiguous, and the following translations have also been proposed: 'Mary the daughter of James the Less and mother of Joses'; 'Mary the wife of James the less and mother of Joses'.[36] Some commentators, like Simon Légasse,[37] think that Mark and Matthew are not referring to three women, as is generally thought, but to four: Mary Magdalene, Mary (wife, daughter or mother) of James the Less, the mother of Joses, Salome. Of course the alternative translations make the Hieronymian theory even more improbable.

Suppose nevertheless that the person designated is indeed Mary, the mother of James the Less and Joses. Is it then plausible to identify James the Less and Joses with the James and Joses of Mark 6.3? The answer must be no. James the brother of the Lord is nowhere called Less or Little, either in the New Testament or in the earliest traditions, where he is generally called James the Just. It seems more probable that Mark used this title to differentiate James from the two other Jameses mentioned earlier. It would also be necessary to explain why James, Joses and their two brothers are most frequently associated with the mother of Jesus. There is hardly any convincing answer. Some think that Joseph will have adopted nephews on the death of their father. Anything is conceivable. But why were these adopted nephews always with their aunt when their mother was still alive?

Even supposing that the James the Less and Joses of Mark 15.40 are those of Mark 6.3, can one demonstrate from the New Testament that they are close relatives of Jesus? It is here that the ingenuity of the supporters of Jerome's theory reaches its height. The precise solution put forward by Jerome seems very improbable, since it is doubtful whether two sisters could both be called Mary. To get round this difficulty, exegetes have proposed several alternative solutions. Some think that 'sister' must be taken in the sense of 'sister-in-law', Mary of Clopas being the wife of Clopas, a brother of Joseph. On the basis of the testimony of Hegesippus it is possible that Clopas was the brother of Joseph. However, the same testimony excludes the possibility that Clopas was the father of James, the brother of the Lord:

> And after James the Just had suffered martyrdom, as also had the Lord, on the same account . . . the son of his uncle, Simeon, the son of Clopas, was appointed bishop; whom all put forward, being a cousin of the Lord, as the second [bishop] . . . [38]

So James, the brother of the Lord, could not have been both the son and the nephew of Clopas. Other scholars suppose on the basis of certain manuscripts that the Gospel of John mentions the presence of four women by the cross (see pp. 21f.). In that case the sister of the mother of Jesus would not be Mary of Clopas. According to a contemporary exegete, Mary, the mother of James the Less and Joses, would be the sister-in-law of the mother of Jesus[39] (without being Mary of Clopas). This sister-in-law, called sister, would be Joseph's sister. Many other solutions have been proposed, each more speculative than the other. They look a makeshift bunch without any logic to it. We therefore have to accept that nothing in the New Testament and the earliest traditions of the church allows us to establish any close and well-defined kinship between the mother of James the Less and Joses on the one hand and the parents of Jesus on the other.

That brings us to the last question. Is it plausible that cousins or other close relatives could systematically be called brothers? The remarks of J. B. Lightfoot still display a caustic common sense: 'But it is scarcely conceivable that the cousins of any one should be commonly and indeed exclusively styled his "brothers" by indifferent persons; still less, that one cousin in particular should be singled out and described in this loose way, "James, the Lord's brother".'[40] There are also other more scholarly arguments. The demonstration by Jerome and his successors is based principally on examples from the Hebrew Bible.

As Hebrew has no word to signify 'first cousin', the Hebrew Bible sometimes uses the word 'brother' *('aḥ)* to denote a cousin. (In this case it can also speak of the son of an uncle.) In some of these instances the Greek translation (the Septuagint) uses the word *adelphos*. Nevertheless, these situations are not frequent and the context always makes clear the precise nature of the kinship in question. Moreover, as J. P. Meier has judiciously remarked, we could not identify them otherwise. But the analogy between the New Testament and the Greek version of the Hebrew Bible is scarcely convincing, despite the repeated efforts of Catholic apologists.[41] Even if the Gospels may sometimes have drawn on sources in Aramaic, they are not translations.[42] And there is no denying the fact that Paul wrote his letters in Greek, probably his mother tongue. Now Greek has the word *anepsios* to denote 'cousin'.[43] Why should not Paul, who knew James personally and must certainly have known the precise nature of his relationship to Jesus, have used this word had they been cousins? J. P. Meier has reviewed the 343 passages in the New Testament in which the word *adelphos* is used. His conclusion is quite definite: 'In the NT, *adelphos,* when used not merely figuratively or metaphorically but rather to designate some sort of physical or legal relationship, means only full or half brother, and nothing else.'[44]

Outside the New Testament we might recall the testimony of Flavius Josephus, who presents James as 'the brother of Jesus'. Now Josephus often uses the word *anepsios* in his works, just like Hegesippus, who makes a clear distinction between brothers and cousins in Jesus' family.

In reality the Hieronymian theory is based on such improbable hypotheses that its chances of being true are virtually nil. To defend this interpretation in practice amounts to claiming that the evangelists and Paul conspired to present a complicated enigma with an obvious but false conclusion, the key to which will first have been provided by Jerome, three centuries later.

Thus the Helvidian theory seems by far the most natural and most convincing. James, and also Joses, Jude, Simon and their sisters, were very probably children of Joseph and Mary.

2

A Galilean Family

A pious family

So James was probably the son of Joseph and Mary. One can suppose that he was born shortly after his older brother Jesus, perhaps several years before the beginning of the Christian era.[1] Let us try to discover a little more about his family and his education.

According to Matthew, Joseph and Mary were living in Bethlehem in Judaea at the time of the birth of Jesus.[2] To escape Herod, who wanted to kill the new-born child, Joseph and his family emigrated to Egypt. On the death of Herod, in 4 BCE, the angel of the Lord called on them to return to the land of Israel. But on learning that Archelaus, Herod's son, was reigning over Judaea, Joseph thought it more prudent to settle in Galilee. The fact that Galilee was governed by Herod Antipas, another of Herod's sons, does not seem to have disturbed him. It is true that Josephus has portrayed Archelaus as a particularly brutal character. In Galilee Joseph chose a village called Nazareth so that the prophecy 'He will be called a Nazarene' (Matt. 2.23) could be fulfilled. Let us hope that the meaning of this prophecy was clearer to Matthew's contemporaries than it is to modern exegetes.[3] Thus according to the Gospel of Matthew, Joseph, who came from Bethlehem, will have settled in Nazareth with his family some years after the death of Herod. So James will have been born either in Egypt or in Nazareth.

The Gospel of Luke tells us a significantly different story. In order to take part in a Roman census, Joseph, accompanied by Mary, who was then pregnant, left Nazareth where he lived and went to Bethlehem, the town of his ancestors, who were of the Davidic line. After the birth of Jesus at Bethlehem, the family returned to Nazareth. Mark and John do not have any account of the birth of Jesus. They present him as coming from Nazareth. John seems explicitly to deny any relationship between Jesus and Bethlehem, since Jesus' opponents refuse to accept that he is Messiah because of his Galilean origin (John 7.40–43).

Matthew's account is not historically impossible. But its structure is too based on fulfilled prophecies for it to be totally credible. Thus the birth at Bethlehem fulfils a prophecy of Micah about where the Messiah, son of David, will be born (Micah 5.1). The exile in Egypt and the return to the land of Israel, which are not attested anywhere else in the New Testament, evoke well-known biblical episodes like the prophecy of Hosea (11.1). Conversely, Luke's account seems barely probable in historical terms,[4] despite the ingenious efforts of traditionalist exegetes to demonstrate the contrary. Luke refers to an edict of Caesar Augustus which orders a census throughout the inhabited Roman world.[5] He seems to put this edict and the birth of Jesus towards the end of Herod's reign. Now we know of no general census of the Roman empire which took place in this period. On the other hand, we do know of a census held in Judaea by Quirinius, governor of Syria, when this region came under direct Roman domination in 6 CE. However, Joseph, who lived in Galilee, had no reason to go to Judaea to register, even if his family came from Bethlehem. According to the Roman custom, individuals were registered where they lived and worked. It seems that Luke has tried to make a historical fact (Joseph's Galilean origin) compatible with a theological construction (the birth of Jesus in Bethlehem). The census would offer a plausible explanation of why the son of an inhabitant of Galilee should have been born in Bethlehem. Matthew doubtless thought it more convincing to make Joseph live in Bethlehem. So in all probability James was born and spent his childhood in Nazareth, a small village in Galilee from which his family originated.[6]

At that time Galilee[7] covered an area of about two thousand square kilometres. Situated on the northern edge of Palestine, it was bordered by Samaria and Scythopolis to the south, Lake Tiberias (or the Sea of Galilee) and the Jordan to the east, the territories of Tyre and Sidon to the north, and Ptolemais and its region to the West. The green hills and valleys of Lower Galilee were a contrast to Upper Galilee to the north, which was more mountainous and less fertile. The population, very largely Jewish, was in the region of 200,000. The Gentiles gathered above all in the two big cities, Sepphoris and Tiberias, the population of which was perhaps above 25,000.[8] At that time Nazareth[9] was a small village in Lower Galilee numbering around 500 people. Situated on the heights, an hour's walk from Sepphoris, Nazareth overhung two important lines of communication, the route from Sepphoris to Caesarea and Jerusalem, and the route linking Tiberias with Ptolemais which went through Sepphoris.

Galilee and Judaea, both of which belonged to the united kingdom of David and Solomon, underwent different historical developments after this kingdom was divided in 925 BCE into the northern kingdom of Israel and the southern kingdom of Judaea.[10] Galilee was included in the kingdom of Israel until its invasion by the Assyrian king Tiglath-pileser III in 732 BCE. From this moment until its conquest by the Jewish king Aristobulus I in 104 or 103 BCE Galilee in practice ceased to be part of what is traditionally called the history of Israel. Despite its name, this was then concentrated on Jerusalem and Judaea. At the end of the seventh century Galilee passed under the control of the Neo-Babylonian empire before being integrated into the Persian empire in 539 BCE. After the conquest and death of Alexander (323 BCE) it came under the domination of Hellenistic rulers, either Lagid (Egypt) or Seleucid (Syria, Persia), until it was annexed by Aristobulus I. Scholarly literature has not managed to agree on how important the Jewish presence in Galilee was during the Persian and Hellenistic periods. The First Book of Maccabees (5.17–23) seems to indicate the existence of a significant Jewish population in the middle of the second century BCE, even if it was a minority one. From the time of its conquest by Aristobulus I, Galilee rapidly became Jewish with the conversion of the Ituraeans and the immigration of Jews from Judaea or elsewhere. Galilee and Judaea again experienced separate destinies on the death of king Herod. Herod Antipas, who figures in the New Testament, inherited Galilee and

Peraea, which he governed until he was deposed by Caligula in 39. He was replaced by (Herod) Agrippa I. Archelaus obtained Judaea, Samaria and Idumaea, the larger part of Herod's kingdom. In 6, he was deposed by the Romans. They administered these territories directly through a prefect, then a procurator, until the beginning of the war with Rome in 66, apart from the brief reign of Agrippa I between 39 and 44.

Galilee has often been presented as a region which, although it had abundant natural resources, remained outside the major commercial and cultural currents of the Greco-Roman world. Ernest Renan certainly contributed to shaping this image:

> From the ruins that remain of its former glories, we can imagine an agricultural people, by no means gifted in art, caring little for luxury, indifferent to the beauties of form, exclusively idealistic . . . In this earthly paradise, which the great revolutions of history had, up to that period, scarcely touched, lived a population in perfect harmony with the land itself, active, honest, joyous, and tender of heart.[11]

Similarly, more recently Geza Vermes[12] has spoken of the 'unsophisticated simplicity' of life in Galilee. As is shown by recent archaeological excavations, particularly in Sepphoris, this image is erroneous.[13] At that time Galilee was a densely populated region with an active economy, crossed by major lines of communication like the *Via Maris*. The historian Magen Broshi estimates that in the time of Jesus, Lower Galilee was one of the most densely populated and developed regions in the Roman empire.[14] The four main valleys which cross Lower Galilee formed excellent trade routes, running in the direction of the great coastal cities of Caesarea, Acco-Ptolemais and Tyre. Sepphoris and Tiberias had all the architectural and cultural characteristics of Hellenistic cities. Although the villages of Galilee were less Hellenized than the cities, they were nevertheless influenced by Hellenistic culture. And if Aramaic was certainly the everyday language of the majority of Galileans, the use of Greek seems to have been quite widespread, above all in the great cities, and particularly for economic, administrative or cultural activities. So it would be wrong to describe Galilee as a Semitic enclave surrounded by very Hellenized regions. In reality, Galilee played a full part in the Greco-Roman world of its time.

The New Testament gives us very little information about Joseph and his family. Apart from the contradictory facts about where he came from, we learn that Joseph was a Jew who observed the Mosaic law, that his family was descended from David and that he practised the trade of a carpenter. Let us look at these three pieces of information in rather more detail.

The Gospel of Matthew (1.19) describes Joseph as a just man, i.e. one who observed the precepts of the Mosaic law. However, the image of Joseph as a very observant Jew comes above all from the section of the Gospel of Luke (2.22–39) which is devoted to the birth and childhood of Jesus. Luke emphasizes the scrupulous observance of the regulations of the law of Moses at the birth of Jesus:

> And when the time came for their purification according to the law of Moses, they brought him up to Jerusalem to present him to the Lord (as it is written in the law of the Lord, 'everything that opens the womb shall be called holy to the Lord') and to offer a sacrifice according to what is said in the law of the Lord, 'a pair of turtle doves, or two young pigeons' . . . And when they had performed everything according to the law of the Lord, they returned into Galilee, to their own city, Nazareth.

A little later we learn that the parents of Jesus went to Jerusalem every year for the feast of Passover (Luke 2.41).

As exegetes have long shown, the author of the Gospel of Luke, who is also the author of the Acts of the Apostles, tends to emphasize the respect for the law shown by Jesus and the first Christians. Moreover it seems doubtful that the author had any privileged information about the religious ceremonies which followed the birth of Jesus. He certainly reconstructed them, sometimes inaccurately, basing himself on his knowledge of the customs practised when the temple still existed. Nevertheless Joseph, like many Galilean Jews, doubtless observed the regulations of the law faithfully. The names of members in Jesus' family confirms its traditionalist Jewish character.

Onomastics, i.e. the study of personal names, gives us

valuable information about the cultural and religious development of the Jews of the ancient world.[15] Thus we know that the first names of some great figures of the Bible were used above all from the third century BCE. After the Maccabaean revolt, for example, above all in Palestine we can see a marked preference for the biblical names borne by the heroes of the rebellion. At that time Simon, Judas, Matthew/Mattathias and Eleazar became extremely popular. Indubitably such a choice demonstrated the attachment of the family to its religious tradition. Such a name associated with the Maccabaean revolt and the Hasmonaean dynasty doubtless also added a nationalist connotation. Greek names were taken above all by rich and educated Jews.

We may recall that Joseph was the name of Jacob's eleventh son, and father of the tribe of the same name, which later divided into two to produce the tribes of Manasseh and Ephraim. It was a common first name in Palestine and in the Diaspora. Mary (Miriam/Mariamme) was the name of Moses' sister. It was the most common female first name in first-century Palestine, perhaps because it had been that of a Hasmonaean wife of Herod the Great. The names of Joseph and Mary's sons equally evoke biblical figures. Jesus (Yehoshua or Yeshua), 'the one who saves', was of course the name of the conqueror of the promised land. James (Jacob/Yacob), the younger son of Isaac, had twelve children whose names denoted the tribes of Israel. Jacob was called Israel after his victorious struggle described in Genesis 32. Curiously, this first name was used more frequently in the Diaspora than in Israel, despite its frequency in the New Testament. Jude/Judas and Simon/Simeon were the names of two of Joseph's sons. They were extremely popular in the first century, probably because two of the heroes of the Maccabaean revolt had borne them. All these choices indicate a family attached to the tradition of Israel and its sovereignty.

James, son of David?

Was James son of Joseph a descendant of king David? The Davidic descent of Jesus and his family, affirmed a number of

times in the New Testament, is a matter of considerable controversy. The designation of Jesus as son of David, i.e. descendant
of David, goes back at least to the 50s, since it appears for the
first time in the Letter to the Romans (1.3), composed around
55 or 56. Paul refers to Christ Jesus 'descended from David
according to the flesh'. According to scholars this qualification
will have been part of a pre-Pauline formula which was widely
accepted at that time. Paul, who attaches little importance to the
Davidic descent of Jesus in his theology, would probably not
have emphasized it had it not then been generally believed. The
fact that Jesus belongs to the same line is also mentioned in
Mark, Matthew and Luke and in Acts and the Second Letter to
Timothy.

Hegesippus, quoted by Eusebius, relates an episode[16] which
shows that the Davidic descent of the family of Jesus was
accepted both by the members of this family and by the Romans
at the end of the first century. According to him, someone
denounced the grandsons of Jude, one of the brothers of Jesus,
as being of the race of David and thus capable of leading or at
least symbolizing a messianic revolt. When the emperor
Domitian, before whom they had been brought, asked them
whether they were really descended from David, the great-
nephews of Jesus said that they were. After interrogating them,
Domitian, judging them no danger, had them released. Despite
some features which are probably legendary, like the personal
interrogation by Domitian, Hegesippus' account is doubtless
based on historical facts.

So it seems probable that the family of Jesus and James at the
end of the first century believed in all good faith that they were
descended from king David. But clearly that does not prove that
they were right to think so. Even accepting that David, monarch
of the united kingdom, is not a mythical figure,[17] it remains
impossible to prove irrefutably that Joseph was his descendant.
On the other hand we can try to determine whether this Davidic
origin is an invention of disciples of Jesus or goes back to a well-
established family tradition.

For many exegetes, above all the most critical, this descent is
only a theological statement devoid of any historical foundation. It would have been imagined by some disciples of Jesus

after their experience of the resurrection. These disciples, convinced of the messianic character of Jesus, would then quite naturally have seen him as the keenly awaited descendant of David, in whom God was fulfilling the promise made to David in II Samuel 7.12–14. Such descent was attributed to important figures like Menahem, one of the leaders of the Jewish revolt in 66, the great Pharisee Hillel, and Rabbi Judah the Patriarch, leader of the Palestinian Jews at the end of the second century: it is impossible either to confirm or deny it. In antiquity, and moreover much later,[18] an appropriately prestigious pedigree was conferred on exceptional individuals. Those concerned, if they were still alive, and their families, had no difficulty in accepting it.

Other experts think it more probable that the Davidic descent of Jesus had been acknowledged before the resurrection. They think that it would in fact be difficult to understand why certain disciples should necessarily have conceived of the resurrection of a man condemned to crucifixion as the enthronement of the Davidic royal Messiah had they not already been persuaded of his Davidic descent and his messianic character. Their experience of the risen Christ would have confirmed their conviction that Jesus was the Messiah rather than created it. Whatever was Jesus' own opinion,[19] this conviction would have been established during his ministry by reason of his personality, his more or less miraculous acts and his message. Some experts think that the disciples, seeing him as the Messiah, would quite naturally have attributed Davidic descent to him in conformity to what was then the most widespread opinion about the identity of the Messiah. Others, like Raymond E. Brown and John P. Meier, think that the Davidic origin of Jesus and his family could be based on a well-established family tradition.[20] They comment that at the time there was no consensus about the nature and identity of the Messiah (see Chapters 3 to 5 below). Not all Jews thought that the Messiah necessarily had to be descended from David. So the disciples should have been able to see Jesus as the Messiah without conferring Davidic descent on him. According to Meier and Brown, they would have had good reason to attribute such an origin to him. Moreover their messianic hope would have been open to easy refutation had there been no serious basis for supposing that Jesus belonged to the line of David. Now Jesus' opponents and the first Christians never cast doubt on this descent. And would the family have tolerated such a belief had it been totally improbable?

Such arguments, sometimes somewhat naive, are far from being completely convincing. However, we cannot exclude the possibility that the Davidic origin of Jesus and James goes back to family traditions. Can we be more positive and rely on the genealogies presented in Matthew 1.1–17 and Luke 3.23–28?[21] Before answering this question we need to investigate the existence and quality of genealogies in the first century of our era.

The importance that the Jews of antiquity attached to their descent is well known. The priestly families, particularly sensitive to the purity of their line, avoided misalliances. We know, particularly from Josephus, that information about the families of priests was deposited in the public archives, both in Jerusalem and in the major centres of the Diaspora. Through these facts families could reconstruct their own genealogy or evaluate that of a family with which an alliance was envisaged. The information provided by Josephus and the other ancient sources is much less clear about lay families. Joachim Jeremias, in his great book on Jerusalem in the time of Jesus,[22] argued that many non-priestly families, above all among the most prestigious and most influential, had relatively trustworthy written genealogies, going back at any rate several centuries. However, such a view is far from being unanimously accepted. Marshall D. Johnson,[23] after a careful analysis of the available sources, concludes that the existence of this type of written genealogy in lay families has not been demonstrated. On the other hand he thinks that, within families, oral traditions certainly made it possible to go back several generations. Johnson's scepticism is probably justified, given the credulity of certain traditionalist exegetes. However, it can be accepted that powerful families, notably those who claimed to be descended from David, must have had genealogies going quite far back into the past.

Conservative exegetes have long thought that the genealogies of Matthew and Luke indubitably proved the reality of the

Davidic origin of Jesus and his family. Such a position is hardly
ever accepted these days, since so many of the problems raised
by these genealogies in particular cannot be answered satisfactorily. First of all it must be remembered that Matthew and
Luke present Jesus' line on the side of Joseph, who according to
these same Gospels is his adoptive father. But at that time legal
paternity, which had priority over biological paternity, conferred all the hereditary rights. So these genealogies also represent the paternal descent of James. Luke's genealogy goes back
to Adam, while that of Matthew stops at Abraham. This choice
derives from theological considerations. But what interests us
more particularly is the list of Joseph's ancestors up to King
David. Now these two genealogies are not only very different,
but in fact completely incompatible, for four main reasons:[24]

1. From David to the exile, Matthew's genealogy goes
   through Solomon and the kings of Judaea, while Luke's
   goes through Nathan, another of David's sons.
2. The two lists meet up again after the deportation to
   Babylon, with Salathiel and his son Zerubbabel.
3. From Salathiel to Joseph, the legal father of Jesus
   according to the evangelists, the two lists present entirely
   different names, none of which is known from elsewhere.
   They do not even agree on the name of Joseph's father.
4. From David to Jesus Luke has forty-two generations as
   opposed to Matthew's mere twenty-eight.

These divergences render futile all attempts at harmonization
between these two genealogies, which are often very ingenious.
The theory sometimes advanced that Luke's genealogy would
represent Jesus' descent on his mother's side is completely
unfounded.

If the two genealogies cannot both be correct, perhaps one
of them nevertheless contains some trustworthy facts. These
two lists have certainly been composed to pass on a theological
message. So they have an artificial aspect which is quite customary in genealogies of the time. According to most scholars,
Matthew's list has a more pronounced theological character
than that of Luke: there are not so many generations, and
they are presented in three groups of fourteen, starting from

Abraham. It includes four women of pagan origin. Moreover, it makes Joseph descend from David by the royal line of Judah, while according to some sources this royal line was extinct some centuries before the birth of Jesus. That is why most of those who have studied these genealogies think that that of Luke has more chance of containing trustworthy historical facts. But if Luke's genealogy seems less artificial, it poses just as many serious problems. For example, the presence of patriarchal names like Joseph, Judah or Simeon among the pre-exilic ancestors seems strange in so far as such names only began to be used after the exile.

The exegete Richard Bauckham has recently defended the historicity of the genealogy given by Luke in an attempt to show that it was based on well-established family traditions.[25] Among his arguments he mentions the testimony of Julius Africanus, a third-century Christian author quoted by Eusebius.[26] After attempting to demonstrate that the genealogies of Matthew and Luke are compatible, Julius Africanus indicates that they come from members of Joseph's family. Again according to him, Herod, whose descent was hardly glorious from a Jewish point of view, had the genealogies of the families with the most prestigious descent destroyed. However, some families, including that of Joseph, will have succeeded in reconstructing their family tree on the basis of oral traditions and documents which escaped destruction. Contrary to what Bauckham thinks, this testimony seems rather to show that the early Christians had difficulty in justifying the authenticity of the genealogies of Jesus, since they had to resort the doubtful argument that documents had been destroyed. As we can see, this summary analysis of the genealogies of Joseph's family can hardly confirm its Davidic origin. Such an origin is certainly not impossible, but is it probable? According to the documents at our disposal it would be rash to make such a claim.

A modest carpenter

Although Joseph was heir to an illustrious line, he is presented to us as a modest carpenter working in an obscure small village. The only reference to Joseph's trade is Matthew 13.55: 'Is

he [Jesus] not the carpenter's son?' According to the majority
of exegetes Matthew will have modified Mark 6.3, where Jesus
is called 'the carpenter, the son of Mary', because for the Jews
the expression 'son of Mary', far from evoking a divine paternity, suggested an illegitimate birth. In that case one would have
supposed that Joseph and Jesus engaged in the same activity.
The Greek word *tekton* is usually translated carpenter, joiner or
mason, but sometimes also craftsman or builder. The earliest
Christian tradition opted for the sense carpenter/joiner. Thus in
his *Dialogue with Trypho*,[27] Justin Martyr (c.110–c.165) says
more specifically that Jesus made yokes and ploughs.

Some scholars, like Geza Vermes[28] and David Flusser,[29] think
that the trade of carpenter could have been used metaphorically,
as is sometimes the case in rabbinic literature, to denote a wise
or knowledgeable man. Jesus the carpenter would thus mean
Jesus the wise man, and would not prove that he and his father
were in fact carpenters. However, there is no indication that
this use of the word 'carpenter' existed in the first century.
Moreover the context in which the word is used does not
encourage such an interpretation. In fact the inhabitants of
Nazareth did not want to emphasize the knowledge of Jesus and
his family, but the fact that they were very ordinary.

Most often Joseph is represented, above all in popular
imagery, as a poor man. Certainly carpenters did not generally
pass as rich men, but the poverty which one can *a priori*
associate with this trade would seem to be accentuated by the
birth of Jesus in a manger. According to Luke, since there was
no room for Mary in the inn, she had to give birth in a crib.
Luke's objective in having Jesus born in a crib was doubtless not
to make his readers pity Joseph's poverty. The birth in a
manger, by evoking certain biblical texts, designated Jesus the
saviour of his people.[30]

The Protevangelium of James, in having him born in a cave,
once again emphasized how destitute Joseph was. But we may
note that in the same work Joachim, Mary's father, is presented
as a very rich man. The sacrifice of two turtle doves (Luke 2.24)
on the occasion of the birth of Jesus indicates more than the
giving birth in a crib how poor Joseph was, since turtle doves
were the offering of the least well off. Another argument put

forward in support of the poverty of Joseph and his family is
drawn from the account of the appearance of Jude's grandsons
before Domitian, which I have already mentioned:

> Then he asked them what possessions they had or what for-
> tune they owned. And they said that between the two of them
> they had only nine thousand denarii, half belonging to each of
> them; and this they asserted they had not in money, but only
> in thirty-nine plethra of land [around twelve hectares], so
> valued, from which by their own labours they both paid the
> taxes and supported themselves. Then they showed also their
> hands, and put forward the hardness of their bodies and the
> callosities formed on their hands from continual working, as
> a proof of personal labour.[31]

If this testimony were trustworthy, it would only prove
that some of the Joseph's great grandsons were very modest
peasants. One may suppose that had Jesus' brothers inherited
anything, as good Christians they would have given it to their
needy fellow-believers.

By contrast, some historians think that Joseph and his sons
were fairly well off. They usually suppose that *tekton* must
be taken in the sense of builder. Joseph will have been a builder
responsible, with his sons and several paid workers, for con-
structing entire buildings. For example, he will have played an
active part in the rebuilding of Sepphoris by Herod Antipas.[32]
Defending this interpretation, George Wesley Buchanan,[33] an
exegete with often provocative ideas, has even suggested that
Jesus and his family belonged to the Palestinian upper class.
Buchanan bases his thesis mainly on a somewhat unconven-
tional interpretation of II Corinthians 8.9:

> For you know the grace of our Lord Jesus Christ, that though
> he was rich, yet for your sake he became poor, so that by his
> poverty you might become rich.

The traditional interpretation of this passage is usually based
on Philippians 2.6–7, a hymn to the glory of Jesus, who aban-

doned his divine condition to take that of a slave and become like human beings. Buchanan, reading this passage quoted from II Corinthians literally and without any *a priori* theological considerations, thinks that according to Paul, Jesus abandoned his material riches to give them to the poorest. Although it was rapidly rejected by almost all exegetes, this interpretation is by no means absurd, above all since the context of this very extract is the collection for the poor in Jerusalem. Buchanan also considers that Jesus' relations with prominent figures and the character of some parables tell in favour of a rich Jesus. He concludes that Jesus' exhortations to abandon riches would have carried more weight had he himself already given an example.

Without going as far as this, we can imagine that Joseph's family was a family of craftsmen living in a degree of comfort, compared to most of the inhabitants of Nazareth, who will have been agricultural workers or farmers working a minuscule plot of land. This was doubtless a family of craftsmen like those from whom many of the sages mentioned in rabbinic literature emerged. Joseph's activities probably included making furniture and other wooden objects and tools, along with carpentry and perhaps even masonry. Some of these activities called for considerable technical knowledge. Moreover it is probable that Joseph and his sons found work at Sepphoris and other important locations in Galilee. The parables of Jesus show us someone who was very familiar with the mechanisms of the monetary economy.

James' education

It would be moving to imagine Jesus, at the age of seven or eight, leading his little brother James, two years younger, by the hand through the narrow and dusty streets of Nazareth. They go to the school called *bet sefer* (house of the book). In such a small village the school will have only been a simple room in the synagogue. James, like all the boys of his age, goes first to lessons given by the *sofer*,[34] who teaches him to read and acquaints him further with the Bible. Because his father has told them to him many times, he already knows the stories of

Abraham, Isaac, Jacob, Joseph, Moses, Aaron, Joshua and other great glories of Israel. Jesus, who has been going to the courses taught by the *sofer* for two years, can already decipher some passages in the Torah when he unrolls the *megillah* (scroll). In two years he will pass into the *bet talmud* (house of study), in which the *masneh* will teach him the oral traditions handed down by the men of old, from generation to generation since Moses. So he will be able to interpret the precepts of the Bible correctly. Like all Jews, Jesus and James will have to lead their lives in scrupulous observance of all the instructions (*halakhah*) taught by the *masneh*. At the age of twelve or thirteen they will leave the *bet talmud*. If they are gifted and interested, they will be able to sit with other adults at the feet of a master of the law in a *bet midrash*. But as Nazareth is too small to have its own *bet midrash*, they will have to go to a neighbouring town. After some years, if they excel, they could even study in Jerusalem with Gamaliel or some other distinguished wise man.

Such a story, which can be found in the traditional biographies of Jesus, presupposes that at the beginning of the first century there was a compulsory system of education in Palestine similar to that which can be reconstructed from the Mishnah, the Tosefta and the Jerusalem and Babylonian Talmuds, the main works of rabbinic literature.[35] The Mishnah and the Tosefta, the oldest of these texts, were completed around 200. Those who believe that there was a general system of education at the beginning of our era mostly rely on information coming from the Jerusalem Talmud, a commentary on the Mishnah finished around 400. According to the Jerusalem Talmud, at the beginning of the first century BCE the high priest Simon ben Shetah ordered that all children should go to school.[36] However, more than one scholar doubts whether this is true. The fact that the Babylonian Talmud traces the origin of compulsory education back to the high priest Joshua shortly before the war against the Romans already makes it suspect.[37] Scholars like Shaye Cohen,[38] far from asking which is the authentic tradition, think that both traditions are legendary, since we have no historical proof of the existence of public schools in Palestine or in the Diaspora in the first century. Josephus and Philo, though emphasizing how familiar the Jews were with the holy scriptures and the law of Moses, nowhere mention such schools. More probably, only the most well-to-do families could provide their children with a tutor. The few schools one could find were not public institutions for young children but private and informal groups of adult disciples around an established master. The great majority of children had to be content with the reading and explanation of the Torah in the synagogue on the sabbath.

Do we have to adopt Shaye Cohen's scepticism, or do we accept that the educational system described in the rabbinic literature already existed at the end of the second temple? On this question depends the view we take of the level of education and literacy in the ancient world at this time. The historian William V. Harris[39] has recently shown that this level was very low. Is it reasonable to suppose that Palestine formed an island of literate people in an ocean of illiterates? Even supposing that teaching and literacy were more developed in Palestine than elsewhere in the Roman empire, is it realistic to imagine that they were the same in Nazareth as in Jerusalem, Sepphoris or Tiberias? Shaye Cohen is probably right to be sceptical.

A more logical way of evaluating the level of James' education is to suppose that it would not have been very different from that of Jesus, as we can deduce this from the Gospels. Although there is much argument over the question, several passages suggest that Jesus read Hebrew,[40] the language of the Bible, and perhaps wrote it. We should recall that the language spoken by the Jews of Palestine was above all Aramaic; the use of Hebrew, which was less widespread, was principally limited to the study of the Torah. Jesus seems to have had a good knowledge of the holy scriptures. His debates with the Pharisees, scribes or Sadducees show that he used the type of argument based on the Bible that we find in rabbinic literature.[41] But it is difficult to decide whether Jesus was a self-taught genius who, thanks to his gifts and his efforts, acquired his knowledge from visiting the synagogue and perhaps, as an adult, some sage, or whether Joseph had sufficient resources to provide him with a satisfactory education. In the first instance, James' instruction would similarly have depended entirely on his personal talents;

in the second, one could presuppose a level of education equivalent to that of Jesus, unless Joseph favoured his firstborn.

Finally, we can try to evaluate James' education by analysing the texts which are attributed to him. This procedure certainly gives significant results in the case of Paul, from whom we have at least seven authentic letters. However, the problem is more complex with James, since the authenticity of the Letter of James, the only New Testament writing to bear his name, is very much in dispute (see Chapter 9). This letter is written in a very correct, indeed elegant, Greek. To suppose that James could have written it without outside help would oblige us totally to reconsider our idea of the social and cultural milieu of Joseph's family. They would have to be imagined as a largely Hellenized family, and sufficiently rich to have the children taught the principles of Greek rhetoric. The Acts of the Apostles (15.13–21) contains a speech which James is said to have made to the Council of Jerusalem. In it James defends the entry of the Gentiles into the church without first being circumcised, with the support of scriptural proofs. This speech shows good knowledge of the Hebrew Bible, of the Septuagint (the Greek translation of it) and of the type of biblical interpretation that we find in the commentaries discovered at Qumran.[42] Thus James is presented by Luke, the author of Acts, as someone who is a true master in the interpretation of scripture. However, it is difficult to determine to what degree James' words reflect his talents as an exegete or merely the skill of Luke or the author of a source which Luke used. Some scholars think that the authority which James enjoyed in the primitive church was in part based on his knowledge of the scriptures. Taking account of his scrupulous respect for the law and the protests of the Pharisees when he was condemned to death, many see him as a man trained in schools inspired by the Pharisees. Others, basing themselves above all on his presumed asceticism, see him closer to the Essenes.[43] However, here again there is no convincing proof.

We have seen that James, like Jesus, belonged to a Galilean Jewish family which faithfully observed the Mosaic law. So we need to investigate the nature of Judaism around the middle of the first century of our era if we want to understand their thought and their actions.

3

What is a Jew?

To assert that Jesus, James and the first Christians, who were all Jews, can only be understood in the context of the Judaism of their time might seem self-evident to many people. But as Francis Schmidt has emphasized in his book on the temple thought-system,[1] this assertion has often been heavily qualified, and even rejected. In the past, many exegetes thought that Hellenism or Gnostic speculations were the real cradle of Christianity. Even now, the American exegetes Burton L. Mack and to a lesser degree John Dominic Crossan make Jesus a kind of wise vagabond, more influenced by Cynic philosophy than by the Bible.[2]

For all that, to regard Judaism as the matrix of the thought and action of Jesus and his disciples does not make them easier to interpret, contrary to what was supposed a few decades ago. At that time the majority of scholars, Jews or Christians, thought that first-century Judaism was a relatively homogeneous and well-defined entity, with which the ideas of Jesus and the first Christians could easily be compared. The Judaism defined as normative was that of the Pharisees, who are well known as the opponents of Jesus in the Gospels. The Judaism of the Pharisees, to whom we cannot attribute with certainty any of the writings of the period that we have, was thought to be very similar to its direct descendant, rabbinic Judaism, as developed in the Mishnah and the two Talmuds. It was thought that rabbinic Judaism, based on the Hebrew Bible and oral traditions, inherited almost unchanged, through the Pharisees, notions of Ezra dating from the fifth century BCE.

This conception of a normative Pharisaic-rabbinic Judaism appeared clearly in the great syntheses of George Foot Moore,[3]

Joseph Bonsirven[4] and Joachim Jeremias,[5] which were developed between the two wars. One can still find it in the most recent composite work edited by S. Safrai and M. Stern, *The Jewish People in the First Century*.[6] Certainly, the existence of other groups like the Essenes and the Sadducees, whose notions were opposed to those of the Pharisees, was known; however, the former were seen more as a picturesque curiosity than as an influential group, and the latter, represented above all in the priestly aristocracy, seemed more interested in the defence of their political and economic privileges than of their religious ideas.

This description related mainly to the Jews of Palestine, especially those of Judaea. The Jews of the Diaspora, who were three or four times more numerous, were thought to have practised a somewhat bastardized Judaism as a result of the influence of the Hellenistic world. Some decades ago, this consensus was demolished by a growing number of researchers, particularly because of the discovery of the Dead Sea Scrolls, recent archaeological evidence and a more critical analysis of texts which had been known for a long time. Thus, following Morton Smith[7] and Jacob Neusner,[8] many scholars doubt the existence of a normative Judaism inspired by Pharisaism in the first century CE in Palestine. Rabbinic Judaism, supposed to be the heir to the Pharisees, never became normative in Palestine, supposing that it ever really became normative, before the third or even the fourth century.

The majority of scholars today see the Judaism of the time of Jesus as very diversified and in process of evolution.[9] Although the Pharisees were relatively few, beyond doubt they formed an influential and respected group when it came to questions of the interpretation of the Mosaic Law.[10] But to give them a dominant position, above all at a political and social level, seems exaggerated and anachronistic. Moreover, historians are increasingly sceptical about the possibility of a faithful reconstruction of Pharisaic doctrines from a much later rabbinic literature. In order to understand the Judaism of this period they seem more inclined to use, in addition to the works of Josephus and Philo, the so-called pseudepigraphical texts, the Qumran literature and the New Testament.

Lastly, the traditional distinction between Palestinian Judaism and the supposedly very Hellenized Judaism of the Diaspora is no longer tenable. As Martin Hengel[11] and others have shown, Palestinian Judaism was widely influenced by Hellenistic culture. Besides, it is sometimes difficult to determine whether some texts come from the land of Israel or the Diaspora. The works of A. T. Kraabel[12] and other historians have shown us the existence of a creative and very diversified Judaism in the lands of the Diaspora. Given the differences in practice and belief, some experts like Jacob Neusner prefer to speak of Judaisms rather than Judaism.

However, this plural seems questionable and moreover does not tell us anything in particular.[13] In fact it leads us to ask what the elements are which make it possible to characterize a system of beliefs and practices as a Judaism. Why are Pharisaism and Essenism Judaisms, and not the cult of Isis? This notion implies that the different sorts of Judaisms had sufficient common features to bear the same generic name. In fact, despite their differences, almost all Jews were agreed on some basic beliefs and practices which distinguished them from the rest of the population. Despite boundaries which were sometimes rather fluid, they formed a relatively well-defined and recognizable entity, both for themselves and for the Gentiles.

The diversity of Judaism at the end of the Second Temple period can largely be explained by the very evolution of the idea of Jew and of Judaism.[14] First of all it should be noted that the word 'Jew' originally denoted a member of the tribe of Judah, and then an inhabitant of Judaea. It was only in the second century BCE that the word began to denote all those who worship YHWH and live according to the principles of the law of Moses. It must be emphasized that this word was used above all by the Gentiles; the Jews preferred to call themselves 'people of Israel'. The term 'Judaism' occurs for the first time in the Second Book of Maccabees (2.21; 8.1; 14.38), composed in the second half of the second century BCE, to define the customs and beliefs of the Jews as opposed to Hellenism. The words 'Jew' and 'Judaism' are thus often used in an anachronistic or incorrect way. I shall continue this bad habit, and ask to be excused for it in advance.

The notion of Jew has three distinct elements:[15] ethnic, linked to descent from Abraham and membership of one of the twelve tribes of Israel; territorial, linked to residence in the land of Israel; and socio-cultural, associated with certain beliefs and customs. Depending on the period, these three elements varied in importance. In the obscure period before the fall of Jerusalem (587–586 BCE) and the exile in Babylon, all three were generally necessary to define a Jew. However, the determining influence of the ethnic and territorial elements has to be emphasized. The ethnic element was basic, as with most of the people of the time. The stranger (*ger*) living amongst the Israelites/Jews benefited from the protection of the law of the country and had to respect its customs. But just as a *metic* could not become an Athenian citizen, so a *ger* had no possibility of being integrated into the people of Israel. By contrast, Jews could marry foreigners and integrate them into their people. Residence in the land of Israel, the territory chosen by YHWH for his people, was also an essential aspect of Israelite/Jewish identity. In I Samuel 26.19 David complains of being unable to honour YHWH since he has been banished from the land of Israel. In Psalm 137 the exiles ask how it is possible to praise YHWH in a foreign land. It is hardly surprising that after the fall of Samaria and the kingdom of Israel in 722 BCE, exiles often melted into the background without maintaining their cultural identity. The people of Israel, like all the other peoples, certainly had its own customs and beliefs. But its members did not define themselves by their customs and their beliefs, any more than the Athenians of the time or the French of today. Besides, the Bible and archaeology show us a great diversity of beliefs and religious practices among the Jews before the exile. Those who worshipped only YHWH were opposed to those, probably the majority of the population, who also took part in the cult of other gods. But these latter were no less Israelites/Jews than the former.

During the exile, the Jews learned to sing the glory of YHWH outside the land of Israel. From that moment the territorial element of Judaism began to become less important, allowing the formation of strong and lasting communities outside Israel. The existence of these communities, which were sometimes flourishing ones, favoured diversity within Judaism. Among many Jews the weakening of the territorial element led to a reinforcing of the ethnic and socio-cultural elements, as we can see in the post-exilic books of Nehemiah and Ezra. Rejecting marriages with foreigners, they tried to preserve the purity of their line. Moreover, the notion of Jewish beliefs and customs became a criterion for identity which, since it was no longer a matter of course as in the past, had to be defined, indeed to be created. The redaction of the Bible, which dates essentially from the Persian period, shows this quest for an identity.[16] The growing acceptance of an exclusive monotheism and the concept of the covenant with YHWH obliged Jews to ask themselves, sometimes anxiously, what was the will of YHWH and how he was to be worshipped. In authorizing the Jews to return home and requiring them to live in accordance with their ancestral customs, the Persian king encouraged this approach. Moreover the adoption of an exclusive monotheism led the Jews to differentiate themselves more from other people. This development was accentuated with the Hellenization of the Middle East following its conquest by Alexander the Great.[17]

This Hellenization must not be conceived of as an imperialistic process in one direction. Hellenistic civilization, the fruit of the encounter between the Greeks and the East, incorporated elements from two cultures. Hellenization led to a degree of homogenization in the east and south of the Mediterranean basin, as Hellenistic culture increasingly became an identity factor which transcended frontiers and traditional ethnic groups. In the classical period the Greeks were linked by common blood, the same language and a similar way of living and thinking. In the fourth century, with the Macedonian expansion, blood lost its importance as compared with language, lifestyle and thought. It then became possible to become a Greek by cultural assimilation. This Hellenization provoked ambivalent reactions among the Jews. On the one hand they absorbed many elements from this new culture, both in the land of Israel and abroad; on the other hand they sought to preserve their identity and their religious particularism. In the third century BCE the Jews of Egypt were able to maintain a subtle balance between these two tendencies: they succeeded in being regarded as Greeks while remaining Jews. Nevertheless, Judaism came increasingly to define itself as a specific way of life and thought as opposed to Hellenism. It then became possible, probably in the second century BCE, to become a Jew by conversion. Neither the ethnic factor nor the territorial factor were any longer thought decisive, at any rate by certain Jews. This new development was also linked with the growing individualization of religion in the Hellenistic world. Little by little religion, formerly a collective and compulsory phenomenon associated with city or ethnic group, became more a matter of personal choice guided by individual aspirations.

Above all in Palestine, the development of Judaism was largely influenced by the events which followed the attempt to Hellenize Judaea undertaken by the Jerusalem elite after 175 BCE.[18] The 'Hellenizers', without repudiating Judaism, wanted to adopt certain Greek institutions and customs. This enterprise led to serious trouble. Some opponents sought the support of the Lagid rulers of Egypt, thus provoking a violent reaction from the Seleucid Antiochus IV, who in 167 BCE decided to ban specifically Jewish practices in Judaea. After many years of struggles and compromise, the revolt started by Mattathias, of the family of Hasmonaeus, and his son Judas called Maccabaeus, resulted in the liberation of Judaea from the Seleucid empire in 141 BCE with the creation of a Hasmonaean kingdom. The Maccabean reaction began to restore traditional customs, in opposition to the Hellenism against which it had fought. Hasmonaean rulers like John Hyrcanus (134–104 BCE) and Alexander Jannaeus (103–76 BCE) considerably extended the territories under their domination. Entire populations were converted more or less voluntarily. This return to ancestral customs, which had to be rediscovered and sometimes even created, prompted the formation of several movements (Pharisees, Essenes and Sadducees), each with its own interpretation of the law. The Roman domination of Palestine, which began in 63 BCE with the capture of Jerusalem by Pompey's legions, served to accentuate the separatist tendencies in areas with an essentially Jewish population, but also certain assimilationist tendencies in the more cosmopolitan cities. In the first century of our era the notions of Jew and Jewish identity raised many questions, and there was by no means a consensus on them. The importance to be attached to ethnic, territorial and socio-cultural factors respectively was very much a matter of dispute. Not everyone defined the practices and customs of the Jews in the same way. The conflicts and debates within the primitive church largely reflect all these problems.

God, his people and his covenant

Judaism is essentially based on a few fundamental concepts accepted by all Jews. These can be summed up as: belief in one God; the revelation of the Torah by God to Israel; Israel defined as the people which lives in accordance with the Torah as a sign of obedience to God. To these elements, for the period preceding its destruction in 70 CE, can be added the Jerusalem temple, the central place of worship.

Judaism is a system of beliefs and practices revealed by God. These revelations have been made directly by him to certain exceptional beings like Abraham and Moses, or are known through the mediation of inspired prophets. They are collected in the Hebrew Bible, called *Tenakh*. According to a tradition which is challenged by many experts today, the canon of the Hebrew Bible as we know it was fixed at the 'council' of Jabneh (or Jamnia) at the end of the first century of our era. The first five books (Genesis, Exodus, Leviticus, Numbers and Deuteronomy), which are especially important, are called the Pentateuch or Torah. The rest of the Hebrew Bible is divided between the Prophets (*Nebi'im*) and the writings (*Kethubim*); the name *Tenakh* given to it is simply made up of the initial letters of the three groups of works it comprises, given vowels to make it pronounceable. The Septuagint, a Greek version of the Bible intended for the Jews of the Diaspora, contains several additional texts.

In the middle of the first century there was probably no single canon accepted by all Jews, apart from the five books forming the Pentateuch, which were unanimously held to be divinely inspired. The numerous references to the 'Law and the Prophets' in the New Testament show that the Prophets must have been widely accepted as holy scripture.[19] The status of the

Psalms and other Writings is more controversial. Some groups could consider texts which did not belong to the present canon to be divinely inspired. In the Qumran community, near to which the Dead Sea Scrolls were found, the First Book of Enoch, Jubilees and the Temple Scroll perhaps enjoyed such a status. We cannot overestimate the importance of sacred texts in the life and piety of the Jews of the first century. Known by all, they were constantly read and commented on in the synagogues. The existence, the intellectual and symbolic universe, the world-view and history of the Jews were largely structured and determined by these texts.

The fundamental element of divine revelation is monotheism, belief in one God. Regardless of the eventful historical evolution of monotheism in Israelite religion, and leaving aside the exalted status given to certain biblical figures, belief in YHWH the one God was universal among the Jews of the first century. Twice every day they had to recite the *Shema*,[20] the most ancient core of the liturgy, which begins by recalling that God is one: 'Hear, O Israel: The Lord our God is one Lord; and you shall love the Lord your God with all your heart, and with all your soul, and with all your might' (Deut. 6.4–5). Belief in one God was accompanied by a prohibition against making cultic images of YHWH and his creatures and, quite naturally, against worshipping other gods. The rejection of idolatry was very deeply rooted in the mentality of the Jews of the time. Above all for the Jews of the Diaspora, it was the most basic element, separating them from their pagan environment. In fact, in the Hellenistic and Roman cities religion touched on the majority of civil, social and family activities. The festivals and other manifestations of civic life were accompanied by worship offered to the deities of the city. The vast majority of Jews, who refused to be associated with these ceremonies, could only be imperfectly integrated into the rest of the population.[21]

In addition to monotheism, Judaism is based on three fundamental concepts which are unanimously accepted: the election of Israel, the covenant between God and Israel, and the Law or Torah. These notions are linked in the following way:

– God has chosen Israel from all the peoples to be his elect people;

- this election is manifested by a covenant between God and Israel which contains a divine promise and, in response, a commitment on the part of Israel;
- God promises Israel a land in which it will prosper for ever;
- in exchange, Israel commits itself to live in accordance with the law given by God, often called the Torah.

Moreover, during the period before the destruction of the temple, a sacrificial system centralized on Jerusalem allowed the remission of the sins of those who had not followed YHWH's instructions correctly.

The two moments of the foundation of this election and covenant are the promise made to Abraham and the exodus from Egypt under the leadership of Moses. In Genesis 17, God institutes his covenant with Abraham. He promises him numerous descendants and the possession of the land of Canaan for ever. In exchange he requires the Israelites to be circumcised. Several centuries later, again according to the Bible, God frees the people of Israel from slavery and leads it to the Promised Land. During the exodus, on Mount Sinai, God reveals to Moses the law which is to guide its existence. Those who respect these commandments benefit from the love and favour of God. Those who transgress them will not be able to escape the divine anger.

Adherence to these beliefs led to the following notions among many Jews:

- The Jewish people is to some degree a people apart, the only people which truly lives according to the will of God;
- By reason of the divine promise, the land of Israel enjoys a quite special importance;
- the misfortunes which afflict Israel are the result of his inability to observe God's commandments;
- despite the faults of Israel, YHWH, remaining faithful to his promise, will intervene to restore its fortunes.

We shall now look rather more closely at the essential preoccupation of the majority of Jews: how must one live in order to respect the will of God?

Living according to the law

What is the law?

To continue to benefit from its election and the divine promise, the people of Israel must follow the law of Moses in their lives. In addition to its ritual and religious aspects, this law encompasses areas covered in our modern society by civil and criminal law and by commercial regulations. The notion of the Mosaic law is complex and often misunderstood. As Philip Alexander has shown very well in a most useful survey of Jewish law at the time of Jesus, 'there is a powerful tendency in NT scholarship to treat the Torah of Moses as an undifferentiated, highly uniform body of law'.[22] In this literature the Mosaic law, derived directly from the Bible, is often seen as a collection of well-defined precepts which are easy to apply. In fact the Hebrew Bible, far from containing a coherent and homogeneous legal system, juxtaposes instructions which derive from different codes. These instructions are usually incomplete, as in the case of marriage and divorce, and sometimes even contradictory, as with priestly tithes and sacrifices. When two commandments clash, a priority has to be decided (see the *corban*, p.87). So in order to be transformed into a coherent legal system which can be applied, the biblical precepts have to be interpreted and completed, even modified. In fact, several conceptions of the law of Moses can be legitimately derived from the Bible. The only homogeneous ancient conception known to us which can be applied is the rabbinic law developed in the Mishnah and the Talmud. To work this out, the rabbis interpreted and completed the majority of the biblical precepts. Some were even modified and indeed dropped because they contradicted others, or because they corresponded to conditions which no longer existed. The rabbinic law even includes elements which have no support from the Bible.

At the time of Jesus and the first Christians there were several rival views of the Mosaic law and therefore several rival ways of living as a Jew. The two views which are least ignored are those of the Pharisees and the Essenes. Although we know of no writings which can be attributed with certainty to the former, their positions are often mentioned in rabbinic literature, on which they exercised a significant influence. We have seen that some scholars, beginning with Jacob Neusner, express serious doubts about the fidelity of the transmission of Pharisaic doctrines in rabbinic literature. The information contained in well-known contemporary documents, the Gospels and the works of Flavius Josephus, are perhaps more trustworthy. The Pharisees were held in particularly high esteem for their knowledge and precise interpretation of the Torah.[23] In addition to the precepts drawn from the Bible, they also applied certain traditions of non-biblical origin, later called traditions of the elders or the oral law. The Pharisees formed a group which put the emphasis on a scrupulous observance of the law, particularly in the sphere of purity, sabbath observance and priestly tithes.

We know some aspects of the Essene view of the law through the Qumran manuscripts and the works of Josephus and Philo. They constituted a movement with marked sectarian tendencies.[24] Their legal system was based on a particularly rigorous and inflexible interpretation of the biblical laws. Even more than the Pharisees, they favoured an extension and a strict application of the laws of ritual purity. For them the law of Moses contained unwritten prescriptions in the Bible which had been specially revealed to the Teacher of Righteousness.

Josephus, the New Testament and the rabbinic literature mention a third group, the Sadducees, whose doctrine is still not at all well known.[25] They seem to have been well represented in the high-priestly families. According to the majority of experts they held to a very literal interpretation of the Torah and rejected the Pharisaic traditions which were alien to the Bible.[26] In rabbinic literature the Sadducees are often opposed to the Pharisees on questions of purity, in connection with which they usually prove to be more strict. But do these texts always refer to the Sadducees we find in Josephus and the New Testament? One might sometimes doubt it. It is possible that the Sadducees restricted the laws of purity above all to relations with the temple. They were also notable for the severity of their punishments.

However, the Essenes, Pharisees and Sadducees were only a minority. The great majority of the population, those whom rabbinic literature scornfully calls the people of the country ('*ammē hā-ārets*), had a different view of the law and practised it differently.[27] From the rigorist perspective of the Pharisees or the Essenes they were characterized by an imperfect knowledge and lax observance of the law, particularly in the spheres of ritual purity and of tithes. This did not necessarily imply any lesser piety on their part.

We hardly know how an ordinary Jew might have practised the Mosaic law, what was allowed and what prohibited, and what punishments might have been inflicted for transgressions. The best-known rules are probably those relating to the temple, its sacrifices and its festivals. These rules were the same for all who took part in the activities of the temple. Those who, like the Essenes, disapproved of its forms of worship had a choice between not taking part and compromising.

Works on Second Temple Judaism concentrate on those aspects of the law which are usually – and wrongly – described as ritual or religious. But the Mosaic law includes elements relating to civil or commercial law like marriage, successions, adoptions, loans, contracts of purchase and sale, and so on. All these matters are regulated in detail in the rabbinic literature. What was the position over them in the time of Jesus and the first Christians? This is a very tricky question, which is hardly touched on by E. P. Sanders in his great synthesis on 'common' Judaism at the end of the Second Temple period.[28] This aspect of the law is referred to above all in studies devoted to the Jews of Egypt in the Ptolemaic and Roman periods, for which we have important documentation.[29] We know that the Jewish communities in Egypt were authorized to live according to their ancestral laws and that they had their own tribunals which judged on the basis of these laws. However, most of the legal documents which have come down to us show that Hellenistic common law was used for family and business matters.

Many scholars think that this situation was peculiar to the Jews of Egypt. In their view, the family and business affairs of the Jews of Palestine were regulated according to the law of the time, which was similar to the rabbinic law. This position has to be qualified in the light of the recent discovery in the Judaean desert of eight marriage contracts dating from the beginning of the second century of our era.[30] Of these eight contracts, five are drawn up in Greek and with one exception conform to Greco-Roman common law. The three others are written in Aramaic and correspond to the rabbinic law of marriage as this is codified in the tractate Kethubot of the Mishnah. These discoveries can only suggest that those who want to determine the nature and extent of the Mosaic law at the time of Jesus and the first Christians need to be more cautious.

However, various elements were regarded as fundamental factors of Jewish identity, transcending differences and conflicting interpretations. These elements are circumcision, the sabbath, the dietary laws and the temple. Each was to be the subject of debates and major conflicts in the primitive church, some of them having a pre-Christian origin.

Circumcision

Circumcision more than anything else at that time conferred and symbolized the quality of being a Jew.[31] Every boy born of Jewish parents had to be circumcised at the age of eight days. Thus the Gospel of Luke (2.21) mentions the circumcision of Jesus on the eighth day. In the Hebrew Bible, circumcision goes back to the covenant of YHWH with Abraham and his descendants (Gen. 17.10–14). It is the mark of this covenant in the flesh:

> You shall be circumcised in the flesh of your foreskins, and it shall be a sign of the covenant between me and you.

Isaac, conceived by Sarah, Abraham's wife, at the age of ninety, was circumcised by his father 'when he was eight days old, as God had commanded him' (Gen. 21.4). It might be added that circumcision was hardly something that distinguished the ancient Israelites from neighbouring peoples, since at that time circumcision was a very widespread practice in the Near East. The Hellenization of the ancient world led to circumcision being seen as an alien custom, generally arousing disgust, scorn or ridicule.[32] The Greeks, who deliberately exposed their naked bodies in gymnasia and public baths, found the uncovered glans particularly repugnant.[33]

Although it was still practised by certain Semitic populations and by the Egyptian priests, in the Hellenistic Near East circumcision gradually came to be considered the distinctive sign of male Jews. Thus at the time of the forcible Hellenization of Judaea under Antiochus IV, women who had had their sons circumcised were put to death along with their infants and those who had performed the operation.[34] With the Maccabaean reaction, circumcision became a major symbol of Jewish identity which for the most part it would have been sacrilege to question or to relativize. For those who wanted to convert to Judaism it was an inescapable rite of passage.[35]

Nevertheless, at the end of the Second Temple period, above all among Hellenized Jews, we find currents of thought aimed at relativizing the importance of circumcision and emphasizing its symbolic character. Such ideas may have favoured the development of Christianity in certain Jewish circles. They were certainly influenced by the metaphorical references to circumcision found in the Hebrew Bible.[36] Thus the prophet Jeremiah speaks of the circumcision of the heart, i.e. of that faithfulness to the word of YHWH without which physical circumcision is nothing.

Philo of Alexandria, while accepting the need for circumcision, sought to justify it in terms acceptable to the Greeks. He begins his treatise *On the Special Laws* (*De specialibus legibus*) with circumcision, according to him the most mocked of Jewish customs.[37] He gives six reasons to justify the practice. Three relate to its beneficial effect on health and procreation. The three others, inspired by biblical metaphors, are allegorical. Thus circumcision makes the circumcised member resemble the heart; it is the symbol of the excision of pleasures and of knowledge. So Philo is not content to say that circumcision is necessary because it is a commandment of God. The barrier between this position and the rejection of circumcision is not such a high one, and some Jews, the number of which is difficult to determine, did not hesitate to cross it. Some refused to have their male children circumcised.[38] Others, in order to integrate themselves more easily with the Greeks, had their foreskins reconstructed by means of a surgical operation called epipasm.[39] Were those who were not circumcised and those who had submitted to this operation still Jews? A number of them had surely abandoned the traditions of their fathers. Others doubtless continued to identify with the Jewish people, content to interpret most of the elements of the law symbolically. Certainly the supporters of an allegorical interpretation of circumcision and other aspects of the Mosaic Law mentioned by Philo in his *De migratione Abrahami*[40] fall into this category. Philo, while approving their interpretation of circumcision, condemns their abandonment of this practice. But he nevertheless considers them to be full Jews. Another Jew, who would be much talked about, also emphasized the symbolic aspect of circumcision when he wrote:

> For he is not a real Jew who is one outwardly, nor is true circumcision something external and physical. He is a Jew who is one inwardly and real circumcision is a matter of the heart, spiritual and not literal (Rom. 2.28–29).

Saul of Tarsus, of the tribe of Benjamin, better known under the name of Paul, wanted to redefine Jewish identity by minimizing the role of circumcision. We shall be discussing this later.

The sabbath

The sabbath was also one of the particularly distinctive aspects of the Jewish way of life. According to the account in Genesis 2.2–3, God, after creating the heavens and the earth and the creatures, rested on the seventh day, which he blessed and sanctified. The Fourth Commandment enjoins the people of Israel not to do any work on the seventh day (Ex. 20.8–11; Deut. 5.12–15). The sabbath, a word denoting 'cessation of work', begins on Friday evening before sunset and ends the next day at nightfall. Apart from a few passages (Ex. 16.30; 31.12–17; 35.1–3; Num. 15.32–36; Jer. 17.19–27), the Bible is somewhat parsimonious over details of what is allowed during this period. Permitted or prohibited activities came to be defined more precisely over the centuries. A typical example was the question whether war could be waged on the sabbath. At the beginning of the war of resistance against Antiochus IV, many pious Jews were massacred because they had refused to defend themselves on this day (I Macc. 2.29–38). On learning this, Mattathias, the leader of the rebellion, and his friends authorized defensive military action.

Some problems arose when two commandments clashed. Thus the Mishnah tractate Pesahim mentions discussions of the conflict between the observance of the sabbath and the work necessary for preparing the Passover lamb: 'One day it happened that 14 Nisan coincided with the sabbath and they did not know whether or not the Passover sacrifice had priority over the sabbath.'[41] It was decided that the Passover sacrifice had priority. Similarly, the circumcision of a newborn child, which is a work, has to take place on the eighth day after birth. What is to be done when this day is a sabbath? In that case circumcision has priority.

Since the issues were by no means simple, we can easily understand how the main movements within first-century Judaism could take opposing views on the sabbath.[42] The Essenes observed the sabbath in a particularly rigorous way. The Sadducees also seem to have been very strict. The Pharisees, whose opinions were not homogeneous, seem to have been comparatively less rigorous. The Gospels clearly reflect disputes about sabbath observance. This observance hardly posed any problems in areas of Palestine predominantly populated by Jews. But things were not the same in the Diaspora where, apart from certain sympathizers who followed their customs, the Jews were the only ones to cease all activity on that day. A number of pagans, like Tacitus attributing the sabbath to the laziness of the Jews, will not have made life easy for them.[43] However, in some cities the Jews who had obtained official recognition of this practice enjoyed concessions, like not having to appear before the tribunals on that day.[44] They had also obtained from Rome exemption from military duties, which also posed other problems, connected with lawful foods.

Dietary laws

To live in accordance with the Mosaic law in fact involved observing a number of dietary restrictions relating to the type of food that could be eaten and the way in which it could be prepared.[45] The best known is the prohibition against eating pork. In the Graeco-Roman world the Jews stood out quite markedly by virtue of this practice, since pork was by far the most widely eaten meat. The symbolic aspect of the animal comes out clearly in the accounts of the martyrdom of Eleazar and the seven brothers, put to death by Antiochus IV because they refused to eat the forbidden meat and thus deny the laws of their fathers (II Macc. 6.18–7.42). Pork is the best-known meat, but the pig was not the only animal that Jews were forbidden. There is a list in Lev. 11.1–47 and Deut. 14.3–21. The blood and certain fatty parts are also proscribed by the Mosaic law. Furthermore, animals had to be killed in such a way as to empty them of their blood. While the observance of these laws posed no problems in the land of Israel, it could prove more difficult in the Diaspora. In fact in the Hellenistic world the meat sold on the markets most frequently came from animals sacrificed to pagan deities. This meat, even if it had been emptied of blood, as was usually the case with Greek sacrificial practices, could not be eaten by Jews because of its association with idols. This particular question gave rise to numerous disputes and controversies among the first Christians. Providing food for Jews, who also avoided buying their olive oil and wine from pagan merchants, could be a difficult business. That is why the Roman authorities sometimes required cities to take appropriate measures in order to have lawful food supplies available.[46]

A demanding morality

To live as a Jew also involved observing very rigorous moral precepts. These, of course, most frequently derived from the Bible. However, some rules which did not have any evident biblical foundation were developed at a later stage.[47] The definition of an appropriate Jewish ethic gave rise to a vast amount of reflection in the first century.[48] Some biblical rules were tightened and it was by no means rare to consider intention as culpable as action. Jewish literature which was apologetic or missionary by nature in particular emphasized the moral virtues of Judaism.

In many spheres the ethic derived from the Mosaic law hardly differed from the pagan ethic of the Hellenistic world. The differences were most marked in the sphere of sexuality and the family. Adultery, prostitution and homosexuality, widely tolerated in the pagan world, were severely condemned among the Jews. The definition of incest was particularly broad, since it included parents-in-law. Abortion and the exposure of new-born children, current in the Greco-Roman world, were forbidden.

Some humanitarian virtues like charity and mercy were emphasized more in Jewish morality. Similarly, a more developed solidarity could certainly have prompted pagans to join Jewish communities.

The temple system

For Jews who did not live too far from Jerusalem, observing the law meant first and foremost taking part in the activities of the temple.[49] As Francis Schmidt has demonstrated, it is difficult to overestimate the importance of the Jerusalem temple in the period in which we are interested. For the one God there was one sanctuary, which was both the centre of the land and its most holy place. The destruction of the temple in 587–586 BCE, its reconstruction after the exile in Babylon, the various desecrations of it, and finally its second destruction in 70 were powerful moments in the history of the Jews in antiquity.

The respect due to the temple and its prestige were magnified by the imposing majesty of the building. Following the work of enlargement and embellishment begun by Herod the Great, the temple had become one of the architectural wonders of the time, arousing the admiration of pilgrims and travellers. Its outer wall enclosed a surface of almost fifteen hectares, the equivalent of fourteen football pitches or five or six Acropolises. Only a few great Egyptian temples like Karnak were more extensive. The sanctuary proper, which was reached by crossing the great Court of the Gentiles, was clad in the most precious materials.

For all its riches and splendour, if we could go back in time, a visit to the temple would not be a pleasant experience. The crush of people, the jostling, the animals being led to the altar, the foul smells, would all make the visit a painful one. And once having reached the inner parts of the temple where the sacrifices took place, the modern visitor would doubtless feel repulsion: the altar and its surroundings, with hundreds of animals having their throats slit and being cut up, would seem more like a vast abattoir than a synagogue or a modern church.

The temple, the centre of Jewish religious life, also played a major political and economic role.[50] During the Roman occupation the high priest had a privileged role *vis-à-vis* the prefect (or procurator after the reign of Claudius). Assisted by the Sanhedrin, a great council of notable men, in practice he enjoyed by no means negligible authority in the administration of Jerusalem and the rest of Judaea, ensuring that public order was kept and also that the tribute claimed by the Romans was paid.

The temple and its personnel benefited from considerable contributions, in both money and in kind, voluntary and compulsory. These contributions, on top of the spending of pilgrims during the great festivals, stimulated economic activity throughout Judaea. The major work of rebuilding the temple provided work for almost 20,000 people. Its completion at the beginning of the 60s created major economic difficulties, which certainly contributed to the outbreak of the war against Rome.

However, it was clearly the religious function of the temple which constituted its unique and basic character. The celebration of worship, with the whole sacrificial system, guaranteed harmony between heaven and earth, between God and Israel. Appropriate sacrifices allowed the Jews, individually or collectively, to put themselves right before God. The rhythm of the everyday life of all the inhabitants of Jerusalem and its neighbourhood was marked by the temple and its ceremonies. At *Pesach* (Passover), *Shavuoth* (the Feast of Weeks or Pentecost) and *Sukkoth* (the Feast of Tabernacles), the three great pilgrimage seasons, pilgrims from the land of Israel and the countries of the Diaspora flocked to Jerusalem. Some scholars think that more than 300,000 pilgrims went to the temple at each of the great festivals, two-thirds of them coming from Palestine.

Here it is important to correct an erroneous view about sacrifices for the expiation of sins which is widespread among traditionalist Christian theologians. In this view, true repentance, which is that of the heart, is opposed to the mechanical and artificial repentance of sacrifices. The former type of repentance, inherited from the prophets, is said to inspire Christianity, whereas the latter, representative of Second Temple Judaism, is thought to mark a lower form of religious practice. However, there is no foundation for such a contrast. The Jews of the Second Temple were well aware that a sacrifice was valueless unless it was accompanied by sincere repentance. Jesus ben Sirach expresses this idea clearly:

Do not offer him [the Lord] a bribe, for he will not accept it; and do not trust to an unrighteous sacrifice (Eccles. 35.11).

Jesus is simply picking up this idea when he calls for reconciliation with a brother who has been offended before presenting an offering in the temple (Matt. 5.23–24).

Leaving aside the question of clean and unclean animals mentioned above, the rules of purity and impurity, so important in Leviticus, were largely linked to the temple and its cult:

Thus you shall keep the people of Israel separate from their uncleanness, lest they die in their uncleanness by defiling my tabernacle that is in their midst (Lev. 15.31).

The Mosaic law defines about ten sources of impurity, the chief of which are corpses, childbirth, sperm, bodily emissions, menstruating women and skin diseases wrongly called leprosy. The temple had to be protected from any blemish. It even had different degrees of holiness corresponding to the appropriate levels of purity, as is shown by the priest Flavius Josephus in his work *Against Apion*:

All who ever saw our temple are aware of the general design of the building, and the inviolable barriers which preserved its sanctity. It had four surrounding courts, each with its special statutory restrictions. The outer court was open to all, foreigners included: women during their impurity were alone refused admission. To the second court all Jews were admitted, and, when uncontaminated by any defilement, their wives; to the third male Jews, if clean and purified; to the fourth priests robed in their priestly vestments. The sanctuary was entered only by the high priests, clad in the raiment peculiar to themselves.[51]

The closer one got to the Holy of Holies, the greater the degree of purity had to be. There was a complex system for eliminating impurities. The slightest were removed by immersion and by sunset; others also required a sacrifice in the temple.

By reason of their priestly activity, the priests themselves had most often to be free of impurity. This was required not only when they officiated in the temple but also when they ate consecrated food (offerings, tithes) within its precincts. The laity, too, had to have an appropriate level of purity when they entered the temple or ate consecrated food. However, in theory the majority of Jews could live their everyday lives in a state of uncleanness as long as they did not go to the temple. Women were most often impure because of giving birth, menstruation and normal sexual relations.

In the period with which we are concerned, certain groups like the Pharisees and the Essenes extended the laws of purity far outside activities associated with the temple.[52] This extension was based on certain biblical passages like Leviticus 19.2, in which YHWH requires all Israel to be holy. The Pharisees indubitably attached great importance to the laws of purity. Jacob Neusner, one of the greatest experts on rabbinic Judaism, thinks that the Pharisees differed from the rest of the population chiefly because they ate their ordinary food in a state of priestly purity. E. P. Sanders, who thinks Neusner's position exaggerated, nevertheless believes that the Pharisees were characterized by a state of purity superior to that of the majority of the population.[53] The Essenes, who, regarding themselves as a priestly and holy community, tried to maintain the highest possible state of purity, were even more rigorous than the Pharisees.

Thus it seems quite clear that, outside their contacts with the

temple and consecrated food, the laity enjoyed considerable lati-
tude in the degree of purity that they wanted to maintain. The
fanatics about purity stood over against those who observed the
minimum requirements.

While the temple with its festivals marked the rhythm of the
life of the inhabitants of Jerusalem and its environs, for the
majority of Jews of the Diaspora it represented only a powerful
symbol or a sometimes distant dream. The richest of them, or
those who lived closest, could hope to go to Jerusalem for one
of the great annual festivals. The rest were content to show their
solidarity and their devotion by paying an annual contribution
of a half-shekel. For the Jews of the Diaspora, the synagogue
was the centre of religious life.[54] Some traditions put the
creation of the synagogue in the Babylonian exile. However, the
earliest material evidence that we have relates only to Egyptian
'houses of prayer' dating from the second century BCE. The
synagogues, houses of prayer and study of the Torah were also
the centre of local community life.

There were also synagogues in the land of Israel. However,
their liturgical activities must have been all the more limited, the
closer they were to the temple. Many scholars contrast synagogue worship, controlled by the Pharisees, with the temple,
dominated by the Sadducees. However, this opinion is wrong
and anachronistic, as Lester Grabbe,[55] E. P. Sanders[56] and many
others have shown. Far from being opposed to the temple, the
synagogues were more a complement than a substitute. No one,
above all the Pharisees, some of whom were priests or levites,
would have dared to pretend that a synagogue could replace the
temple. Furthermore the Pharisees did not exercise any dominant influence on the synagogues. These were governed by
prominent men who belonged to priestly or lay families. Some
of them certainly belonged to the Pharisaic movement, but it is
by no means certain that they formed a majority. In Palestine,
the rabbis of the Mishnah and Talmud, the heirs of the
Pharisees, did not dominate the synagogues before the third or
the fourth century.

We have looked above all at the essential aspects of the mode
of conduct *(halakhah)* of the Jews which were derived from the
law. It must be understood that the disputes between the

different schools or sects related above all to the interpretation of the law, and thus to the way in which the Jews had to lead their lives. The differences, which might seem to us to be trivial, were at that time thought to be fundamental. YHWH had decided to regulate the life of his people in detail. Several interpretations were conceivable in spheres where the will of God did not seem to be very clear. So a choice had to be made, and this choice was crucial.

And afterwards?

Judaism, unlike Christianity, has never been a dogmatic religion the adherents of which have to accept a certain number of clearly defined beliefs. Judaism attaches more importance to religious practice and to life-style than to abstract ideals. Apart from belief in one God, Jews are rarely in agreement on the existence and importance of other articles of faith. Eschatology, i.e. discourse on the ultimate individual and collective destiny of human beings, is a sphere in which no article of faith had normative value in Second Temple Judaism.[57] The most diverse and contradictory conceptions were expressed.

Judaism, like Christianity, often passes for a religion of salvation, i.e. of a quest for eternal life amongst God's elect. Nothing is more mistaken where the religious ideas contained in the Hebrew Bible are concerned. In fact, apart from a few passages which are regarded as late, the Bible does not offer any reason for hoping for a happy life after death, in the form of either the immortality of the soul or the resurrection of the body.[58] When men die, their shade or double goes to lead a wretched spectral existence in a sad subterranean place called Sheol. No distinction is made between the just and the sinners, who are all in the same boat. So there is no reason for hope or rejoicing. Those who respect the ordinances of YHWH are nevertheless recompensed, but during their lifetime, with a long and prosperous life and with many descendants.

The only hope contained in the Hebrew Bible is of a collective kind, and relates only to the living and/or their descendants. It is initially expressed in the promises made to Abraham and Moses. But it takes on quite special importance after the fall of the kingdom of Israel, and above all after that of the kingdom of Judaea and its capital, Jerusalem. The prophets then make themselves the heralds of a new era of spiritual happiness, material riches and political independence. As this new era is sometimes preceded and ushered in by the coming of the Messiah – the one who is anointed by YHWH – it is usually called the messianic era or age.[59] A certain number of prophets conceived of this new era in mainly historical terms, emphasizing the political restoration of Israel. Others announced that this golden age, the final period of humanity, would be bound up with radical cosmic changes in the natural order of things. The inauguration of the messianic era would be preceded by formidable sufferings and persecutions for Israel, which would then culminate in the Day of YHWH. This day, on which his anger would explode, would destroy the nations which oppressed Israel and those of YHWH's people who neglected his commandments. The 'remnant of Israel' and the survivors of the nations who recognize the glory of YHWH will benefit from the blessings of this golden age. The biblical prophets, Isaiah[60] in particular, offered a foretaste of the time of paradise. The exiles of Israel will return to the promised land; the temple and Jerusalem will be rebuilt more magnificently than ever. God will take his place on Zion again and rule over the whole earth. Peace will be manifestly established among the nations, between human beings and nature, and among the animals. Evil, violence and war will disappear for ever. Social justice will triumph. Nature will become immensely fertile. Diseases and infirmities will be cured. God will give, if not eternal life, at least a long and happy existence.

In the time of Jesus and the first Christians, when Israel was under the domination of the Gentiles, such a hope had very deep roots among many Jews, especially the most pious. Academic circles tend to minimize the importance of the messianic hope in this period. But that is to forget too quickly the indisputable messianic elements in the great revolts in Palestine in 66 and 132 and by the Jews in Cyprus, Egypt and Cyrenaica (Libya) in 115. The great prophetic texts did not all envisage this messianic era in the same way. Its supernatural and cosmic aspect was more or less pronounced. According to some, the messianic era, which would be of limited duration, would be followed by YHWH's judgment and the final era conceived of in very supernatural terms; according to others, it would last for ever. For some, YHWH himself would bring about everything; for others he would act through his Messiah.

The role and identity of the Messiah were also the object of numerous and varied speculations.[61] For some, perhaps the majority of the population, this Messiah would be a king of the line of David; for others he would be a prophet like Moses (Deut. 18). Texts discovered at Qumran speak of two Messiahs, a royal Davidic Messiah and a priestly Messiah descended from Aaron. Some identify him with the Son of man spoken of in the books of Daniel and Enoch. However, the great new development as compared with the age of the great prophets is the belief that it would be possible for the just who had died too early to take part in the spiritual and material joys of the messianic age thanks to their resurrection.

This belief, which appeared in some Jewish circles probably during the period of Persian domination, spread increasingly from the beginning of the second century before our era. As a correlative there developed the notion of the immortality of the soul, which was of Greek origin. The two conceptions were sometimes combined: the survival of the soul after death, and then resurrection at the beginning of the final era. The importance attached to individual survival after death is partly explained by the increasing individualization of religion in the Hellenistic world.

Flavius Josephus and the New Testament also attest these sectarian disputes over survival after death. The Sadducees, who kept to the traditional doctrine of the Hebrew Bible, denied the resurrection of the body and the immortality of the soul. The Synoptic Gospels report an episode in which the Sadducees tried unsuccessfully to prove to Jesus the absurdity of the resurrection (Matt. 22.23–33/Mark 12.18–27/Luke 20.27–40). But the Pharisees, like Jesus and the first Christians, believed in the resurrection of the dead, a basic element in their system. The Essenes, who had no doubts about eternal life, lived in the expectation of the end of time. As Émile Puech has demonstrated, the Qumran texts which have recently been translated suggest that the doctrine of the Essenes in this sphere was resurrection and not the immortality of the soul, as several scholars thought. On the other hand, the immortality of the soul was doubtless a widespread doctrine among the most Hellenized Jews of the Diaspora.

Another important aspect of the eschatological doctrines is the identity of those who will benefit from eternal life in the world to come. Here again there were most widespread opinions. The Essenes thought that only the Jews who lived in accordance with their interpretation of the law would be saved. The traditional rabbinic doctrine, expressed in the Mishnah tractate Sanhedrin, is that all Israel has a share in the world to come (a few exceptions follow, but these do not alter the general character of the doctrine). However, we do not know to what degree this position reflects that of the majority of Pharisees in the middle of the first century. We shall see in Chapter 7 the fate that was reserved for the Gentiles; nevertheless, we should note immediately that the salvation of the Gentiles was certainly not an essential preoccupation of the Jews of antiquity.

A Galilean Judaism

Aware of the diversity of Judaism at the end of the Second Temple period, many scholars try to explain the religious conceptions of Jesus and his main disciples in the light of the particularities of Galilean Judaism. This, and not the Judaism of Judaea, is thought to have formed the ground from which Christianity grew. The special character of Galilean Judaism as compared with the more orthodox Judaism of Judaea would be due to the quite special development of this region and in particular to its late (re-)Judaizing at the time of Jesus. A number of scholars conclude from this that Galilee was only very superficially Judaized at the beginning of the first century BCE. On the basis of recent archaeological discoveries some advocates of this theory think that Galilee, very cosmopolitan and strongly Hellenized, was little different from the Greek cities of the Decapolis (Philadelphia, Pella, Gadara, Scythopolis, etc.).[62] Such a position is generally adopted by those who, like Burton Mack, conceive of Jesus as an itinerant cynic-type philosopher. These scholars underestimate the Jewish character of Galilee, though this is widely attested in Josephus and in the New Testament. Moreover, the presence of the material civilization of a Hellenistic kind common to the Mediterranean regions does not necessarily imply a profound cultural influence. Just because the same skyscrapers, supermarkets and television programmes can be found today in New York, Riyadh and Beijing does not mean that we can talk of cultural convergences between these three cities. The majority of scholars, rejecting this approach – though it was popular in the last century – do not question the Jewish character of Galilee. Certainly Gentiles lived there, like the numerous mercenaries in the service of Herod Antipas, but the vast majority of the population was sincerely and profoundly Jewish.

Some historians think that the Judaism of the Galileans was not very sophisticated and was characterized above all by its enthusiasm and its intense nationalism. They make Galilee a hotbed of anti-Roman resistance,[63] believing that the 'Zealots' there combined a sincere zeal for the law with a rejection of any foreign domination, even indirect. One of the major reasons put forward in support of such a conception is the origin of Judas the Galilean, the father of the Zealot movement, which, according to some historians, was an important and continuous factor in the agitation leading to the revolt against Rome. This opinion is warmly endorsed by those who see Jesus and the first Christians as Zealot supporters. However, this seems considerably to exaggerate the agitation in Galilee. Thus while Judas in fact began his career with an attack on Sepphoris in 4 BCE, he carried out most of his later actions in Judaea. It was also in Judaea that his sons Simon and Jacob caused troubles until their execution. Scholars like Sean Freyne[64] and Uriel Rappoport[65] think that Galilee was relatively calm up to the beginning of the war against Rome. Moreover they rightly remark that apart from a brief interval between 44 and 62, Galilee was under the direct rule, not of Rome, but of the Herodian kings.

Dismissing any notion of revolutionary enthusiasm, many scholars, inspired by the traditional image of a rural and un-developed Galilee, emphasize the simple and archaic character

of Galilean Judaism. In their view the majority of Galileans
were *'ammē hā-ārets,* that is to say Jews who were somewhat
lax in their practice of certain aspects of the law. Impervious to
the often Sibylline innovations of the Pharisees, they preferred
to keep to their more simple traditional customs, putting inner
piety and purity above the external manifestations of religion.[66]
Their heroes were not these learned masters from Jerusalem
who bored them with their arguments, but pious and charismatic men like Honi the 'Circle-Drawer', Hanina ben Dosa and
of course Jesus.

We can immediately see how much this image of Galilean
Judaism is inspired by a certain idea of Jesus as a champion of
the Galilean *'ammē hā-ārets* in the face of the Pharisees. Jesus
then becomes a pure product of Galilee, in contrast to James,
the man who observes the law strictly. That is why some
historians envisage that James had his education in Jerusalem in
Pharisaic or Essene circles. And that would immediately explain
why under James the church of Jerusalem lost the true meaning
of the message of Jesus.

This image of Galilean Judaism is based on passages drawn
from the Gospels, the works of Josephus and rabbinic literature.
The scribes and Pharisees who argue against Jesus are often presented as coming from Jerusalem. The Gospel of John shows us
Pharisees who think that the Galileans are ignorant of the law.
Such an accusation is repeated in rabbinic literature. Thus
according to the Jerusalem Talmud (Shabbat 15d), Yohanan
ben Zakkai, a sage from the first century of our era, is said to
have declared that Galilee hated the Torah. That Herod Antipas
built Tiberias on tombs is also said to shows the laxity of the
Galileans in matters of ritual purity.

The Israeli historian Aharon Oppenheimer has firmly rejected
this view.[67] He has shown that the hostile or scornful remarks
about the Galileans to be found in rabbinic literature cannot
reflect the situation in Galilee some centuries earlier. He has
emphasized that, on the contrary, the example of Tiberias cited
by Josephus indicates attentive respect for the laws of purity in
that Herod Antipas found difficulty in populating his new city.
Furthermore, Josephus[68] notes that the Galileans paid tithes and
regularly went on pilgrimage to Jerusalem. Thus Oppenheimer,

followed here by Shmuel Safrai[69] and many other scholars, refuses to contrast a Judaean Judaism of Pharisaic obedience with a more lax Galilean Judaism dominated by the *'ammē hā-ārets*. He thinks that each region had its strict Jews and its *'ammē hā-ārets*, in equivalent proportions. Moreover Oppenheimer and Lawrence Shiffman have noted that when the interpretation of the law in force in Galilee differed from that in Jerusalem, it was often stricter.[70] Perhaps, as Étienne Nodet suggests, that was due to the influence of the Jews from Babylon who emigrated to Galilee under Herod the Great.[71]

So given the present state of our knowledge it seems somewhat futile to want to explain Jesus in terms of the supposedly special features of Galilean Judaism. Similarly, James fits perfectly into the Galilean Judaism of his time.

4

Jesus, James and the Brothers

The New Testament writings give us hardly any specific information about James before he surfaces as one of the heads of the primitive church. We have seen how difficult it was to describe his education. We know nothing of his profession. Was he a carpenter like his father and his brother Jesus? A farmer? A merchant? A scribe? Since Paul indicates that the brothers of Jesus travelled around with their wives (I Cor. 9.5) we can suppose that James was married. If he had children, none seems to have left any traces in the primitive church. To relate the 'hidden life' of James would be fantasy pure and simple. The Gospels give us a glimpse of only one aspect of his life before the crucifixion, though this is a fundamental one: James' relationship with his famous brother. Yet again it must be made quite clear that the Gospels speak of brothers of Jesus, sometimes mentioning their names, but not differentiating James from the others. Readers who are more familiar with the New Testament will certainly remember the famous saying of Jesus on the occasion of his barren visit to Nazareth: 'A prophet is not without honour, except in his own country, and among his own kin, and in his own house' (Mark 6.4). They will also recall the contrast drawn by Jesus between his natural family and his true, spiritual family. The Gospel of John (7.5) seems to sum up the situation by affirming bluntly that 'not even his brothers believed on him'.

For the majority of believers and experts, it is a matter of course that James and his brothers were not disciples of Jesus. They even seem to have shown some hostility towards him. This is attributed above all to Jesus' brothers and to the rest of the family. Rather than regarding Jesus as being divinely inspired, they would have regarded him as a crank. Moreover, since they themselves were profoundly pious and traditionalist Jews, they would have been shocked by the radical nature of his message and his somewhat lax observance of the law. According to some exegetes, this break would even have had major psychological effects on the personality and the message of Jesus. For others, Jesus would have been the person principally responsible for the family conflict; an opponent of traditional patriarchal values, he would have deliberately distanced himself from his family. So the break would have come about over a matter of principle.

Despite their scepticism or their hostility during his ministry, Jesus' brothers, and James in particular, occupied a pre-eminent place in the Christian church. How do we explain this volte-face? Perhaps the Gospels do not tell us the whole truth. The case deserves to be reopened.

A difficult relationship

The Synoptic Gospels

The Synoptic Gospels mention relations between Jesus and his family on two well-known occasions, 'the true kinsfolk of Jesus' and 'the visit to Nazareth'.[1] Both belong to the triple tradition, i.e. they appear in the three Synoptic Gospels. Here is how the Gospel of Mark relates the episode of the true kinship of Jesus. After instituting the Twelve, Jesus goes home:

> Then he went home; and the crowd came together again, so that they could not even eat. And when his relatives heard it, they went out to seize him, for they said, 'He is beside himself' (Mark 3.20–21).

This episode, interrupted by a story in which scribes who have come from Jerusalem accuse Jesus of being possessed by a devil, resumes with the arrival of his close relations. Here once again is this important passage:

> And his mother and his brothers came; and standing outside they sent to him and called him. And a crowd was sitting

about him; and they said to him, 'Your mother and your brothers are outside, asking for you.' And he replied, 'Who are my mother and my brothers?', and looking around on those who sat about him, he said, 'Here are my mother and my brothers! Whoever does the will of God is my brother, and sister, and mother' (Mark 3.31–35).

Mark draws attention both to the attitude of Jesus' family and to Jesus' own reaction. Some traditionalist interpretations try to eliminate all conflict between Jesus and his family. Thus according to Fr Lagrange, a great Catholic exegete from the beginning of the century, Jesus' family was 'moved by his all-consuming activity, which threatened to exhaust his strength'.[2] Their approach is well-intentioned. They ask whether Jesus isn't doing too much. Again according to Fr Lagrange, Jesus, in his reply, emphasizes the superiority of spiritual kinship over natural kinship: 'The sacred duties of the family are not denied. Jesus does not deny his mother. We see only that he attaches more importance to his feelings towards God than to the care with which she looked after him as a child. By putting Mary at the head of the new spiritual family of Jesus, high above all the saints, the church has interpreted his thought.'

Fr Lagrange, like many other Catholic exegetes, was trying in a more or less convincing way to reconcile the mariolatry of his church with a passage revealing somewhat tense relations between Jesus and his next of kin. This type of harmonizing interpretation is nowadays relegated to the sphere of popular devotional literature. It cannot in fact be denied that Mark emphasizes the scepticism, not to say the opposition, of Jesus' family, who think that he has lost his head. For his part Jesus, when told that his mother and his brothers are looking for him, replies dryly and with no ambiguity. He does not want to proclaim that his spiritual family transcends his natural family, but that it replaces it. In denoting those seated around him as his true family, he indicates clearly that his biological family is not among those who are doing the will of God.

Matthew and Luke present this episode in a different light. They nowhere mention that the kinsfolk of Jesus had gone in search of him because he was 'out of his mind'. Moreover, the pericope on the calumny of the scribes is not attached to that on the true kinsfolk of Jesus. Matthew and Luke do not treat this last pericope in the same way. Matthew is close to Mark:

> While he was still speaking to the people, behold, his mother and his brothers stood outside, asking to speak to him. But he replied to the man who told him, 'Who is my mother, and who are my brothers?' And stretching out his hand towards his disciples, he said, 'Here are my mother and my brothers! For whoever does the will of my Father in heaven is my brother, and sister, and mother' (Matt. 12.46–50).

By stretching out his hand towards his disciples, Jesus shows that his mother and his brothers are not part of them. Here is how Luke presents the scene:

> Then his mother and his brothers came to him, but they could not reach him for the crowd. And he was told, 'Your mother and your brothers are standing outside, desiring to see you.' But he said to them, 'My mother and my brothers are those who hear the word of God and do it' (Luke 8.19–21).

Luke reduces the opposition between Jesus and his family. Whereas in Mark his mother and brothers have Jesus called, in Luke they go to him, but cannot get to him because of the crowd. In his reply Jesus is content to define his true family; there is no indication that his mother and his biological brothers are excluded from it.

Let us now look at the way in which the Synoptic Gospels present the second episode, the visit to Nazareth.

Mark (6.1–6) and Matthew (13.53–58) offer similar versions, with only a few differences in detail. Jesus goes to Nazareth, his home village, which he left to settle at Capernaum. He teaches in the synagogue. The congregation, at first impressed, ends by asking where this local man gets his wisdom and his capacity to perform miracles from. But Jesus can do very few wonders there. Amazed at the lack of faith among the people of Nazareth, he tells them, 'A prophet is not without honour, except in his own country, and among his own kin, and in his own house' (Mark 6.4). In the Gospel of Matthew (13.57), Jesus does not mention his kinsfolk.

Luke's account, much longer, differs significantly. The congregation present in the synagogue passes quite inexplicably from admiration to scepticism. Jesus then tells them:

> 'Doubtless you will quote to me this proverb, "Physician, heal yourself; what we have heard you did at Capernaum, do here also in your own country."' And he said, 'Truly, I say to you, no prophet is acceptable in his own country' (Luke 4.23–24).

The scepticism of the inhabitants of Nazareth turns to fury. Jesus, driven from the town, barely escapes death.

Thus the position of Jesus' family is presented differently by each evangelist. For Mark, the family is part of those who have rejected Jesus. Luke, eliminating all references to the house of Jesus and his kinsfolk, does not explicitly include it among the unbelievers. Matthew, preserving the reference to the house but not mentioning the kinship, is more ambiguous and can be interpreted in different ways. The variations that we identified in the discussion of the first episode are confirmed here.

For the majority of exegetes the Gospel of Mark, which is the earliest, reflects an authentic tradition of opposition between Jesus and his closest relations. They think that the evangelist would never have dared to write that the family of Jesus imagined that he had lost his head had this statement not been based on trustworthy traditions. Matthew is said to have modified the Gospel of Mark, his source, so as to reduce the antagonism between Jesus and his kinsfolk. Luke will have made it virtually disappear. The later evangelists will have acted in this way out of respect for the family of Jesus, which occupied a pre-eminent position in the primitive church, and in order to avoid a major contradiction with the accounts of the birth of Jesus. We should not forget that Matthew and Luke, in contrast to Mark, offer accounts of the virgin birth of Jesus in which Joseph and Mary are several times officially notified of the exceptional destiny of the new-born child. Given these divine revelations, the scepticism, indeed hostility, of the family would have been incomprehensible.

This interpretation has not gained unanimous support. Some

scholars, rejecting the priority of Mark in favour of Matthew, think that the latter transmits a more authentic tradition.

Others think that the authors of Matthew and Luke do not draw on the present Mark but on a proto-Mark which is quite different from the Gospel that we know. For the great exegete M.-E. Boismard, Proto-Mark contained neither the episode of the rejection of Jesus at Nazareth nor the search for Jesus by his close relatives because he had lost his mind.[3] First-rate exegetes like Étienne Trocmé, John Dominic Crossan and Werner Kelber, while accepting the priority of the Mark that we have, also challenge the dominant interpretation.[4] For them, the fact that Mark is the earliest Gospel does not imply that it must always be considered the most trustworthy from a historical point of view. As for the episodes which interest us here, they think that Mark, engaging in major redactional activity, substantially remodelled the written sources and oral traditions that he had.[5] So he would have strongly accentuated, even created, the opposition between Jesus and his family. In the Gospel of Mark this antagonism, far from reflecting trustworthy traditions, would represent above all the conflicts between the evangelist's community and the brothers of Jesus, who were so pre-eminent in the churches of Palestine some decades after the crucifixion. In the pericope about the true family of Jesus Mark would also have wanted to emphasize that the brothers of Christ should not benefit from any prerogative linked to their kinship.

Those who support this interpretation base it on a very thorough analysis of the texts. They emphasize the breadth of Mark's redactional activity in order to magnify the opposition between Jesus and his kinsfolk. The placing of the approach of Jesus' kinsfolk is very revealing of the intentions of the redactor. It comes after several miraculous healings and the institution of the Twelve, whom Jesus has chosen to spread his message. Jesus' kinsfolk, far from believing in the miraculous healings, and thinking that he has gone mad, set out to get hold of him. It is at this moment that Mark inserts a passage in which the scribes slander Jesus. They have come down from Jerusalem and thus represent the Jewish authorities, and they claim that Jesus is possessed by Beelzebul when he performs his exorcisms.

Jesus, accusing them of blaspheming against the Holy Spirit, promises them eternal damnation:

> 'Truly, I say to you, all sins will be forgiven the sons of men, and whatever blasphemies they utter; but whoever blasphemes against the holy Spirit never has forgiveness, but is guilty of an eternal sin' – for they had said, 'He has an unclean spirit' (Mark 3.28–30).

The episode of the scribes allows us to understand better why Jesus' family thought that he had lost his mind. To lose one's mind, to become mad, was interpreted as being possessed by a demon. The evangelist skilfully likens the family to the scribes. Like them, it has mistaken the holy spirit for a demon; like them, it is guilty of an eternal sin.[6]

Similarly Luke (8.21), who does not explicitly exclude Jesus' mother and brothers from his true spiritual family, could represent the original form of Jesus' saying. Moreover Logion 99 of the Gospel of Thomas presents a form similar to that of Luke.

Continuing in the same direction, the reference to kinship in Mark (6.4) could be an addition by the evangelist. Luke and Matthew, who do not mention it, would be closer to the earliest tradition, which seems also to be reflected in John and Thomas:

> For Jesus himself testified that a prophet has no honour in his own country (John 4.44).

> Jesus said, 'No prophet is accepted in his own village; no physician heals those who know him' (Gospel of Thomas 31).

So might not the opposition, even the hostility, between Jesus and his family be merely an invention of Mark's? Or has the evangelist simply dramatized the family's scepticism and failure to understand? Let us see if the Gospel of John allows us to settle the matter.

The Gospel of John

We already know that the Gospel of John (7.5) mentions the unbelief of Jesus' brothers: 'For even his brothers did not believe in him.' Before considering the context and meaning of this phrase, let us look at the first reference in John to the brothers of Jesus: Jesus, accompanied by his mother, his brothers and his disciples, goes to Capernaum after performing his first miracle at Cana (John 2.11–12). We should note that Jesus' brothers, in contrast to his mother and his disciples (John 2.2), are not listed among those invited to the wedding at Cana. Some exegetes, like M.-E. Boismard, think that this contradiction is due to modifications made to the authentic Johannine text by someone who revised the Gospel.[7] They think that the disciples are not mentioned in the original text: Jesus is present at the marriage feast with his mother and his brothers, and it is with them that he goes to Capernaum. They use as a basis for this view the fact that some very old versions of John, like that of the Codex Sinaiticus, omit 'and his disciples' in John (2.12).

A very old testimony to the wedding at Cana, the *Epistula Apostolorum*, mentions the brothers of Jesus but not the disciples among those who are invited. Similarly, Chrysostom and Epiphanius read John 2.2 as follows: 'And Jesus was invited to the wedding and his mother was there, and his brothers.' Analysing the account of the wedding at Cana, one cannot but be struck by the artificial character of the dialogue between Jesus and his mother. When his mother tells Jesus that there is no more wine, Jesus replies quite dryly and mysteriously, 'O woman, what have you to do with me? My hour has not yet come' (John 2.4). In spite of that, he nevertheless performs a miracle by transforming water into wine. That is why scholars like M.-E. Boismard and Robert Fortna have suggested that the evangelist used a primitive document in which Jesus performed a miracle at the request of his mother.[8] His mother and his brothers would thus have been associated with the miracle in the initial version.

Let us now move on to John 7, in which the brothers of Jesus are described as unbelievers.

After this Jesus went about in Galilee; he would not go about in Judaea, because the Jews sought to kill him. Now the Jews' feast of Tabernacles was at hand. So his brothers said to him, 'Leave here and go to Judaea, that your disciples may see the works you are doing. For no man works in secret if he seeks to be known openly. If you do these things, show yourself to the world.' For even his brothers did not believe in him. Jesus said to them, 'My time has not yet come, but your time is always here. The world cannot hate you, but it hates me because I testify of it that its works are evil. Go to the feast yourselves; I am not going up to this feast, for my time has not yet fully come.' So saying, he remained in Galilee. But after his brothers had gone up to the feast, then he also went up, not publicly but in private (John 7.1–10).

The evangelist transmits a very negative image of the brothers of Jesus which goes beyond the simple mention of their unbelief. When Jesus says that the world which hates him cannot hate his brothers, he suggests that they are perfectly at ease and accepted in a world dominated by Satan. Moreover the account can give the impression that in urging him to go up to Jerusalem, Jesus' brothers want to throw him to the wolves.

Like the account of the wedding at Cana, John 7.1–10 has a markedly artificial character. The mention of the unbelief of Jesus' brothers is inserted clumsily into the narrative. The redactor seems to offer an explanation, but one does not really understand why the request made by Jesus' brothers manifests their unbelief. Although Jesus says that he will not go to Jerusalem, he ends up going there secretly. Despite everything, on his arrival he teaches openly in the temple (John 7.14). These anomalies suggest that the Gospel incorporates, with modifications, an earlier document which according to Boismard and Lamouille would have read like this:

Jesus was travelling around in Galilee. His brothers said to him: 'Go from here to Judaea so that they can see the works that you are doing. No one acting in secret seeks to get attention. If that's what you are doing, show yourself to the world.' Jesus said to them, 'It is not yet time.'[9]

For our commentators, going up to Jerusalem would be a separate episode. No animosity or unbelief on the part of Jesus' brothers would appear in this reconstruction, though we should remember that it remains a speculative one.

Whatever may be the history of the redaction of the Gospel of John, it is clear that the version that we have presents the brothers of Jesus in an unfavourable light. As Raymond Brown emphasizes, this might seem surprising: 'In any case, the hostile portrait of the brothers of Jesus, without any hint of their conversion, is startling when we reflect that the Fourth Gospel was written after James, the brother of the Lord, had led the Jerusalem church for almost thirty years and had died a martyr's death.'[10] In fact, as Brown and J. L. Martyn have suggested, the best way of understanding such a negative portrait of the brothers of Jesus in the Gospel of John is to interpret it in the light of the conflicts between the Johannine community and the Jewish Christians, disciples of James and his brothers.[11] In this perspective the unbelief of Jesus' brothers takes on a different meaning. In fact nothing in the Gospel of John suggests that James and his brothers do not believe in the miracles that Jesus has already performed or in the exceptional character of his person. But they are unbelievers because they do not understand the identity of Jesus or the meaning of his mission. They see him only as a messianic prophet who, by performing signs, is to restore Israel. They do not take into account the fact that he is far more than that. In short, they are unbelievers because their belief is wrong.

Raymond Brown thinks that this episode must be connected with two other passages in John (2.23–25; 6.60–66). In the first, the evangelist tells us that in Jerusalem at the time of the feast of Passover many people believed in Jesus because of the signs that he did. But, he adds, Jesus did not trust himself to them because he knew them all. In the second, many disciples, scandalized by the eucharistic sayings of Jesus, decided to stop following him. Very impressed by the miracles, the meaning of which they did not understand, and refusing to eat the flesh of the Lord and to drink his blood, they could well have been Jewish Christians with another conception of the eucharist. The Jewish Christians in John (2.23–25; 6.60–66), like the brothers of Jesus who are their inspiration, are unbelievers not because they reject the Christ but because they do not perceive his true nature. We should also note that the Gospel of John, in contrast to the Synoptic Gospels, draws a distinction between the mother of

Jesus and his brothers. Mary, whose image is ambiguous in the episode of the marriage at Cana, appears as a disciple at the crucifixion (John 19.25–27). In this scene, which I have already mentioned, Jesus entrusts his mother to the beloved disciple. Some commentators have seen this as an attack on the brothers of Jesus, with the beloved disciple becoming the true brother of the Lord in their place. But that does not explain the positive image of Mary compared with that of Jesus' brothers. Mary, who died earlier, could perhaps have been less closely associated with the communities of which the evangelist was an opponent.

So John's testimony, which is particularly ambiguous despite appearances, does not provide any decisive answer to our question. It could nevertheless suggest that the brothers of Jesus were sometimes associated with Jesus' ministry.

Some scholars think that the antagonism between Jesus and his family is confirmed by the hostility of Jesus towards the traditional family system. They even tend to think that his presumed break with his family is due more to his attitude than to that of his kinsfolk. But is this certain?

Jesus and the family

Several sayings attributed to Jesus refer to his attitude towards the family. Some, emphasizing the obligation to honour one's parents, are in conformity with the Jewish moral tradition inspired by the Decalogue. The well-known episode of the rich man who wanted to inherit eternal life is a prime example of this (Matt. 19.16–22/Mark 10.17–22/Luke 18.18–23). Here is Mark's version:

And as he was setting out on his journey, a man ran up and knelt before him, and asked him, 'Good Teacher, what must I do to inherit eternal life?' And Jesus said to him, 'Why do you call me good? No one is good but God alone. You know the commandments: "Do not kill, Do not commit adultery, Do not steal, Do not bear false witness, do not defraud, Honour your father and mother."' And he said to him, 'Teacher, all these I have observed from my youth.' And Jesus looking upon him loved him, and said to him, 'You lack one thing;

go, sell what you have, and give to the poor, and you will
have treasure in heaven; and come, follow me.' At that saying
his countenance fell, and he went away sorrowful, for he had
great possessions.

In this passage Jesus emphasizes the obligation to observe the
commandments, including the commandment to honour one's
father and mother. So this is a necessary condition for inheriting
eternal life. It is necessary, but insufficient, since Jesus then
requires the man to give away his possessions. Such a passage
could reflect an authentic tradition. It echoes the attitude that
Jesus is presumed to have had towards riches. Furthermore it is
hard to conceive that the phrase 'Why do you call me good? No
one is good but God alone' could come from a disciple of Jesus.

In another passage common to Matthew (15.3–6) and Mark
(7.8–13), Jesus attacks the Pharisees, who according to him
transgress the commandment requiring filial respect:

And he said to them [the Pharisees]: 'You have a fine way of
rejecting the commandment of God, in order to keep your
tradition! For Moses said, "Honour your father and mother";
and, "He who speaks evil of father or mother, let him surely
die"; but you say, "If a man tells his father or his mother,
What you would have gained from me is Corban (that is,
given to God) – then you no longer permit him to do anything
for his father or mother, thus making void the word of God
through your tradition which you hand on. And many such
things you do' (Mark 7.9–13).

The *corban* was a vow by which one set possessions aside
and dedicated them to the temple. Jesus criticizes the Pharisees,
who think that such a vow is irrevocable no matter what the
wider circumstances. He judges that the author of such a vow
can be authorized to modify it in the future in order not to
infringe the commandment requiring filial piety. We should
note that the position generally approved in rabbinic literature
is similar. In the eyes of some exegetes, these words reflect a
controversy between the Pharisees and members of the primitive
church, and therefore cannot go back to Jesus. However, it

seems doubtful whether Mark, who was writing above all for Christians of pagan origin, would have preserved such an esoteric debate if it did not go back to Jesus.

We should also note that Jesus pronounced a ban on divorce (Mark 10.1–12; Matt. 5.31–32; 19.1–9; Luke 16.18), stating that the married couple form one flesh (Gen. 2.24). There can hardly be any doubt about the authenticity of this prohibition, mentioned by Paul as one of Jesus' teachings (I Cor. 7.10–11).

By contrast, several sayings attributed to Jesus seem to present a very different attitude towards the family.[12] Some call for a form of behaviour which marks a clear break with the precepts of traditional morality. The two most radical aphorisms are to be found only in Matthew and Luke. According to experts, they would belong to the Q document used by these Gospels.

A first aphorism shows the attitude that the disciples must display towards their families. Luke and Matthew offer different versions of it:

He who loves father or mother more than me is not worthy of me; and he who loves son or daughter more than me is not worthy of me (Matt. 10.37).

If any one comes to me and does not hate his own father and mother and wife and children and brothers and sisters, yes, and even his own life, he cannot be my disciple (Luke 14.26).

Matthew contents himself with expressing the primacy of Jesus without putting the traditional family ties in question. Luke presents a far more radical view, which could have come from the mouth of a Cynic philosopher. Here the verb 'hate' is synonymous with rejection, scorn, disdain. It is not that traditional family values are subordinate to the kingdom of God announced by Jesus and already partially manifested in his mission; they are incompatible with it. Most commentators think that Luke's version reflects an authentic saying of Jesus, the most shocking aspect of which Matthew will have erased. In coming to this conclusion they use the criterion of dissimilarity, one of the criteria most regularly used to determine the authen-

ticity of the sayings attributed to Jesus. According to it, sayings
which have no known equivalent in the Jewish world of the
time of Jesus or in the primitive Christian communities are
probably authentic.[13]

Another aphorism emphasizes the absolute priority of Jesus
and his mission (Matt. 8.21–22/Luke 9.59–60). To a disciple
who asked for permission to bury his father before following
Jesus, Jesus gave a reply which is both famous and brutal:
'Follow me, and leave the dead to bury their own dead.'

This aphorism has given rise to numerous interpretations.
The most common one is to interpret the dead (who must bury
their dead) as being those who do not follow Jesus, i.e. those
who are spiritually dead. Thus Jesus requires his disciples to
follow him even if this means scorning the fundamental biblical
obligation to honour one's parents. As C. Coulot writes, this
saying of Jesus is generally regarded as authentic: 'The authenticity of the saying in Matthew 8.22 (Luke 9.60), "Follow me,
and leave the dead to bury their own dead", is hardly put in
question . . . It is also difficult to attribute it to the community.
In fact it contains no Christian reflection. The possibility of
translating the saying back into Aramaic tells in favour of its
antiquity. It is opposed to Jewish morality and piety. It is hard,
obscure and paradoxical. That is why it has to be attributed to
Jesus.'[14]

These last two sayings of Jesus are hardly compatible with
those which prescribe respect for filial obligations. They leave
numerous commentators perplexed. Several approaches have
been suggested by scholars, depending on their view of Jesus.

Those who see Jesus as a gentle sage, loving children and
favouring love of neighbour in the framework of a sublimated
traditional morality, tend to minimize the shocking aspect of his
most radical sayings. This image, which was very much in
fashion in the last century, is not very popular in academic
circles these days.

Nowadays, above all in the United States, it is very much the
fashion to regard Jesus as a wise man who defended unconven-
tional, indeed subversive, values and a corresponding life-
style.[15] Jesus, a veritable David Cooper[16] of antiquity, is said
to have been an opponent of the patriarchal family system,

which oppressed women and children. The supporters of such a Jesus generally dismiss as inauthentic sayings which endorse traditional family bonds. The majority of members of the much-publicized and controversial Jesus Seminar, a group of 'modernist' experts most of whom teach in North America (see pp.103f.), have taken this line.[17]

By contrast, scholars who see Jesus above all as an eschatological prophet think that it is possible to reconcile the different sayings about the family. In their view the radical sayings of Jesus do not indicate a rejection of traditional family values but only their subordination to his mission.

A more thorough analysis of Matthew 10.37 and Luke 14.26 on the one hand and Matthew 8.21–22 and Luke 9.59–60 on the other shows that the third approach is not without merit. The unique and radical character of 'Leave the dead to bury their own dead' has been widely exaggerated by many exegetes. Some, like Martin Hengel, professor at Tübingen, have even seen it as an abrogation of the Mosaic law by Jesus.[18] However, they seem to forget that this very law recognizes exceptions to the obligation for children to give their kinsfolk burial. Thus someone in the process of performing the Nazirite vow (see p.138) by which he has devoted himself to YHWH must not approach a dead body, even if it is that of his father, his mother, his brother or his sister (Num. 6.6–7). The same constraint is imposed on the High Priest (Lev. 21.10–11). The disciples of Jesus doubtless thought of these exceptions when they heard such sayings.

However, Matthew 8.21–22 and Luke 9.59–60 should probably not be interpreted in terms of Leviticus 21.10–11 or Numbers 6.1–8, but rather with reference to certain well-known prophetic actions.

Thus the episode can be seen in parallel to the call of Elisha by Elijah[19] in I Kings 19.19–21. Before following Elijah, Elisha goes to embrace his father and his mother. Jesus' call, which is more important and more urgent, cannot tolerate the least delay. Matthew 8.21–24 and Luke 9.59–60 more directly evoke the words of YHWH to the prophet Ezekiel:

Also the word of Yahweh came to me: 'Son of man, behold, I

am about to take the delight of your eyes away from you at a
stroke; yet you shall not mourn or weep nor shall your tears
run down. Sigh, but not aloud; make no mourning for the
dead. Bind on your turban, and put your shoes on your feet;
do not cover your lips, nor eat the bread of mourners.' So I
spoke to the people in the morning, and at evening my wife
died. And on the next morning I did as I was commanded
(Ezek. 24.15–18).

Thus the message of Matthew and Luke seems to be quite
clear. In order to fulfil the mission required by God, Jesus and
his disciples do not submit to the traditional norms of ordinary
life. If necessary, they can infringe them.

Luke 14.26 is not equivalent to 'Family, I hate you'. This
saying does not express a revolt against the traditional family
but emphasizes the need for the disciples to be ready to detach
themselves from their families so that they can dedicate themselves entirely to Jesus and his mission. This break with the
family also evokes certain biblical passages. In Psalm 69, which
is regarded as messianic in the New Testament, the faithful
victim of his zeal becomes a stranger to his brothers. According
to Deuteronomy 33.9, Levi, before consecrating himself to the
worship of YHWH, broke with his idolatrous family: 'Who said
of his father and mother, "I regard them not"; he disowned his
brothers and ignored his children.' Similarly, YHWH ordered
Jeremiah not to take a wife and thus not to have children, since
these would die and not be buried (Jer. 16.1–7).

While it is probable that Matthew 10.37 and Luke 14.26
on the one hand and Matthew 8.21–22 and Luke 9.59–60 on
the other go back to Jesus, their original form and context
remain uncertain. It would be imprudent to interpret them too
literally, given their prophetic rhetoric. The same prudence is
also desirable in connection with those sayings of Jesus which
emphasize the family conflicts to which his disciples will
become exposed. One is common to Matthew and Luke
(12.51–53):

Do not think that I have come to bring peace on earth; I have
not come to bring peace, but a sword. For I have come to set

a man against his father, and a daughter against her mother, and a daughter-in-law against her mother-in-law (Matt. 10.34–36).

Other sayings take up the same theme, this time against the background of the troubled times which are to precede the destruction of Jerusalem[20] (Mark 13.12; Luke 21.16). During this time of war and natural catastrophe the disciples will undergo numerous severe persecutions: 'And brother will deliver up brother to death, and the father his child, and children will rise against parent and have them put to death' (Mark 13.12).

These words recall the description by the prophet Micah of the troubled times when the faithful have disappeared from the land:

> For the son treats the father with contempt,
> the daughter rises up against her mother,
> the daughter-in-law against her mother-in-law;
> a man's enemies are the men of his own house (Micah 7.6).

Conflicts within families or between friends are among the characteristics of the troubles and disorders preceding the end of time in many other texts of the Hebrew Bible[21] and the intertestamental literature.[22] I Enoch, a compilation of texts generally dated to the last three centuries BCE, offers a typical example of this genre of prophecy:

> In those days, the father will be beaten together with his sons, in one place, and brothers shall fall together with their friends, in death, until a stream shall flow with their blood. For a man will not be able to withhold his hands from his sons nor from his sons' sons in order to kill them. Nor is it possible for the sinner to withhold his hands from his honoured brother. From dawn until the sun sets, they shall slay each other (I Enoch 100.1–2).[23]

Thus the sayings prophesying conflicts within families have a conventional character and tend to exaggerate. Moreover, they reflect above all struggles and persecutions subsequent to the death of Jesus.

This brief analysis of the sayings about the divisions, sacrifices and conflicts within the family caused by the mission of Jesus shows that they largely derive from a traditional prophetic rhetoric.[24] That hardly allows us to draw definite conclusions from them about the attitude of Jesus to the family in general and to his own family in particular. Two other elements confirm this view.

First, the relations between Jesus and his family are not mentioned in Q, which presents the most radical attitude of Jesus and his disciples to the family in general. This literary source, on which both Matthew and Luke, but not Mark, draw, is no longer extant. In Matthew and Luke, which incorporate it, the opposition between Jesus and his own family is less emphasized than in the Gospel of Mark, though there the demands to break with the family are less radical. These demands hardly appear at all in John, whereas the antagonism between Jesus and his brothers is particularly marked. So one would have great difficulty in demonstrating that the opposition between Jesus and those close to him derives from an opposition on his part to the family in principle.

Secondly, the New Testament texts indicate virtually no conflicts between the immediate disciples and their families. Certainly the Gospels show us Peter and his brother Andrew abandoning their fishing nets to follow Jesus (Mark 1.16–18/ Matt. 4.18–20/Luke 5.1–11). But they do not seem to have broken with their family since, shortly afterwards, Jesus goes to Peter's house to cure his mother-in-law (Mark 1.29–31/Matt. 8.14–15/Luke 4.38–39). According to Matthew (20.20–23), the mother of the sons of Zebedee interceded with Jesus on behalf of her sons James and John. This intervention, which does not appear in Mark's account (10.35–40), is probably a creation by Matthew aimed at masking the rivalries among the Twelve. Nevertheless, the fact that the author has made the mother of James and John intervene shows that she may have been associated with the ministry of Jesus.

Moreover, again according to Matthew (27.56), the mother of the sons of Zebedee was present at the crucifixion of Jesus.

The Gospel of John mentions, among the women present at the execution, the mother of Jesus, her sister and Mary of Clopas (if she was in fact different from the sister of Jesus' mother). Supposing, as Hegesippus writes, that Clopas was a brother of Joseph's, that shows that Jesus had not been abandoned by all his family.

Fulfilling their mission does not seem to have disturbed the married life of many of the members of the primitive church. In I Corinthians 9.5 Paul indicates that Peter and Jesus' brothers were accompanied by their wives on their missionary travels. Another indication of the continuation of family relations in the early church is the existence of the widows of the 'Hellenists' mentioned in Acts 6.1–6. These widows must have been sufficiently numerous for their treatment to have become a source of discord. However, I Corinthians 7.12–16 shows us the difficulties experienced by couples only one of whom was a believer. Nevertheless, Paul recommends that couples should not separate. These few examples show clearly that it is prudent not to take too literally the sayings and prophecies of Jesus about the family divisions and conflicts caused by his mission. The same caution should also apply to the relations between Jesus and his brothers.

James, disciple?

This rapid survey invites us to suppose, along with some exegetes, that the traditional conceptions of the relations between Jesus and his family must be regarded with scepticism.[25] Contrary to what is said by various scholars, the nature of these relations cannot reasonably be deduced from the sayings of Jesus about divisions and conflicts in the family, which are difficult to interpret. Similarly, it has emerged that for polemical reasons Mark and John presented relations between Jesus and his family in a particularly unfavourable light. Though perhaps they did not create this conflict completely, beyond question they magnified an antagonism or an event of less magnitude. While serious and lasting opposition seems improbable, the precise nature of the relations between Jesus and his brothers remains difficult to determine. If there was scepticism, was it permanent or transitory? Did the brothers become disciples? Did they take part in Jesus' mission? No definitive answer can be given to these questions. The Gospel of John suggests some association between Jesus and his brothers; Luke, who mentions no opposition, may indicate support for Jesus from his brothers. But it is hardly possible to go further solely on the testimony of the canonical Gospels. The best indication that James may have taken part in Jesus' mission is his major role in the primitive church.

We have seen that according to the author of Acts (1.14), Jesus' mother and brothers were among the first disciples, immediately after the Ascension. However, some scholars think that it is doubtful whether they were among the very first believers. Still, such scepticism certainly cannot be applied to Paul's mention of his meeting with James some years after the death of Jesus (Gal. 1.19). One might reasonably infer from Paul's account that at that time James was one of the most important figures in the Jerusalem church. Most scholars, convinced that James was not a believer in Jesus' lifetime, think that his conversion will have come about as the result of an appearance of the Lord mentioned by Paul in the First Letter to the Corinthians, which is a familiar passage:

> For I delivered to you as of first importance what I also received, that Christ died for our sins in accordance with the scriptures, that he was buried, that he was raised on the third day in accordance with the scriptures, and that he appeared to Cephas, then to the twelve. Then he appeared to more than five hundred brethren at one time, most of whom are still alive, though some have fallen asleep. Then he appeared to James, then to all the apostles. Last of all, as to one untimely born, he appeared also to me (I Cor. 15.3–8).

This list of appearances of the Christ is the earliest that we have. It is certainly earlier than those contained in the Gospels, which are the following:[26]

Matthew: in Jerusalem, Mary of Magdala and Mary the mother of James and Joses (28.9–10); then the eleven disciples (the Twelve less Judas) in Galilee (28.16–20).

Mark: in Jerusalem, Mary of Magdala (16.9); then the two
disciples going into the country (16.12); finally the Eleven in
Galilee (16.14–18).
Luke: two disciples, one called Cleopas, on the way to
Emmaus (24.13–37), and then, on the same day, in Jerusalem, Simon (Peter) (24.33); then in the evening the Eleven
(including Peter) and their companions (24.36–50).
John: Mary of Magdala in Jerusalem (20.14–17); then in
the evening, the disciples (without Thomas) still in Jerusalem
(20.19–24); then, a week afterwards, in Jerusalem, the
disciples with Thomas (20.26–29); finally, later in Galilee,
seven disciples including Peter, Thomas and the sons of
Zebedee (21.1–23).

We should note finally that according to the author of Acts,
who is also the author of the Gospel of Luke, Christ appeared to
the apostles and lived forty days with them in Jerusalem (Acts
1.1–9). We can see immediately how much these lists differ both
in the figures they feature and in their locations.

The differences between the lists in the Gospels and that
in I Corinthians 15 are even more striking. Paul does not
specifically mention any women among those to whom Jesus
appeared. The five hundred brethren, who are completely
unknown to us, do not appear either in the Gospels or in Acts.
Moreover, and this is of more interest to us, Paul is the only one
to mention James. Are the Gospels ignorant of this tradition or
have they chosen not to cite it? The second hypothesis seems
more probable. The traditions reported by Paul are beyond
question older and more authentic than those reflected in the
Gospels. But they are nevertheless very complex to interpret.[27]
Most exegetes think that Paul does not present the appearances
in strictly chronological order. They agree in thinking that in
15.3 to 15.5 (or 15.6) Paul is taking up a traditional formula.
On the other hand, opinions differ widely over 15.7. Some
scholars think that this verse is entirely due to Paul's redactional
activity, using various pieces of information at his disposal.[28]
For others, Paul will have taken up a traditional formula in
whole or in part. According to Jerome Murphy O'Connor, this
will simply have been, 'He appeared to James, then to all the

apostles.'[29] Paul Winter has reconstructed a longer formula: 'He appeared to James, to the apostles and all the brothers.'[30]

Another matter of controversy is the content of the expression 'all the apostles'. Are these the Twelve or a wider group, including or excluding the Twelve, representing the faithful who received their mission from the risen Christ? In the first hypothesis, the formula 'to James, then to all the apostles' could reflect a rival tradition to I Corinthians 15.5. In the second, it could be either a rival tradition or a complementary one. The reason why Paul should have combined two such different traditions has yet to be determined satisfactorily. Be this as it may, the appearance of Jesus to James was already a well-established tradition when Paul wrote I Corinthians at the beginning of the 50s. It is possible that two more or less rival formulae were circulating at this time, one giving the privilege of the first appearance of Jesus to Peter (I Cor. 15.5–6) and the other attributing it to James (I Cor. 15.7). But the historicity of the appearance to James, whatever its nature, seems beyond dispute. It took place very shortly after the crucifixion, since it happened before that to Paul.

The traditional conception according to which James will have been converted following an appearance is one which has no basis in any New Testament or apostolic writing. As Roy Bowen Ward emphasizes, 'nor is there anything here [in I Cor. 15.5–8] to suggest that the appearance to James represented a "conversion"'.[31] In fact, he thinks, Paul seems to present the appearance which he himself was granted despite his unbelief as something exceptional; no text mentions a similar phenomenon in the case of James. Besides, the tradition generally considers that the appearances of Jesus were reserved for his disciples. So, as Richard Bauckham has recently argued, this appearance to James, associated with his conversion only in the imagination of exegetes, suggests that James was perhaps one of the disciples of Jesus.[32]

The apocryphal Gospels of the Hebrews and Thomas reinforce such a hypothesis. We must recognize that the majority of scholars, sceptical about the historical value of the non-canonical Gospels, are reluctant to use them in their researches into Jesus. J. P. Meier's recent book on Jesus reflects such

an opinion.[33] However, an increasing and active minority under
the impulse of prestigious exegetes like Helmut Koester[34] and
John Dominic Crossan refuses to give the canonical writings
priority over some apocryphal works which are just as old.
Crossan defends this approach in *The Historical Jesus*, one
of the most important books on Jesus to have appeared in
recent years, and largely uses apocryphal texts in his reconstruction of the historical Jesus. That is why the evidence of the
Gospel of the Hebrews and the Gospel of Thomas deserves to be
heard.

We have only very partial knowledge of the Gospel of the
Hebrews, now lost, through seven short passages cited in patristic literature. It is generally attributed to Jewish Christians in
Egypt. Most scholars put the date of its composition in the first
half of the second century. Nevertheless, some think that it
could be earlier. In *The Historical Jesus*, Crossan has classified
the early Christian texts, both canonical and apocryphal, by
chronological strata.[35] In his view, three works, including the
Gospels of Thomas and the Hebrews, belong to the earliest level
(30–60 CE). Q would also be part of this chronological stratum,
but not the canonical Gospels. In the recent and distinguished
Anchor Bible Dictionary, Ron Cameron thinks that the most
probable date would be the beginning of the second half of the
first century.[36] The extract which interests us is quoted in
Jerome's *De viris illustribus*:

> And when the Lord had given the linen cloth to the servant
> of the priest, he went to James and appeared to him. For
> James had sworn that he would not eat bread from that hour
> in which he had drunk the cup of the Lord until he should
> see him risen from among them that sleep. And shortly there-
> after the Lord said: Bring a table and bread! And immediate-
> ly it is added: he took the bread, blessed it and brake it and
> gave it to James the Just and said to him: My brother, eat thy
> bread, for the Son of man is risen from among them that
> sleep.[37]

This passage, which mentions the appearance of Jesus to James,
also suggests that James took part in the Last Supper.

Logion 12 of the Gospel of Thomas also takes up this tradition which associates James with his brother's ministry; Jesus even designates James his successor:

> The disciples said to Jesus, 'We know that You will depart from us. Who is to be our leader?' Jesus said to them, 'Wherever you are, you are to go to James the righteous, for whose sake heaven and earth came into being.'[38]

The Gospel of Thomas is a collection of sayings of Jesus without any narrative framework. Even more than the Gospel of the Hebrews it is the object of fascinating and passionate disputes among experts.[39] For the 'traditionalists', this writing will be a document which depends on the canonical Gospels, composed during the first half of the second century. For the 'moderns' it will be totally or largely independent.[40] According to some, the whole work will date from the 50s or 60s. For others, the logia dating from this period will have been supplemented some decades later by others which reflect a more marked Gnostic character. The antiquity of Logion 12, which emphasizes the pre-eminence of James, seems confirmed by the content of Logion 13. There the authority of Thomas would seem to take the place of that of James. Some scholars think that Logion 13 has been added to the initial collection by Christians who wanted to emphasize the authority of Thomas without denying that of James. Thus for Henri-Charles Puech, the presence of Logion 12 is evidence of the probability of an early form of the Gospel of Thomas which is of Jewish-Christian inspiration.[41] The Jewish-Christian character of Logion 12 is clearly manifested in the expression 'for whose sake heaven and earth came into being'. The theme of the righteous one for whom the world was created occurs frequently in Jewish literature. The Syriac Apocalypse of Baruch (II Baruch), a Jewish text dating from the end of the first century, contains a similar concept:

> And with regard to the righteous ones, those whom you said the world has come on their account (II Baruch 15.7).

This logion demonstrates the importance of James clearly:

in Jewish literature, the figures for whom the world had been created include Abraham, Moses and the Messiah.

The traditional conception of relations between Jesus and his brothers thus needs to be treated carefully. The Gospel of the Hebrews and the Gospel of Thomas suggest an alternative version according to which James will have been a disciple of Jesus before the crucifixion. Their testimony, far from being further justification of the pre-eminence of James, could reflect an authentic tradition. The detailed analysis of the New Testament texts that we have engaged in does not allow us to rule out such a version. At all events it would seem probable that relations between Jesus and his brothers were more complex than a superficial reading of the New Testament might suggest. Perhaps, as Richard Bauckham supposes, they developed during the ministry of Jesus.

5

A Famous Brother

We shall probably never know the real nature of the relations between James and his brother Jesus. But we do know quite certainly that shortly after the death of Jesus, James became one of the most important figures in the young Christian movement. So we need to investigate the person and message of Jesus if we are to understand the nature and development of the primitive church and James' position and activity within it.

We have already noted while studying the question of Jesus' brothers and sisters and the nature of the relations between Jesus and his family how difficult it was to reconstruct important aspects of the life and message of Jesus. The image that we perceive in the New Testament texts is coloured by the interpretations of his death and resurrection. The words attributed to him often reflect more the preoccupations of the primitive Christian communities. The nature of the sources at our disposal make the work of the historian arduous and speculative. The letters of Paul, very probably the earliest New Testament texts, offer us little information about Jesus. So every portrait of Jesus is essentially based on the Gospels. The majority of commentators restrict themselves to the canonical Gospels. However, a growing minority, as we have seen, do not hesitate also to use apocryphal texts, particularly the Gospel of Thomas. This decision is not a neutral one, in that some of these writings present a somewhat unorthodox picture of Jesus. But to limit oneself to the canonical Gospels does not make the task any easier, since these do not offer a homogeneous portrait of Jesus.

Even a superficial reading shows that the so-called Synoptic Gospels are very different from the Gospel of John. Thus in the Synoptics, Jesus expresses himself above all by means of parables and aphorisms, while in the Gospel of John he pronounces discourses about himself with a strong theological content. In the Synoptic Gospels his ministry lasts only a year, and important episodes, like the incident in the temple and institution of the eucharist at the Last Supper, take place just before his arrest. The Gospel of John describes a ministry which lasts three years; the incident in the temple and the eucharistic discourse which takes the place of the institution of the eucharist at the Last Supper are put at the beginning of this ministry. The list of differences and contradictions could easily be extended. The majority of experts give priority to the Synoptic Gospels, while recognizing that John often contains some details the historical character of which would seem to be superior.[1]

The Synoptic Gospels also differ considerably among themselves over important aspects of the life and message of Jesus. There are even contradictions within each Gospel which are sometimes very difficult to explain. So while approaching the Gospels critically, historians must determine which sayings and acts of Jesus would seem most likely to be authentic. To do this, they try to identify the earliest levels of the Gospels. Now their identification of these primitive levels largely depends on their hypotheses about the composition of the Gospel texts, particularly the Synoptic Gospels.[2]

We have seen that the majority of scholars follow the so-called 'two-source' theory, according to which Matthew and Luke, probably composed between 75 and 90, depend on both Mark and the so-called Q document. Those who accept this theory give priority to Mark and the hypothetical reconstruction of Q largely developed from passages common to Matthew and Luke. Moreover academic circles have recently become infatuated with Q; some scholars regard it as an earlier and more authentic witness than Mark. Some try to identify the most primitive strata of Q. John Kloppenborg has developed a fashionable theory that Q has various strata, the earliest with the characteristics of wisdom and not apocalyptic.[3] These views have considerably influenced the portrait of Jesus given by Burton L. Mack[4] and John Dominic Crossan.[5]

However, the two-source theory has some weak points which are well known to all exegetes. Most exegetes do not think that these weaknesses are serious enough to tell against this theory; even if it is not perfect, they believe it nevertheless to be superior to its rivals. That is not the opinion of an important group of scholars, above all in the United States, who defend the 'two Gospel' theory, according to which Matthew is the primordial Gospel, Luke depends on Matthew, and Mark used both Matthew and Luke.[6] The supporters of this theory, who do not believe in the existence of Q, thus favour Matthew in reconstructing the historical Jesus.

Other scholars reject both theories because they are incapable of explaining certain significant literary facts. To take account of these, they have developed sometimes complex hypotheses and have inserted several intermediate documents, no longer extant, on which the Gospels in our possession are said to depend.[7] These scholars try to reconstruct these sources in order to identify the most primitive strata of the Gospels.

However, the earliest passages do not necessarily lead to the historical Jesus. They may only reflect the theological conceptions of Christian communities in the 40s or 50s. Similarly, passages thought to be less primitive can transmit authentic traditions. That is why exegetes have developed a whole battery of criteria aimed at estimating the authenticity of the sayings and actions attributed to Jesus.[8] I have already mentioned the criterion of dissimilarity, an uncritical application of which has contributed to producing the portrait of a unique Jesus who breaks with the Judaism of his time and is misunderstood by the primitive church. A related criterion, that of embarrassment, favours sayings which are included in the Gospels although they must have been a source of embarrassment to the primitive church. Among the other most-used criteria one might cite the number of attestations by independent sources and the possibility of rediscovering the original Aramaic form of sayings.

Of course the application of most of these criteria and the importance to be attached to each of them are largely subjective. The roughly fifty experts, mainly American, who make up the Jesus Seminar have classified the sayings of Jesus into four categories, depending on their presumed degree of authenticity.[9] The detailed results of votes show a great diversity of opinions.

Moreover, while exegetes sometimes agree in attributing certain sayings to Jesus, they can differ considerably over their interpretation. To see this, one need only go through some of the works devoted to the parables of Jesus.

Reconstructing the actions of Jesus presents even greater difficulties, since the Gospels are so full of supernatural phenomena and actions fulfilling biblical prophecies.

All these obstacles show the limits of critical analysis. Finally, exegetes and historians have to base their portrait of Jesus on hypotheses and presuppositions which are often arbitrary. At the beginning of the century, the famous doctor, Albert Schweitzer, who was also a great New Testament exegete, analysed the main books on Jesus which had appeared in the nineteenth century. He noted that their authors had a tendency to attribute to Christ the ideas and values which they themselves particularly cherished.[10] Jesus thus became the ideal model that they aspired to imitate. One need only read several contemporary works on Jesus to see that this tendency is far from having disappeared. That is why some exegetes, like the famous Rudolf Bultmann, are very sceptical about the possibility of discovering the historical Jesus.

Others, who are more optimistic, while rejecting the traditional biographical approach with a well-defined chronology and psychological development, nevertheless try to paint a portrait of Jesus. Given the lack of a consensus on the authenticity of his words and actions, it is hardly surprising that these studies come to very different conclusions.[11] Over recent years Jesus has been seen successively as a Zealot revolutionary,[12] a magician,[13] an exorcist,[14] a pious and charismatic *hasid*,[15] a Galilean proto-rabbi,[16] a Pharisaic disciple of Hillel,[17] a cynic sage,[18] a peasant Cynic with a social programme,[19] a subversive wise man,[20] a social prophet,[21] an eschatological prophet,[22] a messianic prophet[23] or a Davidic Messiah,[24] not to mention the different combinations of several of these features. Of course not all these conceptions enjoy the same credit among scholars. At present two portraits are sharing almost equal popularity. For many scholars Jesus was a prophet, whether messianic or not, who proclaimed the imminent arrival of the eschaton, i.e. the final era of humanity, associated with the restoration of

Israel and the defeat of its enemies, the return of the scattered tribes and the universal triumph of YHWH. The supporters of the eschatological Jesus are opposed by those who see him as a master teaching a counter-cultural and subversive wisdom, little by little undermining the archaic and oppressive social structures of Palestine. In their view the primitive church will have transformed this subversive sage into an eschatological agent sent by God.

An important aspect of these portraits which has long divided the experts is the position of Jesus *vis-à-vis* the Mosaic law. Was Jesus a Jew who observed the law, or a transgressor? Were he the former, the later separation of Christianity from Judaism would be hard to base on his message and acts. Were he the latter, Jesus would be responsible for the schism, directly or indirectly. A last aspect which is decisive for the development of the Christian movement is the attitude of Jesus towards the Gentiles. We shall examine all these questions rather more closely.

Why did Jesus die?

The circumstances of Jesus' death are among the most certain facts of his life. It is virtually certain that Jesus was crucified by the Romans on the orders of Pontius Pilate, prefect of Judaea. This information, mentioned in the four Gospels, is confirmed by Josephus and Tacitus.[25] The inscription on the cross indicating the reason for his condemnation was probably 'The king of the Jews'. Moreover the high priest and his allies in the priestly aristocracy doubtless supported the action by the Roman authorities. Everything suggests that Jesus was condemned to death as a messianic pretender capable of disturbing public order. Unless we are to suppose a major judicial error, the theories which make Jesus only a pious and charismatic man, a proto-rabbi, the teacher of an alternative wisdom or even a religious reformer, become incomplete or improbable.

We know, above all thanks to Josephus, of the existence of several contemporaries of Jesus whose career finished in a very similar way. In Acts, Jesus is compared by the Pharisee Gamaliel with two of them.[26] During the appearance of the apostles before the Sanhedrin, shortly after the resurrection, Gamaliel speaks up for their release:

> Men of Israel, take care what you do with these men. For before these days Theudas arose, giving himself out to be somebody, and a number of men, about four hundred, joined him; but he was slain and all who followed him were dispersed and came to nothing. After him Judas the Galilean arose in the days of the census and drew away some of the people after him; he also perished, and all who followed him were scattered. So in the present case I tell you, keep away from these men and let them alone; for if this plan or this undertaking is of men, it will fail; but if it is of God, you will not be able to overthrow them. You might even be found opposing God! (Acts 5.35–39).

Even supposing that he did in fact defend the Christians before the Sanhedrin, Gamaliel probably did not make this speech, which, in keeping with the practice of ancient historians, is a creation of Luke, the author of Acts. Luke composed the speech which seemed to him to be most appropriate in the circumstances, without noting that he was committing an anachronism. So he thought it plausible for Jesus to be compared with the Galilean and Theudas, the main difference lying in the survival of his movement after he had disappeared from the scene.[27]

In 6 CE, Judas the Galilean rebelled against the Romans on the occasion of the census of the population and property ordered by Quirinius, governor of Syria.[28] This census was to be the basis for calculating the fiscal contributions to be made by the inhabitants of Judaea. Judas, thinking that this was a violation of divine sovereignty, launched a major revolution which was put down by the Romans.

Theudas, around 45, led a large crowd as far as the Jordan.[29] Claiming to be a prophet, he asserted that the waters of the river would part at his command. The procurator Cuspius Fadus preferred not to wait for Theudas to exercise his gifts. He sent a squadron of cavalry which put a brutal end to the experiment. Theudas, who probably gave himself out to be the 'prophet like

Moses' predicted by Deuteronomy (18.15–18), thought that God would perform through him a miracle similar to the one which allowed Joshua to cross the Jordan (Josh. 3). This miracle would have announced the restoration of Israel.

The two figures mentioned in Gamaliel's speech certainly aimed at freeing Israel from the grips of the pagans, i.e. at the restoration of divine sovereignty. But Judas trusted more in arms, whereas Theudas hoped above all to benefit from an intervention of YHWH.

The history of other contemporary figures who are not mentioned in Gamaliel's speech also helps to illuminate the message and the action of Jesus. Around 56 a Jew from Egypt, called the Egyptian, came to Jerusalem.[30] Proclaiming himself a prophet, he gathered a large crowd on the Mount of Olives. There he announced that at his command the ramparts of Jerusalem would collapse. The procurator Felix, forestalling him, fell on the Egyptian and his supporters. He killed 400 of them, but the Egyptian managed to escape. Theudas and the Egyptian do not seem to have been isolated cases. According to Josephus, charlatans and impostors, 'on the pretext of a divine inspiration, sought to bring about revolutionary changes and persuaded the mob to abandon themselves to madness'.[31] They took 'people into the desert, telling them that God would show them signs of their deliverance there'. Such adventures usually came to a bad end.

Two other historical figures of the period, John the Baptist[32] and Jesus son of Ananias, also shed light on the activity of Jesus of Nazareth. John the Baptist was beyond question the person who most influenced Jesus. The Gospels present him as an ascetic announcing the imminent advent of divine judgment and calling on all to receive the baptism of repentance for the remission of sins. It is practically certain that Jesus was baptized by John, whose disciple he became. According to the Gospels, Herod Antipas, tetrarch of Galilee, had John executed because he was opposed to his marriage with Herodias, widow of his brother Philip. Josephus presents John the Baptist in a rather different light. John no longer appears as an eschatological prophet but as a good man, inciting the Jews to piety and justice. Nevertheless, the grip that he had on the crowds became such that Herod Antipas finally got alarmed. Fearing that John's eloquence would lead some to rebel, he decided to eliminate him before it was too late. The authorities of the time were not very fond of inspired preachers even when, like Jesus son of Ananias, they had no disciples. This Jesus, a man of the people and a countryman, alarmed the authorities when he went to Jerusalem in 62 or 63 for the Feast of Tabernacles:

> And as he stood in the temple he suddenly began to shout: 'A voice from the east, a voice from the west, a voice from the four winds, a voice against Jerusalem and the sanctuary, a voice against bridegrooms and brides, a voice against the whole people.' Day and night he uttered this cry as he went through all the streets. Some of the more prominent citizens, very annoyed at these ominous words, laid hold of the fellow and beat him savagely. Without saying a word in his own defence or for the private information of his persecutors, he persisted in shouting the same warning as before. The Jewish authorities, rightly concluding that some supernatural force was responsible for the man's behaviour, took him before the Roman procurator. There, though scourged till his flesh hung in ribbons, he neither begged for mercy nor shed a tear, but lowering his voice to the most mournful of tones answered every blow with 'Woe to Jerusalem!' When Albinus – for that was the procurator's name – demanded to know who he was, where he came from and why he uttered such cries, he made no reply whatever to the questions but endlessly repeated his lament over the city, till Albinus decide that he was a madman and released him (*Jewish War* 6, 300–5).[33]

Jesus ben Ananias presents interesting similarities with Jesus of Nazareth. Both prophesied the destruction of the temple; both were interrogated by the Jewish nobility before being taken before the procurator. Jesus ben Ananias was not thought sufficiently dangerous to be put to death. Was this perhaps because he had no disciples and seemed more mad than dangerous? Christian historians and exegetes are often reluctant to use the example of figures like Theudas or the Egyptian to understand the history of Jesus better. Adopting the disdainful tone of Flavius Josephus, they usually consider such individuals as impostors, with a trivial and unoriginal message.[34] But this is a gratuitous assumption. We have no reason to doubt their sincerity. As for their messages, we know absolutely nothing about them. The one thing that is certain is that it would be useless to compare someone about whom one knows a little with others about whom one is almost completely ignorant. However, their history shows that figures claiming to be divinely inspired were by no means rare at the time of Jesus, that they aroused the enthusiasm of the crowds and the fear of the authorities, and that their supporters expected liberating miracles from them.

Now let us return to Jesus and to the events which led directly to his death. Jesus and his disciples had gone to Jerusalem to celebrate the feast of *Pesach* (Passover) and Unleavened Bread, one of the three great annual pilgrimage feasts. Every year, several hundred thousand Jews from Palestine and the Diaspora would go up to Jerusalem. The feast lasted from 14 to 22 Nisan. Many arrived at least eight days before the beginning of the festivities in order to have time to purify themselves. Some stayed with the locals, in Jerusalem and in the neighbouring villages; others set up their tents around the Holy City. Jerusalem and its temple were teeming with pilgrims and animals destined for sacrifice.

Since the religious fervour was intense, the least incident could set off a riot. Moreover, Josephus mentions several serious conflicts which arose on this occasion. Were not the Jews celebrating the exodus from Egypt, i.e. liberation from oppression and slavery? The Romans, who were perfectly aware of the symbolic character of the festival, were on their guard. They co-operated closely with the temple authorities, who also wanted to avoid the slightest trouble.

The first episode marking this last visit is Jesus' entry into Jerusalem sitting on an ass. Those who were present cried out, quoting Ps.118, 'Hosanna! Blessed is he who comes in the name of the Lord! Blessed is the kingdom of our father David that is coming! Hosanna in the highest' (Mark 11.9–10). Jesus' entry into Jerusalem evokes the prediction of Zechariah (9.9) concerning the Messiah:

Rejoice greatly, O daughter of Zion!
Shout aloud, O daughter of Jerusalem!
Lo, your king comes to you;
triumphant and victorious is he,
humble and riding on an ass,
on a colt the foal of an ass.

It is very difficult to decide about the historicity of this episode. Jesus could have chosen to enter Jerusalem mounted on an ass in order to give messianic significance to his action. But one could equally well suppose that the evangelist invented the messianic entry into Jerusalem in order to show the fulfilment of a prophecy. To take up E. P. Sanders' terms, the prophecy could have prompted the event or created the narrative without any event underlying it.[35]

By contrast, few experts doubt the historicity of the second action, which probably sealed Jesus' fate. This is the famous incident in the temple which is usually called the 'cleansing of the temple':[36]

And they came to Jerusalem. And he entered the temple and began to drive out those who sold and those who bought in the temple, and he overturned the tables of the money-changers and the seats of those who sold pigeons; and he would not allow any one to carry anything through the temple. And he taught, and said to them, 'Is it not written "My house shall be called a house of prayer for all nations [Isa. 56.7]"? But you have made it a den of robbers [Jer. 7.11]' (Mark 11.15-17).[37]

The evangelists add that Jesus' outburst alarmed the temple authorities, who decided to put an end to his activities. The Synoptic Gospels also contain a prediction by Jesus of the destruction of the temple (Mark 13.1-4/Matt. 24.1-3/Luke 21.5-7):

And as he came out of the temple, one of his disciples said to him, 'Look, Teacher, what wonderful stones and what wonderful building!' And Jesus said to him, 'Do you see those

great buildings? There will not be left here one stone upon
another, that will not be thrown down' (Mark 13.1–2).

Jesus was even accused, wrongly according to the evangelists,
of having announced that he himself would destroy the temple
and build another not made by human hands (Mark 14.57–58/
Matt. 26.60–61). Whereas most experts doubt whether Jesus
proclaimed that he himself would destroy the temple, they
nevertheless think that he predicted its destruction, perhaps on
the occasion of this incident. As we have seen in the case of
Jesus ben Ananias, there would have been nothing unique about
such a prophecy, which would have provoked the disquiet of
the temple authorities.[38] How is this episode to be interpreted
and reconciled with such a prediction? Several hypotheses have
been proposed.

Some scholars, including S. G. F. Brandon, think that Jesus,
like Judas the Galilean, wanted to free Israel from Roman
domination, using force if necessary.[39] The episode in the temple
would have been an attempt at armed rebellion which the evangelists will have discreetly camouflaged, transforming it into a
theological conflict. There are arguments to support this position. However, it is hard to understand why such violent action
was not immediately suppressed by the temple police and the
Roman cohorts posted on the portico and why Jesus' main disciples were not arrested with their master.

According to an interpretation once popular in Christian
apologetic, the episode will have manifested the rejection by
Jesus of the temple and its sacrifices. By predicting – successfully
– the destruction of the temple, Jesus was thus announcing
the end of the sacrificial system. This conception suffers from
two major weaknesses. First, there is nothing in the Gospels to
suggest that Jesus rejected the temple and its sacrificial system.
The attitude of the primitive community in Jerusalem as
described in Acts does not tell in favour of such a hypothesis.
Secondly, an explicit demonstration by Jesus against the temple
and its sacrifice, in other words against one of the essential
elements of the law, within the temple and during Pesach, far
from winning the sympathy of the crowd as the Gospels suggest,
would certainly have provoked very violent reactions.

The same criticism applies to the theory recently defended by John Dominic Crossan, that Jesus by his action sought to signify symbolically the destruction of the temple.[40] He wanted the destruction of the temple, not for theological reasons, but because of its role in the economic exploitation of the country people.

E. P. Sanders thinks, probably rightly, that Jesus was in no way opposed to the sacrificial system of the Mosaic law.[41] He also thinks that the system did not suffer from any blatant abuse; this is more doubtful. For Sanders, Jesus, as a prophet of the end of time, wanted by his action to signal the imminent destruction of the temple. This would be followed by the coming of the kingdom of God, which would see the building by God of a new and even more magnificent sanctuary. The prophecies of Jesus would have conformed with certain eschatological conceptions which were quite common at the time. Like Theudas and the Egyptian he thought that YHWH would intervene directly in history to liberate his people. Sanders' position has certain weaknesses which have been noted and analysed in detail by several exegetes.[42] The weakest point of his interpretation is without doubt the absence of any major conflict between Jesus and the temple authorities over its functioning. Adopting this point of view, Sanders thus attaches little importance to the nature of the actions of Jesus in the temple.

By contrast, other scholars think that Jesus wanted to purify the temple by attacking the corruption of the high priest and other members of the priestly aristocracy and/or ritual practices that he thought improper. The corruption of the priestly aristocracy is suggested by a passage inspired by the book of Jeremiah: 'But you have made it a den of robbers.' Similarly, the famous parable of the husbandmen (Mark 12.1–12/Matt. 21.33–46/Luke 20.9–19), pronounced shortly before the incident in the temple, can be interpreted as an attack on the priestly aristocracy. Citing numerous texts from the time or immediately afterwards, C. A. Evans has clearly shown that there were many complaints about the greed and dishonesty of the most powerful priests.[43] We also find protests in the literature against the cost of sacrificial practices, which was prohibitive for the poorest Jews. Thus according to the Mishnah, shortly before the war against Rome, Rabban Simeon ben Gamaliel protested against the exorbitant prices of the doves sold for sacrifice in the temple precincts.[44] At that time the dove was the sacrifice of the poor. By obtaining a change in the way in which doves were sacrificed, Simeon succeeded in reducing the demand for them and thus their price. In overturning the places where doves were sold, Jesus perhaps had such abuses in view.

According to other exegetes, Jesus protested above all against practices which in his view defiled the temple. He will have proclaimed a ban on commercial transactions within the temple precincts. V. Eppstein has tried to show that the high priest Caiaphas had authorized such transactions within the temple around 30.[45] According to Eppstein, Jesus will have attacked this new practice, which was hardly in conformity with tradition. However, this hypothesis remains controversial, since the sources relating to the measure are not entirely trustworthy. In the same order of ideas, Bruce Chilton thinks that Jesus will have insisted that the animals sacrificed actually belonged to the person offering the sacrifice.[46] So his action will have been aimed at preventing the sacrifice of animals bought in the temple. Peter Richardson has recently suggested that Jesus overturned the tables of the money-changers to protest against the use of Tyrian coinage which bore the effigy of the god Melkart.[47]

While all these hypotheses seem plausible, none of them can be proved. It is nevertheless reasonable to conclude from them that Jesus probably pronounced a diatribe against the corruption of the chief priests and against certain practices which polluted YHWH's sanctuary. He perhaps predicted that such abuses would lead to the destruction of the temple. Rightly or wrongly his action was understood as a prophetic act. Since Jesus received the approval of part of the crowd, the temple police will have preferred not to intervene.

At the time, many people believed that the Messiah would purify the temple just before the eschaton. Perhaps Jesus hoped that his action would provoke the decisive intervention of God to usher in the messianic era. Thus Jesus was very probably perceived by his supporters as an agent and messenger of God charged with announcing and preparing for the coming of the final era. His status and role at the time of the judgment of Israel and the nations and after the complete inauguration of the kingdom of God must certainly have been argued over by his followers. If some saw him as the expected royal Davidic Messiah, others considered him more as an eschatological prophet whom they might or might not call messianic.

Doubtless the temple authorities did not dwell on all these subtle questions. For them the response was simple: Jesus was simply a dangerous impostor who had to be silenced. They probably thought that he could spark off uncontrollable and dangerous popular reactions, the tragic consequences of which could be suffered by the whole Jewish nation. At any rate, this is what the Gospel of John suggests:

> What are we to do? For this man performs many signs. If we let him go on thus, every one will believe in him and the Romans will come and destroy both our holy place and our nation (John 11.47–48).

Again according to John, Caiaphas the high priest thought that Jesus should be got rid of to avoid major dangers. Pontius Pilate was perhaps already aware of the danger that Jesus represented. Had this not been the case, Caiaphas would surely have had little difficulty in persuading the prefect of Judaea to act, since he was a man who was hardly renowned for his scruples and anxious not to take any risks. Let us now see whether the preaching of Jesus is compatible with the portrait which I have just sketched out.

The kingdom of God

Commentators are almost unanimous in acknowedging that the central element of the preaching of Jesus is the imminent arrival of the kingdom or, better, the reign of God (or, according to Matthew, of heaven).[48] Mark makes the preaching of Jesus begin like this:

> Now after John was arrested, Jesus came into Galilee, preaching the gospel of God, and saying, 'The time is fulfilled, and

the kingdom of God is at hand; repent, and believe in the gospel' (Mark 1.14–15).

The kingdom of God also plays an essential role in the Beatitudes of Matthew (5.1–12) and Luke (6.20–23). Here Jesus announces that the poor and the persecuted will inherit the kingdom of God. The Gospels also contain numerous parables in which Jesus tries to show the nature of the kingdom of God by means of comparisons which are more or less easy to understand. The Our Father also evokes the kingdom of God:

> Our Father who art in heaven,
> Hallowed be thy name.
> Thy kingdom come,
> Thy will be done
> On earth as it is in heaven
>
> . . .
>
> And lead us not into temptation,
> But deliver us from the Evil One (Matt. 6.9–10, 13).

This prayer recalls the Kaddish, a Jewish prayer which probably already existed in the first century. Its general idea is that God reigns in heaven but not on earth, which is dominated by the Evil One. The kingdom of God on earth will come when, rid of the powers of evil, human beings can live in conformity to the will of God.

To understand this concept better we need to turn to the Hebrew Bible, a supreme point of reference for Jesus, as for the other Jews of his time.[49] Quite surprisingly, the expression 'kingdom of God' does not appear anywhere in the Bible. Nevertheless, 'kingdom of YHWH' does appear in I and II Chronicles. On the other hand, the idea that YHWH reigns is expressed rather more frequently, particularly in the Psalms and the prophetic writings. The kingdom of YHWH is usually associated with the restoration of Israel, the judgment of the nations and the messianic era, which will see the God of Israel triumph over all. After the defeat of Israel's enemies, 'YHWH will become king over all the earth . . . Then every one that survives of all the nations that have come against Jerusalem shall go up year after year to worship the King, YHWH Sabaoth, and celebrate the feast of booths' (Zech. 14.9,16).

The book of Isaiah also evokes the kingdom of God after the liberation of Jerusalem and the restoration of Israel:

> How beautiful upon the mountains are the feet of him who brings good tidings, who publishes peace, who brings good tidings of good, who publishes salvation, who says to Zion, 'Your God reigns.' Hark, your watchmen lift up their voice, together they sing for joy; for eye to eye they see the return of the Lord to Zion. Break forth together into singing, you waste places of Jerusalem; for the Lord has comforted his people, he has redeemed Jerusalem (Isa. 52.7–9).

In the Hebrew Bible the notion of the kingdom or the reign of God refers indubitably to the final era of humanity, sometimes described as the messianic era. The same eschatological connotation can often be found in literature which is chronologically closer to Jesus. Two significant examples are the Testament of Moses and the Psalms of Solomon. The former seems to have been composed in Palestine in the first century of our era on the basis of other older texts which could go back to the Maccabaean revolt. Here is how the kingdom of God manifests itself at the end of time:

> Then his kingdom will appear throughout his whole creation. Then the devil will have an end. Yea, sorrow will be led away with him. Then will be filled the hands of the messenger, who is in the highest place appointed. Yea, he will at once avenge them of their enemies. For the Heavenly One will arise from his kingly throne. Yea, he will go forth from his holy habitation with indignation and wrath on behalf of his sons. And the earth will tremble, even to its ends will it be shaken . . . For God Most High will surge forth, the Eternal One alone. In full view will he come to work vengeance on the nations. Yea, all their idols will he destroy. Then you will be happy, O Israel! . . . And God will raise you to the heights. Yea, he will fix you firmly in the heaven of the stars, in the place of their habitations. And you will behold from on high. Yea, you will see your enemies on the earth (Testament of Moses 10.1–10).[50]

The messenger is probably not the Messiah but Michael, the guardian angel of Israel. The material universe, the enemies of Israel and the devil are apparently destroyed. The final dwelling place of the people of God is in heaven.

The Psalms of Solomon, originally written in Hebrew at the end of the first century BCE, also refer to the kingdom of God. Psalm 17 evokes the eternal reign of God over the nations. The author calls on God to raise up a royal Messiah, son of David. As representative of the reign of God over Israel and the nations, the Messiah, inspired by the Holy Spirit, having driven away the enemies of Israel and gathered together a holy people, will purify Jerusalem and reign in justice and wisdom. This Messiah, son of David, appears more as a just and wise king than as a warrior king. Purity, justice, wisdom and peace will characterize the kingdom of God through its Messiah. In contrast to the Testament of Moses, the new era here is terrestrial and not celestial. But its eschatological nature is also beyond question. The analysis of other texts of the time, like certain Qumran manuscripts, would confirm the eschatological character of the kingdom or reign of God in post-biblical literature.

Thus for most Jews at the time of Jesus, the expression 'kingdom of God' had an eschatological meaning. It quite certainly evoked a decisive intervention on the part of God aimed at freeing his people from pagan domination. It also announced the judgment of sinners and the wicked, and the establishment of a new world in conformity to the biblical prophecies. In this ideal world all, Jews and Gentiles, will honour the God of Israel and respect his will.

Can we attribute such a conception of the kingdom of God to Jesus?

Since the beginning of critical studies of Jesus in the eighteenth century, this question has divided scholars. In the nineteenth century they tended to minimize, indeed to reject, the eschatological aspects of Jesus' message. Jesus was seen above all as a sage, teaching superior moral values with a universal scope.[51] On the basis of a dubious interpretation of Luke 17, the kingdom of God was conceived of as the realization of a process of moral transformation of the individual, a change taking place within each person. Around 1900, Johannes Weiss and Albert

Schweitzer, criticizing these conceptions, interpreted the person and message of Jesus in the context of the apocalyptic literature of his time. Jesus, the teacher of morality, became an eschatological prophet deeply anchored in Jewish tradition. This interpretation, with more or less substantial modifications, was to hold the field until the 1980s.

Since then, following the work of J. D. Crossan, Marcus Borg, B. L. Mack and the Jesus Seminar, with which these three scholars are closely associated, we have been seeing a return in force of the conception of a non-eschatological Jesus, above all in the USA. For these exegetes, Jesus was above all a teacher who taught a kind of counter-cultural and subversive wisdom, inspired by cynical philosophy. In this view, based in part on recent readings of the parables of Jesus, the kingdom of God becomes the symbol and manifestation of a social transformation brought about by his ministry. In a recent book, J. D. Crossan sums up this view as follows:

> Jesus called his programme the presence of the Kingdom of God, but that expression must be interpreted primarily in the light of what he himself did and what he also challenged his companions to do. It did not mean for Jesus, as it could for others, the imminent apocalyptic intervention of God to set right a world taken over by evil and injustice. It meant the presence of God's kingdom here and now in the reciprocity of open eating and open healing, in lives, that is, of radical egalitarianism on both the socioeconomic (eating) and the religiopolitical (healing) levels.[52]

Such a modernist interpretation is certainly more seductive for modern men and women. Moreover, given the growing influence of apocalyptic fantasies in church congregations, we can understand why many universities, above all in the United States, want to minimize the eschatological character of Jesus and his message. But this fashionable conception seems implausible for the following reasons:

(a) As J. P. Meier has clearly shown in his recent book on Jesus, some of his sayings, the authenticity of which seems indubitable, have an incontestably eschatological character;

(*b*) The designation of the Twelve by Jesus, generally regarded as historical, becomes difficult to explain outside the eschatological context of the return of the twelve tribes of Israel;

(*c*) It is doubtful whether the message of Jesus would have been understood by the people of Galilee had his conception of the kingdom of God been so novel and original. The sophisticated interpretations of some modern scholars seem particularly problematical;

(*d*) The circumstances of the death of Jesus become difficult to understand unless we think in terms of a judicial error or, like B. L. Mack and R. J. Miller, we deny the historicity of the Gospel accounts of the death of Jesus;

(*e*) Even taking account of the impact of the visions of the risen Jesus, the markedly eschatological character of the primitive church is inexplicable. The letters of Paul, written about twenty years after the death of Jesus, show that this eschatological character cannot be considered late and secondary.

So it seems that the kingdom of God as proclaimed by Jesus must be understood as an eschatological phenomenon. Jesus appears as a messianic prophet announcing a new and final era. In speaking of the kingdom of God he used a somewhat rare expression to denote a familiar concept. The scholars who reject this characterization bring out the fact that Jesus is most often depicted by the evangelists as a teacher of wisdom. But to define Jesus as a messianic prophet is not in complete contradiction to his teaching. The concept of Messiah, which relates to a king who is son of David, a prophet like Moses or a priest, is most often associated with justice, wisdom and the law. Thus 'the prophet like Moses' of Deuteronomy 18.17–19 brings a message which is divinely inspired:

And YHWH said to me [Moses], 'They have rightly said all that they have spoken. I will raise up for them a prophet like you from among their brethren; and I will put my words in his mouth, and he shall speak to them all that I command him. And whoever will not give heed to my words which he shall speak in my name, I myself will require it of him.'

Similarly the priestly Messiah (Messiah of Aaron) who accompanies the Davidic Messiah (Messiah of Israel) in some Qumran texts is sometimes regarded as the final interpreter of the law.[53]

The royal Davidic Messiah of Psalms of Solomon 17 also stands out for his wisdom, his justice and his holy and pure word. The question of a Messiah who brings inspired teaching would thus seem to be firmly rooted in various traditions in the time of Jesus.

Furthermore the message brought by Jesus has some particularly remarkable characteristics. For him the kingdom, though it is not yet manifested in all its force, is already partially revealed through his ministry, and in particularly his healings and exorcisms. At the time of Jesus many people thought that illnesses were caused by demons. The healings of Jesus thus manifested the victory of God over the forces of evil.

But if it is by the finger of God that I cast out demons, then the kingdom of God has come upon you (Luke 11.20).

It is very probably thanks to his healings that Jesus was seen as an eschatological agent. His reply to a question from John the Baptist about his identity is to be interpreted in this sense:

Now when John heard in prison about the deeds of the Christ, he sent word by his disciples and said to him, 'Are you he who is to come, or shall we look for another?' And Jesus answered them, 'Go and tell John what you hear and see: the blind receive their sight and the lame walk, lepers are cleansed and the deaf hear, and the dead are raised up, and the poor have good news preached to them. And blessed is he who takes no offence at me' (Matt. 11.2–6).

This text, which evokes Isaiah (35.5–6; 61.1–2), presents remarkable similarities with a recently published Qumran manuscript (4Q521).[54] This manuscript mentions a Messiah whom the heavens and the earth will obey. Through him God will proclaim the good news to the poor, heal the wounded, revive the dead, raise up the humble. Emile Puech thinks that the Messiah in question is a royal Davidic Messiah.[55] Basing himself on Isaiah 61, John J. Collins thinks it more probable that this is an eschatological prophet anointed by YHWH.[56]

The kingdom of God was already present to some degree through the teaching of Jesus. By putting it into practice, Israel would come closer to the will of God, thus hastening the coming of God's kingdom in all its power. Jesus seems to have addressed his preaching primarily to those who were remote from God, to those who for religious or social reasons were rejected by the powerful or the self-righteous. Beyond question he wanted to bring together the whole people of Israel and break down the barriers and privileges which divided them. Following the tradition of the poor of Israel, he thought that wealth was an obstacle to true piety. He said that one could not worship both God and mammon. So he called on his disciples to give up their possessions. The poor, the humble and the oppressed would inherit the kingdom of God. But by his teaching Jesus also revealed that he thought that this was the true interpretation and profound meaning of the law of Moses.

Jesus and the law

Jesus' teaching on the law of Moses is a controversial question and one which is a key to understanding both him and the primitive church.[57]

For a very long time the traditional position of many Christian exegetes has been that Jesus abrogated the law of Moses. By several times transgressing some of the most basic elements of this law, like the sabbath and the rules of purity, he unambiguously proclaimed his rejection of it. Such a view is still widespread among believers today. According to a milder version, Jesus transcended the law without abrogating it. On his own authority he substantially revised it, doing away with some precepts and reinterpreting others in a quite radical way. The high priest, the scribes and the Pharisees would thus have got rid of a rather impudent heretic. These traditional conceptions are now being criticized by an increasing number of scholars,[58] who think that the interpretation of the law taught by Jesus was within the limits of what was tolerable in the middle of the first century.

The question is an important one and provokes passionate reactions. In fact, if Jesus was a Jew who respected the law and had no intention of abrogating it, it is harder to justify the way in which it was later abandoned by the church. That is why those who defend the traditional view often nurture apologetic after-thoughts. Every effort is made to show that Jesus went beyond the bounds of this law. To this end his view of the law is compared both with a hypothetical normative law inspired by the Pharisees, supposed to be in force at this time, and with all the precepts of the Bible. Now we have seen that it is incorrect to speak of a normative interpretation of the law in the first century and that at this time a certain number of biblical commandments had ceased to be observed. So it is not surprising that Jesus was thought guilty of having transgressed the law. Using the same criteria, a similar judgment could be passed on all the Jews of his time.

Exegetes who adopt a more objective and more 'historical' approach are nevertheless confronted with a relatively complex problem in that the Gospels do not present a homogeneous picture of Jesus. Thus according to Matthew 15.10–20 and above all Mark 7.14–23, he seems to reject the uncleanness of certain foods, abandoning a basic element of the law. By contrast, in Matthew 5.17–19 and Luke 16.17 Jesus calls for the observance of the whole of the law:

> Think not that I have come to abolish the law and the prophets; I have come not to abolish them but to fulfil them. For truly, I say to you, till heaven and earth pass away, not an iota, not a dot, will pass from the law until all is accomplished. Whoever then relaxes one of the least of these commandments and teaches men so, shall be called least in the kingdom of heaven; but he who does them and teaches them shall be called great in the kingdom of heaven (Matt. 5.17–19).

However, this extract from Matthew, which is included in the 'Sermon on the Mount', is not always interpreted as a concern on the part of Jesus to observe the Mosaic law, because of the six 'antitheses' which follow (Matt. 5.20–48). The antitheses, in which Jesus opposes his message to the traditional teaching, are often seen as the sign of an abrogation of the Mosaic law. Each antithesis begins with 'You have heard . . . But I say to you . . . ' In particular Jesus forbids divorce and oaths, likens desire to adultery and calls for love of enemies.

We should first note that the positions of Jesus on divorce and oaths have an equivalent in the Qumran community, which no one accuses of apostasy.[59] Moreover, each time Jesus expounds a more rigorous teaching than that of the Hebrew Bible. He seems to suggest that the mere observation of biblical precepts is not enough to attain the level of perfection that he requires of his disciples. Far from signalling the abrogation of the law, Jesus, according to Matthew, reveals its meaning and true spirit. This is not a replacement, but a deepening made necessary by the imminent arrival of the kingdom of God. As W. D. Davies and D. Allison write in their important commentary on Matthew: 'The enduring validity of OT legislation is presupposed: the Torah remains valid. So the old legislation is not being annulled and replaced by new legislation. What is added over and above the tradition is something altogether different – a new attitude, a new spirit, a new vision.'[60] Matthew 5.16–19 certainly aims to show that the antitheses must be interpreted in this way: just like the Teacher of Righteousness for the Qumran community, Jesus, for his disciples, appears as the final interpreter of the law.

An important bone of contention between Jesus and his opponents seems to have been the nature of acts permitted during the sabbath, on which, as we have seen, there was no consensus. In particular Jesus was accused of performing healings on the sabbath day[61] (Mark 3.1–6/ Matt. 12.9–14/Luke 6.6–11). After a thorough analysis of Jesus' attitude to the sabbath and practices prevailing in his day, E. P. Sanders notes that the controversies related to relatively minor points and that each time Jesus justified his position with arguments drawn from the scriptures. He concludes that the conduct of Jesus and his disciples was within acceptable limits in the Judaism of this time, even if the Pharisees could take offence at it.[62] So these were disputes over interpretation in a sphere where the Bible is hardly explicit. For example, in undertaking, indeed choosing, to perform healings on the sabbath, Jesus rejected the interpretation of the Pharisees, who justified them only in emergencies, but without contradicting any biblical precept.

The Pharisees criticized Jesus for keeping company with sinners and publicans, even going so far as to share in their meals. This attitude is sometimes considered, wrongly, to be a transgression of the law. The meaning of the word 'sinner' in the Synoptic Gospels is very uncertain.[63] The term would not seem to denote particular wicked and impious individuals but Jews who from the point of view of the sectarian groups did not observe the law in a sufficiently rigorous way.[64] The famous *'ammē hā-ārets* would beyond doubt fall into this category. Similarly, the publicans were usually thought badly of in very pious circles because of the abuses and injustices habitually associated with their activity. But these publicans, *personae non gratae* in Pharisaic or Essene circles, were neither marginal nor pariahs. Beyond doubt they had their contacts among the powerful. Since the Pharisees certainly did not spend their time criticizing all sinners and those who kept company with them, we might suppose that they attacked Jesus because he thought himself to be divinely inspired and allowed himself to teach his interpretation of the law without having the training or appropriate references. One might also suppose that they attacked Jesus in particular because before he began his preaching he had been associated with groups which observed the law very strictly.

Moreover, according to many scholars, Jesus would have transgressed the laws of purity, which were so important in the Judaism of the time. He would have broken the law by taking his meals with unclean hands, i.e. hands which had not been washed (Mark 7.1–5/Matt. 15.1–2/Luke 11.37–38). However, two elements must be emphasized which allow us to put this event in an appropriate context. First of all, according to Mark and Matthew, it was the disciples and not Jesus who did not wash their hands, and this could suggest that the accusations relate to Christian communities after the death of Jesus. Then washing hands before meals is not prescribed in the Hebrew Bible. This is an ancient tradition of extra-biblical origin followed by many Jews, including the Pharisees, but not by all, in the time of Jesus. Washing one's hands before meals was one of those elements of the oral law of the Pharisees criticized by Jesus or his disciples.

Much more fundamental is the abolition of the dietary laws of Leviticus 11, which according to many traditionalist exegetes Jesus is said to have proclaimed. According to Mark, Jesus declared:

Hear me, all of you, and understand; there is nothing outside a man which by going into him can defile him; but the things which come out of a man are what defile him (Mark 7.14–15).

The redactor of Mark (7.19) concludes, not illogically, that Jesus had declared all food clean, thus rejecting the distinctions between clean and unclean animals in Leviticus 11. In abolishing the instructions in Leviticus 11 Jesus could not but attack all the laws of cleanness. The authenticity of these words and the validity of their interpretation by Mark is certainly a basic question, both for defining the message of Jesus and for describing the development of the primitive church. Furthermore, we shall more than once have to ask about the continuity between the conceptions of Jesus, those of the Jerusalem community and those of Paul.

A number of exegetes think it improbable that Jesus proclaimed the abrogation of the dietary laws of purity.[65] Some think that Mark 7.14–15 is a saying which is to be attributed not to Jesus himself but to the primitive church. Others think that Mark beyond doubt interpreted sayings of Jesus similar to Mark 7.14–15 wrongly or tendentiously. They point out that Matthew 15.1–11 takes up this passage of Mark, but without drawing such radical conclusions from it. It seems that exegetes have good reason to doubt whether Jesus ever rejected Leviticus 11. His adversaries, who were so prompt to denounce his departures from their conception of the law, never charged him with this rejection, nor is it mentioned at his appearance before the Sanhedrin, shortly before his condemnation by Pilate. Moreover to proclaim the abrogation of Leviticus 11 in the villages and small towns of Galilee would certainly have provoked violent reactions. Furthermore, how can we imagine someone who proclaimed the abrogation of the laws of purity teaching in the temple at the time of *Pesach*? He would surely have soon been stoned. It would have been a bit like Salman Rushdie eating roast pork in the great mosque of Mecca at the time of Ramadan. Moreover, controversies within the primitive church over the admission of Gentiles and table relations between Jewish Christians and pagan Christians would be totally incomprehensible had Jesus manifested such a break with the law. If he did so, it was evidently without Peter and the main disciples noticing it! The Acts of the Apostles, on the occasion of the episode of the conversion of the centurion Cornelius, present Peter as confessing that he has never eaten anything common or unclean (10.14; 11.8). Lastly, in his confrontation with Peter at Antioch, related in the Letter to the Galatians, Paul would not have failed to mention such an abrogation to support his thesis, had he known of it. James Dunn's conclusion seems to me to be hard to refute: 'Such testimony as to the earliest community's continuing faithfulness on the matter of food laws and table fellowship provides one of the strongest reasons for questioning whether Jesus was as clearly as radical on the subject of the food laws as Mark 7.15 and 19 indicate.'[66]

If Mark 7.14–15 is based on an authentic saying of Jesus which has been incorrectly interpreted by the evangelist, what could its true meaning be? Several readings have been proposed. Some scholars think that Jesus, like the prophets of times past, was simply emphasizing the priority of ethics over ritual, without abandoning the latter. Others think that Jesus was expressing the idea that some things do not make one unclean by reason of an intrinsic impurity, but because they have been so designated by God. So it is the transgressing of the prohibition which makes one unclean, and not the object to which it relates. Such a view can also be found among the rabbis.[67]

The Gospels several times show us Jesus observing the law quite naturally. As the law demands (Num. 15.38–39; Deut. 22.12), fringes hung from the four corners of his garment (Mark 6.56; Matt. 9.20; 14.36; Luke 8.44). After healing a leper, Jesus asked him to show himself to the priest and to offer for his purification what Moses prescribed (Mark 1.44/Matt. 8.4/Luke

5.14). He approved the levying of tithes (Matt. 23.23/Luke 11.42), voluntary contributions to the temple (Mark 12.41–44/ Luke 21.1–4) and the tax of half a shekel.[68] He visited synagogues, and regarded Deuteronomy 6.5 and Leviticus 19.18 as the two greatest commandments.

Thus in all probability Jesus behaved like any practising Jew, not putting any of the basic aspects of the law in question. Jesus defended a view of the law in which the moral element had priority over the ritual aspect. In concrete, that was shown in legal terms when two biblical commandments were in opposition. Jesus had to disagree with the legal conceptions of the Pharisaic and Essene movements which encouraged divisions and exclusions within the people of Israel. However, as E. P. Sanders has well shown in his magisterial *Jewish Law from Jesus to the Mishnah*, the conflicts which set him over against Pharisees and other groups did not relate to fundamental points. These disagreements were no deeper than those which set the Essenes over against other movements within the Judaism of the time, or even sometimes divided the Pharisees. Jesus never had the intention of rejecting the law of Moses, or even of creating a new religion. What we know of the piety and practices of the primitive community of Jerusalem make this hypothesis even more improbable.

Jesus and the Gentiles

Did Jesus preach the imminent arrival of the kingdom of God to the Gentiles? Given the controversies in the primitive church about the mission to the pagans, this question takes on quite special importance.

The final redactors of the Gospels were all in favour of a mission to the Gentiles. Thus on the principle of dissimilarity, any attitude to the contrary which is attributed to Jesus in the Gospels has a good chance of being authentic.

At the end of the Gospel of Matthew, Jesus, after his resurrection, calls on his disciples to preach the good news among the Gentiles:

Go therefore and make disciples of all nations, baptizing

them in the name of the Father and of the Son and of the Holy
Spirit (Matt. 28.19).

However, during his ministry Jesus, according to Matthew,
explicitly restricted his mission to the people of Israel:

Go nowhere among the Gentiles, and enter no town of the
Samaritans, but go rather to the lost sheep of the house of
Israel (Matt. 10.5–6).

For truly, I say to you, you will not have gone through all the
towns of Israel, before the Son of man comes (Matt. 10.23).

I was sent only to the lost sheep of the house of Israel (Matt.
15.24).

These three statements probably reflect Jesus' attitude. Given
the sayings attributed to the risen Jesus, the evangelist would
certainly not have preserved them had he not considered them
authentic. He would not have hesitated to attribute the mission
to the Gentiles to Jesus had he known trustworthy traditions to
this effect. Matthew, like the other Gospels, contains some cases
of the healings of Gentiles by Jesus. These healings, which are
not historically improbable, do not imply a mission outside
Israel.

The version of the Gospel of Mark that we know was written
mainly for Christians of pagan origin; nevertheless it retains
traces of a negative attitude on the part of Jesus towards the
Gentiles in an episode which also occurs in Matthew
(15.21–28). During a long journey in pagan territory. Jesus was
approached by a women whose small daughter was possessed
by a demon:

Now the woman was a Greek, a Syrophoenician by birth, and
she begged him to cast the demon out of her daughter. And he
said to her, 'Let the children first be fed, for it is not right to
take the children's bread and throw it to the dogs.' But she
answered him, 'Yes, Lord; yet even the dogs under the table
eat the children's crumbs.' And he said to her, 'For this saying
you may go your way; the demon has left your daughter.'

And she went home, and found the child lying in bed, and the demon gone (Mark 7.26–30).

It is difficult to believe that the saying 'Let the children . . . to the dogs' is not authentic, since it is so opposed to the spirit and the message of the Gospel of Mark. It is not clear why the author has included it in his Gospel. This phrase was perhaps used by Christian communities opposed to a mission to the Gentiles. Mark, who could hardly ignore it, tried to neutralize its most pejorative aspects by following it with the healing of the small Syrophoenician girl. So it seems almost certain that Jesus, even if he visited and indeed healed Gentiles, did not have a high opinion of them, and carried out his mission exclusively among the children of Israel. The fact that Peter, James and the other leaders of the Jerusalem community hesitated for a long time before launching a mission among the Gentiles clearly shows that Jesus had not given instructions to this effect. Disciples less familiar with the person and ideas of Jesus like the Hellenists, Barnabas and Paul were certainly the ones who initiated the mission to the Gentiles. Paul clearly indicates in Romans 15.8 that 'Christ became a servant to the circumcised to show God's truthfulness, in order to confirm the promises given to the patriarchs'. In Galatians 1.11–17 he emphasizes that it is Christ himself who has revealed to him his mission among the pagans, not men. Such a comment would have been superfluous had Jesus himself decreed this mission during his ministry.

Did Jesus think that the Gentiles would be admitted to the kingdom of God? Some of his sayings (Matt. 8.11–12/Luke 13.28–29) have often been interpreted in this sense. Even supposing that Jesus believed that when the kingdom of God came the Gentiles would join the people of Israel in worshipping YHWH, he would only be doing so in conformity to numerous biblical prophecies (see pp.151–2).

6

An Uncertain History

The history of the first decades of the church is known to us above all through the letters of Paul and the Acts of the Apostles.[1] The letters of Paul are certainly fundamental documents, since they come from a direct witness and a key figure in the events to which they refer.[2] Of course they must have priority in any historical reconstruction. But they are complex writings which have to be handled with care and can only provide bits of information. Several difficulties await the researcher. First of all, of the thirteen letters attributed to Paul in the New Testament (in the Jerusalem Bible, Hebrews is counted among Paul's letters, but that is not customary in Anglo-Saxon countries), only seven are regarded as authentic by all the experts (Romans, I and II Corinthians, Galatians, Philippians, I Thessalonians and Philemon). The authenticity of II Thessalonians, Ephesians and Colossians is ruled out by the majority of scholars. That of the three last letters (I and II Timothy and Titus) is very widely rejected. Moreover some epistles, like II Corinthians, seem made up of several letters. Besides, Paul did not write his letters to tell us about the history of emergent Christianity or to present his theological views or those of his opponents in a systematic way. These are committed texts, of an apologetic kind, polemic or pastoral, meant as a response to particular problems. Paul presents, sometimes in a tendentious way, only the events and ideas necessary for his demonstrations. All exegetes know how difficult it is to reconstruct Paul's own thought, that of his opponents, and the course of certain events, from his letters.

All these difficulties in interpretation reappear in the Letter to the Galatians, Paul's letter which contains most information about the history of the primitive church and which is most often linked to the Acts of the Apostles. This is a polemical and apologetic text written at the beginning of the 50s and addressed to a Christian community in Galatia, in present-day Turkey, which was founded by Paul. In Paul's absence, this community was visited by Jewish-Christian missionaries who, questioning his authority and his apostolic message, called for the circumcision of Christians of pagan origin. In Galatians Paul tries to justify his authority and the validity of his message. At the same time he criticizes the views of his opponents. His account of events as important as the Council of Jerusalem and the incident in Antioch must be interpreted in the light of his objectives. Thus the considerable amount of valuable information contained in the letters of Paul is too partial, incomplete and often obscure to allow us to make a faithful and consecutive reconstruction of the history of the primitive church.

In contrast to Paul, the author of the Acts of the Apostles, conventionally called Luke, had the ambition to write a history of the Christian movement. Luke divided his account into two parts. The first, the Gospel of Luke, is devoted to the birth, ministry, death and resurrection of Jesus. The second, the Acts of the Apostles, deals with the development of the Christian movement during the three decades following the death of Jesus. In a prologue similar to those written by historians in the Hellenistic period, Luke indicates that he has decided 'after having followed all things closely for some time past, to write an orderly account' (Luke 1.3). Thus the Acts of the Apostles offers us a chronological and ordered history which, whether considered critically or not, forms the backbone of almost all histories of the primitive church. For readers who are not so familiar with this document I shall offer a brief synthesis of it, concentrating on the passages devoted to the church of Jerusalem and to James.[3] Some events which will be discussed in more detail later will only be mentioned briefly here.

An edifying account

The Acts of the Apostles begins after the resurrection of Jesus. Jesus remained for forty days with the apostles whom he had chosen. He spoke to them of the kingdom of God and told them to remain in Jerusalem to wait for the realization of the divine promises which he had given them. He announced that they would soon be baptized in the Holy Spirit. To those who asked him when he would restore the kingdom of Israel, he replied that it was not for human beings to know the date; this depended on God alone. Then he told them:

> But you shall receive power when the Holy Spirit has come upon you; and you shall be my witnesses in Jerusalem and in all Judaea and to the end of the earth (Acts 1.8).

With these words, Jesus ascended into heaven and disappeared. Two men clothed in white, perhaps Moses and Elijah, announced to the apostles that he would return in the same way. The eleven apostles – we should remember that Judas had betrayed Jesus – then returned to Jerusalem and went up to the 'upper room' where they usually lived. They were assiduous in prayer with some women, including the mother of Jesus, and his brothers (1.14). The brothers of Jesus, whose names we are not given, appear for the first time in the account. Shortly afterwards, on the initiative of Peter, it was decided to nominate a replacement for Judas. Two candidates were presented. Lots were drawn, and Matthias became one of the twelve apostles (1.26). Shortly after his election, at Pentecost, the Holy Spirit announced by Jesus was given.

Pentecost, i.e. the fiftieth day after the Passover, is a name for the feast of Weeks (*Shavuoth*), one of the great Jewish pilgrimage festivals celebrating the gift of the Torah to Israel on Mount Sinai. When the disciples were gathered in the same place, they heard a noise like that of a violent gust of wind:

> And there appeared to them tongues as of fire, distributed and resting on each one of them. And they were all filled with the Holy Spirit and began to speak in other tongues, as the Spirit gave them utterance (2.3–4).

A crowd of pious Jews who had come from every nation was attracted by the noise. Each heard the apostles speaking in his own language. Peter, then making his first great missionary speech, explained the significance of the event:

> Men of Israel, hear these words: Jesus of Nazareth, a man attested to you by God with mighty works and wonders and signs which God did through him in your midst, as you yourselves know – this Jesus, delivered up according to the definite plan and foreknowledge of God, you crucified and killed by the hands of lawless men. But God raised him up, having loosed the pangs of death, because it was not possible for him to be held by it . . . This Jesus God raised up, and of that we are all witnesses. Being therefore exalted at the right hand of God, and having received from the Father the promise of the Holy Spirit, he has poured out this which you see and hear . . . Let all the house of Israel therefore know assuredly that God has made him both Lord and Christ, this Jesus whom you crucified (2.22–36).

To all those who asked what they were to do, Peter replied:

> Repent, and be baptized every one of you in the name of Jesus Christ for the forgiveness of your sins, and you shall receive the gift of the Holy Spirit (2.38).

On that day three thousand people were baptized. From Acts 2.42 to the end of Acts 5 the account is devoted to the organization of the Christian community in Jerusalem, its missionary progress and the threats and intimidations of the Jewish authorities. Several themes emerge from these sections which, as numerous exegetes have shown, contain more than one doublet.

Peter still appears as the spokesman of the Twelve. He is the only one to make speeches. Apart from Peter, John is the only apostle mentioned by name.

The apostles (i.e., the Twelve) go regularly to the temple, where they pray and spread the word of God (2.46; 3.1; 5.12; 5.42). They perform many signs and wonders (3.1–10; 5.12–16), like Peter's healing of a man lame from birth. The Jews are very impressed and are converted by the thousand (4.4; 5.14). The believers live together and have all their possessions in common (2.44–45; 4.34–35). Each one receives according to his needs (2.45; 4.35); Ananias and Sapphira, his wife, who had concealed some of their possessions when entering the community, are struck down and die (5.1–11). One does not play around with the Holy Spirit.

The apostles are continually harassed by the Jewish authorities, who criticize their teaching and their proclamation, in the person of Jesus, of the resurrection of the dead. They are twice arrested and then interrogated by the Sanhedrin (4.1–22; 5.17–42). They are released on condition – which is evidently not respected – that they no longer teach in the name of Jesus. At their second appearance before the Sanhedrin, the Pharisee Gamaliel intervenes on their behalf. Many scholars think that these two arrests relate to the same event.

Acts 6.1–8.3 is devoted to the episode of the martyrdom of Stephen, which is both enigmatic and important. This is the occasion for the first discord within the Jerusalem community. The Hellenists, i.e. the disciples whose mother tongue was Greek, complained to the Hebrews that their widows were being neglected in the daily service of tables. At the request of the Twelve, who wanted to devote themselves to the word of God, the assembly of the faithful designated seven men, including Stephen and Philip, apparently all Hellenists, to be responsible for serving tables (6.2–5). Stephen, supposed to be in charge of them, nevertheless performed great wonders among the people. Accused – according to Luke, wrongly – of having spoken blasphemies against Moses and the law, he was brought before the Sanhedrin. In his defence, the longest speech in Acts, Stephen related the history of Israel, accusing the Jews of not having observed the law and having resisted the prophets. Moreover, citing Isaiah, he emphasized the uselessness of the temple, since 'the Most High does not live in dwellings made with hands' (7.48). The population, enraged, stoned Stephen. Paul then appears for the first time in Acts as a witness to this murder, of which he approves (7.58–8.1). The persecution of the Jerusalem church continued. All its members, with the exception of the apostles, took refuge in the countryside of Judaea and Samaria (8.1–3).

The good news then began to be proclaimed outside

Jerusalem. In Samaria, many were baptized by Philip, one of the Seven (8.4–13). Learning that Samaria had accepted the word of God, the apostles sent Peter and John there. Thanks to them, the Samaritans, who had been baptized only in the name of Jesus, received the Holy Spirit (8.14–18). Luke doubtless wants to emphasize that the apostles controlled the missionary activity of the Hellenists. With the evangelization of Samaria, the Good News spread outside the Jewish community. But the Samaritans, without being truly Jews, were not Gentiles. They regarded themselves as Israelites descended from the tribes of Ephraim and Manasseh, retaining the Pentateuch as their holy book. Up to the time of its destruction by John Hyrcanus in 128 BCE, the temple where they worshipped YHWH had been located on Mount Gerizim. In the time of Jesus and the first Christians, relations between Jews and Samaritans were particularly tense.

Then Philip baptized an Ethiopian eunuch (8.26–39). The episode evokes Isaiah 56.3–5, where the prophet announces that the eunuchs, excluded from the cultic assembly of Israel in Deuteronomy 23.2, would take part in the messianic era if they respected the word of God. Exegetes ask whether the Ethiopian eunuch was a Jew or a godfearer, i.e. a Gentile who acknowledged the God of Israel while observing certain aspects of the Mosaic law. In the original tradition, the Ethiopian was perhaps a Gentile. Nevertheless Luke, who does not present this episode as the first conversion of a Gentile, seems to have seen him as a Jew marginalized by virtue of his infirmity, who became a full member of the people of God through his baptism. For Luke, Peter would have the privilege of the first conversion of a Gentile, the centurion Cornelius.

After the episode of the eunuch, Acts describes the conversion of Paul, the persecutor, on the road to Damascus (9.1–19). Luke attaches quite special importance to this conversion, since he relates it twice more (22.5–16; 26.9–18). After his baptism, Paul preached in Damascus. Driven out by the Jews, he went to Jerusalem, where Barnabas introduced him to the apostles (9.26–30). Chapter 10 and the first part of ch.11 are devoted to a fundamental event, the conversion of the centurion Cornelius by Peter. Cornelius was a pious man and a godfearer. One day he had a vision in which the angel of God asked him to bring Peter to his home (10.1–8). The latter, after a divine vision, did not hesitate to go to Cornelius. He told him and his people:

> You yourselves know how unlawful it is for a Jew to associate with or to visit any one of another nation; but God has shown me that I should not call any man common or unclean (10.28).

While Peter was expounding the good news to them, the Spirit fell on those present, both pagans and Jews. And all spoke in tongues. Peter, judging that the water of baptism could not be refused to those who had received the Holy Spirit, ordered that they should be baptized in the name of Jesus Christ (10.44–48).

On his return to Jerusalem, the circumcised brothers criticized Peter for having entered the house of pagans and having eaten with them. He then explained to them how God had guided his action (11.1–18).

Luke then relates the foundation of the church of Antioch by the Cypriots and Cyrenaeans who had fled Jerusalem after the murder of Stephen. There these last also baptized Greeks, i.e. pagans (11.19–21). It was at Antioch that the disciples were first called Christians. Barnabas was sent by the church of Jerusalem to supervise the situation. He left to seek Paul out in Tarsus, in order to help him. Somewhat later the two went to Jerusalem to bring help to the brothers in Judaea, who were threatened by a famine (11.27–30). At the same moment (Herod) Agrippa I, king of Judaea, had James, the son of Zebedee, put to death by the sword. Peter was also arrested, but managed to escape with the help of the angel of the Lord. Once free, he asked for James and the brothers to be informed. Then he left for another place (12.17).

Chapters 13 and 14 are devoted to the first great missionary journey of Paul and Barnabas, to Cyprus and the numerous cities in the south of what is now Turkey. Their missionary activity usually followed the same pattern. They first went to the local synagogue, where they convinced the Jews and god-fearers whom they found there. But the hostility of some Jews forced them to leave the city or to concentrate their preaching on the Gentiles.

Chapter 15 deals with the very important Council of Jerusalem. A serious conflict broke out at Antioch at that time. People who had come down from Judaea were teaching Christians from the Gentile world that they had to be circumcised if they wanted to be saved. To settle this dispute, it was decided to send Paul, Barnabas and some others to the apostles and elders in Jerusalem. There the apostles and elders met to examine the question. Peter, with very Pauline arguments, spoke out against the circumcision of the Gentiles.[4] Then the author of Acts indicates, without quoting their words, that Barnabas and Paul related the wonders performed among the pagans. Finally James, the brother of the Lord, spoke. After quoting holy scripture, he concluded, like Peter, 'that we should not trouble those of the Gentiles who turn to God' (15.19). He decided to impose only four obligations on them: to abstain from anything that had been polluted by idols, from illegitimate unions, from what had been strangled, and from blood. These obligations were taken up in the 'Apostolic Decree', which the apostles and the elders, in accord with the whole church, sent to the Gentiles of Antioch, Syria and Cilicia.

After the Council of Jerusalem, Paul becomes the hero of Acts which, right to the end, is devoted to his travels. After parting company with Barnabas because of a conflict over John called Mark (15.36–40), Paul visited numerous regions and cities including Philippi (16.12–40), Thessalonica (17.1–10), Beroea (17.10–15), Athens (17.15–18.1) and Corinth (18.1–18). After a long stay in Corinth he then resumed his journey and went, among other places, to Ephesus (18.19–21), Caesarea (18.22), Jerusalem (18.22) and Antioch (18.22–23). After that he returned to Ephesus, where he spent a long time (19.1–40). Then he decided to pay another visit to Jerusalem, hastening in order to arrive there before Pentecost (19.21; 20.16). Paul undertook this journey, the reasons for which are never specified, despite forebodings (20.18–38) and the warnings of some (21.4, 11–12). He and his companions were received gladly by the Jerusalem brothers (21.17). The next day, Paul went to the house of James, where all the elders were met. He told them of the success of his mission to the Gentiles. They rejoiced at it and gave glory to God. Then James and the elders told Paul that thousands of Jews, zealous supporters of the law, had embraced the faith. They warned him that many of these brothers had heard that he was urging the Jews living among the pagan Christians no longer to follow the law of Moses (21.20–25).

To prove that these rumours were unfounded, they asked Paul to finance and perform with four Jewish Christians the final rites of a Nazirite vow.[5] According to Numbers 6.1–21, by this vow a Jew consecrated himself to God. He committed himself during the period of the vow to drink neither wine nor fermented drinks, not to cut his hair and not to touch a dead body. According to Acts, Paul had already made such a vow at Cenchreae (18.18). This demonstration of piety had little effect. Paul was recognized in the temple by Jews from Asia, who accused him of having introduced Gentiles into the holy place (21.27–29). The Roman soldiers saved him from a lynching. After his arrest he appeared successively before the Sanhedrin, the Roman procurator Felix and king Agrippa (22–26). Each time he proclaimed his innocence, emphasizing that he had always been a Jew who respected the law and that he had never proclaimed anything 'but what the Prophets and Moses had said must happen'. Having asked to appear before Caesar because he was a Roman citizen, he was sent to Rome, where he tried, with slight success, to convince the Jews (28.17–27). He concluded from this that the pagans would listen (28.28). Paul continued to proclaim the kingdom of God for two years (28.30). Luke does not tell us whether he was condemned to death or was able to leave Rome to pursue his mission.

Whom to believe?

What are we to think of the account in the Acts of the Apostles?[6] Until the beginning of critical analyses of the New Testament, the historical value of Acts was accepted without discussion. Histories of the primitive church were written by supplementing, in the most judicious way possible, the account in Acts with facts from the letters of Paul.[7] The contradictions between these documents were either ignored or harmonized more or less happily. While this approach still inspires numerous popular works and some more scholarly works of a fundamentalist kind, it is no longer thought acceptable by modern criticism.

Whatever the historical value of the information presented in Acts, first of all its very incomplete and selective character must be underlined. Concentrating essentially on Peter and Paul, Acts has very few facts on most of the figures of the early church, including James, the brother of the Lord. Acts does not tell us anything about the Christian communities of Galilee, Egypt, eastern Syria or Mesopotamia. Similarly, we know nothing at all about the foundation of the church of Rome. The development of the Jerusalem church and Peter's career after the Council of Jerusalem hardly seem to interest Luke. The omissions by the author of Acts can be explained in several ways. The absence of trustworthy information is one possible explanation in certain cases. In many others Luke doubtless chose not to mention events which he thought insignificant. But we also have good reason to suppose that some information has been ignored because it embarrassed Luke, since it contradicted the message that he wanted to pass on.

Beyond question Luke sinned by omission. But can we trust him over the events that he does relate? Some scholars link the truthfulness of Acts with the highly debatable identity of its author. Those who attribute its composition to Luke, the companion of Paul, judge the account to be relatively trustworthy. They think that as a direct witness to some of the events that he described, and having benefitted from numerous first-hand testimonies, Luke surely knew what he was talking about. Other scholars, for whom the author of Acts would be an anonymous Christian of the following generation, are more sceptical about its historicity. In reality, even if it were demonstrated that the author of Acts was a travelling companion of Paul, that would not necessarily make his account much more trustworthy and impartial. Some scholars have tried to reconstruct the written sources used by Luke in order to evaluate the historicity of Acts better. With the possible exception of a travel diary written in the first person, most think that it is in practice impossible to reconstruct these sources, since they have been so worked on by the author of Acts.[8]

The best way of assessing the historical reliability of Acts is therefore to compare the information which it contains with what we find in the letters of Paul. These letters allow us to test – if not the whole of Acts – numerous facts relating to Paul, his missionary journey and his relations with the Jerusalem church. Beyond question, an important part of the information contained in Acts is confirmed by the letters of Paul. Whether he knew some of Paul's letters (as several scholars think[9]), whether he himself was one of Paul's travelling companions, or whether he made use of good-quality oral or written sources, the author of Acts had a good knowledge of the missionary activity of the apostle to the Gentiles.

However, there are a certain number of contradictions between Acts and the letters of Paul. Some concern points of detail, others very significant aspects, like the portrait of Paul and his visits to Jerusalem. In a famous article which appeared in 1966, Philippe Vielhauer drew attention to the important difference between the portrait of Paul painted by the author of Acts and that which emerges from the letters of Paul.[10] It is difficult to imagine that the Paul of Acts, so respectful of the law of Moses, could have composed such a radical a work as the Letter to the Galatians. Very characteristic features of his thought as it appears in his letters are absent from the speeches which Luke attributes to him. Strangely, the most Pauline speech in Acts is the one made by Peter at the Council of Jerusalem. In fact Acts only presents to us Paul the Jew with the Jews; it does not know the Paul who abandoned the practice of the law to preach among the Gentiles, as Paul himself describes in I Corinthians 9.20–21:

To the Jews I became a Jew, in order to win Jews; to those under the law I became as one under the law – though not being myself under the law – that I might win those under the law. To those outside the law I became as one outside the law – not being without law toward God but under the law of Christ – that I might win those outside the law.

Another major discrepancy is the number of visits made by Paul to Jerusalem.[11] These are particularly crucial for establishing the chronology of Paul's journeys and the Jerusalem church.[12] As we have seen, Acts mentions five visits of Paul to Jerusalem after his conversion (9.26–30; 11.29–30; 15.4–29; 18.22; 21–26).

Paul's letters allow us to identify only three of these certainly. The visit mentioned in Galatians 1.18–20 certainly corresponds with that described in Acts 9.26–30. However, the two accounts differ significantly. Paul's account is particularly concise:

> Then after three years I went up to Jerusalem to visit Cephas, and remained with him fifteen days. But I saw none of the other apostles except James the Lord's brother. (In what I am writing to you, before God, I do not lie.)

Since Paul is proclaiming his good faith, we can deduce that other versions of this visit were circulating in Galatia. This visit, which took place three years after his 'conversion', thus happened between 33 and 38, most probably in 37.

According to Paul, his visit was brief and confidential. Among the dignitaries of the church he saw only Peter and James. Moreover, it seems doubtful that he preached in Jerusalem. In the account in Acts, the apostles, at first sceptical about the conversion of the former persecutor, agreed to receive him and trust him, thanks to Barnabas. Afterwards, Paul preached with them in Jerusalem. But this visit, longer and less private than in Paul's account, ended badly, since Paul had to flee in order to escape a plot hatched by Jews of the Diaspora. The reader has the feeling that perhaps Paul is not telling us everything, and that Luke is probably telling us more than he knew. But his account has the merit of suggesting that perhaps the visit did not go off without incident.

In his letter to the Galatians, Paul tells us that his second visit took place fourteen years afterwards. He does not make it clear whether this was fourteen years after his conversion or after his visit, but the second hypothesis seems more probable. Since in antiquity the first and last years were counted as whole years even if they had almost ended or hardly begun, this visit took place at the earliest in 43 and at the latest in 52. On the basis of other elements, the majority of scholars put it in 48 or 49, after Paul's first missionary journey. Paul's account, which I shall quote in full, is of very great importance for reconstructing the history of the primitive church:

> Then after fourteen years I went up again to Jerusalem with Barnabas, taking Titus along with me. I went up by revelation; and I laid before them (but privately before those who were of repute) the gospel which I preach among the Gentiles, lest somehow I should be running or had run in vain. But even Titus, who was with me, was not compelled to be circumcised, though he was a Greek. But because of false brethren secretly brought in, who slipped in to spy out our freedom which we have in Christ Jesus, that they might bring us into bondage – to them we did not yield submission even for a moment, that the truth of the gospel might be preserved for you. And from those who were reputed to be something (what they were makes no difference to me; God shows no partiality) – those, I say, who were of repute added nothing to me; but on the contrary, when they saw that I had been entrusted with the gospel to the uncircumcised, just as Peter had been entrusted with the gospel to the circumcised (for he who worked through Peter for the mission to the circumcised worked through me also for the Gentiles), and when they perceived the grace that was given to me, James and Cephas and John, who were reputed to be pillars, gave to me and Barnabas the right hand of fellowship, that we should go to the Gentiles and they to the circumcised; only they would have us remember the poor, which very thing I was eager to do (Gal. 2.1–10).

Reconciling this account with Acts is one of the favourite sports of exegetes and historians. As Jacques Dupont has demonstrated, every kind of solution, possible or impossible, has been proposed.[13] The most traditionalist exegetes, anxious to preserve the historical veracity of Acts, generally try to show that the visit described in Galatians 2.1–10 corresponds to Paul's second visit related in Acts 11.26–29.[14] We may recall that according to Acts 11.26–29, Paul and Barnabas went to Jerusalem to bring help to their brothers in Judaea, who were facing famine. For these exegetes, the third visit in Acts, that of

ch.15, which will have taken place after the writing of the Letter
to the Galatians, is not mentioned in any of Paul's letters. Such
a solution abuses both logic and chronology. Galatians 2.1–10
is more suggestive of the Council of Jerusalem in Acts 15 than
the visit in Acts 11.26–29. In the two accounts Paul and
Barnabas go to Jerusalem, where they discuss with the heads of
the church the admission of Gentiles without circumcision. In
both cases, the decision arrived at is not to require circumcision.

There are certainly more or less significant differences
between these two texts. In Acts, Paul and Barnabas go to
Jerusalem after a conflict in Antioch, while in Galatians it is a
revelation of Paul which leads them to go there. Titus is not
mentioned in Acts. The meeting with the pillars seems to be
more of a private matter in the letter, whereas in Acts it has a
very public and official character. Acts says nothing about
dividing up missionary activities between Paul and Barnabas on
the one hand and James, Peter and John on the other. Moreover
Luke knows nothing of any responsibility of Paul towards the
'poor' of Jerusalem. These difficulties, though important, could
simply reflect the fact that the two texts were produced with
different objectives. The problem of the Apostolic Decree is
more delicate. In Acts it imposes four obligations connected
with the Mosaic law on Gentiles entering the church. Not only
does Paul says nothing of these obligations, but he emphasizes
again that nothing was added to his gospel, which seems to
exclude them. Scholars generally think that the Apostolic
Decree was not adopted at this meeting, but later.

If Galatians 2.1–10 corresponds to the Apostolic Council in
Acts 15, what becomes of the second visit of Paul related in Acts
11.26–29? Some scholars simply suppose that Paul did not mention this visit in Galatians because he did not think it very
significant. Such 'forgetfulness' would seem improbable, given
that Paul attests before God that he is not lying. By pointing out
such an 'omission' his opponents could have cast doubt on the
truthfulness of the rest of the account. Since attempts aimed at
harmonizing Acts and the letter to the Galatians seem futile, we
have to accept that Paul's second visit in Acts is due either to
Luke's imagination or to a misinterpretation of his sources.

Many scholars, adopting this latter hypothesis, think that

Acts 11.26–29 and Acts 15 are two parallel reports, both dealing with the visit mentioned by Paul in Galatians 2.1–10. A chronological problem then arises. Is this visit to be put, with Acts 11.26–29, before Paul's first great missionary journey, or with Acts 15 just after it? Most scholars think, probably rightly, that the meeting could not have taken place before the first missionary journey.

The fourth stay in Jerusalem, mentioned in passing (Acts 18.22), is not corroborated by Paul's letters and, besides, seems improbable. However, we should note that certain sound exegetes like Simon Légasse[15] and Gerd Lüdemann[16] think that the Council of Jerusalem took place at that time, i.e. after the second great missionary journey, in 51 or 52. So Luke would have reported the same visit three times.

There is no doubt about Paul's last stay in Jerusalem (Acts 21–26), which was so decisive for him. Paul announces it, with some apprehension, in his letter to the Romans. His main motive, which is to deliver the collection made for the 'saints' of Jerusalem, does not appear in Acts apart perhaps from two allusions (24.17,26), which are incomprehensible to readers who do not know Paul's letters. Despite the great ingenuity employed by some scholars, Acts and the letters of Paul can hardly be reconciled over Paul's visits to Jerusalem. This certainly does not reinforce the historical validity of Acts.

Several events which occupy an important place in Paul's letters have been omitted by Luke, although he certainly knew them. The most notorious of these omissions are the conflicts affecting the communities of Corinth (I and II Corinthians) and Galatia (Galatians) and the incident in Antioch where, shortly after the Council of Jerusalem, Peter and Paul clashed bitterly over Jewish and pagan Christians eating together (Gal. 2.11–14). Paul reproached Peter for having ceased to share a table with pagan Christians during a stay in Antioch, after the arrival of people from James's entourage. Luke doubtless preferred not to mention this episode, decisive though it was in the history of the primitive church, because it contradicts his vision of a harmonious church.

The Acts of the Apostles contains a number of facts about Paul and his journeys which have no equivalent in the letters.

The truthfulness of much of the political, geographical or institutional information, and the realism and precision of some details, lead many historians to be very positive about the reliability of the accounts in which they appear. Others, who are more sceptical, point out that, in Luke's time as in ours, people wrote excellent historical romances.

All in all, a comparison between Acts and the letters of Paul prompts some reservations about the historical truthfulness of Acts. While much information would seem trustworthy, some often important information is inaccurate or presented tendentiously. Moreover, Luke has certainly omitted significant facts which would have shed a different light on his account.

However, Paul's letters allow us to test only one part of Acts. With the exception of the question of persecutions of the Christians, they are of no use in connection with the first eight chapters of Acts. On the basis of the internal coherence of the account, modern criticism is sceptical about the reconstruction made by the author of Acts. Concrete information is sparse and sometimes repeated. We may suppose that Luke had only incomplete sources, difficult to harmonize and to put in chronological order. He filled out the meagre facts at his disposal with abundant speeches. As Henry Cadbury[17] and Martin Dibelius[18] have shown, these speeches are the works of the author. Like classical historians, he has put into the mouths of characters words which he thought appropriate for the circumstances. At the same time, the speeches comment on and explain the situations and the meaning of the account. Given the poverty of Luke's sources, more than elsewhere his reconstruction has been influenced by theological considerations.

So it is generally accepted that the author of Acts has worked both as a historian and as a theologian. He has carefully chosen events worth relating. And his account has been constructed in such a way as to transmit a theological message.[19] A comparison of Acts with Paul's letters allows us to see Luke's objectives and theological presuppositions better.

Luke seeks above all to show the universal progress of the Christian mission from Jerusalem to Rome in conformity with the prophecy of Jesus (Acts 1.8). According to a widespread view, the author of Acts emphasizes above all the success of the mission to the Gentiles which develops after the failure of the mission to the Jews.[20] Following the works of the Scandinavian exegete Jacob Jervell,[21] many scholars now recognize that Luke's message is more subtle. Up to the end of Acts the word of salvation brought by Jesus leads many Jews, above all in Palestine (2.41,47; 4.4; 5.14; 6.1,7; 21.20), but also in the Diaspora (13.43; 14.1; 17.4, 11; 19.9; 28.24), to join the movement. The mission to the Gentiles is presented more as the continuation and expansion of the mission to the Jews than as its replacement. Although Paul appears as the prime mover of the Christian mission among the Gentiles, Luke emphasizes that it was begun by Peter following a divine revelation and approved by the whole of the Jerusalem church. Luke emphasizes the faithfulness of the church, including Paul, to the Jewish tradition. The Jewish Christians continue to observe the law with zeal, and the pagan Christians, in keeping with the dispositions of the Apostolic Decree, recognize its authority in some way. Thus Luke wants to give the image of a united and harmonious church. Some conflicts are omitted; others, if they are mentioned, appear in a very watered-down form.

Paul, presented as a Jew with great respect for the tradition of his ancestors, is certainly the hero of Acts. However, hero though he may be, he never appears as a decisive authority. Thus at the Council of Jerusalem he does not seem to take part in the final decision, which is left to James, Peter and the other apostles and elders, whatever their relative importance may be. At the time of his last visit to Jerusalem, Paul submits to the instructions of James and the elders without discussion. For Luke, he and his mission are thus dependent on the church of Jerusalem, which is the supreme authority for all Christians.

The portrait of James, which is more ambiguous, raises questions about Luke's intentions. James is introduced in a laconic and surreptitious manner by Peter after he has escaped the jailers of Agrippa I: 'Tell James and the brothers' (Acts 12.17). Luke does not specify the identity of this James, who clearly occupies a prime position in the church of Jerusalem. The reader can deduce that this is not James son of Zebedee, since he has just been beheaded. There is nothing to indicate that this is not one of the other three Jameses previously mentioned in the

Gospel of Luke and Acts.[22] In fact, it is only by using other sources that the modern reader can identify him with James the brother of Jesus. It is impossible to deduce this information from Luke and Acts, since while these writings indicate the existence of brothers of Jesus, they never mention their names.

While accepting that the kinship between James and Jesus must have been well known to Luke's readers, we cannot but be astonished that Luke has not mentioned it. Perhaps he did not want to emphasize the weight carried by kinship with Jesus in the early church? Although the majority of commentators think that Peter is designating his successor here, there is nothing to prevent us from supposing that James already occupied first place. Luke never explains why or how James attained a pre-eminent position. He does not mention the appearance of Jesus to James, which to judge from I Corinthians 15.5–7 and the Gospel of the Hebrews was of public notoriety. So why such a silence?

Jacob Jervell thinks that James and the sources of his authority were sufficiently known by Luke's readers for him not to have to mentioned them.[23] However, this silence arouses the suspicions of S. G. F. Brandon[24] and Etienne Trocmé.[25] They think that Luke perhaps chose to ignore important events which he found embarrassing or which did not fit with his conception of the development of the church. We shall have occasion to return to this question.

Whatever may have been the beginning of his 'career', James is the only figure in Acts whose authority is never put in question. At two decisive moments (Acts 15 and 21) he is the dominant figure in the taking of a decision which affects all. Jacob Jervell has given a good explanation of the role played by James in these two chapters. James, whose faithfulness to Judaism was beyond dispute in the primitive church, provides support for Paul. By not requiring the circumcision of pagan Christians and justifying his position by holy scripture, he guarantees the orthodoxy of Paul's gospel *vis-à-vis* the law. Similarly, by asking Paul to finance Nazirite vows, he implicitly gives him a certificate of good conduct.

However, the identification of Luke's intentions and theological presuppositions should not lead us, like some hypercritical exegetes, to put in question or reject systematically all the elements which confirm them too ideally. Similarly, it would be wrong to explain most of the major omissions in Acts by saying that they are embarrassing and go against the meaning of the account which Luke wants to give. Acts is certainly a complex text, which contains numerous historical facts and others which are more doubtful. Sorting these out is difficult and often arbitrary, hence the tendency – which is all too human – shown by more than one historian to accept the elements that confirm his theses and to reject the others. The history of the primitive church is very like a minefield the plan of which has been lost. Nevertheless, we shall attempt to cross it, tackling a question which more than anything else divided the primitive church: the conversion of the Gentiles.

7

How Can One Be Christian?

The Acts of the Apostles and the letters of Paul present us with a primitive church which is particularly preoccupied and divided by the different problems relating to the evangelization of the Gentiles. Is the Good News to be preached to them? If so, is it necessary for them to be converted to Judaism if they want to become Christians? If that is not indispensable, what then becomes of their status *vis-à-vis* the Mosaic law and the Jewish Christians? The question is an important one. If circumcision is required of Gentiles, Christianity will remain a sect or a reform movement within Judaism. If it is not, the status of Christianity becomes more uncertain, and serious problems of identity are raised. The development of the primitive church seems to have been dominated by conflicts which produced answers to these questions.

James is known to us above all for the predominant place which he occupied at the heart of these controversies. Of course that does not imply that James was not involved with other decisions and conflicts which were perhaps just as important for him. But they are largely unknown to us. The debates about the Gentiles can only be understood in the context or relations between Jews and Gentiles at the end of the Second Temple period.[1]

Jews and Gentiles

The literature about the origins of Christianity usually describes the attitude of Judaism towards the Gentiles at the end of the Second Temple period by these three assertions:

- the Gentiles were intrinsically impious and wicked, and would only obtain salvation if they converted to Judaism;
- the Jews of the first century of our era engaged in intense missionary activity in order to save pagans by converting them;
- the Mosaic law forbade Jews to have dealings with Gentiles: in particular, eating at the same table was prohibited.

Such generalizations, which are increasingly being challenged, are largely incorrect. First of all, Judaism did not present a single and well-defined position on the Gentiles, their salvation and the nature of appropriate social relations with them. On the contrary, the Jews expressed opinions and adopted forms of behaviour which differed considerably depending on the period, the place and the circumstances. Only if we appreciate this diversity do the specific features of Christianity and the development of the primitive church become comprehensible. The Hebrew Bible, which so markedly shaped the world-view of Jews in the first century, itself expresses a great variety of opinions about the Gentiles. Today, thanks to the progress of critical analysis, we know that the Bible is made up of numerous texts from different periods which reflect very different conceptions and religious practices. Most of these texts have been widely worked over by successive redactors. However, the Jews of the first century, like certain fundamentalists in our day, did not conceive of the Bible as the product of a long and complex historical evolution. For them it was a uniform revelation of the divine word and divine truth. Because of its diversity, it could therefore inspire and justify numerous often contradictory conceptions.

Most often we find a relatively tolerant attitude towards the pagans and idolatry.[2] Certainly there are often manifestations of hostility, indeed of cruelty. However, this hostility is mainly directed against the pagans who worship other gods in the land of Israel and against those who, outside Israel, are opposed to the plans of YHWH. The Israelites were concerned to stamp out idolatry above all in the land which YHWH had given them. The Gentiles are not generally thought to be intrinsically impious or wicked. Indeed very often they are cordially invited to bring their sacrifice to YHWH's temple. Since they have not made a covenant with YHWH, they do not have to observe the law of Moses. In the biblical texts which mention belief in the existence of the gods of other peoples, it seems quite natural that these peoples should be able to worship their own gods, since 'all the peoples walk each in the name of its god' (Micah 4.5). YHWH is not offended at this as long as Israel is not contaminated by these cults. Thus in Amos 1.3–2.3 idolatry is not one of the crimes censured by YHWH in the nations that he is going to destroy. When, after the exile, YHWH was progressively regarded as the only and universal God, the pagans were thought to be as naive as they were impious. Furthermore, why should YHWH be offended at their idolatry if he himself had given the sun, the moon and other stars to the pagan nations to worship (Deut. 4.19)?

This tolerance is also evident in passages where the salvation of the Gentiles is mentioned. Since, with rare exceptions, notions of retribution after death and eternal life do not appear in the Hebrew Bible, the salvation of the Gentiles is expressed by their survival at the judgment of the nations and their participation in the messianic era. According to the prophets, YHWH will exterminate the impious Israelites and the enemies of Israel. But this extermination is not usually total, since passages with a messianic inspiration often mention the existence of Gentiles in the final era. Many texts announce that the glory of YHWH will be revealed to all nations. These nations will go to Jerusalem to worship the God of Israel and take part in the messianic feast:

It shall come to pass in the latter days that the mount of the house of YHWH shall be established as the highest of the mountains, and shall be raised above the hills; and all the nations shall flow to it (Isa. 2.2).

I am coming to gather all nations and tongues; and they shall come and see my glory (Isa. 66.18).

On this mountain YHWH Sabaoth will make for all peoples a feast of fat things, a feast of wine on the lees (Isa. 25.6).

At that time Jerusalem shall be called the throne of the Lord, and all nations shall gather to it, to the presence of YHWH in Jerusalem, and they shall no more stubbornly follow their own evil heart (Jer. 3.17).

Such texts, which would easily be multiplied,[3] are fundamental to understanding the development of primitive Christianity. But they do not offer a clear answer to a key question: during the messianic era, will the Gentiles become proselytes, i.e. be completely integrated into Israel by having themselves circumcised and adopting the law,[4] or will they preserve their national identity and their customs while abandoning idolatry and glorifying YHWH?[5]

For while such a tolerant concept was dominant, some texts certainly reflect a very negative attitude towards the Gentiles. This attitude is particularly evident in Leviticus,[6] Ezekiel, Ezra and Nehemiah. These books, influenced by the need for some Israelites to maintain their cultural and religious identity during and after the exile, emphasize the holiness of the land of Israel and its people, who must remain pure and free of all stain. The Gentiles are generally considered to be intrinsically unclean and evil, since they refuse to follow the ways of YHWH. The aliens who live in the land of Israel must largely conform to the law, even if they do not join the Israelite community through circumcision.[7]

Opinions about the Gentiles at the end of the Second Temple period reflect the same diversity; it seems that negative attitudes became increasingly important because of the Roman domination of Palestine. Undeniably the great majority of Jews censured idolatry and other practices generally associated with it, like adultery, homosexuality and infanticide. But the gravity of idolatry and its consequences were the object of the most varied interpretations. Four typical positions can be reconstructed on the basis of extra-biblical Jewish literature composed between the third century BCE and the third century CE.[8]

According to the first the Gentiles, who have deliberately refused to submit to the law, are intrinsically wicked and impious by virtue of their idolatry and their general and continual uncleanness; their conduct is abominable, diabolical; it offends YHWH, who denies them any hope of salvation. The Book of Jubilees (22.16–22) clearly expresses this position:

> Their [the nations'] deeds are defiled, and all of their ways are contaminated, and despicable, and abominable. They slaughter their sacrifices to the dead, and to the demons they bow down. And they eat amongst tombs . . . And for all those who worship idols and for the hated ones there is no hope in the land of the living: because they will go down to Sheol. And in the place of judgment they will walk, and they will have no memory upon the earth.[9]

Those who have not been circumcised on the eighth day are lost, which suggests that for the author of Jubilees the conversion of the Gentiles was not an option – though perhaps the conversion of their newborn was. To judge from the main sectarian manuscripts discovered in the caves near Qumran, the Essenes largely shared the views of the author of Jubilees, a work which moreover has been found in the caves. They thought that the Gentiles, like the Jews who did not belong to their movement, were wicked and dirty creatures, condemned by God to extermination. Any association with them was strictly prohibited.

Some Pharisees expressed similar opinions, if we are to suppose that the rabbinic literature reflects their views in this area. A passage of the Tosefta (Sanhedrin 13.2), a work dating from the beginning of the third century, relates a disagreement between Rabbi Eliezer ben Hyrcanus and Rabbi Joshua ben Hananiah, two Pharisaic sages of the end of the first century. The former thinks that no Gentile will have access to the world to come, i.e. will obtain salvation in God's judgment. The latter thinks that the righteous among them will be saved. Thus for Rabbi Eliezer ben Hyrcanus, no Gentile will be saved unless he is circumcised and becomes a proselyte. But contrary to the author of Jubilees and the Essenes, Rabbi Eliezer probably did not think that conversion was impossible – though that does not mean that he was keen for it to happen. We may suppose that this first position would have met with wide approval during periods of pagan oppression in Palestine.

Rabbi Joshua represents the second position. According to this, the majority of Gentiles, guilty of idolatry and other grave sins, will only be saved if they become proselytes. However, those who respect the basic moral principles of the Mosaic law – a kind of natural law applicable to all humankind – will be able to benefit from the divine mercy. Whatever their virtues, these righteous will only be able to conform fully to the will of God if they convert. This position, which beyond question underlies the proselytism of some Jews, must have been quite widespread in the first century.

The two latter positions also accept, though for different reasons, that a larger or smaller number of Gentiles will be saved.

According to the third,[10] which is to be found in some apocalyptic texts like I Enoch and the Testaments of the Twelve Patriarchs, all humankind, both Jews and Gentiles, is subject to the influence of the evil principle. The superiority of Israel is only illusory. All human beings are equally guilty. But YHWH will be stricter on Israel, to whom he has taught his way. By his intervention, God will deliver humanity from evil. The rare individuals who have done good and have been merciful will not experience the effects of the divine wrath.

> Through his kingly power, God will appear, dwelling among men on the earth, to save the race of Israel, and to assemble the righteous from among the nations (Testament of Naphtali 8.3).[11]

This pessimistic view does not generally lead to proselytism.

The fourth position, which is to be found above all in texts coming from the Hellenistic Diaspora, is characterized by great tolerance towards the Gentiles. Idolatry, contrary to some practices, is not generally regarded as a sin. Thus the author of the Testament of Abraham, probably an Egyptian Jew of the first century, condemns homosexuality among the Gentiles, but not idolatry. In his eyes, at the last judgment Jews and Gentiles will be judged according to the same criterion, which is their respect for universal moral values. The *Letter of Aristeas*, while favouring the separation of Jews and Gentiles, also thinks that the salvation of both Jews and Gentiles depends on their moral conduct. The Jews will not enjoy any particular privilege. The law is nevertheless precious for its pedagogical value. But its teaching hardly differs from that of traditional Greek wisdom. The *Letter of Aristeas* even contains the idea that Jews and Greeks worship the same God under different names.

It is impossible to assess how representative each position was. But it is important above all to note that the opinion of the Jews about the Gentiles was not uniformly negative and that many people thought that the best of the latter would accede to the world to come. So we may conclude that a large number of Jews were not preoccupied with the conversion of the Gentiles, thinking either that they were in any case lost, or that the most virtuous of them would be saved even without being converted.

This review of the most typical positions stated by the Jews on the Gentiles leads us to qualify considerably the widespread view that the Judaism of the first century was profoundly missionary.[12] According to this view the Jews, convinced of the superiority of their way of life and their beliefs, and regarding themselves as a light which was to lighten and save humanity, exerted great efforts to convert the pagans. The supporters of this theory back it up with a group of more or less relevant arguments: the existence of a Jewish propaganda literature, the measures taken by the Roman authorities to thwart Jewish proselytism, the difficulty of explaining the important Jewish population of the time by natural demographic growth, and literary evidence, Jewish or pagan, emphasizing the expansion of Jewish customs among the Gentiles.

Some antisemitic remarks of Seneca and a saying of Jesus are often cited among the chief evidence for this proselytism:

> The customs of this accursed race have gained so much influence that they are now accepted everywhere. The conquered have given their laws to the conquerors (Seneca, *De superstitione*).

> Woe to you, scribes and Pharisees, hypocrites! for you traverse sea and land to make a single proselyte (Matt. 23.15).

Recently, after a rigorous analysis of these arguments, Scot

McKnight,[13] Edouard Will and Claude Orrieux,[14] Martin Goodman[15] and some other scholars have challenged the view that the Judaism of this period was essentially proselytizing. Without denying the existence of isolated efforts and individual conversions, they reject the notion of an organized Jewish mission, active and systematic. These scholars, perhaps pushing their revisionist effort a bit far, have probably underestimated the diversity of the positions over proselytism. However, it seems likely that the conversions, which were certainly less numerous than used to be thought, were not actively sought by the majority of Jews or by many Gentiles, and that proselytes were not always well received. In the Diaspora, many Jews were ready to allow Gentiles to take a more or less close part in their religious activities, even if they did not urge them to convert. Doubtless these sympathizers allowed the Jewish communities to integrate into their cities better. Without being converted, the sympathizers, generally known as godfearers,[16] attended the synagogues and observed certain practices derived from the Mosaic law.[17] Most Diaspora Jews were probably very ready to accept that, even though they had not been converted, the godfearers would gain their salvation if they led virtuous lives.

Josephus refers to these latter when he mentions the Greeks attracted by the ceremonies of the Jews of Antioch:

> The number of Greeks whom they attracted to their religious ceremonies did not cease to grow, and in a way they made them part of their community (*Jewish War* 7.45).

Similarly Juvenal, but in a very different spirit, is probably referring to the godfearers, whom he distinguishes from proselytes:

> Some by a father revering the sabbath begotten
> pray but to clouds and divine power of heaven in worship,
> holding the flesh of the pig to be like flesh of humans,
> which their father forbids. The foreskin they circumcise early
> (*Satires* 5.14,96–99).

The father is a godfearer and the son becomes a proselyte. Some scholars make these godfearers a well-defined and homogeneous category. However, as S. D. Cohen has shown,[18] the literary and archaeological sources at our disposal prove rather that the concept could denote very different situations. At one extreme it included rich individuals who funded certain activities of the Jewish community of their city for political reasons, without taking part in worship of YHWH or abandoning that of the traditional gods. At the other extreme were people who were very integrated into a synagogue, having ceased to worship the gods of the city and observing certain aspects of the Mosaic law.

According to the third common opinion, because of legal constraints, contacts between Jews and Gentiles were limited to the strict minimum.[19] The Jews avoided the Gentiles; they did not enter Gentile houses or have Gentiles into their own. Eating together, which signified greater intimacy, was in practice impossible. This view is essentially based on certain Jewish texts which dissuade Jews from having contact with Gentiles or forbid it altogether, and texts from pagan authors which note the Jewish separatism or criticize Jews for it.[20] This reticence was due to a religious ban associated with the uncleanness of Gentiles. Those who defend this view think that the words attributed to Peter in Acts (10.28) are a good description of the situation in this period:

> You yourselves know how unlawful it is for a Jew to associate with or to visit any one of another nation.

This view, which reflects the actual situation only very imperfectly, must be heavily qualified. There seems no denying that, in contrast to the ancient Israelites, the Jews of the first century BCE generally regarded the Gentiles as unclean.[21] The fact that the Gentiles were not authorized to go beyond the Court of the Gentiles in the temple shows this. However, it should be noted that this prohibition did not imply a very serious impurity. As E. P. Sanders comments, its only consequence was a ban on penetrating deeper into the temple.[22] That did not prevent Jews from entering into contact with Gentiles if they wanted to go into the courts forbidden to them. In fact the question of the uncleanness of the Gentiles is extremely complex.

The Jews of the period most often considered that the Gentiles were not subject to the biblical system of impurity. However, they expressed very different views on the nature, the gravity, the extent and the transmission of their impurity, on the means of purifying oneself from it, and on its consequences. According to a widespread opinion, the impurity of Gentiles deriving from their character as such was associated with their idolatry and their presumed immorality. To understand the consequences of the biblical impurities, it is necessary to distinguish two different situations. Certain unclean foods, like pork and other meats, are explicitly prohibited by the Bible. Other impurities which can hardly be avoided are tolerated, even encouraged. They are removed by clearly defined rites of purification. Thus although corpses make one unclean, Jews must bury their dead parents. Although sperm is a cause of uncleanness, in practice procreation is a biblical obligation. By reason of these impurities, and others which it was difficult to avoid, the Jews often found themselves in an unclean state. So we must not conclude, as some Christian exegetes do, that since the Gentiles were a source of impurity, the Jews were forbidden to have dealings with them. It seems very probable that the Jews, for whom the regulations about purity concerned above all their relations with the temple, most often attached only limited importance, at the practical level, to the impurity of the Gentiles. Since they were themselves unclean most of the time, this was doubtless not a major factor in their decision whether or not to associate with Gentiles. However, by reason of the dietary regulations of the Mosaic law, they certainly refused to eat with Gentiles if they were not certain that the food served was fit to be consumed. This constraint could oblige them to bring their own food. Of course this problem did not arise when they invited Gentiles to their homes.

The Jews who wanted to extend the rules of cleanness to their everyday life, considering that they had to be pure as often as possible, certainly adopted a less 'relaxed' attitude. The most radical, the Essenes, avoided the Gentiles and their products as far as possible. They judged it necessary to bathe after any contact with a Gentile – this was also the case after contact with a Jew who did not belong to their movement. They certainly refused to share tables with Gentiles, doubtless thinking that this was an implicit biblical prohibition, equivalent to that of idolatry. Many Pharisees/sages adopted a similar attitude, if we can trust the earliest rabbinic literature.[23] For them, to share a table with Gentiles amounted to idolatry and eating with the dead.[24] However, other Pharisees were ready to receive Gentiles and even to visit their homes, in the latter case taking all necessary precautions not to eat unsuitable food.[25] In fact the earliest rabbinic texts (Mishnah, Tosefta) indicate a substantial level of social interaction between Jews and Gentiles.[26] Even if this literature essentially reflects situations dating from the second century, there is no reason to suppose that the rabbis of this period were much more lax than the Pharisees of the first century.

It thus seems very probable that a significant number of Jews, even in the land of Israel, thought that no religious prohibition prevented them from associating with the Gentiles. Of course they could desire to limit their contacts for personal reasons, whether cultural, social or political. In practice it is impossible to assess the real extent of social interaction between Jews and Gentiles. Nevertheless, beyond doubt they were more limited in the land of Israel than in the countries of the Diaspora, by reason of the sacred character of the territory and the numerical predominance of the Jewish population.

Some Diaspora communities, particularly in Asia Minor, seem to have been particularly well integrated with the rest of the population.[27] The Jewish community of Sardes, in present-day Turkey, was not concentrated in any specific district of the city.[28] In Alexandria, although two districts were essentially inhabited by Jews, it was not rare to find a Jew living among Gentiles in the three other districts of the city. In Alexandria, as in the other great Hellenistic cities of the time, the Jewish elites aspired to an education in the gymnasium and attended the theatre and athletic games.

Moreover, we have seen that some Gentiles were closely associated with synagogues. It is probable that many of these god-fearers continued to take part in the traditional cults of their city. It is enough to mention a certain Julia Severa, who built a synagogue at Acmonia when she was high priestess of the imperial cult. Similarly, mixed marriages, while not being particularly numerous, need not have been rare. We need mention only the mother of Timothy, Paul's companion, married to a Greek who apparently did not convert for the occasion (Acts 16.1). Everything suggests that the level of social interaction between Jews and Gentiles in the Diaspora was significant and not limited to the godfearers.

The beginnings of the mission to the Gentiles

The diversity of opinions on the Gentiles in first-century Judaism explains the conflicts and controversies within the primitive church. To understand them, we need to know that in questions relating to salvation, two essential beliefs distinguished the Jews belonging to the Jesus movement from other Jews. First, they were convinced that only those who believed that Jesus was the Messiah, or an eschatological agent of the same type, and that YHWH had raised him, would be saved. The Jews who did not recognize Jesus were thus rejecting the word of God. They were cutting themselves off from God in the same way as if they had denied the status and the words of Moses. Virtuous behaviour and faithful observance of the law would not be enough to save them. The second essential belief was that humanity had to a large degree already entered into the final eschatological era. This would not be manifested fully until the return of Christ on earth (the Parousia). In such a situation the traditional questions concerning the Gentiles called for a new approach and sometimes new solutions.

Let us examine in detail how the young Christian community approached and resolved the three basic questions which, as we have seen, it faced:

– Has the Good News to be preached to the Gentiles?
– If so, are circumcision and the practice of the Mosaic law to be required of Gentiles who accept the Good News? Must they then become proselytes?

– Supposing that circumcision is not necessary, what is their status *vis-à-vis* Jewish Christians and the Mosaic law?

Two New Testament writings, the Acts of the Apostles and the Letter to the Galatians, tell us about the beginnings of the Christian mission to the Gentiles up to the Council of Jerusalem. The Acts of the Apostles contains an account which is long and detailed, but full of legendary elements and constructed in such a way as to justify certain theological conceptions. The Letter to the Galatians offers a perhaps more trustworthy account, but one which is unfortunately very incomplete and partial.

We have seen that according to Luke, the primitive church of Jerusalem had initially restricted its preaching to the Jews of the Holy City. Christian missionary activity spread outside Jerusalem following the expulsion of the Hellenists. In his account of the propagation of the faith, Luke distinguishes three decisive stages: the conversions of Samaritans, of an Ethiopian eunuch, and of the centurion Cornelius. Philip, one of the Seven, was responsible for the first two, symbolizing the adherence of believers on the periphery of Judaism. In fact the Samaritans, who were circumcised and regarded the Pentateuch as their sacred book, were perceived as schismatic Jews/Israelites by the Judaism centred upon the Jerusalem temple. Whatever may have been the identity of the eunuch, supposing that he existed, Luke regards him not as a Gentile but as a marginal Jew who is excluded by reason of his infirmity. The conversion of the Samaritans and the eunuch is part of the reconstitution of the true Israel desired by Jesus.

For Luke, the conversion of Cornelius by Peter is a decisive event since he is the first Gentile to join the community. We should note that Cornelius was converted without first being circumcised, i.e. without first having become a Jewish proselyte. This account, despite its legendary features, is perhaps based on a real fact, but Luke has so reworked the sources and traditions at his disposal that any historical reconstruction has become almost impossible. The episode nevertheless raises interesting questions when one compares it with the reports of the Council of Jerusalem presented in Acts 15 and Galatians 2.1–10.

At the time of the Council, Paul's opponents thought that baptized Gentiles could only be saved if they had themselves circumcised. In the Cornelius episode, the apostles and brothers in Jerusalem do not censure Peter for having baptized Cornelius without first having him circumcised, but for having gone into his house and eaten with him (Acts 11.3). Peter himself, thinking 'how unlawful it is for a Jew to associate with or to visit any one of another nation', only agreed to visit the centurion after a vision. Curiously, this vision, which seems to imply the abrogation of the dietary laws of cleanness, is understood by Peter to signify that God accepts Jews and Gentiles who fear him and practise justice in the same way.[29] In this episode, the Jerusalem church appears particularly strict on matters of purity until Peter's vision, not envisaging having dealings with the Gentiles, and thus not being able to convert them. As Etienne Nodet of the École Biblique in Jerusalem emphasizes,[30] in this area it does not seem very different from the Essene sect.

Independently of the conversion of Cornelius, Luke tells us that when disciples from Cyprus and Cyrene came to Antioch, they addressed Greeks (Acts 11.20). These missionaries were among the Hellenists driven from Jerusalem after the martyrdom of Stephen. Similarly, although Luke does not specifically say this, one can imagine that circumcision was not required of the Greeks to whom the word of the Lord was preached. Then Barnabas, delegated by the Jerusalem church, and Paul, the companion whom he had chosen, made a long missionary journey on behalf of the church of Antioch during which they converted numerous Jews and Gentiles to the Good News. It was after their return to Antioch that they had to go to Jerusalem, because of a dispute with people from Judaea who taught the pagan Christians of Antioch that 'unless you are circumcised according to the custom of Moses, you cannot be saved' (Acts 15.1). So in Acts, the conversion of Gentiles without the need for circumcision is initiated both by Peter and by the disciples of the church of Antioch. Then Paul and Barnabas, on behalf of this church and under the supervision of Jerusalem, converted numerous Gentiles until the day when some Jewish Christians from Judaea questioned these missionary efforts.

In the Letter to the Galatians, Paul tells us a significantly different story. He states that God has specially designated him to go to preach among the pagans and that he did not consult anyone:

> But when he who had set me apart before I was born, and had called me through his grace, was pleased to reveal his son to me, in order that I might preach him among the Gentiles, I did not confer with flesh and blood, nor did I go up to Jerusalem to those who were apostles before me, but I went away into Arabia; and again I returned to Damascus (Gal. 1.15-17).

Then, after a brief stay in Jerusalem (Gal. 1.18-20), he again went to Syria and Cilicia. Fourteen years after this first visit he went to Jerusalem again, 'by revelation', to expound the gospel that he was preaching among the pagans. Thus Paul presents his gospel, i.e. the conversion of pagans without requiring circumcision and observance of the Mosaic law, as a personal innovation, conceived through a revelation. He emphasizes that he did not consult the apostles and even suggests that they were not conversant with his gospel when he expounded it to them (Gal. 2.2). He leads one to believe that Peter and the others were solely involved in evangelizing the circumcised. Paul mentions Barnabas only on the occasion of his second visit to Jerusalem, for the Council. So he presents himself as a solitary and independent missionary among the Gentiles.

It is difficult to reconcile his account and that of Acts. Paul is *a priori* a more trustworthy witness than the author of Acts. However, we need to take the often tendentious and apologetic character of his letters into account. Paul certainly overestimated his role and his independence in the evangelization of the Gentiles. In order to thwart the attacks of his opponents in Galatia, he wanted to emphasize above all that his evangelistic mission had been revealed to him by God and that he had exercised it independently of any human authority. That he was the first to convert pagans is doubtful. That he was the first to agree to baptize them without requiring them to be circumcised is possible, but difficult to prove.[31] But what doubtless distinguished Paul and his missionary companions was the absolute priority that he accorded to the evangelization of the pagans. For Paul, the basic feature of the eschatological era which was opening with the resurrection of Christ was the possibility for the Gentiles to obtain their salvation and join the people of God. More than anyone else, Paul was influenced by the universalistic message of certain prophets, particularly Isaiah.

The Letter to the Galatians and the first eleven chapters of Acts suggest that the salvation and conversion of the Gentiles were not the priority of the Jerusalem church. Like Jesus, its members were above all preoccupied with the salvation of Israel. As the account of the conversion of Cornelius indicates, many of them must have thought the evangelization of the Gentiles inconceivable, in that they refused to enter into contact with them. Moreover, some could have thought that the Gentiles would be damned anyway. Others perhaps supposed that such evangelization was premature and that the Gentiles would be converted *en masse* to the word of God on the return of Jesus.[32] If some members perhaps evangelized Gentiles, they therefore probably also required them to be circumcised. Thus the historicity of the conversion of Cornelius before the Council of Jerusalem seems very doubtful. Moreover it would make Paul's account in the Letter to the Galatians difficult to understand. Finally, it would amount to accepting that the Council of Jerusalem discussed a question which had previously been settled after the conversion of Cornelius.[33]

We may ask why, over the years, the evangelization of pagans by Paul and Barnabas without the requirement of circumcision did not provoke a negative response from Jerusalem. George Howard[34] has suggested that the Jerusalem church was unaware of the practices of the church of Antioch. However, such a hypothesis, which can legitimately be derived from the Letter to the Galatians, seems improbable. Many exegetes think that the church of Jerusalem became more sensitive to this mission to the Gentiles following the adherence of many Jews who observed the law very strictly and as a result of the pressure exerted by the zealot movements in Jerusalem. We shall have occasion to return to these arguments, but they do not seem entirely convincing. It seems more credible that most of the Jewish

Christians of Jerusalem will initially have thought this mission marginal and exceptional. Moreover the eschatological enthusiasm of the first years of the church doubtless made this anomaly easier to accept. In time, when the exception became the rule, many people began to feel uneasy. The fact that many uncircumcised former pagans belonged to the Christian movement could have dissuaded many Jews from joining it. As Paula Fredriksen suggests,[35] some Jewish Christians could have thought that the mission to the Jews was enjoying only limited success because YHWH disapproved of such practices.

The Council of Jerusalem

The meeting called (wrongly) the Council of Jerusalem is known to us from a short and ambiguous passage in the Letter to the Galatians and the long and detailed account in Acts. Paul's testimony, despite its character, which is partial in both senses of the word, is our basic source. The historical value to be attached to the account in Acts is much argued over. Boismard and Lamouille, for example, think that Acts 15.1–34 was composed on the basis of the Letter to the Galatians and the account of the conference which will have followed the conversion of Cornelius, contained in another document (the sequel to Acts 11.1–18).[36] According to this hypothesis, Acts 15 would have no independent historical value. By contrast, other scholars are ready to accept the same passage, including the speeches attributed to James and Peter, as historical. So a good deal of scepticism is needed.

The Council was probably more like the small private meeting described by Paul than the solemn assembly, complete with protocol, imagined by Luke. The three pillars, i.e. James, Peter and John, plus perhaps some other dignitaries, including the false brethren mentioned by Paul, were present on behalf of the mother church. Barnabas, Paul and some others represented the church of Antioch. The discussion was certainly very heated, and the final compromise sufficiently ambiguous not to put an end to the debate.

The principle of a mission to the Gentiles does not seem to have been raised at this meeting. However, some Jewish

Christians argued that the new Christians had to become proselytes, i.e. be circumcised and observe the Mosaic law. The majority of them thought, like many other Jews, that since circumcision was the mark of the people of God, there could be no salvation without it. It is possible that others, while accepting that some Gentiles could be saved, thought that new members of pagan origin had to be circumcised, since in their view the Gentiles, having gained their salvation, had to become proselytes in the final age. And this final age was in process of being established.

Paul and Barnabas argued that the Gentiles who had recognized the God of Israel and his Messiah Jesus would be saved without the need for circumcision. Such an opinion would not have been questionable to the many Jews who readily accepted that some Gentiles could accede to the world to come. But apparently many Jewish Christians did not share this point of view. Neither Galatians 2.1–10 nor Acts allows us to reconstruct Paul and Barnabas's argument. Certainly it did not have the very radical character of the Letter to the Galatians, in which Paul questions the nature and role of the law and denies that God makes any distinctions between the Jews and the Gentiles who have recognized Jesus. If Paul had likened conversion to Judaism to passing under the law of slavery (Gal. 5.1) and had proclaimed that circumcision was nothing (Gal. 5.6; 6.15), the patience of the pillars would probably soon have reached its limit.

Paul doubtless mentioned that his gospel came from a divine revelation, and this, we can readily imagine, will not have convinced many of his opponents. Barnabas and he certainly emphasized that the success of their mission was the best testimony to the validity of their view. On hearing the Good News, numerous pagans had acknowledged YHWH and his Messiah, at the same time abandoning their idolatrous practices. Since these pagans engaged in ecstatic practices like glossolalia (speaking in tongues), they had received the Holy Spirit. Their membership of the community confirmed that the messianic age had already manifested itself. Moreover, while the prophets had proclaimed that during the eschaton the Gentiles would worship the God of Israel, they had rarely indicated whether the

Gentiles would join the people of Israel by becoming proselytes. Taking into account the often fluid status of the Gentiles during the messianic era, Barnabas and Paul must have argued that the uncircumcised Christians would form the people of God alongside the Jewish Christians, i.e. the true Israel.

Acts contains the speeches which Peter and James are said to have given at the Council of Jerusalem. Peter spoke first:

> Brethren, you know that in the early days God made choice among you, that by my mouth the Gentiles should hear the word of the gospel and believe. And God who knows the heart bore witness to them, giving them the Holy Spirit just as he did to us; and he made no distinction between us and them, but cleansed their hearts by faith. Now therefore why do you make trial of God by putting a yoke upon the neck of the disciples which neither our fathers nor we have been able to bear? But we believe that we shall be saved through the grace of the Lord Jesus, just as they will (Acts 15.7–11).

Two aspects of this speech have long struck exegetes. First, it seems to refer to the conversion of Cornelius as described by Peter in his speech in Acts 11.5–17 and to be a continuation of that speech. More important, exegetes since the Tübingen school and Renan have noted the very Pauline character of Peter's words. Like Paul in Galatians 1. 15–16, Peter indicates that he has been chosen by God to proclaim the Good News to the Gentiles. Acts 15.10 evokes the 'yoke of slavery' of Galatians 5.1. Acts 15.11 evokes Galatians 2.16 and Ephesians 2.8. So Peter, like Paul in the Letter to the Galatians, is stating that God makes no distinction between Jews and Gentiles, that the law is a yoke, and that only faith saves. The argument attributed to Peter is probably more 'Pauline' and radical than that of Paul at the Council of Jerusalem. Traditionalist scholars conclude from this that Peter shared Paul's theological views. Others deduce that Peter never spoke the words attributed to him by the author of Acts. This latter constructed a speech inspired by Paul in order to show that Peter fully endorsed Paul's theology.

Let us see if James' words tell us any more about his position at the Jerusalem assembly:

Brethren, listen to me. Symeon [Peter] has related how God first visited the Gentiles, to take out of them a people for his name. And with this the words of the prophets agree, as it is written,

> After this I will return,
> and I will rebuild the dwelling of David, which has fallen;
> I will rebuild its ruins,
> and I will set it up,
> that the rest of men may seek the Lord,
> and all the Gentiles who are called by my name,
> says the Lord, who has made these things known from of
>   old.

Therefore my judgment is that we should not trouble those of the Gentiles who turn to God, but should write to them to abstain from the pollutions of idols and from unchastity and from what is strangled and from blood. For from early generations Moses has had in every city those who preach him, for he is read every sabbath in the synagogues (Acts 15.13–21).

James' argument is based essentially on a quotation from Amos 9.11–12 drawn from the Septuagint.[37] We should note that the Hebrew version of the Bible that we have, which differs significantly from the Greek translation of the Septuagint, makes James' argument impossible.[38] James begins by emphasizing that it is God himself who has decided to choose among the pagans a people consecrated to him. Then he quotes Amos 9.11–12 quite precisely. This text indicates that in the messianic era, when the house of David is restored, the pagans will seek the Lord, i.e. will acknowledge him. James suggests that since Jesus has raised up the house of David, it is all right for Gentiles to turn to God. The text of Amos does not specify whether these Gentiles who acknowledge God must become Jews, i.e. be circumcised and live according to the law of Moses. James thinks that it is enough for them to respect four important prohibitions derived from this law which are taken up in the Apostolic Decree approved at the end of the meeting. According to most exegetes, this speech, which is based on a Greek translation of the Bible, could hardly have been pronounced by James, who was doubtless more familiar with the Hebrew original. However, the arguments derived from Amos could have been used by Paul, Barnabas or one of their companions. Perhaps James accepted, taking up this quotation or another, that during the messianic era the Gentiles who had acknowledged God did not need to be circumcised. This is a tricky point to establish.

All we know is that the discussion was lively and difficult. James, Peter and John, who originally had probably asked for Titus, Paul's companion, to be circumcised, were finally convinced that they need not demand this. Paul and Barnabas thought that a general principle had been established. But did the pillars also think so? Did they not rather see Titus as an exception which was not to be repeated too often? Perhaps they thought that if the non-circumcision of Gentiles was tolerable, their circumcision was preferable.

Paul indicates that a division in the Christian mission was also decided on: Barnabas and he would go to the pagans, while James, Peter and John evangelized the Jews.

According to Luke, the Council ended with the approval of the Apostolic Decree, which we shall discuss shortly.

The decision of the Council of Jerusalem is most often regarded as the key factor which led to the expansion of Christianity. For Christian apologetic it manifests the superiority of Christian universalism over Jewish particularism. By opening the gates of salvation to the Gentiles, the gospel, in the spirit of the biblical prophets, was to make the true God known to the four corners of the earth. This view is exaggerated. The Gentiles could be converted to Judaism, and many first-century Jews accepted that unconverted Gentiles could obtain their salvation. Moreover, early Christianity presented a sectarian aspect, absent from a number of Jews of the time, to the degree that those who did not share its faith, whether Jews or Gentiles, were damned.

The Apostolic Decree

According to the Acts of the Apostles, James ended his speech at the Council of Jerusalem by stating the obligations to be imposed on the pagan Christians:[39]

> But should write to them to abstain from the pollutions of idols and from unchastity (*porneia*) and from what is strangled (*pnikton*) and from blood (Acts 15.20, Eastern text).

The Apostolic Decree sent to the Gentiles of the churches of Antioch, Syria and Cilicia restates James' conclusions, the expression 'the pollutions of idols' being replaced by 'meat sacrificed to idols *(idolothytes)*' (Acts 15.29).

These prohibitions are also restated in Acts 21.25 in the same terms as Acts 15.29. The so-called Western text of Acts lists significantly different prohibitions. Thus Acts 15.29 in this version mentions the following prohibitions:

> To abstain from meat offered to idols, from blood and from unchastity, and not to do to others what one would not want to have done to oneself.

The Western text knows nothing of meat from animals that have been strangled and includes the Golden Rule in its negative form. It is clearly about rules of a moral kind in which the prohibition of blood refers more to murder and violence than to the eating of meat. According to most experts this version is later than that of the Eastern text, which reflects prohibitions specifically connected with the law of Moses. But contrary to what many exegetes state, the Apostolic Decree in this version does not only have a ritual aspect. It also contains moral aspects which cannot be dissociated from it.

The nature and object of the Apostolic Decree have given rise to a vast and complex literature. Most commentaries think that the Decree specifies the minimum conditions imposed on pagan Christians so that the Jewish-Christians can agree to have dealings with them and share their table. According to the most common opinion it should be dissociated from the Council of Jerusalem; it will have been adopted on the initiative of James to settle the conflict which occurred at Antioch and inspired by the conditions imposed on godfearers associated with the synagogues.[40] Such an interpretation runs contrary to the sense which can be got out of a reading of Acts 15. In this passage the question posed is: can the Gentiles who believe in Jesus be saved if they do not become Jewish proselytes? The answer given by James is: they can be saved if they respect the conditions imposed by the Apostolic Decree. Thus according to Acts 15 the Decree specifies what the pagan Christians must do to obtain their salvation. Markus Bockmuehl of the University of Cambridge is doubtless right in thinking, contrary to the majority of scholars, that this was indeed the objective.[41] At the same time, as Charles Perrot has emphasized, the Decree defined the status of the 'Christian god-fearers'.[42]

The clauses of the Apostolic Decree have often been compared with the commandments given to Noah, the Noachic commandments.[43] These commandments, derived from Gen. 1–11, correspond to the ethical obligations which all human beings had to accept before the law was revealed to Moses on Mount Sinai. The earliest mention of these commandments is to be found in Jubilees 7: justice, covering one's nakedness, worshipping the creator, honouring father and mother, loving one's neighbour, the prohibition of unchastity and impurity, the rejection of violence, a ban on eating blood. The Jews of antiquity, for whom the Mosaic law applied only to the people of Israel, usually thought that the Gentiles who observed certain universal moral rules would be saved. These rules frequently derived from the Noachic commandments addressed to all humankind before the revelation on Sinai. Thus a whole current of rabbinic thought accepted that Gentiles who conformed to the Noachic commandments would have a right to the world to come. The first definition of these commandments in rabbinic literature is to be found in the Tosefta (Aboda Zara 8,4): 'Seven commandments were given to the children of Noah: concerning the establishment of courts of justice, idolatry, blasphemy, fornication, the shedding of blood, theft and limbs torn from a living animal.' While other definitions have been proposed, including up to thirty commandments, it can be noted that three basic crimes constitute the essence of these rules: fornication, idolatry/blasphemy, and shedding blood. Moreover, as Bockmuehl has indicated, they correspond to the three offences which according to a rabbinic decision of the second century Jews were never to commit, even if their refusal to do so cost them their lives.[44] Like the Noachic commandments, the Apostolic Decree proscribes fornication and idolatry. But it seems to attach more importance to a ban on eating blood and meat which has not been prepared correctly.

It is generally accepted that the four prohibitions of the Apostolic Decree are perhaps more inspired by the rules which in the Bible apply both to the people of Israel and the one who resides within it (the *ger*). These rules, which occur mainly – but not exclusively – in Leviticus 17–18, number more than four. However, Terrance Callan has shown that there is a close parallel between the prohibitions of the Decree and four basic prohibitions of Leviticus which are formulated as follows:[45] 'Everyone who . . . will be cut off from his people.' That signifies that the infringement of these prohibitions means death both for the *ger* and for the Israelite. The pollutions of idols, i.e. mainly the meat sacrificed to them, but also anything to do with idolatry, evoke Leviticus 17.8–9; 20.2–3. Unchastity (*porneia*) doubtless refers to the sexual prohibitions of Leviticus 18: adultery, unions between close relatives, homosexuality, bestiality, and perhaps intercourse with a woman during menstruation. The prohibition against eating blood, the principle of life, is the object of Leviticus 17.10–12. The prohibition relating to *pnikton* (meat from an animal that has been strangled, i.e. one that has died and not been slaughtered according to the principles of the law) is more difficult to identify, and the parallel with Leviticus 17.13–14 in Callan's scheme is less convincing. It is probable that the prohibition against blood and *pnikton* both relate to the ban on eating or drinking blood and the various prohibitions associated with it: meat coming from animals which have died naturally, have been improperly slaughtered (i.e. suffocated or strangled), or have been torn apart by a wild beast. As several scholars have emphasized, the prohibition against blood must also have covered blood crimes.

In the Bible, the prohibitions of Leviticus 17 and 18 were imposed on the Israelites and the Gentiles residing among them because they forbade practices which were an abomination to YHWH and which, moreover, defiled the land of Israel. Dwelling in the land over which the God of Israel reigned, and living in the midst of his people, the Gentiles had to respect his will and not pollute his domain, on pain of death. Although it was not the main aim of the prohibitions, they could facilitate cohabitation between Israelites and Gentiles, perhaps including table-fellowship – except for the Passover meal. The main risk entailed by the Gentiles infringing these prohibitions was not that the Israelites would be made unclean but that YHWH would be offended, with the terrible consequences which that brought down upon those who had contravened the rules and those who had allowed them to do so.

We can imagine that, going by the situation in pre-exilic Israel, the authors of the Apostolic Decree thought that the Gentiles who, having acknowledged the God of Israel and his Messiah Jesus, were going to enter his kingdom, had to avoid practices which he abhorred in order not to offend him and defile his domain. They thought that no pagan Christian could hope to live under the reign of God without respecting at least the clauses of the decree. Thus already from now on, and later, when the kingdom of God manifested itself in all its power, while the Jewish Christians had to continue to live in accordance with the law of Moses, the pagan Christians had at least to respect the clauses of the Decree which incorporated the most essential aspects of the divine law.

Beyond question the Apostolic Decree made relations between Jewish Christians and pagan Christians easier, but did it allow them to eat together? Most experts, according to whom this Decree was adopted to make such eating together possible, of course reply in the affirmative. But Charles Perrot[46] and Christian Grappe,[47] according to whom the aim of the Decree has nothing to do with eating together, think that, far from authorizing this, it excluded it. They are probably right in thinking that the Decree was not aimed at settling problems of eating together. However, they perhaps go too far in considering that it did not help eating together at all, since according to them all the Jewish Christians refused to eat with the Gentiles, even if the latter respected the clauses of the Decree.

We have seen that many Jews did not hesitate to invite Gentiles to share their table. They would surely have been less disposed to visit them unless they could be certain that the dietary laws would not be transgressed.[48] More Jews would agree to share tables with Gentiles who respected the clauses of the Apostolic Decree, and were thus less suspect of idolatry. Nevertheless, many others, above all in the land of Israel, would doubtless have refused to eat with these Gentiles for reasons of purity. We may also suppose that had the Decree been aimed at making it possible for Jews and Gentiles to eat together, it would have included the prohibition against eating the food forbidden by Leviticus 11. Otherwise, we have to accept that the Decree did not allow the Gentiles to receive Jewish Christians at home.

Most exegetes, supposing that the object of the Decree was to allow Jewish Christians and pagan Christians to eat together, think that it cannot have been adopted at the Council of Jerusalem, since that would have made the incident at Antioch incomprehensible. They also put forward the following arguments:

- In Galatians 2.6 Paul emphasizes that the pillars did not add anything to his gospel;
- For reasons of principle, Paul would never have approved the Apostolic Decree;[49]
- Paul would have mentioned the Decree in I Corinthians 8–10 had he known it.

These exegetes generally conclude that the Decree was elaborated in Paul's absence to settle the problem of eating together which had emerged in Antioch.

We have seen that the first argument is doubtful to the degree that the aim of the Decree does not seem to have been to settle the question of Jewish Christians and pagan Christians eating together. Nor do the other arguments have the force generally attributed to them, as Bockmuehl and others have shown.[50] As Charles Perrot has recently argued, we cannot rule out the possibility that the Apostolic Decree was approved at the meeting in Jerusalem mentioned in Galatians 2.1–10 and Acts 15.4–29. If that was the case, the consequences of the Decree for Jews and Gentiles eating together were not perceived in the same way by all those who took part in this meeting.

Trouble at Antioch

The incident which took place at Antioch shortly after the Council of Jerusalem went to show how fragile the compromise negotiated with the pillars was: there was difficulty in reconciling the contradictory positions.[51] The only mention of this conflict in the New Testament is in Galatians 2.11–14:

> But when Cephas came to Antioch I opposed him to his face, because he stood condemned. For before certain men came from James, he ate with the Gentiles; but when they came he drew back and separated himself, fearing the circumcision party. And with him the rest of the Jews acted insincerely, so that even Barnabas was carried away by their insincerity. But when I saw that they were not straightforward about the truth of the gospel, I said to Cephas before them all, 'If you, though a Jew, live like a Gentile and not like a Jew, how can you compel the Gentiles to live like Jews?'

This brief passage, so fundamental to our understanding of the history of the primitive church, has stimulated the imagination of exegetes, who have proposed the most diverse and contradictory reconstructions and interpretations. It is true that many crucial points remain obscure, even if the main lines of the incident are clear. Peter, who was living in or passing through Antioch at the time, and the Antiochene Christians of Jewish origin, were taking their meals with the Christians of Gentile origin. After the arrival of certain people from James' entourage (or sent by him), Peter stopped sharing a table with the pagan Christians, and was imitated in this by the other Jewish Christians, including Barnabas. Paul reproached Peter for having modified his behaviour, not for religious motives, but out of fear of the circumcised. The one who was living as a pagan was now forcing the pagan Christians to Judaize. At that time to Judaize *(ioudaizein)* usually meant becoming a Jew.[52] But this word sometimes referred to the adoption of certain Jewish customs, circumcision apart.[53]

For many scholars, the crisis at Antioch was sparked off by Peter and the other Christians of Jewish origin abandoning the Mosaic dietary laws. That is why, according to Paul's expression, they were living as pagans. Marcel Simon and André Benoît sum up the most widespread view like this:

> In order not to paralyse the life of a mixed community and in particular to make possible the celebration of the eucharist, which was generally linked with a brotherly meal, those converted from Judaism found it natural, following Paul's example, to abandon the dietary laws.[54]

However, exegetes of the first order like James D. G. Dunn[55] and E. P. Sanders[56] find it hardly credible that Peter, Barnabas and other Christians of Jewish origin should have all abandoned their religious heritage so completely. We must in fact remember that the abandonment of the dietary laws, a basic element in Jewish practice, hardly differed from complete apostasy. That would be particularly surprising in the case of Peter, who was responsible for the mission among the Jews. Is it conceivable that Peter, who, at the Council of Jerusalem, had reluctantly admitted that the pagan Christians could be saved without becoming Jews, should so soon afterwards have thought that the Jewish Christians could dispense with such an essential element of the Mosaic law? Such a rapid development seems improbable. That is why, according to Dunn and some other scholars, those sent by James charged the Jewish Christians of Antioch, not with transgressing major prohibitions, but with not following the law sufficiently rigorously.[57] Perhaps they were only too confident when they were eating with Gentiles. Perhaps they observed certain rules of purity less rigorously than others. In accusing Peter of living like a pagan, Paul, the old Pharisee, was doubtless talking like sectarian Jews when they spoke of other Jews applying the law less strictly.[58]

Thus according to this interpretation, James will have sent a delegation to Antioch to urge Jewish Christians to follow the dietary laws more strictly. If the pagan Christians wanted to share tables with the Jewish Christians, they had to conform to the demands of the Mosaic law about food. So to use Paul's expression, they were forced to Judaize. This reconstruction is not very convincing. We cannot rule out the possibility that those sent by James thought the behaviour of Jewish Christians towards the dietary laws lax. But if the problem had been only a lack of rigour on the part of the Jewish Christians, it is doubtful whether the arrival of the people from James would have led them to refuse to share a table with pagan Christians. We may suppose that the eating together would have taken place in the houses of Jewish Christians, or even in those of Gentiles who agreed to serve food in complete conformity with the law. Moreover this interpretation attributes to the word 'Judaize' a meaning which not only is not the most natural one, but also is hardly compatible with the context of the Letter to the Galatians. Paul's opponents in Galatia, who called for the circumcision of the pagan Christians, had doubtless mentioned the incident at Antioch to justify their position.[59] Had Peter not forced the pagans to be circumcised, Paul would have been clumsy to use so strong a word as 'Judaize'.

So it seems than the problem at Antioch did not concern so much the food as the company, i.e. sharing a table with non-Jews. James and his envoys were thus criticizing the fact that Jewish Christians and pagan Christians were eating together. D. R. Catchpole and other exegetes have put forward the hypothesis that those sent by James came to Antioch to bring the Apostolic Decree.[60] According to them, this Decree, enacted by James in the absence of Peter and Paul, established the conditions to be imposed on pagan Christians to allow them to share a table with Jewish Christians. The imposition of these constraints derived from the law of Moses would have provoked Paul's anger. This seductive interpretation hardly accords with the account given by the interested party. First of all, Paul in no way suggests that those sent by James brought a message addressed to pagan Christians. On the contrary, it seems that the discussions at Antioch initially concerned the behaviour of the Jews. Then, this interpretation presupposes that the object of the Decree was to allow Jewish Christians and pagan Christians to eat together which, as we have seen, was certainly not the case. Lastly, had those sent by James enjoined the pagan Christians to respect the Apostolic Decree if they wanted to continue to share the table with Jewish Christians, it is probable that many of them, without doubt old godfearers, would have agreed to do so. Peter and the other Jewish Christians would not have been separated from all the Gentiles, but only from those who refused to conform to the clauses of the Decree.

Since the arrival of those sent by James led to a complete cessation of table relations between Christians of Jewish and Christians of pagan origin,[61] we have to ask why they required the Jewish Christians of Antioch to adopt such behaviour. Some scholars think that this injunction was motivated more by strategic considerations than by basic religious motives. In his commentary on the Letter to the Galatians, F. F. Bruce reconstructs their message like this:

News is reaching us in Jerusalem that you have habitually been practising table-fellowship with Gentiles. This is causing grave scandal to our more conservative brethren here. Not only so: it is becoming common knowledge outside the church, so that our attempts to evangelize our fellow-Jews are being seriously hampered.[62]

Bruce does not ask why Peter, who was responsible for the mission to the Jews, did not himself take account of the risk that this behaviour was posing to his missionary activity. According to many scholars, the envoys had also warned Peter and the Jewish Christians of Antioch that the 'nationalist' zealots were threatening to take reprisals against the Jerusalem church if its provocative attitude continued. By indicating that Peter kept his distance from the Gentiles 'for fear of the circumcised', Paul meant that he feared the zealots, and not James and his envoys, as many commentators think.[63] This interpretation is in part based on a possible parallelism with Galatians 6.12, where Paul accuses his Judaizing opponents of preaching circumcision to avoid persecutions. We can understand why some exegetes and theologians endorse this type of reconstruction. In this perspective the Jerusalem church was not opposed to the 'true gospel' favoured by Paul. It required the policy of eating with the Gentiles, approved by all at the Council of Jerusalem, to be suspended provisionally in order to ensure the success of the mission to the Jews and for reasons of security. This hypothesis seems above all to satisfy theological considerations. It is probable that some Jews contested the practices of the Christians of Antioch. But whether this was the main reason for the cessation of eating together is doubtful. Besides, can one seriously think that James, a deeply pious man living in the expectation of the messianic age, who was later to die a martyr, would have compromised with his principles so as not to have any more trouble with the zealots?[64]

So the most plausible interpretation is that James and those close to him refused to share a table with pagan Christians as a matter of principle. We have seen that there was nothing in the law to prevent Jews from eating with Gentiles if the food served was permissible. However, above all in the land of Israel, numerous Jews avoided taking food with those who were uncircumcised.[65] Many did so for essentially cultural, social or political reasons. We should not forget the major symbolic role attached to eating together in antiquity. To these reasons was often added a desire not to be defiled by the impurity that attached to the Gentiles. According to the most widespread view, this impurity derived from their idolatry. Although this was not the most common view, it is probable that some people thought that the Gentiles could also be subject to some of the impurities which affected the Jews. Perhaps James thought that even if the pagan Christians had in principle abandoned their idolatrous beliefs and practices, they still maintained too many links with idolatry, albeit involuntary and indirect, for him to be able to eat with them.[66] Perhaps he thought that they could be subject to other impurities. Given the profoundly sacred aspect of common Christian meals, particularly at the celebration of the eucharist, one might think that he wanted Jewish Christians to take part in this meal in a state of high ritual purity, which would exclude the presence of pagan Christians, even if the latter respected the clauses of the Apostolic Decree.[67] Even if we cannot define his reasons precisely, the position

of James and his envoys accords with what we know of the
Jewish conceptions of the time. It certainly puts them among
the Jews who were particularly preoccupied with questions of
purity.

So we can suppose that the position of those sent by James
could be summed up as follows:[68] 'Just because certain pagans
have acknowledged YHWH and his Messiah does not mean
that they should become full members of the people of God, the
eschatological Israel. The Jews who have acknowledged Jesus,
those who form the true Israel, must maintain their identity and
respect a certain level of ritual separatism *vis-à-vis* these pagan
Christians.' Peter, contrary to what some exegetes think, put up
little resistance to this request from those sent by James. The
words used by Paul to describe Peter's behaviour suggest more
of a side-step or a prudent retreat than a bitter struggle. Paul
accuses Peter of having changed his attitude towards pagan
Christians, not out of conviction, but to preserve good relations
with James and those close to him. However, it would not be
reasonable to regard Paul's interpretation as being completely
credible, since he had every interest in showing that Peter,
contrary to what his behaviour suggested, was himself basically
in agreement with Paul's own view of a unified community.
We certainly cannot rule out the hypothesis that Peter was
convinced by the arguments of those sent by James. At all
events, Peter's attitude influenced Barnabas and the other
Jewish Christians of Antioch decisively, and this doubtless
increased Paul's anger towards him.

The question debated at Antioch initially related to the
Jewish Christians. Of course it had an important impact on the
pagan Christians. By forcing the pagans to Judaize, i.e. to
become Jews, was Peter signifying that the agreement made in
Jerusalem was abrogated, and thus that the mission to the
Gentiles without any requirement of circumcision was termi-
nated? Did the pagan Christians have to convert to Judaism if
they wanted to gain salvation? It does not seem that the agreement was revoked;[69] but it was certainly spelled out in terms
which reflected the views of James and not those of Paul. In fact
Paul does not rebuke Peter for having gone back on the
Jerusalem agreement, but for having hypocritically changed his

attitude towards eating with the pagan Christians, a question which perhaps had not been raised in Jerusalem. Moreover it has to be noted that in his account of the incident Paul does not criticize either James or his representatives. From this we can deduce that he was hardly surprised at their position over the former pagans, a position which he knew to be in conformity with their interpretation of the Jerusalem agreement. In their view the mission to the Gentiles without the requirement of circumcision had to be kept separate from the mission to the Jews. Certainly the pagans who acknowledged YHWH and his Messiah could be saved. But that did not make them members of the people of Israel, descendants of Abraham. For them to achieve this status, for them to be able to live in communion with the Jewish Christians, they had to have themselves circumcised and to live as Jews.

It is the incident at Antioch which reveals most clearly the differences between James, Peter, Barnabas and the great majority of Jewish Christians on the one hand and Paul on the other. For the former, the Christians,[70] or, to use their terminology, the Nazarenes or those who follow the Way, were first and foremost Jews who had acknowledged Jesus. They formed the true Israel, the eschatological assembly of Israel.[71] We may doubt whether they described baptized pagans as Nazarenes. They were only the godfearers, who would be saved. They were not integrated into the true Israel, but only associated with it. By refusing to share a table with them, the Jewish Christians were showing that they did not think them complete Christians. If they wanted to be fully integrated into the community of the Nazarenes, they had to be circumcised and live according to the law of Moses. Doubtless that is what Paul was referring to when he was criticizing Peter for forcing the pagans to Judaize.

Paul's views were quite different. For him, faith in Jesus had to have priority over all ethnic and 'national' differences. The Christians, i.e. all those who have been baptized in Christ, all those who have put on Christ (Gal. 3.27), form a single community. In Christ 'there is neither Jew nor Greek, slave nor free, male nor female' (Gal. 3.28). That does not mean that there are no longer Jews or Greeks, that there are no longer men or women. It means that these differences have no importance *vis-à-vis* God and Christ. Thus the Jewish Christians, instead of regarding themselves as Jews who believed in Jesus, i.e. as Christian Jews, had to identify themselves as Christians of Jewish race or customs, i.e. as Jewish Christians.[72] In the same way, for Paul the pagan Christians of Antioch were Christians of Greek nationality or customs. By keeping away from the table of the Gentiles, by refusing to share the Lord's Supper with them, the Jewish Christians of Antioch were breaking up the unity of the Christian community. By requiring the pagan Christians to become Jews, the Jewish Christians were accepting distinctions between Jews and non-Jews which according to Paul the death of Christ had abolished.

Contrary to a view which was once very widespread, there is no doubt that Paul did not have the last word in Antioch. Had he succeeded in convincing Peter and the Jewish Christians of the city, Paul would not have failed to emphasize this success in his letter to the Galatians. By refusing to fall into line, Paul ceased his collaboration with Barnabas and left Antioch to pursue his missionary activity alone.

After Antioch

Was the break between Paul and the pillars of the church which came about at Antioch superficial and temporary, or profound and definitive? The experts offer contrasting answers. According to a widespread view, the crisis which erupted at Antioch was only of short duration. Despite their theological differences, Paul and the leaders of the Jerusalem church found a kind of *modus vivendi*, each pursuing their mission in a climate of confidence and mutual respect.[73] The Judaizing opposition to Paul derived from Jewish Christians acting independently of James and Peter. For many scholars, these adversaries are to be identified with the 'false brethren' (Gal. 2.4) who opposed Paul at the Council of Jerusalem. From 1831 on, Ferdinand Christian Baur and his disciples of the Tübingen School attacked this type of harmonizing conception by interpreting the first two centuries of the Christian movement as a merciless struggle between Petrine and Pauline communities.[74] They emphasized the incessant conflicts between

Peter and James on the one hand and Paul on the other. This interpretation was fiercely contested by the majority of exegetes, for good and not so good reasons: sometimes they did not want to concede that the Holy Spirit had not uniformly inspired the glories of the primitive church. After being discredited for a while, this view has recently been taken up again, in more or less mild forms, by some first-rate exegetes.[75]

How we answer this question of the nature of the break which took place at Antioch largely depends on the identity and the message of Paul's opponents in Galatia, at Corinth and Philippi.[76] Were Paul's opponents Judaizers,[77] i.e. did they require pagan Christians to be circumcised and submit to the law? If they were Judaizers, did they think that this circumcision was necessary for the salvation of Gentiles who had acknowledged Jesus, or did they think that though it was not indispensable, it was preferable? Were these opponents acting on the orders of James and Peter? If this was the case, were they following their instructions? The answer to these questions is complex, since we have no writing from Paul's opponents. We only have Paul's testimony, which is hostile and partial.

We may recall that at the beginning of the 50s, Jewish-Christian missionaries visited in Paul's absence communities in Galatia which he had founded. They required the pagan Christians in them to be circumcised and to live as Jews. Paul, annoyed at their success, which threatened to ruin his efforts, sent a particularly virulent letter to the Galatians. He warned them that Christ would be no use to them if they had themselves circumcised (Gal. 5.2) and that they would obtain their salvation through faith in Christ and not by practising the law (Gal. 2.16). The first two chapters of Galatians are centred on relations between Paul and the Jerusalem church – particularly James and Peter, its main pillars. Paul relates his two visits to Jerusalem and the incident at Antioch. He emphasizes both his autonomy from the pillars and the fact that they have approved his gospel. His opponents had certainly presented a different version of relations between Paul and the pillars. Doubtless they had emphasized that Paul, who was dependent on the Jerusalem church, also had to preach the circumcision of the Gentiles.[78] Galatians 1 and 2 would be hard to understand if Paul's opponents in Galatia had not appealed to the authority of James and/or Peter.[79] Contrary to the affirmations of numerous exegetes, there is nothing in the letter to the Galatians which allows us to think that they did not respect their instructions.[80] At Antioch, Peter, following James' policy, had urged the pagan Christians to Judaize, i.e. probably to have themselves circumcised and to live as Jews. In Galatia, the Jewish-Christian missionaries required them to be circumcised, doubtless justifying their position by Peter's behaviour in Antioch. Even if Paul accuses Peter of hypocrisy, he nowhere writes that later he changed his view. Moreover, the irony with which he speaks of the pillars (Gal.2.6) suggests that relations with them had hardly improved since the incident. And if Paul had suspected that his opponents in Galatia were not representing the position of James of Peter faithfully, he would not have failed to emphasize this.

We must now investigate the nature of the message of Paul's opponents. Did they refuse to accept any possibility of salvation for the Gentiles unless they became Jewish proselytes, thus going back on the Jerusalem agreement? It is difficult to answer this question, since we can only reconstruct the position of the Jewish-Christian missionaries from Paul's criticisms; Paul himself knew it only indirectly, via the Galatians. Moreover it seems that what was discussed in Galatia was less the abstract question of the salvation of the Gentiles[81] than the identity and the behaviour of the people of God, the eschatological Israel, and the way in which one could share in it.[82] Whatever may have been their position on the salvation of pagan Christians who had not been circumcised, it seems clear that, like James, they did not appreciate the missionary message and practice of Paul.

The message of the Judaizing missionaries could be summed up like this:[83] 'You have acknowledged the God of Israel and his Messiah Jesus. That is very good. It will perhaps allow you to gain your salvation. But it is only one stage, a first step.[84] To become a full member of the people of God, to share in descent from Abraham, to form a single community with the Jews who have accepted Jesus, you must be circumcised, as the scriptures say, and live in accordance with the law of Moses.[85]

Paul promises you that through the power of the Holy Spirit, your conduct will be exemplary outside the law and that will guarantee your salvation at the Last Judgment. He even claims that by allowing yourselves to be led by the Spirit you are not under the law. But look at your confusion, your moral disarray. You risk perdition. Have yourselves circumcised and live in accordance with the law of Moses. In this way your conduct will be completely in conformity with the will of God.' For the Judaizing missionaries, as a sign of belonging among the descendants of Abraham, circumcision was a step forward, an objective; for Paul, at least where Gentiles were concerned, it was incompatible with the gospel:

> Now I, Paul, say to you that if you receive circumcision, Christ will be of no advantage to you . . . You are severed from Christ, you who would be justified by the law; you have fallen away from grace (Gal. 5.2–4).

For Paul, not only was the circumcision of the Gentiles unnecessary, it was even harmful. According to him, the death and resurrection of Christ had caused a cosmic upheaval, a kind of new creation. They had radically changed the role and nature of the law, the identity and the prerogatives of Israel, the economy of salvation for both Jews and Gentiles. Through Christ, the promises made to the Gentiles (Gen. 12.3; 18.18) were finally to be realized by all those who had faith. Since the death and resurrection of Christ allowed the Gentiles to gain their salvation outside the law, the Gentiles, by wanting to submit to the law, were refusing to see the true meaning of the death of Jesus. So he would have died for nothing (Gal. 2.21). The Jewish-Christian missionaries were doubtless more impressed by the steadfastness and assurance of Paul than by his interpretation of the Bible. For them, Jesus first and foremost realized the promises made to Israel in the context of its covenant with YHWH, made concrete by circumcision and respect for the law.

Paul's troubles were far from being at an end. He was to encounter other difficulties in Corinth and at Philippi in Macedonia. The identity of the missionaries attacked by Paul in

II Corinthians (especially 10–13) is the subject of many arguments. For some scholars these missionaries were Judaizers
appealing to the Jerusalem church;[86] for others they were charismatic preachers coming from the markedly Hellenized Jewish
Diaspora.[87] II Corinthians tells us that missionaries with letters
of commendation visited the Christian community in Corinth,
probably around 55. They put the authority of Paul in question
and proclaimed 'another Jesus' and a different gospel. They
emphasized their Jewish origin. The Corinthians were impressed
by their eloquence, their visionary experiences and their miraculous powers. There is hardly any doubt that these visitors were
Jewish Christians. However, many exegetes think that they
were not Judaizers, since Paul does not mention any request
for the circumcision of Gentiles. But C. K. Barrett and other
scholars have shown convincingly that this argument was not
decisive and that these missionaries, proclaiming another
gospel, were doubtless Judaizers.[88] According to the most
probable hypothesis, they appealed to the authority of James
and/or Peter. Paul's vagueness about their identity tends to
reinforce this view.

The Letter to the Philippians was probably composed in
Ephesus around 55. In Philippians 3 Paul warns his brothers in
Philippi against 'these dogs, evil-workers, those who mutilate
the flesh'. They 'live as enemies of the cross of Christ . . . Their
end is destruction, their god is their belly, and they glory in their
shame.' Paul emphasizes that the law and the gospel are incompatible, and treats circumcision with vulgarity and scorn. There
is hardly any doubt that the missionaries of whose visit to
Philippi Paul was afraid were Jewish Christians, proud of being
circumcised and recommending pagan Christians to imitate
them. The parallelism between the arguments and the attacks in
Philippians 3 and those in Galatians and II Corinthians suggest
that in these three letters Paul was referring to adversaries who,
if not identical, were at least defending similar positions.

The analysis of these three letters suggests that the opponents
of Paul in Galatia, Corinth and Philippi were 'Judaizing' Jewish-
Christian missionaries. These missionaries wanted to counter
the effects of Paul's message and mission, which they thought
harmful. Contrary to Paul, they preached a more traditional

conception of the history of Israel, its covenant with YHWH and the role of the law. Doubtless they wanted the pagan Christians to adopt the customs of Israel, if possible going as far as circumcision and complete integration with the people of God. While a primary 'conspiracy theory' is to be avoided, it would be surprising if this strong opposition during the years following the incident at Antioch was only the fruit of chance and circumstances. It is more reasonable to think that it was prompted and organized from one place, in all probability Jerusalem. It would be equally surprising if it had developed without the agreement of James. Other features seem to confirm such an interpretation.

First of all we can note that the incident at Antioch has left deep marks on several Christian traditions. The Pseudo-Clementine literature, of Jewish-Christian inspiration, accords an important place to this incident, which is seen as a major and lasting break between Paul and the Jerusalem church.[89] At the beginning of the second century the ultra-Paulinist Marcion, who became a heretic, emphasized the virulence and persistence of the conflict between Paul and the pillars of the church.[90]

Etienne Trocmé has shown how Paul organized his missionary enterprise in such a way as to escape the influence of the Jerusalem church.[91] Paul first of all concentrated on isolated regions which had not yet been evangelized. It was only after a missionary base devoted to him had been established that he went to major centres like Corinth or Ephesus. There he could not resist the attacks orchestrated by Jerusalem. Finally, the apostle to the Gentiles no longer had a choice: if he wanted to continue with his mission he had to go to Jerusalem to seek a compromise with James. As a sign of goodwill and reconciliation Paul brought with him the fruit of a collection to which he had committed himself at the Council of Jerusalem.

Some scholars think that this collection, bearing witness to Paul's respect for the 'saints' of Jerusalem and the unity of the church, makes the hypothesis of strong opposition improbable.[92] This argument is hardly decisive. Paul could not allow himself to break with the church of Jerusalem. The fact that he asked the Christians of Rome (Rom. 15.30–31) to pray that the saints of Jerusalem would accept his collection shows the existence of a certain hostility on their part, of which Paul was perfectly aware.

The nature of relations between Paul and James would be easy to define if we had a trustworthy account of the last visit to Jerusalem by the apostle to the Gentiles. But the only evidence of this visit, that in Acts, clearly needs to be regarded with caution:

When we had come to Jerusalem, the brethren received us gladly. On the following day Paul went in with us to James; and all the elders were present. After greeting them, he related one by one the things that God had done among the Gentiles through his ministry. And when they heard it, they glorified God. And they said to him, 'You see, brother, how many thousands there are among the Jews of those who have believed; they are all zealous for the law, and they have been told about you that you teach all the Jews who are among the Gentiles to forsake Moses, telling them not to circumcise their children or observe the customs. What then is to be done? They will certainly hear that you have come. Do therefore what we tell you. We have four men who are under a vow, take these men and purify yourself along with them and pay their expenses, so that they may shave their heads. Thus all will know that there is nothing in what they have been told about you but that you yourself live in observance of the law' (Acts 21.17–24).

Luke does not conceal the fact that certain disturbing rumours about Paul were circulating in Jerusalem. Of course James and the elders, convinced that Paul remained a Jew faithful to the law, did not believe a word of them. The reader of Acts has no reason to doubt this, since Luke has always presented Paul as scrupulously observing the law. But the reader of Paul's letters may ask whether the accusations against him did not have some foundation, if the support and confidence which James seems to show are not a creation of the author of Acts, who is always inclined to affirm the unity of the primitive church. Paul's position on the role and significance of the law since the crucifixion and resurrection of Jesus, above

all for the Jews, is a question which divides experts today.[93] The
Second Letter of Peter (3.16) shows that Paul's thought was
already felt difficult to understand some decades after his
death. It is doubtful whether it was much clearer to his contemporaries. But it would be surprising if the great majority of
Jerusalem Christians, who remained faithful to the law, would
not have been profoundly shocked on reading Paul's letters or
listening to his teaching. While, as I Corinthians 7.20 ('Every
one should remain in the state in which he was called') suggests,
Paul certainly did not incite Jews who had been converted
to abandon the law, he did not seem to think their practice of
the law fundamental to their salvation, nor to attach much
importance to their Jewish character or to circumcision (I Cor.
7.19; Gal. 5.6).[94] Moreover, he required them not to observe
prescriptions which could limit contacts with pagan Christians
and thus break the unity of the Christian community. Paul
could legitimately be regarded as an apostate, since he admitted
that he was not subject to the law (I Cor. 9.20–21; Phil. 3.8–9).
Paul doubtless did not observe certain ritual aspects of the law,
at any rate when living among Gentiles.[95] In asserting that, at
least for Gentiles, Christ and the law were incompatible (Gal.
5.1–5), he was certainly opposing the most common Jewish-
Christian views. Similarly, by redefining the covenant between
YHWH and Israel, the role of the law and the identity of Israel
in a radical and questionable way, Paul could not fail to alienate
many Jewish Christians. Moreover his letters contain negative
assessments of the law (Gal. 5.1) and vulgar expressions about
circumcision of which Juvenal and Tacitus would not have
disapproved. Despite the more conciliatory aspect of the Letter
to the Romans, which emphasizes the specific nature and prerogatives of Israel (Rom. 9–11) and the positive character of the
law, it is hardly surprising that many of the Jewish Christians of
Jerusalem did not receive Paul with open arms.[96]

It is difficult to conceive that the James presented to us by
the Letter to the Galatians and the Acts of the Apostles, who
was faithful to the law, could have shown Paul his support.
Whatever its precise nature, from James' point of view the
agreement made at Jerusalem had had harmful and unforeseen
consequences. His opposition seems to be confirmed by the

probable fate of the collection. The fact that the author of Acts, so eloquent about Paul's last visit to Jerusalem, says nothing about this collection, the main object of Paul's journey (I Cor. 16.1–4; Rom. 15.25, 31), suggests that it was not accepted by James and the elders. Luke certainly would not have failed to mention its acceptance, which would have been further evidence of the unity of the church. However, it is possible that before making a decision on the collection James asked Paul to show his faithfulness to the law by taking part in a Nazirite vow. But this plan did not work out as expected, and Paul was arrested in the temple. Various commentators even think that some Jewish Christians, perhaps including James, will have contributed directly or indirectly to Paul's arrest and that the Christian community of Jerusalem would not have wanted to do anything to help him thereafter. But here we are entering into the realm of historical romance, where James and the Jewish Christians are not usually given good parts.

8

James, the First Pope?

Who gives the orders?

In the controversies over the entry of Gentiles into the church and their relations with Jewish Christians, Acts and the Letter to the Galatians attribute considerable authority to James, seemingly greater than that of Peter. Questions of power and authority in the primitive church are of more than academic interest, since the Roman Catholic Church bases the supremacy of the Pope, the Bishop of Rome, on the primacy of Peter. According to Catholic doctrine, Peter, who was designated the foundation and the ultimate authority of the apostolic church (Matt. 16.13–20), maintained his primacy throughout his life and transmitted it to his successors as bishop of Rome.

Of course the Catholic Church is sensitive to anything that could cast doubt on the primacy of Peter. Some of the Reformers did not fail to emphasize, in their struggle with Rome, that the primacy of Peter and the church of Rome did not fit well with the pre-eminence of James at the time of the Council of Jerusalem. The book *Peter: Disciple, Apostle, Martyr*,[1] by the great Protestant scholar Oscar Cullmann, published in 1952, provoked passionate reactions because it maintained the pre-eminence of James, as opposed to Peter, after 43 or 44. Though today the debates are less lively,[2] the question nevertheless remains a delicate one.

Exegetes have proposed three main schemes to account for the balance of power and its development in the primitive church.[3] These schemes are constructed around the roles of Peter, James and the Jerusalem church.

According to the first, very traditionalist, scheme, up to his martyrdom Peter was the dominant authority in the Christian movement.[4] Initially, at the head of the Twelve, he governed the church from Jerusalem. Together, while limiting their missionary activity to Jerusalem and neighbouring regions, they co-ordinated and supervised more distant missions. In 43 or 44 Peter, persecuted by Agrippa I, had to quit the Holy City, leaving direction of the local church to James. He then devoted himself entirely to missionary activities far from Jerusalem, but remained the pre-eminent authority in the movement until his death. After the departure of Peter the church of Jerusalem, while retaining an important role, nevertheless lost its primacy. For many Catholic exegetes and historians who are particularly attached to this interpretation, the church's centre of gravity shifted with Peter, moving from Jerusalem to Antioch and ending up in Rome, where it has remained. Because of the undisputed pre-eminence of Peter, conflicts were rare and quickly settled.

The second scheme differs little from the first until the beginning of the 40s. However, those who defend it are more inclined to emphasize the collegial character of the government by the Twelve. Following the departure of Peter from Jerusalem in 43 or 44, or perhaps shortly before, James replaced Peter not only as head of the Jerusalem community but also as the supreme authority of the Christian movement. Peter, under the authority and supervision of James, devoted himself to directing the Christian mission among the Jews. James, as head of the mother church, thus became the most influential and most respected authority in the movement. Some scholars see him as a kind of first pope, exercising effective power over the other churches. Others regard him more as a *primus inter pares,* with little means of imposing an authority which was more moral and spiritual than real outside some churches depending on Jerusalem. This scheme has been defended, with more or less important variants, by numerous Protestant scholars including Oscar Cullmann,[5] Maurice Goguel,[6] Etienne Trocmé,[7] Martin Hengel[8] and Christian Grappe.[9]

According to the last scheme, Peter and James were essentially the leaders of one church which, while important, was not dominant. They were more local leaders, whose authority hardly went beyond the limits of their community.

This model emphasizes the decentralized and very diversified character of the primitive church in terms of beliefs and practices.[10] Those who defend it largely use the canonical and apocryphal Gospels along with Q to trace the history of the independent 'trajectories' which constituted primitive Christianity. They usually presuppose the existence of autonomous communities associated with Q and the Gospel of Thomas. Such a conception, if it is possible at all, is very difficult to prove with the sources at our disposal. That is why we shall concentrate above all on the first two schemes.

Let us return, then, to what the Acts of the Apostles tells us. According to Luke, the Twelve, with Peter at their head, as witnesses to the preaching of Jesus and his resurrection, constituted the supreme authority in the Jerusalem church, at any rate until Peter's departure. This authority extended to the other Christian communities. Peter took the initiative in the main decisions and acted as spokesman of the Twelve. Sometimes his authority seemed beyond dispute, as in the episode of Ananias and Sapphira. Sometimes, as in the conversion of Cornelius, it could be put in question and decisions were taken collegially.

The formation of the Seven and the preaching of the Hellenists suggests the constitution of a group which was separate, but still under the supervision of the Twelve. Most commentators think that Peter's escape and departure from the Holy City marked the beginning of a major change of direction in the Jerusalem church, since at that time Peter designated James his successor at the head of the mother church.[11] This interpretation, though plausible, is not certain. Perhaps Luke only wanted to show that James was already the head of the Jerusalem community. In that case, Peter's words prove that he reocgnized his authority. At all events, Luke indicates that the transition was a harmonious one.[12] The dominant position of James announced in Acts 12.17 only became fully manifest at the Council of Jerusalem. Regardless of the historicity of Acts 15, James, by speaking last, summing up the discussion and proposing the decision which figures in the Apostolic Decree, appears as the one who is presiding over the assembly.

He announces his decision with the word *krino*, a term often used in legal writings to signify 'I decree', 'I judge' or 'I decide'.

Here it probably does not mean 'I advise' or 'I recommend', as is supposed by exegetes aghast at the possibility that Acts could attach more importance to James than to Peter. It is this preoccupation which has incited a copyist to weaken the word *krino* by adding 'for my part' in an ancient version. Some scholars also try to reduce the pre-eminence of James by noting that the Apostolic Decree is attributed to the apostles and the elders. It is true that James is not mentioned on his own account. But no one else, including Peter, is either. The very Catholic *Jerusalem Bible*, in the note on Acts 15.19, has to admit that 'James guides the debate, and the apostolic letter simply takes up the terms of his declaration'. From earliest times Catholic exegetes have often claimed that James presided over the discussions as head of the local church which organized them. But this is an argument which convinces only the convinced.

Peter and the other apostles disappear from Acts after the Council of Jerusalem. As Paul becomes the unchallenged hero of Acts after chapter 15, many scholars deduce that Luke attaches only reduced importance to the Jerusalem church. But this conclusion is certainly too hasty. By way of comparison, all the accounts of the discovery and conquest of the New World have Christopher Columbus, Balboa, Cortés or Pizarro as hero. But although these figures had considerable autonomy because of the difficulties in communication at the time, they nevertheless had to give an account, sometimes after a delay, to the Spanish sovereigns. Similarly, despite his forebodings, Paul had to go to Jerusalem in 56 or 57, when the mother church was governed by James and a college of elders. There is nothing in Acts to indicate that this church had lost its primacy.[13] Paul reported to it the results of his mission and submitted without discussion to the instructions of James and the elders. These latter, after drawing attention to the vigour of the Christian mission among the Jews, emphasized that they also exercised their authority over the Gentiles by mentioning the Apostolic Decree again. So there is nothing to show that, with the departure of Peter, the Jerusalem church with James at its head lost its pre-eminence.

Luke's account refers to elders or presbyters. The first mention of them is in Acts 11, at the time of the visit of Paul and

Barnabas to Jerusalem. Then, in Acts 15, they seem to govern the church of Jerusalem with the apostles. In Acts 21, on the occasion of Paul's last visit, since the apostles have disappeared, the elders alone govern this church, with James at their head. The identity of these elders and their relation to the apostles poses a complex problem the solution to which is uncertain, since we do not know to what degree Luke has followed or modified his sources. Many scholars think that ten or fifteen years after its creation, the Jerusalem church formed a council of elders to assist or replace the twelve apostles, who had died or left on missions. Richard Bauckham[14] even supposes that since the Twelve had rapidly ceased to exist as an entity, the remaining apostles had integrated this council of elders. By contrast, R. Alastair Campbell thinks that the college of the Twelve continued to exist for a long time,[15] its members at one point taking the name of elders. Other scholars, who are more critical, think that Acts does not give us any trustworthy information about the organization of the Jerusalem church.

Contrary to what many traditionalist historians suppose, Acts hardly confirms the first scheme, in that Peter disappears after the Council of Jerusalem and the mother church retains a certain pre-eminence. Acts also contradicts the third scheme. Only the second seems to correspond to what Acts tells us about the primitive church. Let us see if the letters of Paul confirm these conclusions.

All the letters of Paul that we have seem to date from the 50s. That is why they give us little information about the first fifteen or twenty years of the church. One of the most disconcerting elements in these letters when they are compared to the Acts of the Apostles is the almost complete absence of the Twelve. They are mentioned only once, in I Corinthians 15.5, when Paul, probably citing an established formula, relates the appearance of Jesus. In this very complex passage, which I have already mentioned (above, pp.95–7), Paul indicates that Jesus appeared to Cephas, then to the Twelve, then to more than 500 brothers, and finally to James and all the apostles, before appearing to him. However, the integrity of the passage has been challenged by some scholars, who think that 'the Twelve' has been added by a copyist who wanted to harmonize the text with the Gospels and Acts.[16] The quasi-absence of the Twelve from the letters of Paul suggests that at best this group played only an ephemeral role after the death of Jesus.

I Corinthians 15.5-8 has caused gallons of ink to flow. We have seen that it was very difficult to deduce from it a chronological sequence of appearances of Jesus. We know that several scholars think that two rival traditions, one relating to Peter and the other to James, could have been fused in Paul's formula. We may note that these exegetes are more inclined to accept the authenticity of the tradition attributing to Peter the honour of the first appearance. It is worth noting above all that Peter and James are the only ones to be mentioned by name, which perhaps reveals that their pre-eminence was greater in the 40s or 50s than at the time of the appearances.

The passage in the letters of Paul which is most often taken into consideration in determining the balance of power in the church some years after the resurrection is the brief account given by Paul of his first journey to Jerusalem in Galatians 1.18-20 (see p.181). Paul indicates that he went to Jerusalem to visit Peter, that he spent two weeks with him, and that he did not see any other apostles except/but only James, the brother of the Lord. Almost all exegetes conclude from this that Peter was the pre-eminent authority in the movement at the time, and that James already occupied a sufficiently elevated position for Paul not to be able to stay in Jerusalem without having to meet him.[17] Oscar Cullmann[18] and other scholars think that Galatians 1.18-20 is the most certain evidence we have about the pre-eminence of Peter before his departure from Jerusalem. But is it truly certain? Scholars seem to find it perfectly natural that the person with whom Paul, a secondary figure from the Antioch community, spends two weeks in Jerusalem, should necessarily be the chief dignitary of this community. That is possible, but not certain. We have seen that this passage must be interpreted with the greatest caution. That Paul attests before God that he is not lying must put us on our guard. Paul is trying to correct a version of his visit to Jerusalem which he thinks wrong. So if he is not lying, he is certainly not telling us all, and what he does tell is probably presented in a way which suits him. Paul wants to emphasize his independence *vis-à-vis* the Jerusalem church

and the private and 'informal' character of his stay. His opponents in Galatia doubtless had to claim the contrary. Paul writes
that he saw no other apostles apart from Peter and, supposing
that he considered him an apostle, James. Numerous exegetes
conclude from this that the other apostles had gone on mission.
But is that certain? And if they were not all absent, why did Paul
not see them all? Perhaps Paul wanted to minimize his meeting
with James because it was not to his advantage.[19] One could
equally think, like Bengt Holmberg,[20] that in the Letter to the
Galatians Paul was seeking above all to place his authority and
mission in relation to Peter, perhaps because Paul's opponents
in Galatia appealed particularly to him.

As I have already indicated, Galatians 1.19 does not show
clearly whether or not Paul regarded James as an apostle. We
may recall that for Paul the apostles were not restricted to
the Twelve.[21] Though his definition of an apostle is ambiguous
and evolved over time, it nevertheless contains two essential
elements: the apostle has to have seen the risen Lord and to have
been mandated by him or another recognized authority to
preach the Good News. If the best Greek scholars of our day are
not agreed on the meaning of Galatians 1.19, can we infer from
this that the passage was equally ambiguous to the recipients of
the letter, whose mother tongue was Greek? At all events, this is
what James D. G. Dunn,[22] the distinguished Scottish exegete,
suggests, thinking that in this way Paul wanted to express polite
reservations about the attribution of the status of apostle
to James. But contrary to what Dunn supposes, perhaps the
ambiguity is not so much disparaging as revealing of the special
status of James as 'brother of the Lord'. In fact the same ambiguity characterizes I Corinthians 9.5: 'Do we not have the right
to be accompanied by a wife, as the other apostles and the
brothers of the Lord and Cephas?' Paul grants the brothers of
the Lord, like Peter, a special status, but without apparently
denying them the title apostle.

Given the ambiguous and incomplete character of Galatians
1.18–19, the authors of an important composite inter-
confessional work on Peter rightly conclude that while the
pre-eminence of Peter seems to be suggested by this passage, it
cannot certainly be deduced from it.[23] On the other hand, one

can suppose that he was the most important person for those who wanted to gain information about Jesus and his message. This was very probably the reason why Paul visited him.

Many scholars think that the primacy of Peter in the first period of the church which seems to emerge from Acts and the letters of Paul is confirmed by the Gospels. They stress that the Gospels, with the exception of that of John, emphasize the primacy of Peter among the disciples of Jesus.[24] But pre-eminence before the death of Jesus does not necessarily imply the same rank afterwards. Some conservative scholars think, basing themselves on Matthew, that Jesus himself designated his successor:[25]

And I tell you, you are Peter, and on this rock I will build my church, and the powers of death shall not prevail against it. I will give you the keys of the kingdom of heaven, and whatever you bind on earth shall be bound in heaven, and whatever you loose on earth shall be loosed in heaven (Matt. 16.18–19).

For the Catholic Church, these verses are the basis for the pre-eminence of Peter and his successors in the government of the church and the establishment of true doctrine. Most exegetes, while recognizing their Semitic character, think that they cannot go back to Jesus.[26] If this were the case, it would be difficult to understand why they only appeared in the Gospel of Matthew. Some ancient authors thought that it was out of modesty that Peter never handed down these sayings of Jesus to his disciple Mark, according to tradition the author of the Gospel which bears his name. Although developed from old traditions, Matthew 16.17–19 was doubtless composed by a Jewish-Christian community in which Peter was held in particularly high esteem.

In the Letter to the Galatians, Paul emphasizes that he began and developed his missionary activity independently of the Jerusalem church, while Acts suggests the opposite. The truth doubtless lies somewhere in between. The Jerusalem church hardly ever intervened in the affairs of other communities. But in cases of conflict it had the last word, since its spiritual authority was so great. At all events, that is what clearly emerges from the passages in Galatians devoted to the Council of Jerusalem and the incident at Antioch, which offer the best evidence about the government of the church around the 50s. Despite his desire to show his autonomy, Paul can hardly disguise the pre-eminence of the Jerusalem church or the decisive character of the meeting with its heads for his future mission.[27] If they did not accept his gospel, it would mean that he would have run in vain (Gal. 2.2). While Paul did not for a single moment doubt the validity of his message, he must have thought that he did not have sufficient authority to impose it against the views of James, Peter and John, the pillars of the church. Even if he tries to present the Council of Jerusalem as a meeting between churches of equal importance, the superiority of Jerusalem is clear. In indicating that Titus was not obliged to be circumcised, Paul indicates that the pillars would have had the authority to require this.

It was undeniably Jerusalem which took the final decision, and the agreement, far from showing the equality of the parties, underlined the pre-eminence of the mother church. This agreement contained an obligation for the church of Antioch to be concerned for the poor of Jerusalem (Gal. 2.9). The Antioch community, probably the richest, had to come to the aid of that of Jerusalem. This latter certainly welcomed new members who had given up their regular professional activity. The few possessions that they could bring to the community must have rapidly been exhausted. We can imagine that when well-to-do adherents did not join it, the Jerusalem church found it difficult to support the needs of certain of the faithful. But apart from its financial aspect, this obligation imposed on the church of Antioch probably had a symbolic role. It indicated the pre-eminence of the church of Jerusalem. Perhaps it was likened to the contribution of a half-shekel which every Diaspora Jew had to send each year to the temple.

Paul implies that the church of Jerusalem was dominated by three pillars: James, Peter and John. This expression suggests that James, Peter and John were considered pillars of the Jerusalem community, which was identified with the temple of the end of time.[28] That it had only three pillars[29] would be explained by Jewish traditions according to which the world and the community of Israel rested on three patriarchs, Abraham, Isaac and Jacob. The Community Rule, one of the main Qumran manuscripts, similarly mentions the presence of three priests in the council of the community. Many scholars think that the church of Jerusalem was led from the start by three pillars who were initially Peter and the two sons of Zebedee. James the brother of Jesus will have taken the place of James the son of Zebedee after the latter's martyrdom. Such a hypothesis, essentially based on the pre-eminence accorded to Peter and the son of Zebedee as disciples of Jesus in the Synoptic Gospels, is not confirmed by the letters of Paul or Acts. The metaphor of pillars evokes Matthew 16.18, in which Jesus, conferring primacy among his disciples on Peter, describes him as a rock (the Greek meaning of his name). It also recalls the term *oblias,* which according to Hegesippus was applied to James and meant 'rampart of the people and of justice'.[30] This word *oblias,* which the experts cannot identify, would be the corruption of a Semitic original.[31] Many scholars suggest that it should be seen as a corruption of Obadyahu, who, under Ahab, is said to have saved the prophets of Israel (I Kings 18.3–15). Other scholars point out that 'rampart of the people' is the expression which, in the Septuagint, denotes the prophet Obadiah/Obadyahu (Obad. 1.1). By contrast, Richard Bauckham thinks that it is derived from the word signifying 'wall' in Isaiah 54.12 (wall of the people).[32] Thus we would have here a metaphor linked to the new Jerusalem. So James, the rampart, would have to be connected with Peter, the rock, the two figures enjoying a unique status in the eschatological community of Jesus.

We cannot fail to note that James is the first of the pillars to be mentioned. Everyone today is aware of the considerable importance attached to the order of names in any document. It was no different in antiquity. So it is practically certain that Paul mentioned James first because of his pre-eminence. The copyists who have put Peter before James in some very early versions were perfectly aware of his. Traditionally historians and exegetes have explained the order of names by the fact that James was the head of the local church where the meeting took place.[33] As with Acts 15, this argument seems particularly weak. Indubitably Paul's account confirms the primacy accorded to James by Luke in his version of the Council of Jerusalem.[34] That in Galatians 2.7 Paul mentions Peter as the chief missionary to the Jews does not in any way imply pre-eminence over James. As Martin Hengel indicates,[35] it merely shows that James exercised only a limited missionary activity, since he was presiding over the destiny of the church from Jerusalem, its eschatological centre.

The pre-eminence of James is confirmed by Paul's account of the famous incident at Antioch (Gal. 2.11-14). This account, discussed at length in the previous chapter, has been a source of embarrassment for many theologians and exegetes. In fact here we see the people from around James imposing their views on Peter. These individuals, who doubtless represented James, had sufficient authority for Peter and Barnabas to adopt their position. But it is above all the account of the conflict between Peter and Paul which has caused consternation to generations of exegetes and theologians.[36] Here we see Peter, the 'first pope', the rock of the church, firmly taken to task by Paul for his laxity, and his hypocrisy after his retreat from eating with Gentiles. How embarrassing! Clement of Alexander went so far as to claim that the Cephas of the Antioch incident was a namesake of the famous apostle. Origen, John Chrysostom (354-407) and Jerome thought that the incident was staged by Peter and Paul, who were in agreement on the essentials. Augustine, who is clearer, never denied the reality of the conflict. He even drew a lesson from it aimed at the edification of the faithful: inferiors must correct their superiors when they depart from the gospel truth. We should note that the fathers of the Reformation did not forget to use this interpretation to justify their revolt against papal authority.

It is clear that at the time of the incident at Antioch, the church of Jerusalem with James at its head was exercising a decisive influence on the church of Antioch and on Peter, who had become an itinerant missionary. Paul had the choice between submission and breaking with the authorities. He chose to break with them and carry on his own missionary activity, which became increasingly difficult and controversial.

Many scholars think that the church of Jerusalem and James saw their prestige and their influence declining considerably from the beginning of the 50s. They imagine a community confronted with attacks by Jewish zealots, closed in on itself, and more preoccupied with its survival than with the propagation of the gospel. The authority of James would have been increasingly challenged by Jewish Christians zealous for the law, who were mainly responsible for the offensives against Paul in Galatia, at Corinth and Philippi. Such a reconstruction, which has very little basis, hardly seems plausible. We saw in the previous chapter that the Judaizing missionaries who visited several important communities founded by Paul were probably acting on the instructions of James. Their mission was undeniably crowned with some success, making it increasingly difficult for Paul to act. He hardly had any other option than to go to Jerusalem and to seek new virgin lands to fulfil his missionary work. However, as he feared, the visit to Jerusalem became a catastrophe and ruined his plans.

Correctly interpreted, the Pauline letters, which agree with Luke's account, bear witness that the church of Jerusalem continued to exercise its domination even after Peter's departure. Paul's letters, like Acts, thus seem to support the second scheme, which affirms the pre-eminence of James – at all events from the Council of Jerusalem onwards – and the church of Jerusalem. But how did James attain such a position?

The rise of James

Most scholars who accept the primacy of James at the time of the Council of Jerusalem think that the 'transfer of power' between Peter and James took place on Peter's departure from Jerusalem (Acts 12.17). The supporters of this view can be put into two schools.

According to the first, Peter, obliged to flee from Jerusalem, designated James as his successor at the head of the mother church. James, in occupying the prime place in the mother church, quite naturally became the pre-eminent authority of the Christian movement. Devoting himself solely to his missionary activity, Peter, though he still enjoyed considerable prestige, saw his influence diminish as he moved away from the centre of power. No particular conflict set Peter against James, and the transition was made with the agreement and blessing of all. Richard Bauckham,[37] who proposes this type of explanation, thinks that James, in contrast to the son of Zebedee and Peter, escaped Agrippa I's persecutions not because his attitude towards the law was stricter, but because at that time he was not sufficiently important to draw attention to himself. This interpretation is plausible. But many scholars find it too harmonious to be totally convincing.

According to the second school, the passing of power would reflect a major theological development within the Jerusalem church. According to some scholars who defend this view, the church of Jerusalem, when it was dominated by Peter and the other apostles, showed a relatively lax attitude towards the law and the Gentiles. Peter had convinced the church to accept the baptism of the centurion Cornelius without requiring him to be circumcised (Acts 10.1–11.18). According to Professor Martin Hengel of the University of Tübingen, the 'liberalism' of the former Galilean fisherman 'probably derived from the fact that as a disciple he was particularly close to Jesus and that, at a later stage, he could not forget the freedom shown by his master'.[38] According to this interpretation, Stephen and the Hellenists were even more radical.[39] These last, a true link between the radicalism of Jesus and that of Paul, were persecuted because of their very critical attitude towards the law and the temple, which derived both from the teaching of Jesus and from the new economy of salvation entailed by his resurrection. However, following the death of Stephen, these subversive characters were soon expelled from Jerusalem. After their departure, the church of Jerusalem under the leadership of Peter, while losing its 'revolutionary' *avant-garde*, nevertheless retained its laxity towards the law. However, the Jewish authorities, influenced by the nationalist zealots or under pressure from them, were increasingly less tolerant of this noisy, unorthodox little sect. In order to satisfy the Jews who were most zealous for the law, King Agrippa had James the son of Zebedee executed, and Peter saved his head only in the nick of time. After these persecutions and the departure of Peter from Jerusalem, power quite naturally passed into the hand of James and other traditional Christians, who were the only ones able to remain in the Holy City. James, who had not been a disciple of Jesus, was unable to perceive the radical character of his message.[40] Those who support this view also emphasize that the church of Jerusalem had welcomed into its midst many Jews, including priests, who observed the law very faithfully (Acts 6.7). As André Lemaire, of the Ecole pratique des hautes études, has written, it was this group, with James at its head, which formed the dominant element of the Jerusalem church:

> The Hellenist community of Jerusalem and the members of the Twelve had been persecuted and exiled. After 43, only the traditionalist Hebrews were left in Jerusalem. They had put at their head James, the 'brother of the Lord', one of the members of Jesus' family; he was surrounded by a council of elders in conformity with the traditional organization of Jewish communities.[41]

However, some exegetes think that the process of selection was not due entirely to external factors. In their view, the arrival of numerous traditionalist Jews led to a 'change of majority' in the Jerusalem community. The liberal tendency represented by Peter was increasingly challenged by the most conservative Jewish Christians. Christian Grappe[42] thinks that the decisive event which provoked Peter's fall was the scandal caused by his very lax attitude in the Cornelius affair. Thus the replacement of Peter by James will have been largely independent of the persecution of Agrippa I, which will simply have accelerated a process that was already well advanced.

This view has the merit of providing a plausible explanation for Luke's silence over the transition between Peter and James. However, it must nevertheless be considered with caution, since its foundations are very fragile. Moreover it fits perhaps all too well with the implicit thesis of many of its defenders, namely the continuity between Jesus, Paul and the post-apostolic church. In fact, according to this thesis, there would not have been any major break between Jesus, the earliest Jerusalem community led by Peter and the apostles, Paul, and the later church, completely detached from Judaism. The radical message of Jesus, fully understood by the Hellenists and by Paul, bore within it the germs of the later schism with Judaism. From 43 or 44 James and the Jerusalem church formed a kind of unfortunate Judaizing parenthesis. We can understand why many exegetes, all too happy to be able to show that James was not a disciple of his brother, accept John 7.5 and Mark 3.20–35; 6.4 without asking too many questions.

Indeed, James had not understood the message of Jesus properly, since he had not been one of his disciples. After the death of James and the irremediable decline of the Jerusalem church, this Judaizing conception of Christianity gave place to Paul's interpretation, which was more faithful to the teaching of Jesus. Some exegetes are not far from quietly thinking what Renan wrote in the last century:

James in particular, who was surnamed 'the Just' or 'the brother of the Lord', was one of the most exact observers of the law ever. If that singular man was really the brother of Jesus, he must have been at least one of those inimical brothers who abjured him and wished him arrested . . . To sum up, the Jerusalem church had become increasingly remote from the spirit of Jesus. The dead weight of Judaism had borne it down. Jerusalem was an unwholesome centre for the new faith and would have ended up by destroying it.[43]

This interpretation is fundamentally based on two assertions: first, the primitive community of Jerusalem, under the direction of Peter and the apostles, showed a relatively lax view towards the law; secondly, Peter and James professed significantly different attitudes towards the law.

Three main arguments are usually put forward in favour of the first proposition: the radical attitude of Jesus towards the law, which will have influenced Peter and the other close disciples; the persecutions of the Jerusalem community; and the relatively liberal attitude of this community towards the conversion of the Gentiles during the first fifteen or twenty years of its existence.

We saw in Chapter 5 what we must think of the first

argument. There is nothing to indicate that Jesus put the law of Moses, including its sacrificial system, fundamentally in question. In criticizing a few popular interpretations, he hardly differed from other teachers of his time.

According to the second argument, the persecutions of the Jerusalem church would be explained by its lax attitude towards the law.[44]

The first persecutions as described in Acts do not seem to have been particularly violent. The apostles, Peter and John in particular, appeared before the Sanhedrin (twice?), which ordered them to stop preaching, though the Pharisee Gamaliel intervened on their behalf. Since Peter and the apostles are presented as very pious Jews, the reasons for their appearance(s) are not very clear. To claim that someone was the Messiah and that only those who considered him to be such would be saved was not a crime at this time. At all events, no one persecuted the Essenes, who accorded an exalted status to their Teacher of Righteousness and who thought that only those who lived according to their instructions would be saved. Many scholars conclude from this that the hostility of the Jewish authorities, contrary to what Luke suggests, would originate in more serious motives, like a very critical attitude towards the law and perhaps the temple, inspired by the teaching of Jesus.[45] In fact, the opposition encountered by the Jerusalem community could easily be understood without recourse to the hypothesis of such radicalism. It is enough to take into account several indisputable elements in the death of Jesus and the beginnings of the church.

Whatever may have been the precise nature and extent of their responsibility for the arrest and condemnation of Jesus, it is almost certain that the high priest Caiaphas and other eminent priests approved of these actions. Far from regarding Jesus as the Messiah or an inspired prophet, in all probability they saw him as a dangerous impostor leading the people to its ruin. In their view, the wonders attributed to him had to be attributed to the regular use of magic. Doubtless they were less preoccupied with his interpretation of the law than with his capacity to arouse the enthusiasm of the crowds, hence the disquiet of the Romans. Moreover, Jesus had perhaps insulted the high priest and some other dignitaries by setting himself against their greed.

Once this Jesus had been crucified, his disciples, far from returning to a peaceful anonymity, began to relate everywhere that he had appeared to them. They claimed that Jesus was the one whom 'God exalted at his right hand as Leader and Saviour, to give repentance to Israel and forgiveness of sins' (Acts 5.31). The priestly authorities must have considered the attribution of such an exalted position to an impostor crucified with their blessing as an insult and a challenge to their legitimacy. The provocation was all the greater since many among the eminent priestly families were Sadducees who did not believe in the resurrection of the dead. Moreover, these impudent people, instead of going to proclaim their message in the desert of Judaea or the mountains of high Galilee, were doing so under their noses, in the temple. Finally, a messianic proclamation of this type could easily give rise to disturbances of public order and bring down Roman repressions. What is surprising is not that the disciples of Jesus were maltreated by the Jewish authorities, but that this did not happen to a greater degree.

The second persecution, which ended with the death of Stephen and the departure of the Hellenists from Jerusalem, is particularly mysterious (Acts 6.1–8.3). A conflict divided the Christians of Jerusalem, setting the Hellenists from the Diaspora against the Hebrews. The motive invoked by Luke, namely the treatment of the Hellenist widows, seems to conceal more serious causes. Stephen, one of the Hellenists, accused – wrongly, according to Luke – of speaking against the law and the temple, was brought before the Sanhedrin. In his defence, he emphasized his loyalty to the law of Moses. The traditional opinion, according to which Stephen rejected the temple, is being challenged today.[46] Nevertheless, he was stoned. Most experts think that Luke has transformed a spontaneous lynching of Stephen by several members of the synagogue into an official and legal condemnation by the Sanhedrin.[47] As Craig C. Hill has shown, we have virtually no trustworthy information about the martyrdom and the ideas of Stephen.[48] He and the Hellenists are a kind of pet theme in the history of the primitive church, each historian interpreting the episode in the way which best suits his thesis. At all events, whatever the reason for the conflict between Stephen, the Hellenists and their opponents, it does not seem to have affected Peter and the other apostles.

The third persecution mentioned in Acts, which culminated in the execution of James son of Zebedee, is particularly interesting to us, since for many scholars it lies at the origin of the rise of the brother of Jesus to be head of the Jerusalem community. We have seen that according to Acts, Agrippa I had James son of Zebedee executed by the sword. 'Seeing that this pleased the Jews' (Acts 12.3), he had Peter imprisoned, though Peter was able to escape with the help of an angel. Those who do not believe that angels open prison doors can suppose that Peter escaped through the complicity of a warder or that he was released by Agrippa I. We have seen that for many experts this persecution was caused by the lax attitude of some Jewish Christians towards the law, in particular in the sphere of relations with the Gentiles. By contrast, Oscar Cullmann[49] and, more recently, the historian Daniel R. Schwartz[50] think that the motives for these persecutions were mainly political. They point out that beheading was above all a penalty for political crimes. Moreover, Cullmann thinks that the brevity of the mention of the martyrdom of James in Acts is surprising. Was not the son of Zebedee the first of the Twelve to die as a martyr? Cullmann deduces from this that Luke perhaps did not want to dwell at length on an execution the motives for which embarrassed him, since they were political.

Schwartz supposes that Agrippa I will have acted at the request of the emperor Claudius, or in order to show support for him following the troubles caused in Rome by the Christians in 41, which would have led to their expulsion.[51] Similar messianic agitation might also perhaps have developed at Antioch[52] and Alexandria.[53] Agrippa I would have had his eye above all on James son of Zebedee and Peter, because of their particular ardour. Do not the Gospels emphasize the aggressive and irascible character of the sons of Zebedee, to whom Jesus gave the name 'sons of thunder' (Mark 3.17)? And did not Peter, according to John 18.10, cut off the ear of the high priest's servant at the moment of Jesus' arrest? So we can suppose that they will have attracted the wrath of Agrippa because of their vigorous words or perhaps because of certain seditious acts. Thus it does not seem that we can conclude that, up to 43 or 44, the persecutions against the primitive church of Jerusalem were provoked by any radical attitude towards the law, perhaps with the exception of those which struck the Hellenists.

By contrast, the same experts think that the respite which the Jerusalem church would have enjoyed between 43–44 and 62 would have been due to its religious conformity and the good relations between James and the Pharisees. Such an argument is hardly any more convincing. Those who put it forward tend to forget that James died as a martyr in Jerusalem and that, as Paul suggests (I Thess. 2.14–15), life was not always easy for the churches of Judaea, which are supposed to have been so tranquil. Moreover the Pharisees, with whom perhaps James had good relations, did not make the law in Jerusalem. So it seems futile to want to demonstrate an ideological evolution of the Jerusalem church from the persecutions which affected it.

According to the third argument in favour of a certain laxity in the primitive Jerusalem community with regard to the law, when the Jerusalem church was governed by Peter, it had adopted a liberal attitude towards the adherence of the Gentiles. In addition to the persecutions which we have just discussed, two factors would confirm such behaviour: the conversion of Cornelius and the absence of any opposition on the part of the Jerusalem church to Paul's' missionary efforts before the debates which provoked the meeting of the Council of Jerusalem.

We have seen that the historicity of the conversion of Cornelius, at any rate before the Council of Jerusalem, is doubtful. Moreover, as I have demonstrated, it does not seem that we must regard the relatively benevolent attitude of the Jerusalem church towards the mission to the Gentiles as a mark of laxity towards the law. Did not the pillars, with James at their head, accept the principle of the conversion of the Gentiles without circumcision? There is no reason to support that the Jerusalem church was less liberal in 48/49 than at the beginning of the 30s.

The supporters of the thesis of the 'Judaization' of the

Jerusalem community explain it in part by the adherents of many Jews, even priests, who observed the law faithfully. These Jews, often of Pharisaic or Essene obedience, would have been Paul's opponents at the Council of Jerusalem. But we may ask why they would have joined the Christian community of Jerusalem if its view of the law had been so radical and its practice so lax. It is more probable that they had joined the Christian movement because it allowed them to satisfy their messianic aspirations while faithfully respecting the law.

Even before the discovery of the Dead Sea Scrolls, scholars had noted how similar certain Essene ideas and practices were to those of the primitive community of Jerusalem as this is described in the Acts of the Apostles.[54] Since this discovery, the similarities have become clearer. The most striking similarity is in the sharing of possessions practised, according to Acts (2.44–45; 4.32–35, 36–37; 5.1–11), by the primitive church of Jerusalem, and which characterized the Essene movement.[55] Nevertheless, most experts think that the sharing of possessions in Acts is only a fiction on the part of Luke aimed at his Hellenized readers. In his idealized portrait of the Jerusalem church, Luke would have imagined an organization in keeping with the model of utopian society developed by the Pythagoreans and Plato.[56] It has to be said that a number of exegetes who are politically conservative hardly appreciate the idea, often taken up by socialists at the end of the last century, that the first Christians were able to form a kind of communist society.

However, it seems more probable, as Brian Capper[57] has recently argued, that the primitive church of Jerusalem had a communal system or a sharing of goods similar to that of the Essenes and inspired by it. This system, which will have been partly voluntary, doubtless did not involve all the possessions of the new members. Still, as the story of Ananias and Sapphira shows, deceit over possessions was severely punished, as it was among the Essenes.

There are many other parallels between the Essenes and the primitive Jerusalem community. Some are probably less significant, since they involve beliefs and practices which were widespread at the time. However, others are more relevant. Thus we can note that the Acts of the Apostles and the Qumran texts sometimes use the same expression, 'the Way', to denote the community's form of life and thought. The manner in which Matthias is elected to the college of the Twelve (Acts 1.15–26) has analogies with Essene practices. The account of Pentecost (Acts 2.1–13) attaches quite special importance to the Feast of Weeks. Now the Essenes associated *Shavuoth* with the celebration of the covenant and the gift of the law. As Christian Grappe emphasizes, the fact that the church is thought to have begun on the day on which the Qumran community repeated the covenant and accepted new members is 'an interesting coincidence'.[58] The similarities between the common Essene meal and the Christian eucharistic meal have often been noted. Similarly, the Essenes, like the first Christians, scorned riches and emphasized poverty. The term 'the poor' (*'ebyonim*) which sometimes denotes the Essenes was perhaps used in the Jerusalem community. We find it later to denote the members of some Jewish-Christian communities, the Ebionites.

Recent archaeological discoveries and some literary evidence suggest the existence of a Essene quarter in Jerusalem situated in the south-east of the city, near the ramparts and the Essene Gate in particular.[59] Moreover, according to Christian traditions which go back to the beginning of the second century, the earliest Christian community in Jerusalem would have been established on Mount Zion, near the Essene quarter. Such proximity, if proved, could have facilitated contacts between communities. The first Christians, some of whom had probably formerly been Essenes, doubtless borrowed Essene ideas and concepts, sometimes modifying them.[60] This influence on the primitive church is probably not an indication of its progressive Judaization. On the contrary, it shows that from its origin this community faithfully observed the law.

So there is little reason to suppose that the primitive Jerusalem community with which Peter and James are associated did not observe the law faithfully. As is noted by François Blanchetière[61] of the University of Strasbourg, the first Christians hardly differed from other Jews in the milieu in which they lived, apart from their belief in Jesus and some other practices of their own. The supposed Judaization of this community represented by James' assumption of power hardly existed except in the imagination of exegetes.

James and Peter

Of course this does not mean that all the members of the Jerusalem church interpreted and observed the law in an identical way. The diversity noted in the Palestinian Judaism of the time must have been to some degree reflected in this community. Perhaps Peter and James did not share the same views in every area of the law. Nevertheless, their differences were probably not as important as many scholars think. A number of scholars tend to present James as a conservative or a traditionalist opposed to Paul, the ultra-liberal, while Peter, the moderate or centrist, adopts a compromise position between the two. Converted Pharisees, ultra-conservatives, flank James on the right. Some experts even put James in the camp of these ultra-conservatives. By contrast, others see him as a liberal not far removed from Paul.

This approach implies that we could easily classify the Jews of the first century by the rigour which which they observed the law. Thus we would have a whole range, from the quasi-apostate to the extremely strict Essene, going through the lax, the liberal and the moderate. Such a classification, which is largely imaginary, can hardly be achieved because of the great diversity of interpretations of the law and the difficulty of classifying them by their degree of rigour. For example, how are we to classify the Sadducees, whose *halakhah*, which was very rigorous in some areas, remained silent on other aspects which were thought important by the Pharisees? Where do we put the *hasidim*, those pious spiritual figures whose behaviour is sometimes so special? What are we to make of Jesus, who is sometimes compared with these *hasidim*: so strict in some spheres like divorce and oaths, and less rigorous in others like the Sabbath? Many scholars deduce James' attitude towards the law from his position on two questions relating to the Gentiles: their salvation and table relations between Jews and Gentiles.[62] But we have seen that the law is not interested in the problem of the salvation of the Gentiles and does not give any categorical instructions about table relations between Jews and Gentiles. At the Council of Jerusalem, James accepted that it was not necessary to be a Jew to be saved. This opinion was shared by many of the Jews of his time, including some Pharisees who observed the law strictly. We also know that James did not favour table relations between Jews and Gentiles, though we cannot say whether it was an absolute prohibition or a general rule of conduct to which there could be some exceptions. However, here again James' position hardly differs from that of numerous Palestinian Jews, whether they observed the law like the Essenes or like the *'ammē hā-ārets*.

The positions of James on some questions relating to the Gentiles hardly allow us to determine his conception of the law and the rigour with which he observed it. Some scholars think that James was close to the Pharisees, since they were offended by his condemnation and execution. As we shall see in Chapter 10, the only conclusion which could reasonably be drawn from the protests of the Pharisees is that James was not guilty of any major transgression of the Torah. To deduce more than that would be speculation. Other scholars derive their view of James as a very strict legalist from a semi-legendary portrait painted by Hegesippus:

This man was holy from his mother's womb, drank no wine nor strong drink, nor ate anything in which was life; no razor came upon his head, he anointed himself not with oil, and used no bath. To him alone it was permitted to enter the holy place; for he wore nothing woollen, but linen garments. And alone he entered into the sanctuary, and was found on his knees asking forgiveness on behalf of the people, so that his knees became hard like a camel's, for he was continually bending the knee in worship to God, and asking forgiveness for the people. In fact, on account of his exceeding great justice he was called 'the Just ' and 'Oblias', which is in Greek 'bulwark of the people' and 'justice', as the prophets show concerning him.[63]

The expression 'holy from his mother's womb' indicates that James was specially called by God.[64] Jeremiah (1.5), Isaiah

(49.1) and John the Baptist (Luke 1.15) were singled out in the same way. His refusal of wine and the razor, added to this holiness 'from his mother's womb', characterizes James as a nazir to the life, i.e. as one wholly dedicated to YHWH. This nazirate recalls the participation in the vow of the four men required by James of Paul at the time of his last visit to Jerusalem (Acts 21.23–24). James' vegetarianism and his rejection of oil and baths shows his asceticism. The prohibition of oil, which we find among the Essenes, is also evidence of important requirements in matters of purity.

Hegesippus presents James as a high priest, since he was the only one who could go into the sanctuary. This feature is surprising, in that Joseph's family is nowhere considered priestly, which would also be in contradiction to his presumed Davidic origin. Moreover James was never high priest. Was Hegesippus perhaps taking up a tradition which, making Jesus the new Moses, would have made James the new Aaron, and thus the first high priest of a new dynasty? He might also be recalling views inspired by the Essenes according to which Jesus would have been the royal Messiah, son of David, and James the priestly Messiah, son of Aaron. Be this as it may, it seems that Hegesippus wanted to give the impression that the true high priesthood of Israel had been transferred to James and his successors at the head of the Jerusalem church. The surname James the Just, very old since it appears in the Gospel of the Hebrews and the Gospel of Thomas, doubtless refers to the great piety of James and his faithfulness to the law. Thanks to these virtues, he had been justified before God, i.e. saved. The surname 'the Just' for James is perhaps also linked to his martyrdom, the theme of the martyrdom of the just being popular at the time.[65]

The most striking aspects of this portrait are on the one hand the asceticism of James and on the other his immense piety and religious fervour, manifested by long prayers in the temple. Hegesippus' description certainly contains many legendary and hagiographical elements. But it is quite wrong to suppose, as some scholars do, that it has no historical basis. There are hardly any valid reasons for doubting that James was a pious Jew who was faithful to the law, in particular in the sphere of

purity and worship in the temple. The image that can be derived
from Acts and the letters of Paul is not opposed to such a portrait. But that hardly allows us to determine James *halakhah*,
i.e. the way in which he conceived of the law and applied it. His
halakhah was certainly sufficiently close to that of the Pharisaic
and Essene movements to allow a dialogue, even if an angry
one, and the adherence of certain members of these groups.
If, as H. D. Betz thinks, the Sermon on the Mount reflects the
views of the primitive church of Jerusalem, it could constitute
valuable evidence about James' *halakhah*.[66] It emphasizes the
need to respect all the precepts of the law. But the disciples
of Jesus must not be content with interpreting the law and
putting it into practice as the Pharisees do (Matt. 5.20). We
should note that the latter are not criticized for an excessively
rigorous interpretation of the laws of purity and of the sabbath.
They are accused, rightly or wrongly, of attaching too much
importance to the outward manifestations of piety and not
being sufficiently rigorous in their conduct, particularly in their
relations with others.[67] The 'Sermon on the Mount' teaches that
there must be respect not only for the letter of the law but also
for its spirit, characterized by two basic principles: love of God
and love of neighbour.

The attacks on the Pharisees, the virulence of which evokes
that of the debates between Essenes and Pharisees, or even
between different Pharisaic schools, must be interpreted in the
context of a struggle between rival groups. But at all events they
show that the Jewish Christians of Jerusalem wanted to define
themselves by what in their eyes constituted a deepening of
the law and its moral demands. The 'Sermon on the Mount'
conjures up a community in quest of ethical perfection, a perfection which many contemporaries must have judged incompatible with a normal social life, but which was justified by the
imminent arrival of the kingdom of God. The same rigour was
certainly applied to the 'ritual' aspects of the law, even if
Essenes or Pharisees could have thought some elements of
James's *halakhah* lax or heterodox.[68]

The Christian theological tradition has often contrasted the
true and superior religion of Jesus and the Christians, based on
authentic piety and love of neighbour, with the sterile legalism

of the Jews, based on scrupulous respect for ritual law conceived of as an end in itself. Although this caricature has largely been discredited today, many theologians and exegetes still have difficulty in conceiving that a scrupulous respect for ritual precepts could go hand in hand with a profound piety and an ethic centred on love of others, an ethic, moreover, of which the first Christians did not have the monopoly. Often they can only imagine James as a legalistic Jew barely stamped with the spirit of Christianity, or as a true Christian who has learned to relativize the importance of the ritual commandments. However, for James, as for most of the Jews of his time, whether or not they belonged to the Jesus movement, the ritual and ethical aspects of the law could not be dissociated, nor were they contradictory, since the whole of the law manifested the will of God.

Peter, for his part, is often seen as a relatively liberal Jewish Christian, above all because of his open behaviour towards the Gentiles on the occasion of the conversion of Cornelius and during his stay at Antioch before the incident (Gal. 2.11–14). We have seen that it would be rash to want to draw too many conclusions from the account of the conversion of Cornelius. Moreover, we have also seen that the fact that Peter, at Antioch, shared a table with pagan Christians does not have the radical character that some scholars attribute to it. In this respect Peter was no different from many other Jews. Without perhaps having the rigour of James, he observed the law faithfully. Just like James, Peter, at least after the incident at Antioch, was opposed to Paul's mission. Without excluding the possibility of a personal rivalry, we have to accept that the hypothesis of a major theological conflict between Peter and James and the forced replacement of the former by the latter at the head of the Jerusalem church is very speculative.

A family affair

There is perhaps no need to seek out dubious explanations in order to understand the pre-eminence of James. He probably occupied first place in the primitive church by reason of his kinship with Jesus. There is nothing surprising about such a rank in a society in which the dynastic principle was so deeply implanted. Outside the royal Hasmonaean and Herodian families, we find a form of quasi-dynastic succession among the high priests with the family of Hanan; in the Pharisaic and rabbinic schools; and even among the rebel Zealots with the family of Judas the Galilean. In a messianic movement like primitive Christianity, in which the Davidic descent of Jesus was affirmed, the primacy of the brother of Jesus, who was also a descendant of David, would seem natural.

The importance attached to kinship with Jesus in the primitive church is confirmed by the elevated position reached by other members of the family of Christ. To judge from I Corinthians 9.5, the brothers of Jesus and James were influential figures, engaged in major missionary activity. One letter of the New Testament bears the name of Jude, one of the brothers of Jesus. According to Eusebius, after the death of James, his cousin Simeon, son of Clopas, was designated head of the Jerusalem church.

> After the martyrdom of James and the taking of Jerusalem which immediately ensued, it is recorded that those apostles and disciples of the Lord who were still surviving met together from all quarters and, together with our Lord's relatives after the flesh (for the most part of them were still alive), took counsel, all in common, as to whom they should judge worthy to be the successor of James; and, what is more, that they all with one consent approved Symeon the son of Clopas, of whom also the book of the Gospels makes mention, as worthy of the throne of the community in that place. He was a cousin – at any rate so it is said – of the Saviour; for indeed Hegesippus relates that Clopas was Joseph's brother.[69]

The grandsons of Jude who according to Hegesippus were brought before Domitian by reason of their Davidic descent, 'ruled the churches, inasmuch as they were both martyrs and of the Lord's family'.[70] Quite apart from kinship with Jesus, the fact that they belonged to a Davidic line explains the pre-eminent position of the members of Jesus' family, who played a significant role in the churches of Palestine and neighbouring regions long after the death of Jesus. The notion of a dynastic Christianity is certainly nothing new. Maurice Goguel, following Adolf von Harnack, Johannes Weiss and Eduard Meyer, emphasized its importance:

> But when the brothers of the Lord rallied to him, the idea occurred to some that those who were members of the natural family of Jesus because they were connected to him by ties of blood ought to take his place provisionally. This introduced an element into Christianity, in one of its forms at least, which has justly been compared by Eduard Meyer to the part that the caliphate played in the beginnings of Islam. 'It is extremely significant,' he writes, 'that in the earliest days of Christianity, as in Islam and Mormonism, as soon as the prophet had died, a dynastic element appeared and tried to assert itself. The brothers of Jesus are held to have a share in the same divine power as the Master and themselves assert this claim.' We can justifiably say that a dynastic Christianity supplanted apostolic Christianity at Jerusalem in 44. This fact throws light on the meaning of the polemical point implied in the references made by Mark and John to the attitude of the brothers of Jesus towards him during his ministry.[71]

Maurice Goguel, like many other historians, makes 44 the decisive moment of the change of power. But evidence of this apostolic Christianity led by Peter and replaced by dynastic Christianity is very thin. The role of the Twelve, with Peter at their head, as the ruling authority of the primitive church is based solely on the first chapter of Acts, the historical trustworthiness of which is limited. Paul's letters never indicate that the Twelve formed an executive organ, even if they show clearly that Peter was one of the heads of the primitive church. Only a speculative interpretation of Galatians 1.18 suggests his primacy some years after the death of Jesus. If we attach only reduced historical value to the first chapters of Acts, we have to accept that the primacy of Peter is based essentially on Galatians 1.18, a brief and ambiguous passage.

Is it not more reasonable to suppose that the revolution of 43 or 44 is perhaps simply a delusion, and that the primacy of

James is prior to Peter's departure from Jerusalem? Several traditions coming from very different Christian movements present James as the first head of the Jerusalem church. We have seen that the Gospel of Thomas and the Gospel of the Hebrews make James Jesus' successor. These two Gospels reflect traditions which, if they are hardly more authentic than that expressed in Matthew 16.17–19, are probably as old. It is generally thought that Logion 12 of Thomas is a reply from the disciples of James to the Gospel of Matthew in which the primacy of Peter is asserted. But the opposite is just as likely.[72] Similarly, the list of appearance of Jesus in I Corinthians 15.5–7 suggests the existence at the beginning of the 50s of a tradition giving James the privilege of witnessing the first appearance of Jesus. Eusebius in his *Church History* quotes passages from Hegesippus and Clement of Alexandria which emphasize the primacy of James from the beginnings of the church. They have already been mentioned in the introduction and I shall quote them here, together with others in which Eusebius indicates his own opinion or reflects non-specific sources.

Hegesippus

Together with the apostles, James the Lord's brother succeeded to [the government of] the church (2.23.4).

Clement

He [Clement] says that Peter and James and John after the ascension of the Saviour did not lay claim to glory, as men who had been preferred in honour by him; but selected James bishop of Jerusalem (2.1.3).

To James the Just and John and Peter the Lord after the resurrection committed the 'gnosis'; they committed it to the other apostles (2.1.4).

Eusebius

And they turned to James the Lord's brother, to whom the apostles had entrusted the throne of the episcopate at Jerusalem (2.23.1). This same James, then, whom the men of old surnamed the Just on account of his excellent virtue, was the first, it is related, to be entrusted with the throne of the episcopate of the church at Jerusalem (2.1.2).

Now the throne of James, who was the first to receive from the Saviour and the apostles the episcopate of the church at Jerusalem . . . has been preserved to this day (7.19).

According to Hegesippus, who is perhaps handing down very old traditions of the churches of Palestine, James received the government of the church with the apostles. He thus suggests a bicephalous-type structure, with James on the one hand and the apostles on the other. However, Gerd Lüdemann, professor at the University of Göttingen, thinks that the expression 'with the apostles' could have been added by Eusebius to make this information more orthodox.[73] Similarly, one might suppose that in his last mention of the accession of James to the head of the Jerusalem church Eusebius has added 'and the apostles' to a source (perhaps Hegesippus) which indicates that Jesus himself had given James this position. Such a source could be contained in Epiphanius's *Panarion*.[74] At all events, for Hegesippus, James – alone or in the company of the apostles – governed the church from its origin.

As Scott Kent Brown has emphasized in his thesis on the traditions relating to James, the two passages attributed to Clement of Alexandria show that he regarded James as the most important person in the primitive church.[75] The first extract indicates that for Clement the position of bishop of Jerusalem was certainly the most prestigious charge in the primitive church. In this passage Clement, who certainly did not know more than we do about the origin of James' pre-eminence, is probably offering an elegant answer to the apparent contradiction between the traditions which emphasize the importance of Peter and the sons of Zebedee as the favourite disciples of Jesus and those which present James as the first head of the church after Easter. The second extract seems to suggest that James was chosen because he was the first to receive the true knowledge from Jesus.

It is interesting to note that Hegesippus and Clement, unlike many modern scholars, do not seem to attach much importance to the accounts in Acts. Eusebius, writing more than a century after Hegesippus and Clement, also thinks that James had been the first bishop of Jerusalem. However, he seems to subordinate him to the apostles, who give him his authority. Thus he adopts the Catholic conception of the apostolic succession. Epiphanius in his *Panarion* also mentions that 'James was installed immediately as first bishop'.[76]

We saw in the Introduction that several Gnostic writings attribute first place in the church after the death of Jesus to James. The Pseudo-Clementine literature, of Jewish-Christian inspiration, takes up similar traditions.[77] According to the most primitive part of the Clementine *Recognitions* (1.27–71), Jesus nominated James first bishop of Jerusalem.

It is particularly striking that such diverse traditions agree in regarding James as the first head ('bishop' is anachronistic) of the Jerusalem church. Given the pre-eminence of the mother church, that amounts to affirming the primacy of James from the start.[78] In contrast to the churches of Antioch and Rome, the Jerusalem church did not claim the patronage of Peter. There is nothing to indicate that these traditions only reflect the pre-eminence of James in the 50s, as the majority of experts think. They could very well represent an older primacy.

The sources at our disposal indicate that Peter and James played a major role in the first years of the church. However, they do not allow us to reconstruct, even in the crudest way, the nature and development of the relations of power in the primitive church. One can only offer a few general and somewhat speculative comments. After the appearances of Christ, numerous disciples doubtless settled in Jerusalem in expectation of his return. It is very possible that James and the other brothers of Jesus remained in Galilee, and that James only established himself in Jerusalem a few years later. Similarly, we cannot exclude the possibility that James and Peter were leaders of different communities in Jerusalem.

In this eschatological fervour, questions of pre-eminence among the disciples surely must have seemed secondary. No one had to think of investing one of the faithful with undivided authority, since the absence of Jesus was considered so temporary. Doubtless Peter and James enjoyed considerable influence and prestige, the one because he had been the closest disciple of the master, and the other because of his kinship with Jesus. Other communities were created rapidly in Palestine and then in the countries of the Diaspora, some being relatively dependent on Jerusalem, others more autonomous. Around the 40s, when the return of Christ was being awaited and the Christian communities were developing successfully, the need for a more hierarchical and centralized power structure made itself felt. James, brother of Jesus and, according to the faithful, like him of the line of David, quite naturally established himself at the head of this messianic community, regardless of the prestige of Peter. His profound piety and perhaps his knowledge of the law and the scriptures must have made his pre-eminence even more incontrovertible. Nor can we exclude the possibility that James' charisma and his qualities as leader also helped his rise to the head of the church. By contrast, we must not forget that several passages suggest that Peter had certain character defects. Perhaps we must not draw too many conclusions from Luke's account and his silences. Maybe his intention was not to reduce James' role or to hide embarrasing events. Perhaps he was only trying to develop a history which was coherent and theologically significant for him on the basis of the disparate and contradictory traditions that he had at his disposal.

To describe James as the first pope is perhaps an exaggeration, and certainly anachronistic. However, if any figure in the primitive church merits this designation, he certainly does.[79]

9

A Strawy Epistle

The author of the first of the seven so-called Catholic Epistles of the New Testament introduces himself as 'James, a servant of God and of the Lord Jesus Christ, to the twelve tribes in the Dispersion' (James 1.1). Despite its apparent modesty, the expression 'servant of God' in the Hebrew Bible denotes significant figures.[1] Such a solemn and majestic introduction thus emphasizes the author's importance. Only two members of the primitive church called James seem to have had sufficient stature to introduce themselves in this way: the son of Zebedee and the brother of the Lord. Origen, followed by Eusebius, identified this James with the brother of the Lord, and most exegetes have accepted their opinion.[2] Does that mean that here we have indubitable testimony to James' thought?

Unfortunately, above all since the development of New Testament criticism in the eighteenth century, the authenticity of the letter has been put in question by numerous experts. They think that the author of this work would have been an unknown Christian who put himself under the spiritual authority of James in order to give more weight to his message. Pseudepigraphical works, very common at the time, were in no way considered frauds or forgeries. On the contrary, they showed the homage of the anonymous author to the prestigious figure whose signature and sometimes ideas he was borrowing. If the Letter of James is a pseudepigraph, at best it could offer only indirect testimony to James' thought.

This letter, perhaps the most enigmatic document in the New Testament, has aspects which leave scholars perplexed. Those to whom it is addressed are not designated in any specific way. The text does not refer to any precise event which makes it possible to date it and define its context. The letter presents itself as a series of moral exhortations inspired by traditional Jewish wisdom. The mentions of Jesus are so few and their christology is so rudimentary that some scholars, like F. Spitta and Louis Massebieau, have put forward the hypothesis – rejected nowadays – that this is a text from a Jewish author unconnected with the Jesus movement which will have been slightly modified by a Christian redactor.

Scholars today can be divided into three main categories.[3]

The first and most numerous group thinks that the Letter of James is a pseudepigraph by a Christian who comes from the liberal Judaism of the Diaspora.[4] The work would date from the end of the first century or the beginning of the second. Antioch, Alexandria and Rome are most often put forward as places of origin. The views expressed by the letter would have only a slight link, if any at all, with James' thought. The major controversies over Gentile membership of the church and respect for the law of Moses are regarded as things of the past.

The second group comprises experts for whom the work would be a pseudepigraph coming from Jewish-Christian circles in Palestine or Syria, still influenced by James and his ideas.[5] According to some of them, the letter would partly consist of authentic writings by the brother of the Lord.

Experts in the third group attribute the authorship of the letter to James. This text then becomes an indispensable document for discovering the thought and personality of the brother of the Lord. This position, which has experienced a notable return to favour, above all in evangelical circles, is generally coupled with the argument that the differences between James and Paul have largely been exaggerated by many exegetes and church historians.[6]

A disputed letter

The external attestations to the letter allow us to fix the latest possible date of its composition and the nature of its reception and dissemination in the churches.[7] The earliest explicit quotation that we know of is in Origen. He includes the letter among the holy scriptures, while admitting that his opinion is not unanimously shared. However, his testimony suggests that the letter is considerably earlier that the beginning of the third century. According to Eusebius, Clement of Alexandria – Origen's teacher – wrote a commentary on the Letter of James. Since the writings of Clement which have come down to us never mention this letter, most experts have tended to doubt the testimony of Eusebius. Nevertheless, similarities with works very much before the quotation by Origen suggest an early date of composition. The Letter of James has quite marked affinities with the First Letter of Peter, Clement of Rome's First Letter to the Corinthians, and the Shepherd of Hermas. The parallels with I Peter, a canonical text composed at Rome during the last decades of the first century, imply more the use of common traditions. On the other hand, the similarities with I Clement, which is dated between 95 and 98, and above all with the Shepherd of Hermas, composed at Rome at the beginning of the second century, could be due to the fact that the authors of these two works used the letter of James.[8] If these conclusions are accepted, the letter could date back to before the 90s.

After Origen, the letter was increasingly regarded as an inspired book in the Greek churches of Alexandria and Palestine. Eusebius in his *Church History* mentions that the letter of James, though read publicly in many churches, is not accepted as authentic by all. Athanasius, in 367, includes it in his list of sacred texts. Explicit evidence in the Latin churches is later. The Letter of James is not part of the canon of Muratori, established by the church of Rome around 200. The earliest quotation comes from Hilary of Poitiers (died 366). Through the influence of Jerome and Augustine (354–430) the letter found wider dissemination and increased prestige. It was recognized as canonical at the Councils of Rome (382), Hippo (303) and Carthage (397, 419). For a long time unknown or ignored in the church of Syria, it appears for the first time around 412 in the Peshitta, the Syriac translation of the Bible.

The very early attestations of the letter are thus few or uncertain. For a long time misunderstood or challenged, it took time to establish itself as holy scripture throughout the Christian world. While these features do not allow us to challenge its authenticity, they do not tell in its favour. The sources used by the letter can also give us some indication of its date of composition and thus of the possibility of James being its author. I mentioned earlier some texts which show similarities to the letter of James. However, it seems improbable that the author of the letter knew them. Experts who support a dependent relationship think that the opposite is more probable. As we shall see later, it is possible that the author of the letter had read certain writings of Paul. The relations between the letter and the Synoptic Gospels have recently become a sphere of active and promising research. In fact the letter contains numerous teachings which, while attributed to James, recall sayings of Jesus of the kind reported in the Synoptic Gospels. The parallels are particularly abundant with Luke and above all Matthew, especially in the 'Sermon on the Mount'. But since the similarities are more conceptual than literary, most exegetes think that the author of the letter did not know any of the Gospels in their present form. After a minute analysis of relations between the letter and Q, as far as it can be reconstructed, Patrick J. Hartin has concluded that the author of the letter was familiar with this text.[9]

Comparisons with other similar passages in the Gospels suggest that the author of the letter knew oral traditions which in some cases were also used by Matthew, who modified them somewhat. We should note that, contrary to the evangelists, the author of the letter has interpreted the traditions about Jesus in accordance with the model of traditional Jewish wisdom as this appears particularly in Proverbs, Ecclesiasticus and the Wisdom of Solomon.[10] Thus the letter, or a substantial part of the elements that make it up, could be earlier than the Gospels of Matthew and Luke, which were probably composed in the 80s. If these conclusions are accepted, a connection between the letter and the brother of Jesus, who died in 62, would not be impossible chronologically.

A cultivated author

The letter of James is written in good Greek: along with that of the letter to the Hebrews, the best in the New Testament. The vocabulary is rich, the syntax correct and the style sometimes elegant. The author seems to be familiar with the basic rules of rhetoric. He uses the Septuagint, which may explain his quite frequent semitisms. So his mother tongue was probably Greek, and he must have had a very respectable literary education. That is why for a long time the great majority of experts have thought that such a work could not have been written by a Jew with a modest background, coming from a small village in Lower Galilee.

However, nowadays specialists generally adopt a more qualified position. We know that the use of Greek was widespread in Lower Galilee at the time of James and his brother. So it is probable that James, like Jesus, knew Greek. In *Do You Know Greek?*,[11] J. N. Sevenster has asked whether James, a Galilean of humble origins, could have written the letter which bears his name. After a long study of the Hellenization of Palestine, Sevenster has concluded that this is not impossible. However, 'not impossible' does not mean 'probable', and we are certainly allowed to remain sceptical. In fact to accept that the brother of James could himself have written the letter would lead us to reconsider the social and cultural status of Joseph's family and the type of education received by James and Jesus.

Be this as it may, reflections on the style of the letter are perhaps not decisive in determining its authenticity. We cannot in fact exclude the possibility that James produced this text with the help of a secretary whose Greek was better than his own.[12] Similarly, the problem no longer arises if one supposes that the letter was written by a disciple of James, basing himself on some of James' writings or sayings.

Nothing so far has allowed us to reject the authenticity of the letter or the possibility that it was written by one of James' disciples and could reflect James' thought. But it would be presumptuous to say any more before studying its content. The results of such an analysis will have to be used carefully, since the information about James that we have is so limited and sometimes contradictory. The authenticity of the letter will certainly be reinforced, without being definitively demonstrated, if its content accords with what other sources teach us about James.

One of the most surprising aspects of the letter is its very rudimentary christology. Jesus is only mentioned twice. And these mentions hardly allow us to determine what the author thought of the person of Christ and his role. The resurrection and its significance are not mentioned anywhere. So we are far from the theological speculations of Paul or the Gospel of John. Some experts think that the very undeveloped christology of the letter indicates a work composed soon after the death of Jesus. Thus in their view it could reflect the conceptions of James or the Jerusalem church. Most scholars, though, who do not see the need to associate an undeveloped christology with a very primitive work, consider – rightly, it would seem – that there is no basis for such a conclusion. The eschatological character of the letter, with its conception of the imminence of the Last Judgment, could also suggest a primitive work connected with the Jerusalem church.[13] But this element is far from being decisive, since late texts sometimes emphasize the imminence of the Last Judgment. The conclusions that can be drawn from the main themes of the letter are more fruitful.

Woe to the rich!

The Letter of James is probably the writing in the New Testament in which the poor are most exalted and the rich are most severely condemned. Two long passages are particularly representative of the views of the author. In the first he attacks the partiality shown in favour of the rich in certain assemblies:

My brethren, show no partiality as you hold the faith of our Lord Jesus Christ, the Lord of glory. For if a man with gold rings and in fine clothing comes into your assembly, and a poor man in shabby clothing also comes in, and you pay attention to the one who wears the fine clothing and say, 'Have a seat here, please,' while you say to the poor man, 'Stand there,' or 'Sit at my feet,' have you not made distinctions among yourselves, and become judges with evil thoughts? Listen, my beloved brethren. Has not God chosen those who are poor in the world to be rich in faith and heirs of the kingdom which he has promised to those who love him? But you have dishonoured the poor man. Is it not the rich who oppress you, is it not they who drag you into court? Is it not they who blaspheme that honourable name by which you are called? If you really fulfil the royal law according to the scripture, 'You shall love your neighbour as yourself,' you do well. But if you show partiality, you commit sin, and are convicted by the law as transgressors (James 2.1–9).

The author is describing a situation in which the poor are treated less well than the rich. He is all the more indignant since God particularly exalts the poor as heirs of the kingdom of God. A more severe condemnation of the rich comes shortly before the end of the letter:

Come now, you rich, weep and howl for the miseries that are coming upon you. Your riches have rotted and your garments are moth-eaten. Your gold and silver have rusted, and their rust will be evidence against you and will eat your flesh like fire. You have laid up treasure for the last days. Behold, the wages of the labourers who mowed your fields, which you kept back by fraud, cry out; and the cries of the harvesters have reached the ears of the Lord of hosts. You have lived on the earth in luxury and in pleasure; you have fattened your hearts in a day of slaughter. You have condemned, you have killed the righteous man; he does not resist you (James 5.1–6).

To appreciate the views of the letter, we have to recognize that in the Hebrew Bible poverty is not generally a virtue nor wealth a vice. Material prosperity is supposed to be a reward for a virtuous life. The rich are most often condemned only when they have accumulated their possessions in a dishonest way or when they profit from their wealth to oppress or humiliate the weakest. However, we can note in some later texts of the Bible or in writings not included in the biblical canon a tendency to identify piety and poverty and to exalt the poor. Some psalms shows this view:

He raises the poor from the dust,
and lifts the needy from the ash heap,
to make them sit with princes,
with the princes of his people (Psalm 113.7–8).

The Psalms of Solomon, an extra-canonical work dating from the first century BCE, take up this notion:

> For you are good and merciful, you are the refuge of the poor (5.2).

> And God will have pity on the poor for the joy of Israel (10.6).

Some Qumran texts also reflect this tendency, which can be found in Matthew, and above all Luke, as well. Thus the remark 'Has not God chosen those who are poor in the world to be rich in faith and heirs of the kingdom . . . ?' (James 2.5) evokes the Beatitudes of Matthew and Luke, particularly the first Beatitude in Luke: 'Blessed are you poor, for the kingdom of God is yours.'

The rejection of riches is extreme and there is no appeal against it. The author is not content, as many biblical texts are, to condemn the rich who are remote from God. The rich are by definition sinners whose condemnation is certain. These curses recall those of I Enoch (94.6–11; 96.4–8; 97.8–10), and certainly evoke several passages in the Synoptic Gospels in which Jesus emphasizes the incompatibility between having possessions and the kingdom of God (Matt. 6.24; 19.16–26; Luke 16.13; 18.18–27; Mark 10.17–24), or condemns the rich inexorably, as in the Beatitudes of Luke:

> Woe to you that are rich, for you have received your consolation.
> Woe to you who are full now, for you shall hunger (Luke 6.24–25).

The author seems to be an heir to the tradition of the poor of Israel as this is expressed by Jesus in the Beatitudes. The members of the Jerusalem church, so closely associated with James, probably belonged to this tradition. According to the Acts of the Apostles, they shared their possessions and were so needy that they required the help of other communities. Paul speaks of the 'needs of the saints of Jerusalem who are in poverty' (Rom. 15.26). We have some reason to suppose that 'poor' was one of the words which the Jewish Christians of Jerusalem used to denote themselves. Moreover, as we have seen, scholars like H. D. Betz think that Matthew's 'Sermon on the Mount' and its equivalent in Luke derive from the views of the Jerusalem community. So it is very plausible that the passages we have considered could reflect James' views.

Let us see if the identification of the context of the letter allows us to confirm this hypothesis.

Some scholars, like Martin Dibelius in his great commentary, consider that the letter is no more than a series of moral exhortations with no reference to any specific situation. The scene in the assembly will only be a fictitious example. The condemnation of riches is not to be associated with any well-defined historical conditions. By contrast, Etienne Trocmé thinks that the author is expressing his indignation against the Pauline churches, in which the social inequalities are marked and respect for the rich is the order of the day:

> The pauperism of the author bristles against the favour thus done to the rich. The energy with which our writer reacts here, excessive at first sight, suggests that the social ideal of the Jerusalem church still affects him, at least in theory. He dreams of a church where, short of a complete sharing of possessions, a rigorous egalitarianism would mask the differences in fortune or rank existing between the faithful. By contrast, the letters of Paul and the second half of the book of Acts several times give the impression that, forced to a rapid break with the synagogue, the Pauline church relied on the well-to-do notables who gave them the places, the protection and perhaps the financial resources they needed to live . . . Thus it was above all in churches of this tendency that respect for a certain hierarchy and attachment to well-to-do brothers threatened to have an effect on worship.[14]

According to Etienne Trocmé, the letter will have been written towards the end of the first century by a Christian influenced by the social ideal of James and the Jerusalem community.

However, for other scholars, above all in American evangelical circles, the epistle, far from reflecting the situation of the Pauline churches twenty or thirty years after the death of James and Paul, is a perfect description of social and political conditions in Judaea at the time of James.[15] Josephus has left us with the picture of a Palestine affected by serious political, religious, economic and social troubles, especially after the death of King Agrippa I, which led to the war against the Romans. In this climate of anarchy, the great priestly families and their allies were actively involved in the exploitation of peasants already oppressed by the Roman occupation. They even enriched themselves at the expense of priests of modest standing by taking the tithes which were the latter's due.[16] These conflicts, aggravated by famines, favoured the development of endemic brigandry. The situation would reflect this situation of growing oppression of the poor and unjust enrichment of the powerful. The Christian communities of Palestine, which suffered from this exploitation, nevertheless had to show consideration for the more fortunate of their members in order to be able to benefit from their financial support. James, who according to the advocates of this view would be the author of the letter, or merely the writings which inspire it, shows his solidarity with the poor and is indignant at their treatment in the Christian communities. His condemnation extends to all the rich. However, he advises the poor not to try to change their condition by using violence. He recommends patience until the coming of the Lord:

> Be patient, therefore, brethren, until the coming of the Lord . . . As an example of suffering and patience, brethren, take the prophets who spoke in the name of the Lord. Behold, we call those happy who were steadfast.

James, like the prophets of old, rises up against oppression and injustice. But contrary to the zealots of his time, he rejects revolutionary violence. James B. Adamson sums up this portrait of James as follows: 'Yet despite his rejection of revolution, James is neither passively quietist nor blindly fatalistic: he has a vigorous social conscience, is sensitive to all types of discrimination and oppression, and does not hesitate to attack social ills whenever he sees them. At the same time, his approach is peaceful and nonviolent.'[17] According to some scholars, this attitude would have been one of the main reasons for the death sentence on James from the Sanhedrin (see Chapter 10).

Such a James would surely have sympathized with Martin Luther King or Emile Zola. But can this portrait, so seductive for social reformers, be deduced from the letter? Is this ingenious reconstruction convincing? We may doubt it. Palestine in the middle of the first century certainly did not have a monopoly of the oppression of the poor in the Roman empire. We even need a good dose of imagination to connect the episode of partiality in assemblies with the situation of the Christian communities in Palestine twenty or thirty years after the death of Jesus. The few details which suggest this region more specifically are not decisive.[18] However, a Palestinian origin cannot be ruled out. It would explain why Origen probably got to know the letter during his stay in Palestine. Such an origin does not, however, imply that James wrote the letter in the 40s or 50s.

Experts with equal competence may suggest quite different contexts for the composition of the letter, and this at least counsels caution. The attitude of the author towards rich and poor is certainly influenced by the tradition of the poor of Israel and by the words of Jesus as they are handed down in the Beatitudes of Matthew and Luke. Such an attitude can probably be attributed to James or to one of his disciples. But it is hardly possible to demonstrate this in a more affirmative way.

James and the law

Many scholars think that the position of the letter *vis-à-vis* the law is a decisive element in evaluating its authenticity. However, having noted the importance of the law for the author of the letter, they emphasize that he presents its ethical aspects without ever mentioning the ritual elements. Some conclude that the letter comes from a community in which the conflict over circumcision and questions of purity is in the past and the law is reduced to moral principles. Thus James, so preoccupied with questions of purity, would not be the author of the letter.

For other exegetes like J. B. Adamson and P. Davids, the letter's lack of interest in ritual questions would not be an obstacle to its authenticity.[19] It would merely indicate that James was an open and 'liberal' Jewish Christian, quite near to Paul. In their view 'the James who was very legalistic over the ritual aspects of the law, with whom the author of the letter is sometimes contrasted, is nothing but a fiction devoid of any historical reality'. But is it certain that the letter was composed by someone who accords only secondary, indeed negligible, importance to the ritual aspects of the law? The letter describes the law as 'the perfect law of liberty':

> But he who looks into the perfect law, the law of liberty, and perseveres, being no hearer that forgets but a doer that acts, he shall be blessed in his doing (1.25).

The expression 'perfect law of liberty', which has no precise equivalent in the New Testament, is particularly disconcerting and ambiguous. It can certainly refer to the Mosaic law. This is described as 'perfect' in Psalm 19 and in some non-biblical Jewish texts. Even if – as Martin Dibelius has shown – the concept of the law of liberty is of Stoic origin, it is not alien to early Judaism.[20] For some Stoics, human beings obtain liberty by living in accordance with the law which governs the cosmos. Philo of Alexandria, in whose eyes the principles of the Mosaic law reflect the order of nature, affirmed that to live under the law of Moses brought liberty. This notion also appears in rabbinic Judaism. According to *Pirqe Avot*, a collection of sentences dating from the second century, Rabbi Joshua ben Levi said 'that no man is free except he who gives himself to the study of the law'.[21] Moreover the notion of happiness in the practice of the law, which is already well expressed in Psalm 119, is very common in the Judaism of the first centuries of our era. Thus the expression 'perfect law of liberty' and the few lines which follow could well come from a Jew who had no connection with the Christian movement and lived in the first or second century.

However, given the indubitably Christian character of the letter, it is more probable that 'the perfect law of liberty' refers to the Mosaic law interpreted and made perfect by Jesus.

But this notion in turn can be understood in at least two ways. It can express a conception similar to that of the Gospel of Matthew, according to which the ritual precepts of the law are maintained. But it can also suggest the Pauline conception of the law of the Spirit, which brings freedom from the law of sin and death (Rom. 8.2). As in the Letter of Barnabas, this second interpretation will most often be understood as a liberation from the ritual constraints of the Mosaic law. Let us see if the longest passage on the law in the letter allows us to settle the matter:

> If you really fulfil the royal law, according to the scripture, 'You shall love your neighbour as yourself,' you do well . . . For whoever keeps the whole law but fails in one point has become guilty of all of it. For he who said, 'Do not commit adultery,' said also, 'Do not kill.' If you do not commit adultery but do kill, you have become a transgressor of the law (2.8–11).

The author attaches quite special importance to the precept 'You shall love your neighbour as yourself,' stated in Leviticus 19.18. This priority recalls the words of Jesus in Matthew 7.12/ Luke 6.31 and in Matthew 22.34–40/Mark 12.28–31/ Luke 10.25–28:

> So whatever you wish that men would do to you, do so to them; for this is the law and the prophets (Matt. 7.12).

> [A Pharisee] asked him a question, to test him. 'Teacher, which is the great commandment in the law?', and he said to him, 'You shall love the Lord your God with all your heart, and with all your soul, and with all your mind. This is the great and first commandment. And a second is like it, You shall love your neighbour as yourself. On these two commandments depend all the law and the prophets' (Matt. 22.35–40).

To consider love of neighbour as the essence, the summary or the royal commandment of the law certainly does not imply the abrogation of ritual aspects of the law, as is witnessed by the popularity of this conception in rabbinic literature. According to Rabbi Akiba, 'You shall love your neighbour as yourself' is the greatest principle of the law (Sifra 18.89b). A famous anecdote about two famous sages, contemporaries of king Herod, takes up the same idea.

A certain heathen came before Shammai and said to him:
'Make me a proselyte, on condition that you teach me the whole Torah while I stand on one foot.'
Thereupon he repulsed him with the builder's cubit which was in his hand.
When he went before Hillel, he said to him:
'What is hateful to you, do not do to your neighbour: that is the whole Torah, while the rest is commentary thereof. Go and learn it.'[22]

The rabbis, who were far from denying the ritual precepts of the Mosaic law, thus did not hesitate to see a moral commandment as its summary or essence.

The author of the letter then affirms the obligation to perform the whole law. A well-known passage from the 'Sermon on the Mount' in Matthew 5.17–19 (see p.122) immediately comes to mind.

Similarly Paul, in Galatians 5.3, emphasizes that everyone who is circumcised has to observe the whole law. We should note, however, that Paul uses precisely this argument to dissuade the Galatian Christians, who are of pagan origin, from having themselves circumcised. The author of James, like the author of the Gospel of Matthew, does not consider this obligation a constraint.

To indicate that the whole law must be observed, rabbinic literature often recalls that some apparently unimportant or insignificant ritual precepts must be respected with just as much attention as the great moral commandments. Thus James 2.10 suggests that the whole of the law, including its ritual aspects, must be observed. One could therefore expect the author in his demonstration to cite as an example someone who, while respecting the major commandments, ignores minor ritual precepts. The author would have concluded that this person was nevertheless a transgressor of the law. Now disconcertingly he appeals to two commandments in the Decalogue. To conclude that someone who avoids adultery but commits murder transgresses the law is a lame argument if one wants to emphasize that the law is one. In fact this example seems to show that the author is referring less to the obligation to observe the precepts of the law, both small and great, than to the theme of the twofold nature of human beings, who are subject to the spirit of evil as well as the spirit of good. The Testaments of the Twelve Patriarchs – a Jewish writing, according to some scholars of Essene origin, dating from the second half of the second century BCE – contain significant parallels:

> Another steals, commits injustice, exploits and has pity on the poor; he too has a double face, but all is wicked . . . He kills many people and has pity on some; that too is to have a double face, but all is evil (Testament of Asher 2.5–7).[23]

Be this as it may, in affirming that the law is one, the letter emphasizes the great moral commandments of the Decalogue and Leviticus (19.12–18),[24] which seem to constitute the essence of the perfect law of liberty. But can we conclude, as many experts do, that the author of the letter reduces the law to its moral precepts?[25] Like Andrew Chester, we may doubt this:

> The fact that nothing is said, for example, about food laws, circumcision, or the temple is not conclusive, since if James belongs to a firmly Jewish-Christian tradition, the natural assumption (unless it is specifically challenged) would be that Jewish practice and observance of the law would continue. Hence the silence here should not be over-interpreted: the question remains open.[26]

We can be more affirmative if we note that several more or less contemporary Jewish texts outside the Christian movement concentrate above all on the ethical aspects of the Mosaic law, ignoring or hardly mentioning its ritual aspect. That is the case with the *Sentences* of Pseudo-Phocylides, a series of moral exhortations derived mainly from Leviticus 19. The Testaments of the Twelve Patriarchs make so few references to the ritual precepts that many experts have long thought that they are a Christian text. However, since fragments have been discovered at Qumran, it is generally thought that the text as we have it is an originally Jewish work, to which some easily identifiable Christian interpolations have been added.

Thus there is nothing against supposing that the notion of the law expressed in the letter comes from a Jewish Christian who has remained faithful to the whole of the Mosaic law. This view, quite close to that of the Gospel of Matthew, could very well come from James or one of his spiritual heirs. The exaltation of the law can be interpreted as a reaction to Paul's critical conceptions. The expression 'perfect law of liberty' would be a response to the association made by Paul between the law and slavery:

> For freedom Christ has set us free; stand fast therefore, and do not submit again to a yoke of slavery (Gal. 5.1).

And that would not be the only major opposition between the letter of James and Paul.

James and Paul

The Letter of James is famous above all for its brief passage on justification. Following Martin Luther, many exegetes and theologians have criticized the letter for what they see as the anti-Pauline character of this passage. However, an increasing number of scholars think that the author of the letter is not attacking Paul, with whom he is in basic agreement, but a 'libertine' interpretation current in certain Pauline churches. Before discussing these questions, I shall cite the whole of the passage in question:

> What does it profit, my brethren, if a man says he has faith but has not works? Can his faith save him? If a brother or sister is ill-clad and in lack of daily food, and one of you says to them, 'Go in peace, be warmed and filled', without giving

them the things needed for the body, what does it profit? So faith by itself, if it has no works, is dead. But some one will say, 'You have faith and I have works.' Show me your faith apart from your works, and I by my works will show you my faith. You believe that God is one; you do well. Even the demons believe and shudder. Do you want to be shown, you foolish fellow, that faith apart from works is barren? Was not Abraham our father justified by works, when he offered his son Isaac upon the altar? You see that faith was active along with his works, and faith was completed by works, and the scripture was fulfilled which says, 'Abraham believed God, and it was reckoned to him as righteousness'; and he was called the friend of God. You see that a man is justified by works and not by faith alone. And in the same way was not also Rahab the harlot justified by works when she received the messengers and sent them out another way? For as the body apart from the spirit is dead, so faith apart from works is dead (James 2.14–26).

The Letter of James is beyond doubt responding to Pauline conceptions. Unquestionably, the formula 'a man is justified by works and not by faith alone' (James 2.24) refers to Galatians 2.16 and Romans 3.27–28:

You who know that a man is not justified by works of the law but through faith in Jesus Christ, in order to be justified by faith in Christ, and not by the works [the practice] of the law, because by works of the law shall no one be justified (Gal. 2.16).

Then what becomes of our boasting? It is excluded. On what principle? On the principle of works? No, but on the principle of faith. For we hold that a man is justified by faith apart from works of the law (Rom. 3.27–28).

Moreover the opposition between works and faith is so alien to traditional Jewish thought and so specific to Paul's theology that it is hardly conceivable that the author could have raised this question without any reference to Paul's ideas.

The author of the letter first of all thinks that the notion of faith cannot be dissociated from works. Without the latter, he writes, faith is dead. The obligation for Christians to put their principles into practice and the fact that they will be judged by the result are perhaps the main theme of the letter.[27] The author is very close to the biblical conception according to which faith (*emuna* in Hebrew) cannot be dissociated from its concrete manifestations.[28] In fact, the Hebrew concept translated 'faith' does not signify belief in a dogmatic truth, as in Christian confessions of faith; it expresses both faithfulness to God and his word and trust in God, i.e. the assurance that God will keep his promises to his people.

The Israelites show their faithfulness/faith by leading their lives in conformity with divine instructions. According to this conception it does not make sense to oppose works to faith. However, in Hellenistic Judaism the Greek word *pistis* which translates the Hebrew *emuna* also takes on the meaning of dogmatic belief, namely belief in one God. It is this conception that we find in Paul, but in the sense of belief in Jesus.

The author of the letter first refers to the notion of faith as belief. Belief in one God, the basic principle of Judaism, means nothing if it is not accompanied by actions which are the manifestation of that belief. We should note that the author, in a way apparently unexpected to anyone who attacks Pauline views, refers to monotheistic belief, common to Jews and Christians, and not to belief in Jesus Christ, which is specifically Christian. Then he uses the example of Abraham to show that faith, in the sense of faithfulness/trust, is inseparable from works. Abraham shows his faithfulness by agreeing to sacrifice his son on the altar. It is at that moment that the faith of Abraham becomes perfect: 'Now I know that you fear God, seeing you have not withheld your son, your only son, from me' (Gen. 22.12). It is in trials that the faith of Abraham has been tested and confirmed. Genesis 26.4–6 similarly emphasizes the faithfulness/obedience of Abraham:

> I will multiply your [Isaac's] descendants as the stars of heaven . . . because Abraham obeyed my voice and kept my charge, my commandments, my statutes and my laws.

For Genesis (22 and 26), as for the Letter of James, faith is recognized only by the doing of works. Faith without works is nothing.

In using this example of the sacrifice of Isaac, the Letter of James is certainly replying to the arguments drawn by Paul from Genesis 15 to prove that justification by faith alone derives from the holy scriptures. In Genesis 15 God promises Abraham numerous descendants. Then he justifies him because he trusts in this promise which could not be fulfilled in human terms because of the advanced age of his wife. Paul emphasizes that Abraham was justified before he performed the least work required by God, whether this was circumcision or the offering of his son Isaac. So he can affirm that Abraham was justified by faith without works.

Martin Luther, and many exegetes and theologians after him, concluded quite naturally from their reading of the letter that it was attacking the Pauline conception of justification by faith by defending that of justification by works. That earned it the somewhat infamous title 'strawy epistle'. Luther understands perfectly that Paul is criticizing above all the doctrine of justification by works of the law, i.e. the practice of the law, while the author of the letter suggests works of charity and piety. Nevertheless, Luther considers that justification by the practice of the law is a particular case of justification by works, which he defines as a doctrine of salvation according to which human beings, through their own meritorious actions, hope to gain their salvation by pleasing God. In his criticism of this doctrine, Luther likens the Jews who think that they can gain their salvation by scrupulous respect for the Mosaic law (the works of the law) to Catholics who have the same objective in accumulating good actions. For Luther, those who think that they can be saved by their own merits deprive God of his sovereign prerogative by transforming him into a debtor. This conception is the antithesis of the true Christine doctrine of justification by faith. Faith alone can put a person in a situation acceptable to God. By faith a person puts all his trust in God, hands himself over entirely to God's grace, accepts the Good News and its promises. We can thus easily understand Luther's hostility towards the Letter of James, which attaches so much importance to works.

However, Luther's opinion on Paul's thought, for a long time dominant above all in Protestant academic circles, has now been challenged by the new approach favoured by exegetes like E. P. Sanders[29] and J. D. G. Dunn.[30] Many Christian exegetes and theologians are increasingly ready to recognize, here following their Jewish colleagues, that the Jews of the first century did not seek to gain their salvation by accumulating good points through the scrupulous observance of the Mosaic law. They observed the Mosaic law because it was an essential element in the covenant with YHWH and accorded with his will. They very often accepted that their earthly works would not suffice at the judgment, where they would therefore have to rely on the grace and mercy of God. In fact Paul does not reproach the Jews for seeking their salvation in meritorious acts like the performance of precepts of the law, even if some passages in his letters could suggest this; in essence he charges them with not believing in Jesus Christ and the new economy of salvation brought by his death and his resurrection. In a word, he does not blame them for being Jews, but for not becoming Christians.

Similarly, Paul is not against his Jewish-Christian opponents because of the importance they attach to meritorious works. He criticizes them for not understanding the consequences of the death and resurrection of Jesus Christ for the conditions of salvation and for the role of the law of Moses, for the Jews and above all for the Gentiles. According to Paul, the death and resurrection allow all those who have faith in Christ, Jews and Gentiles, to be saved independently of their relation to the Mosaic law: 'a man is not justified by works of the law but only through faith in Jesus Christ' (Gal. 2.16). In Christ, the distinctions between Jews and Gentiles previously manifested by adherence to the law of Moses or rejection of it no longer exist (Gal. 3.28). Paul defines faith as belief that Jesus is Lord and that God has raised him from the dead (Rom. 10.9). While he is opposed to the practice of the law by pagan Christians, by contrast he emphasizes, several times, the importance of works of love, the manifestation of an authentic faith (Gal. 5.6, 13–25; I Cor. 13.13; Rom. 12.3–13, etc.). In the light of these considerations many contemporary exegetes think that Luther and those whom he has influenced have exaggerated the anti-

Paulinism of the Letter of James. Whereas Paul opposes salvation by faith to salvation by doing the law, the letter emphasizes that faith cannot be true faith unless it is accompanied by works of charity and piety. Paul, these exegetes add, would have approved of this idea, even if he would have put it differently. Thus either the author of the letter did not know Paul's thought well, or he is attacking the erroneous conceptions of certain disciples of the apostle to the Gentiles, who thought that having faith dispensed them from rigorous moral conduct.

The defenders of the first hypothesis generally think that James will have written the letter in the 40s, on the basis of incomplete information about Paul's thought. According to the supporters of the second hypothesis, the letter would not mention the debates relating to the practice of the law because it would date from a time after the death of James, when these questions had been settled in favour of an abandonment of the Mosaic law.

It would seem doubtful that the author of the letter did not understand Paul's thought well enough. As Gerd Lüdemann has indicated, he probably knew Galatians and Romans, the language of which he picks up almost exactly.[31] So the first hypothesis can be excluded. Nor can we seriously suppose that the author of the letter and Paul were largely in agreement. Such an interpretation is difficult to demonstrate, since what we know of James' thought is very incomplete, and Paul's doctrine is so complex or obscure that the experts hardly agree on its nature. In fact, regardless of the opinion of modern exegetes and theologians on relations between the thought of Paul and that of the Letter of James, it seems quite clear that its author did not think much of Paul's ideas on justification. Otherwise, why would he have used such anti-Pauline formulae and arguments? Why would he constantly have argued for the priority of works over faith? Why would he have emphasized the need to respect the whole law? The author criticizes Paul because Paul gives undue priority to belief over conduct. Some of Paul's statements must have seemed to him to be particularly dangerous for many of the faithful:

If you confess with your lips that Jesus is Lord and believe in your heart that God raised him from the dead, you will be saved (Rom. 10.9).

For 'every one who calls upon the name of the Lord will be saved' (Rom. 10.13, quoting Joel 3.5).

His position suggests a saying from the 'Sermon on the Mount':

Not everyone who says to me, 'Lord, Lord,' shall enter the kingdom of heaven, but he who does the will of my Father which is in heaven (Matt. 7.21).

Paul thought that after baptism, and under the influence of the Holy Spirit, the nature of new Christians would be transformed in such a way that they would have no difficulty in conforming with the will of God. The author of the letter was certainly not so optimistic about the effects of this transformation. He warned the Jewish-Christian communities which he was addressing of the dangers of Paul's ideas. It is not enough to believe in Jesus; it is also necessary to apply his teaching, including respect for the law. It is by this that everyone will be judged.

A Jewish-Christian testimony

The Letter of James is indubitably a complex and ambiguous document. There is no feature in it which allows us to reject it as inauthentic. However, the language, style and structure of the letter make it more probable that it was composed by a Hellenized Jewish Christian in the 60s or 70s. The redactor, who certainly inherited a number of traditions associated with James and the Jerusalem church, perhaps composed it on the basis of texts written by James. So this letter, too, perhaps allows us to learn some aspects of James' thought. One can emphasize in particular the exaltation of the poor and humble and the condemnation of the rich, a very positive attitude towards the law and its obligations, the priority accorded to works and the need to live in conformity to the teaching of Jesus. The letter presents a very different view of human salvation from that of Paul. Paul concentrates on the crucifixion and resurrection of Christ as basic eschatological and cosmological events which radically modify the role and nature of the Mosaic law and the conditions of salvation. According to the author of the letter, it is essentially following the teaching of Jesus that allows one to be saved.

Christians have to respect all the commandments of the law in a deep and exemplary way. Their conduct towards God and their neighbour must be perfect. The letter approves of constancy in trial, acts of charity, sincerity, mercy and poverty. It condemns jealousy, breaking one's word, pride, hypocrisy and slander. Believers have to approach God with humility, submit to him, unhesitatingly ask him for wisdom. They must not usurp God's place by judging their neighbours. These demands are addressed to a community living in expectation of the last judgment and the coming of the Lord.

Finally the letter reveals a Christian community nurtured by biblical traditions and fully integrated into the Judaism of its time. The notion of a separation between belief in Jesus and Judaism would certainly have been incomprehensible to its author.

The Death of a Just Man

Presumed innocent

The best evidence of the death of James that we have is the passage in Josephus, *Jewish Antiquities* 20, 197–203, which I quoted in the Introduction (above, p. 2). In 62, taking advantage of a vacancy in Roman power between the death of the procurator Festus and the arrival of his successor Albinus, the high priest Hanan, after convening a Sanhedrin, had James stoned along with some other people for transgressing the law. Josephus adds that this condemnation offended those inhabitants of Jerusalem who were the most moderate and most precise in observing the law. They secretly requested Agrippa II to order Hanan to stop behaving like this. Some even went to meet Albinus to let him know that Hanan had convened a Sanhedrin without his authorization, which he had no right to do. Albinus, furious, expressed his anger, urging Agrippa II to depose Hanan. We may recall that although Agrippa II had no jurisdiction over Judaea, which was then under Roman domination, he was nevertheless invested with power to nominate and dismiss high priests.

So the death of James occurred when for about fifteen years Palestine had been inexorably sunk in chaos and anarchy.[1] The troubles which broke out after the death of Agrippa I (44), when his kingdom returned to direct domination by Rome, were speedily repressed, and under the procuratorship of Tiberius Alexander (44–48) the province experienced a period of relative peace. The situation deteriorated with Cumanus[2] (48–52) and above all Felix (52–59/60), a procurator whose negligence was equalled only by his greed. The zealots, those fierce 'nationalists' whose zeal for the law would not tolerate the least pagan domination in the land of Israel, became increasingly active and popular. Since the armed bands which ravaged the countryside had temporarily been subjugated by Felix, violent opposition was demonstrated above all by the action of the *sicarii*. These last, armed with daggers, assassinated those who collaborated with the Romans – usually in the thick of dense crowds, so as better to disguise themselves. The high priest Jonathan, known for his moderate views, was among their victims.[3] Popular opposition also manifested itself in the form of those inspired 'prophets' who, like Theudas and the Egyptian (see above, pp.104–8), were convinced that God had sent them to restore Israel and would provide them with any necessary aid.

At the same time, serious internal disagreements were tearing the priestly class apart. In their struggle for power, the richest and most powerful priests launched a reign of terror with armed gangs. It was under the procuratorship of Felix that Paul was arrested by the Romans after being almost lynched by Jews who were particularly zealous for the law. Festus, Felix's successor, who was dismissed from his post by Nero, struggled to restore public order with more good will than success. Sicarii, brigands and false prophets continued to foment trouble and anarchy. It was shortly after the death of Festus that Hanan, who had recently been nominated high priest, saw a propitious moment to rid himself of James and some other opponents.

For a long time scholars have clashed over the motive for the condemnation of James as this can be deduced from Josephus' text. For most of them, the answer depends on explanations for the action of the most moderate and most precise observers of the law, i.e., according to Josephus' terminology, the Pharisees.[4] For some, the protests had nothing to do with the fairness of the verdict on James.[5] For others, the Pharisees were complaining because they thought the condemnation unjust.[6]

According to the first view, the Pharisees were offended and approached Agrippa II and Albinus because Hanan had not respected the procedure fixed by the Roman for the convening of the Sanhedrin. This interpretation is in part based on a different rendering of the passage generally translated 'for he had already acted unjustly before', namely 'for he had not performed the first stage correctly'. This variant would indicate that Hanan's fault was essentially that he convened the Sanhedrin in an irregular way.[7] We may be amazed that the doctors of the Mosaic law had scruples over procedural questions imposed by the Romans, which were completely alien to the law. Those who support this view retort that the Pharisees were acting in this way not out of an immoderate respect for the law imposed by the occupying power but in order to rid themselves of an enemy or to dissociate themselves from an action which was judged anti-Roman. This latter hypothesis has been developed by E. Mary Smallwood in particular:

> This gesture of independence, though no doubt welcomed by the nationalists, alarmed the more moderate Jews and the Pharisees, who, to avoid the possibility of being included in any punishment which Agrippa or the new procurator might mete out, hastened to dissociate themselves from it by complaining to both of them (secretly, for fear of nationalist reprisals), that Hanan had acted *ultra vires*.[8]

The action of the Pharisees *a priori* would not give us any explicit information about their position over the verdict itself. Nevertheless, the supporters of this interpretation often draw from it the fallacious conclusion that if the Pharisees were protesting for reasons of form, it meant that they were agreed on the basic fact, i.e. the condemnation itself. This conclusion can certainly fortify exegetes concerned to show that James did not observe the law very faithfully, or little inclined to accept any solidarity between James and the Pharisees. But it seems more reasonable to suppose that the latter disapproved of the verdict. Unless they were completely hypocritical or opportunist, they would hardly have been urged to complain about the high priest had they approved the condemnation of James.

Even if this first conception is not impossible, it is difficult to reconcile with the sense of Josephus' account. This clearly connects the nature of the verdict with the severity of the doctrine of the Sadducees,[9] to which Hanan adhered:

> Hanan the Younger ... had a proud character and remarkable

courage; he followed the doctrine of the Sadducees, who are inflexible in their perspective compared with the other Jews . . . Since Hanan was such a man and he believed that he had a favourable opportunity because Festus was dead and Albinus still on the way . . .

Hanan did not visibly seek to profit from the vacancy in power to achieve an anti-Roman gesture. Above all he wanted to have death sentences that the procurator would not have countenanced pronounced by the Sanhedrin in conformity with the Sadducean code. The Pharisees doubtless showed their discontent either because they judged James innocent or because, while judging him guilty, they did not think that his fault merited death. Josephus, by indicating the disagreement of the 'most precise observers of the law', probably wanted to emphasize not the irregularity of the convening of the Sanhedrin in terms of the rules imposed by the Romans but the injustice of the verdict in relation to the law of Moses as this was interpreted by the most widely-recognized experts. That those who complained to Albinus cited this faulty procedure can be explained by lack of interest on the part of the procurator in questions relating to their law and by their desire to have vengeance on Hanan.

Thus the most logical interpretation of the Josephus text suggests that the transgression of the law for which James was condemned to death was, according to the Pharisees, either non-existent or insufficiently serious to merit such punishment. That is why they protested. They did so in secret so as not to attract the wrath of a powerful adversary. We can certainly ask, along with many historians, whether the severity of the punishment did not conceal other motives than the supposed transgression of the law.

A truncated text?

It is possible that Josephus himself provided more information about the death of James, since we have some reason to suppose that the text of the *Jewish Antiquities* that we have does not correspond precisely to the original, which a copyist was allowed to truncate. In fact, according to Origen, Josephus considered the destruction of Jerusalem to be the well-deserved punishment of the Jews for the unjust death of James.

> The same author, although he did not believe in Jesus as Christ, sought for the cause of the fall of Jerusalem and the destruction of the temple. He ought to have said that the plot against Jesus was the reason why these catastrophes came upon the people, because they had killed the prophesied Christ; however, although unconscious of it, he is not far off the truth when he says that these disasters befell the Jews to avenge James the Just, who was a brother of 'Jesus the so-called Christ', since they had killed him who was a very righteous man.[10]

In the same work, Origen refers a second time (*Against Celsus* 2.13) to this judgment of Josephus. He also mentions it in his *Commentary on Matthew* (10.17). Strangely, the passage cited by Origen does not appear in the versions of Josephus that we have. To explain such an absence scholars have proposed three hypotheses: either Origen is wrong, or he has read a manuscript interpolated by a scribe, or Josephus in fact connected the death of James with the destruction of Jerusalem and its temple.

Many experts prefer the first hypothesis. In their view, Origen will have attributed to Josephus a commentary which he would have read in Hegesippus. Ancient authors often quoted texts from memory, since they did not have large libraries. It is true that their memory, which was very well trained, vastly exceeded that of modern scholars.[11] But they could certainly be wrong. Origen, quoting a passage from memory, would have attributed it to another author. Despite his immense intellectual faculties, Origen was certainly not shielded from such an error. But is it reasonable to suppose that he could have been confused about such a basic passage three times? Since Josephus only refers twice to Jesus and the first Christians, Origen, like all the church fathers, must have known the two passages in question perfectly.

So can we then suppose, as other scholars do, that Origen

possessed a version of the *Jewish Antiquities* edited by a Jewish-Christian copyist? This scribe, perhaps concerned to exalt James, would have thought it more credible to attribute the destruction of the temple to his martyrdom, which was relatively recent, than to the early death of Jesus. The main argument against this hypothesis is the difficulty of understanding why the copyist should only have focussed on James, while keeping the scepticism about Jesus expressed by Josephus according to Origen.

That leads us to consider the third hypothesis quite possible.[12] But in that case a satisfactory reply has to be given to two difficult questions. First of all, why did Josephus, who was not a Christian, attribute the fall of Jerusalem to divine punishment for the death of a man as just as James? Then, why did a Christian copyist later suppress a reference which was so flattering to James?

S. G. F. Brandon, who supposes that the Christian scribe will have suppressed a good deal of important information, has proposed an ingenious solution.[13] Basing himself on the Acts of the Apostles (6.7; 21.30), he thinks that numerous priests and other Jews, inspired by zealot ideas, had joined the Christian movement. These priests, who were poor and seditious, would have been among those whom the priestly aristocracy had deprived of their tithes, thus reducing them to famine.[14] Again according to Brandon, Hanan had James condemned because he supported the priests. The passages in Josephus suppressed by the copyist contained information to this effect. The reasons for the death of James as Brandon imagines them, though speculative, seem quite plausible. However, we may be surprised that Hanan took advantage of the absence of the procurator to proceed with executions of which the latter would doubtless have not disapproved.[15] Moreover, it seems surprising that the most moderate Jews complained about the condemnation of individuals who supported the zealot movement.

Brandon has no difficulty in responding to the second of the questions raised above. It is easy to understand how a Christian copyist could have wanted to suppress passages which presented James as a friend of the zealots. However, he has more difficulty in finding a satisfactory answer to the first. In his view, Josephus would have connected the fall of Jerusalem with the death of James because the latter had provoked the dismissal of Hanan, an energetic and brave man, capable of mastering the situation. This somewhat arbitrary answer hardly accords with what Josephus, according to Origen, would have written. Apparently it was not the dismissal of Hanan which he criticized but the unjust death of James. Moreover, the fall of Jerusalem was the simple consequence not of the death of James but of his punishment: this includes a moral judgment which Josephus doubtless would not have made had he considered James as a rebel or one of their supporters. If there is no proof that James and the deprived priests had been zealots, there is nothing to prevent our thinking that James criticized the greed of the priestly aristocracy, thus drawing its wrath upon himself.

So perhaps we should accept that Josephus, like other Jews of the time and despite his reservations about Jesus, held James in high esteem. He certainly could have seen his condemnation as at least one of the flagrant injustices which provoked the divine wrath, even if was not the only one. The protests of the more moderate people following this execution suggest that James, far from being a friend of the zealots, was more a supporter of peace. Perhaps Josephus thought that the death of such a figure was prejudicial to the opponents of the struggle against Rome. A Christian scribe could have wanted to edit the original text of the *Jewish Antiquities*, since in it James was held in higher esteem than Jesus and was particularly valued by part of the Jewish population of Jerusalem. At a point when relations between Jews and Christians were at best tense and at worst terrible, such good reports of the time of James could have been disturbing.

Even supposing that the Josephus text has been mutilated, it seems improbable that the original would have contained new features about the reasons for the death of James. Hanan doubtless profited from the absence of the procurator to have James condemned to death for religious reasons. The Pharisees and perhaps others who had great respect for the law thought the condemnation unjust or too harsh. They complained about the severity of the verdict to Agrippa II. Some of them, in order to have their revenge on Hanan, even protested to the new procurator, accusing the high priest of having acted irregularly over the Roman rules. Josephus suggests that some Pharisees showed, if not sympathy, at least some neutrality towards James and the Jerusalem church. This attitude is reflected in certain passages in the Gospels and Acts.[16] Let us see if Christian evidence tells us more about the death of James.

Confused evidence

There are several accounts of the martyrdom of James in Christian tradition.[17] Clement of Alexandria, quoted in Eusebius, is particularly brief:

> There were two persons named James: one, the Just, he who was cast down from the pinnacle and beaten to death with a fuller's club; the other, he who was beheaded.[18]

We should note that in this version James was not stoned, but beaten to death with a fuller's club after being thrown down from the temple. The fuller's club became a major feature of the iconography of James.[19] Hegesippus, also quoted by Eusebius, offers a much more detailed account:

> When, therefore, many also of the rulers were believers, there was an uproar among the Jews and Scribes and Pharisees, for they said, 'There is danger that the whole people should expect Jesus as the Christ.' Coming together, therefore, they said to James, 'We beg you, restrain the people, for it has gone astray to Jesus, imagining that he is the Messiah. We beg you to persuade all who come for the day of the Passover about Jesus, for we all put our trust in you. For we bear you witness, as do all the people, that you are just and that you do not accept the person of any. So persuade the multitude not to go astray over Jesus. For truly the people and we all put our trust in you. Stand, therefore, upon the pinnacle of the temple, so that from your lofty station you may be evident, and your words may easily be heard by all the people. For on account of the Passover all the tribes, with the Gentiles also, have come together.'

So the aforesaid scribes and Pharisees set James upon the pinnacle of the temple and cried aloud to him, saying, 'O just one, in whom we ought all to put our trust, since the people have gone astray after Jesus who was crucified, tell us what is the door of Jesus.' And he replied with a loud voice, 'Why do you ask me about the Son of Man, since he sits in heaven at the right hand of the mighty power, and shall come on the clouds of heaven?' And when many were fully persuaded and gave glory at the testimony of James and said, 'Hosanna to the son of David,' then once more the same scribes and Pharisees said among themselves: 'We do ill in affording such a testimony to Jesus. Let us rather go up and cast him down, that being afraid they may not believe him.' And they cried aloud, saying, 'Ho, ho, even the just one has gone astray!' And they fulfilled the scripture that is written in Isaiah, 'Let us take away the just – for he is troublesome to us. Therefore they shall eat the fruit of their doings.' Going up, therefore, they cast the just one down. And they said to each other, 'Let us stone James the Just.' And they began to stone him, for the fall did not kill him. But turning he kneeled down and said: 'I beseech you, O Lord God, Father, forgive them, for they know not what they do.' And while they thus were stoning him, one of the priests of the sons of Rechab the son of Rechabim, who had witness borne to them by Jeremiah the prophet, cried aloud, saying, 'Stop! What are you doing? The just one is praying on your behalf.' And one of them, a fuller, took the club with which he beat out the clothes, and brought it down on the just one's head. Thus he was martyred. And they buried him at the spot beside the temple, and his monument still remains beside the temple. He has become a true witness both to Jews and Greeks that Jesus is the Christ. And immediately Vespasian attacked them.[20]

Thus according to Hegesippus, James enjoyed considerable prestige among the Jews by virtue of his justice. Strangely, the scribes and Pharisees asked him to use his authority to persuade the crowd not to be led astray over Jesus. Far from speaking against Jesus, James the Just, perched on the pinnacle of the temple, bore witness to him and convinced many of his listeners.

Appalled, the scribes and Pharisees threw him from the top of the temple. Since he survived such an impressive fall, he was stoned and then finished off by a fuller's club.

Hegesippus' account as it appears in the *Church History* is an obscure and confused mixture of historical and legendary facts which it is difficult to separate from one another. It is equally difficult to determine whether Eusebius possessed the authentic text of Hegesippus or a version which had already been edited,[21] and to what degree he has retouched the text that he had in paraphrasing it. It is quite possible that the tradition about the popularity of James and the success of the Christian movement in Jerusalem has a historical basis. More surprising is the fact that the scribes and Pharisees asked James to deny his faith. Since Hegesippus probably did not invent such a ludicrous story, perhaps it contains a grain of truth, but so distorted that it has become unrecognizable.

The death of James after being thrown from the top of the temple seems very improbable. Contrary to the account by Josephus, his death seems due more to popular action than to a condemnation by the Sanhedrin. Responsibility for the crime is attributed to the Pharisees and the scribes, and not to the high priest. Along with most historians, we can conclude that Hegesippus' evidence has little historical value. The same goes for other Christian accounts[22] of the martyrdom of James derived from that of Hegesippus or a common source. The text of Josephus, laconic though it may be, seems much more trust-worthy.

Let us now see whether the circumstances of the death of James are illuminated by the first persecutions of the Christians by the Jewish authorities.

A settling of accounts in the temple

I have already mentioned several times the persecutions by the Jews of their fellow-believers who joined the Jesus movement. We have seen that the notion of persecution covers quite distinct situations, and that it ranged from annoyances, threats and calumnies, via corporal punishment like the thirty-nine lashes of the whip delivered by the synagogues, to murder, legal or illegal.

The persecutions mentioned in the letters of Paul and Acts can be put into four groups:

- the first persecutions of Peter and the apostles (Acts 4 and 5);
- the killing of Stephen and the persecution of the Hellenists (Acts 6.8; 8.3);
- the execution of James son of Zebedee and the imprisonment of Peter ordered by Agrippa I (Acts 12.1–18);
- the different persecutions suffered by Paul.

The first persecutions of the Jerusalem community, which were hardly brutal, seem to have been initiated by the high priest and the Sadducees. We have seen that they resulted above all from the annoyance and disquiet of the priestly authorities, caused by preaching based on the messianic exaltation of a crucified impostor. There is nothing that allows us to think that Peter and the apostles showed a critical attitude towards the law and the temple, for which they would have been punished.

The killing of Stephen, the first Christian martyr, remains surrounded by mystery despite the long account devoted to him by the Acts of the Apostles. It is possible that Stephen was lynched because of attitudes towards the law and/or the temple which were thought offensive, but this has not been established. His death probably prompted or forced other Hellenists to leave Jerusalem.

James son of Zebedee was certainly beheaded on the orders of Agrippa I, king of Judaea, for political reasons. Though Agrippa seems to have sought to favour the Sadducees during his reign, it is difficult to determine to what degree they were associated with James' execution.

The sometimes violent opposition encountered by Paul during his missionary journey and on his last visit to Jerusalem is easier to understand, thanks to his letters. Most of the Jews who did not become Christians must have criticized him in the same way as his Jewish-Christian opponents, with no mitigating circumstances. Doubtless they criticized his abandonment of certain Mosaic precepts while he was living among the pagan Christians (I Cor. 9.19–23), and his radical reinterpretation of the role of the Torah in the history of Israel. Rumours circulated that he was forcing the Jews to renounce their ancestral customs

(Acts 21.21). On being recognized in the Jerusalem temple by Diaspora Jews, he barely escaped lynching.

We have noted the great variety of persecutions, of those responsible for them, and of their motives. These more or less severe persecutions were initiated by the high priest and his allies in the Sanhedrin, by King Agrippa I, or by the crowd. Their motives were sometimes religious and sometimes political. It seems clear that the condemnation of James, contrary to that of his namesake the son of Zebedee, can hardly be attributed to political behaviour which was judged seditious. Similarly James, unlike Paul and perhaps Stephen, probably did not cause offence over the law. However, his condemnation may be connected with the persecutions of Christians in two ways.

It is possible that James, as the supreme authority of the church, was held responsible for the transgressions of the law of which Paul was accused. Hanan would have chosen a favourable moment to punish him. According to Etienne Trocmé,[23] it will have been the zealots who forced Hanan to put James to death. But Hanan's fiery and autocratic character, as it emerges from Josephus' writings, hardly makes such pressure necessary. This interpretation of the death of James suggests a plausible explanation for one of the enigmas in Hegesippus' account. The high priest perhaps asked James not to deny his faith in Jesus, but to break solidarity with Christians of Jewish origin who were too lax over the law and with pagan Christians, and he refused to do this. The Pharisees would have thought it particularly unfair that James was condemned for transgressions of the law which he himself had not committed.

We can also suppose that the condemnation of James reflects the hostility of Hanan towards the family of Jesus and his other disciples, who continued to revere an insolent impostor whose death had been approved by Hanan's father and brother-in-law. Furthermore, we may think that the high priest's hostility was exacerbated by the success of James' missionary activity among the Jews of Jerusalem. Similarly, James and other Christians, like Jesus, perhaps criticized the high priest and the priestly aristocracy vigorously for their improper practices and their greed.

Most scholars suppose that the other individuals killed at the same time as James were Christians. This is not the opinion of Maurice Goguel, who thinks that those punished along with James were not his fellow-believers;[24] otherwise the Christian tradition would doubtless have preserved their names. Goguel thus supposes that Hanan's action was not aimed specifically at Christians, but at rivals: 'Since it was only James who was seized by the high priest, James' personal influence, not that of the church, must have alarmed him.'[25] Goguel even sees this execution as the consequence of a rapprochement between the church and Judaism. It is because James' influence went beyond the bounds of the Christian community that the high priest wanted to get rid of him. While this interpretation is not impossible, it is still speculative.

In fact, Hanan must surely have had good reasons for getting rid of James. It is probably futile to try to separate his personal animosity towards James from his hostility to Christians. If we want to make sense of the tradition transmitted by Hegesippus, James was perhaps regarded by the Christians as the high priest of the renewed cult of the eschatological Israel. This was doubtless not appreciated by the high priest in office.

However, no matter what the precise reasons for the condemnation of James may have been, his death evidently had an effect on the development of the young Christian movement.

Conclusion

The Legacy of James

The heirs

James was the most eminent representative of a primitive church deeply rooted in the Jewish tradition. He regarded his brother Jesus as the eschatological agent chosen by YHWH to proclaim the imminent arrival of the kingdom of God, and to call on the children of Israel to repent. This new era in which the will of God would be respected would see the restoration of Israel. James awaited the return of Jesus, exalted to the right hand of God after his resurrection. His return would signal the resurrection of the dead, the judgment by God and the inauguration of his kingdom. Jesus, like a new Moses, had revealed the true and definitive interpretation of the law, which was to be put into practice with the utmost rigour. James thought that, through Jesus, the promise made to Israel was in process of being fulfilled. Known for his faithful observance of the law, he could not conceive that the role and the importance of the law could have changed. Apart from his belief in the exceptional status and mission of Jesus and some specific ritual practices, nothing distinguished him from many of the Jews of his time. He regarded himself as a pious Jew, a member of the Israel of the end-time. He would certainly have been surprised had someone told him that he adhered to a new religion.

James was opposed to Paul and his message, which implied a redefinition of the identity of Israel and the role of the law. Paul envisaged a unified community of Jews and Gentiles which transcended the traditional frontiers and the specific character of Judaism. James thought this conception unacceptable. Perhaps he thought that there was a risk that it would transform a renewal movement within Judaism into a new religion cut off from its roots. James is often regarded as the symbol of a fossilized Christian community, incapable of perceiving the radical character of the message of Jesus and all the implications of his resurrection. James' incomprehension is often attributed to the fact that he was not a disciple of Jesus before the resurrection. We have seen that this assertion is far from being certain. Moreover if James was not perhaps moving in the direction of history, there is nothing that allows us to think that he did not transmit faithfully the role and the message of Jesus, which he had interpreted in conformity with traditional Jewish conceptions. At the time of his execution the communities who recognized his authority beyond doubt constituted the great majority of the Christian world.

The movement of Jesus' disciples took the death of James very hard. It is perhaps no chance that it has left more historical traces than that of Peter or Paul. With the disappearance of James, the Christian community lost a leader whose authority and decisions were respected widely, if not unanimously. Paul's example shows how difficult it was, even for such an energetic and talented preacher as he was, to depart permanently from the line of conduct laid down by James and the church of Jerusalem. Simon, son of Clopas, a cousin of Jesus and James, was then nominated head of the Jerusalem church. However, it is doubtful whether he enjoyed the same prestige and the same authority as his predecessor.

The destruction of Jerusalem and its temple in 70 certainly put an end to the undisputed primacy of the mother church and his leader. Regardless of whether the majority of the members of this church perished during the capture of Jerusalem, as S. G. F. Brandon supposes, or whether they could have taken refuge in Pella,[1] as a disputed tradition affirms, the fact remains that the destruction of Jerusalem marked the beginning of the irreversible decline of its church. A Jewish-Christian community re-formed in Jerusalem soon after the capture of the city by the Romans, but it never regained the pre-eminence or the prestige which it had before the war. Thus Christianity lost its geographical, spiritual and doctrinal centre of gravity. The churches of Antioch, Rome and Alexandria gained increasing autonomy and influence. When after the revolt of Bar Kokhba

(132–135) Jerusalem became a pagan city forbidden to Jews, under the name of Aelia Capitolina, the local church trans-formed itself into a Gentile community, thus breaking with its Jewish-Christian heritage.

It is undeniable that almost all the Christian texts dating from the last three decades of the first century and a large part of those composed at the beginning of the second century show the massive influence of Jewish concepts and forms of thought. If we follow Cardinal Daniélou in conceiving of Jewish Christianity as a form of Christian thought which expressed itself in frameworks borrowed from Judaism,[2] there is no doubt about its dominant character up to the middle of the second century. On the other hand, if Jewish Christianity is defined, as I have defined it, in terms of Jewish observance and identity, its importance after the fall of Jerusalem becomes much more diffi-cult to evaluate.

According to a widespread view, the destruction of Jerusalem in 70 led to the marginalization of the Jewish Christians in a church which had largely accepted the view of Paul and was increasingly dominated by Christians of pagan origin. Maurice Goguel sums up the common view like this:

From the time when the Christian community took refuge at Pella, the mist which covers the history of Palestinian Christianity grows still thicker. It will be found that for two or three centuries or a little longer Jewish Christianity remained only as the sect of Ebionitism and vegetated, surviv-ing by itself before disappearing, 'obscurely and miserably', as Mgr Duchesne says.[3]

Other commentators recall that the Jewish Christians were expelled from the synagogues controlled by the rabbis, the heirs of the Pharisees, by means of the *Birkat Haminim*[4] (benediction against the heretics). According to this interpretation, we would then be seeing the separation between Judaism and Christianity. The Jewish Christians, rejected by the Jewish communities and increasingly less tolerated by the 'mainstream church', would thus have had the choice between three main options: to return to the Jewish synagogue, abandoning their faith in Jesus Christ;

to become integrated into the mainstream church, and stop observing the Mosaic law; or to form separate communities on the periphery of the mainstream church in which the law continued to be practised.

Those who chose the first two options left no trace. Those who adopted the third are known to us under the name of Ebionites or Nazarenes. Fossilized remnants of the primitive church, they were soon regarded as heretics.

Such a panorama, or at all events its chronology, is increasingly being put in question by contemporary exegetes and historians. While the crisis of 70 doubtless reduced the importance of the Jewish Christians, it seems probable that they were able to maintain their supremacy, if not numerical, at least ideological, for some decades yet, establishing beliefs and practices. According to a happy expression of Jacob Jervell's, they formed a 'mighty minority'.[5] This novel conception largely derives from a new interpretation of several texts of this period, including the Gospels of Matthew and Luke. For a long time the majority of exegetes thought that the Gospel of Matthew came from a community detached from the Mosaic law. It was supposed that numerous passages which proclaimed the observing of the law were 'de-activated' traditions, since the members of this community had abandoned the ritual commandments of the Mosaic law and retained only its moral precepts.

Today, more and more commentators think that the author of this Gospel was a Jewish Christian who respected the whole of the law as Jesus had interpreted it.[6] He regarded himself as a Jew and thought that the Christian movement made up the true Israel. His community, essentially composed of Jewish Christians, confronted the rabbinic synagogues, doubtless with very limited success, in order to gain new members from among the Jews. It tried, perhaps still timidly, to convert pagans. It is difficult to discover whether or not it required circumcision and practice of the Mosaic law from baptized pagans.

Similarly, rejecting the traditional opinion[7] that the Gospel of Luke and Acts were composed by a pagan Christian belonging to a community detached from the Mosaic law, more and more exegetes think that Luke was a Jew, or a markedly Judaized godfearer, who belonged to a church in which the Jewish

Christians were numerous.[8] In this community, Christians of Jewish origin continued to observe the Mosaic law, while the former pagans respected the obligations imposed by the Apostolic Decree. The Jewish Christians certainly formed the dominant ideological element which fixed beliefs and practices in this community. The Didache, a text from the second half of the first century, also comes from a mixed community:

> See that no one leads you astray from this way of instruction, for he teaches you without God. If you can bear the whole yoke of the Lord, you will be perfect; if you cannot, do what you can. As for food, take what you can bear, but keep strictly from meat offered to idols: that is worship of dead gods.[9]

In this community the ideal for Christians coming from the Gentile world was to 'bear the whole of the yoke of the Lord', i.e. to become Jews, but if they could not, they were asked to 'Judaize' as much as possible, above all over food. Meat offered to idols was absolutely forbidden, as was stipulated by the Apostolic Decree. We may be allowed to suppose that this policy was inspired by the ideas of James.

Texts like the Letter of Jude, II Peter, the Apocalypse of John and the Letter of James certainly come from communities which were totally or largely Jewish Christian, and these communities showed a great diversity of beliefs and practices.

Jewish Christians were numerous above all in Palestine, in Syria, in Jordan and very probably in Egypt. The origin of the Christian community in Egypt is one of the great mysteries of the history of primitive Christianity. We know almost nothing about the church of Alexandria before the end of the second century. The tradition which attributes its foundation to the evangelist Mark, the companion and disciple of Peter, is probably legendary. The Acts of the Apostles, which does not show the least interest in the expansion of the church in Egypt, nevertheless mentions 'a Jew named Apollos, a native of Alexandria', who preached in Ephesus (Acts 18.24–26). According to Luke he was 'an eloquent man, well versed in the scriptures'. However, he knew only the baptism of John and, if he 'spoke and taught accurately the things concerning Jesus', Priscilla and Aquila had to explain the Way to him more accurately. Luke clearly did not approve of the doctrine of Apollos. He is also mentioned in I Corinthians 1.12 as one of the preachers to whom the Christians of Corinth appealed.

There is hardly any doubt that a powerful Christian community formed rapidly in Egypt, where almost a million Jews were living out of a total population of between seven and eight million.[10] As S. G. F. Brandon suggests, it is probable that the church of Alexandria, which had a Jewish-Christian majority, was closely dependent on the Jerusalem church. That is perhaps the reason why this region never figures in Paul's missionary plans. According to Brandon, numerous Jewish Christians from Palestine would have joined this church after the fall of Jerusalem. The Gospel of the Hebrews, which gives James the privilege of the first appearance of Jesus, doubtless comes from Alexandrian Christianity. Most Jewish Christians of Alexandria probably suffered the fate of almost all the Jews of Egypt. They were decimated in the great revolt of 115–117.

The Jewish Christian communities of Palestine were considerably weakened by the Bar Kokhba revolt and its repression. Justin, the great Christian apologist who was born in Palestine around 100, attests persecutions by Bar Kokhba of the Christians who refused him allegiance.[11] We may suppose that the Roman repression drew little distinction between the Jewish Christians and the other Jews.

The domination of the Jewish Christians in the church came to be increasingly contested from the beginning of the second century on. The pagan Christians, who had a vast majority in many communities, sought to make their point of view heard and wanted to mark their distance from a Jewish world which rejected them. A number of former pagans came to conceive of Christianity as a religion separate from Judaism, some even wanting to cut the ties completely by rejecting the Old Testament. The Jewish Christians, markedly affected by the catastrophes in Egypt and Palestine, were then rapidly marginalized in a largely pagan Christian church.

One passage from Justin's *Dialogue with Trypho*, dating from the second century, which is full of information, reveals to what extent the position of the Jewish Christians in the church had deteriorated in a few decades. Justin, who came from Palestine and taught in Ephesus and in Rome, knew the Jewish and Christian worlds of his time well. In this work, he enters into dialogue with the (imaginary?) Jew Trypho:

Trypho: But if some one, knowing that this is so, after he recognizes that Jesus is the Christ, and has believed in him and follows him, wishes also to observe these [Mosaic] institutions, will he be saved?

Justin: In my opinion, Trypho, he will be saved if he does not strive in every way to persuade other men – I mean those Gentiles who have been circumcised by Christ and freed from error – to observe the same things as himself, telling them that they will not be saved unless they do so . . .

Trypho: You could say 'In my opinion such a man will be saved' only if there are people who claim that such will not be saved.

Justin: There are such people, and people who do not venture to have any dealings with or to extend hospitality to those who have been mentioned. I do not agree with them. But if some, through narrow-mindedness, wish to observe such institutions as were given by Moses . . . as well as hoping in this Christ . . . yet choose to live with the Christians and the faithful, not inducing them either to be circumcised like themselves, or to keep the Sabbath, or to observe any other such ceremonies, then I think that we ought to accept them and associate with them . . . But if, Trypho, some of your race, who claim to believe in this Christ, compel those Gentiles who believe in this Christ to live in all respects according to the law given by Moses, or choose not to associate with them . . . I do not acknowledge them. But I believe that even those who have been led astray by them to observe the legal dispensation along with their confession of God in Christ will certainly be saved if they continue to confess the Christ of God. However, I firmly dispute that those who have confessed and known this man to be Christ, yet have gone back for some reason to the legal dispensation, and have denied that this man is Christ, and have not repented before death, shall be saved.[12]

At the Council of Jerusalem, the Jewish Christians asked themselves whether Christians from among the Gentiles could be saved if they were not willing to be circumcised and to observe the Mosaic law. A century later, it was the pagan Christians who were asking themselves whether a Christian who observed the law of Moses could gain his salvation. This is an amazing reversal of the situation. Justin, contrary to others, accepts that such Christians could be saved unless they forced pagan Christians to live in accordance with the law of Moses. Similarly, whereas a century earlier numerous Jewish Christians hesitated about having dealings with pagan Christians, now many pagan Christians were refusing to associate with Christians of Jewish origins. The pagan Christians visibly dominated the church in the middle of the second century and fixed the rules. However, the Jewish Christians were far from representing a negligible number of people. Some, as Justin tells us, were sufficiently influential or convincing to prompt pagan Christians to become proselytes.

We may also note that the Jewish Christians did not agree on the attitude to adopt to non-Jewish Christians. Some required circumcision and the practice of the law from them; others agreed to associate with them even if they were not circumcised. A century later, we find the same positions as at the incident at Antioch, which clearly shows that relations between Jewish Christians and pagan Christians had not found a solution which was unanimously recognized. Justin also mentions the case of Christians of Gentile origin who, after adopting the Mosaic law, have denied Christ and become 'orthodox' Jews again. He thus indicates that the frontiers between pagan Christianity, Jewish Christianity and 'orthodox' Judaism were very permeable.

Justin suggests that the Christian communities could be divided into four major categories over observance of the law:

- communities which were totally detached from the Mosaic law, in which Jewish Christians were not tolerated unless they had given up living according to the law of Moses;
- mixed communities in which some members practised the law without forcing or urging others to follow them;
- mixed communities, probably predominantly Jewish-

Christian, in which the pagan Christians were urged to become Jewish proselytes;
– communities to which only Christians who lived according to the law of Moses were admitted.

In time, the communities of the first type largely established themselves and the others either disappeared or became very much minorities – apart from certain areas of Syria, Palestine, Transjordan and probably Arabia.

We still do not have a very good idea of the theological views of the Jewish Christian communities. Whereas the fathers of the mainstream church have left us a voluminous literature, as direct evidence of the doctrines of the Jewish Christians we have only some extracts from the Gospels that they used and the Pseudo-Clementine literature, which has been largely revised and is difficult to interpret. It is also probable that some Jewish-Christian writings have been preserved by being integrated into Islamic texts. That is doubtless the case with the Jewish-Christian source used by the Muslim author of the Gospel of Barnabas,[13] which we know only through a version in Italian dating from the sixteenth century. Shlomo Pines also thinks that he has identified a Jewish-Christian source in a text of 'Abd al-Jabbar.[14]

Sometimes the church fathers mention the Jewish Christians, frequently called Ebionites, and their doctrines. But these are usually polemical texts, often ill-informed and sometimes confused. The beliefs and practices of the Jewish Christians, which have sometimes evolved over time, hardly seem homogeneous.[15] In general the church fathers distinguished two categories of Jewish Christians. The first thought that Jesus had been a man among men, born of Joseph and Mary, adopted and consecrated by YHWH as *Christos* at his baptism by reason of his exceptional justice (his piety and his other meritorious acts). The second, described as Nazarenes by Epiphanius and Jerome,[16] less heretical by the criteria of orthodoxy, accepted that Jesus was born of a virgin and the operation of the Holy Spirit. However, they hardly seemed to agree on his possible pre-existence or on the character and extent of his divine nature. Most Jewish Christians, with the exception of the Nazarenes of

Epiphanius and Jerome, rejected the writings of Paul, whom they considered an apostate. They contrasted the true doctrine which James, Peter and the other disciples received from Jesus himself with the false doctrine which Paul had received after a doubtful vision. These communities generally attributed a very elevated status to James.

The majority of Christian heresiologists connected the birth of these Jewish-Christian sects with that of the Gnosticizing heresies at the end of the first century and beginning of the second. Origen, more perceptive, noted that Jewish Christianity, far from representing a late deviation, went back to the first Christians:

> He [Celsus] asserts that 'deluded by Jesus, they have left the law of their fathers, and have been quite ludicrously deceived, and have deserted to another name and another life'. He failed to notice that Jewish believers in Jesus have not left the law of their fathers, for they lived according to it . . . Moreover, Peter seems to have kept the customs of the Mosaic law for a long time, as he had not learnt from Jesus to ascend from the letter of the law to its spiritual interpretation . . . It was appropriate that those sent to the circumcision should not abandon Jewish customs.[17]

While there is hardly any doubt that the Jewish-Christian movements of the second, third and fourth century were the heirs of the primitive church of Jerusalem, the reconstruction of the beliefs and doctrines of this community from the uncertain and heterogeneous information that we have is a highly speculative exercise. It is probable, as James D. G. Dunn,[18] Hans-Joachim Schoeps[19] and other experts think, that the anti-Pauline Ebionites with an adoptionist[20] christology were the more direct heirs of James and the earliest church. However, Ray Pritz has recently argued that the Nazarenes described by Epiphanius and Jerome were the true descendants of the primitive community of Jerusalem, the Ebionite current forming after a schism shortly after the migration to Pella.[21] This theory, which affirms the orthodox christology of the primitive community and the absence of major antagonisms between it and Paul, is very speculative, since it is largely based on confused and late evidence dating from the end of the fourth century. Nevertheless it suggests that the diversity of later Jewish-Christian movements to some degree reflects the diversity of currents within the primitive church.

Not all Christians had the same tolerance as Justin. The heirs of the primitive Jerusalem community were quite often regarded as heretics. For Jerome,[22] the Jewish Christians were neither Jews nor Christians, while Epiphanius[23] thought that they were only Jews and nothing more.

The Jewish Christians, who laid claim to their Jewish identity, had long formed one of the movements which were struggling for supremacy within the Jewish community.[24] However, over time their chances of success diminished. The Messiah whom they proclaimed still had not returned and the movement which claimed him was more flourishing among the Gentiles than among the Jews. None of that can have helped the Christian mission to the Jews. When heterodoxy was no longer tolerated, with the victory of the rabbinic movement in the third or fourth century most Jews regarded the Jewish Christians as heretics.

They did not disappear completely from the historical scene. We see them reappear on the occasion of an event of considerable importance, the birth of Islam. In fact, as the historian of religion Hans-Joachim Schoeps wrote, Islam indubitably brought together the Jewish-Christian heritage:

> There is no doubt about the indirect dependence of Muhammad on Jewish Christianity. The result of this is a paradox with a truly world-historical dimension; while Jewish Christianity disappeared in the Christian church, by contrast it was preserved in Islam, where it has found a place to our day in some of its directing impulses.[25]

Islam took up the Ebionite notions of prophetic succession and the true prophet – this no longer being Jesus, but Muhammad. Schoeps, as Henry Corbin emphasizes,[26] was certainly right in thinking that the revelation of the Qur'an was inspired by the Jewish Christianity of Jerusalem. However, he was probably wrong to suppose, like most scholars, that the

Jewish-Christian communities disappeared in the fifth century. Some of them seem to have been very much alive at the moment of the genesis and development of Islam.

An embarrassing figure

The image and prestige of James in large measure followed the vicissitudes of Jewish Christianity. We have seen that the Jewish-Christian communities had especially exalted him. His primacy clearly appears in the Gospel of the Hebrews and in the Clementine *Homilies* and *Recognitions*. In the Clementine *Homilies*, Peter recognizes the supremacy of James, whom he calls 'the lord and bishop of the holy church'.[27] He ends a letter containing his recommendations with the phrase: 'I have just indicated clearly what has seemed to me good: for you, my lord, to take as is fitting the measures that you judge opportune.'[28] He proclaims that all teaching must be approved by James: 'That is why, above all, remember to flee every apostle, doctor or prophet who has not previously submitted his preaching carefully to James called the brother of my Lord, and charged with governing the church of the Hebrews in Jerusalem.'[29] Granted, these texts contrast the true teaching of James and Peter with the lies propagated by Paul. In the Clementine *Recognitions*, Jesus himself designates James his successor.[30] James was also the object of great veneration in some Gnostic communities who chose him as patron. Far from indicating that James professed Gnostic ideas, this shows rather the Jewish-Christian origin of such groups. We can easily imagine how Jewish Christians, after the destruction of the temple and the rejection of Jesus by almost all Israel, denied their Jewish roots. Moreover since Christ delayed returning to earth, they would have spiritualized the notion of the kingdom of God.

The mainstream church could not ignore James either; he is one of the rare figures among the first Christians to be mentioned several times in the New Testament. Moreover, thanks to Hegesippus and Clement of Alexandria, and to Eusebius who quotes them, several traditions emphasizing the importance of James were disseminated widely in the Christian world. The pagan Christian church of Jerusalem, which certainly handed on its traditions to Hegesippus, continued to honour James, its 'first bishop'. With the spread of the liturgy which bears his name in the Eastern churches, James maintained an effective presence. Moreover the Jerusalem church was able to benefit from the authority of James to improve its status. Initially subordinate to Caesarea, at the Council of Chalcedon (451) the episcopate of Jerusalem was elevated to the rank of patriachate, thus joining Rome, Antioch, Constantinople and Alexandria.

However, for the master-minds of the mainstream church, James became a source of embarrassment, a kind of anomaly in the history of the church as they wanted to reconstruct it. First of all, James was everywhere called brother of the Lord, whereas Jesus was no longer supposed to have had brothers. Secondly, he was difficult to fit into the scheme of apostolic succession, according to which Jesus had handed down his authority and the true doctrine to the twelve apostles, who had themselves established bishops to govern the different churches. The pre-eminence of James as it emerges from an impartial reading of the New Testament and other traditions does not fit well with the primacy of Peter and other apostles. To defend it could only displease the church of Rome, which justified its pre-eminence by that of Peter, its presumed founder. In his classic work on the apostolic succession, Arnold Ehrhardt shows how the Jewish-Christian tradition of the primacy of James, handed down in particular by Hegesippus, was swept away by the defenders of the pre-eminence of Peter and Rome:

> Irenaeus . . . tacitly dropped the primacy of St James, who is so conspicuously absent from his work against all the heresies. There is no doubt that Rome had, at that time [around 200], a doctrine of the succession of her Popes after St Peter and St Paul, which the Roman Church was not prepared to subordinate to the primacy of St James, especially as his succession had been interrupted by the destruction of Jerusalem under Hadrian.[31]

Furthermore, the nature and source of the authority of James, who was not generally considered to be one of the Twelve, left the church fathers particularly perplexed, as we can see by reading Eusebius' *Church History*. Lastly, James, the supporter of observing the Mosaic law and of the separation between Jewish Christians and pagan Christians, could hardly have been pleasing to a church whose origin was above all pagan and detached from the law. James was certainly against the grain of history. So he was relegated to the role of figurehead.

The ingenious Jerome found a solution which settled the 'James problem' for more than fifteen centuries in the Roman Catholic Church. By supposing that James was only a first cousin of Jesus, he resolved the question of the kinship between James and Jesus. By identifying him with James, son of Alphaeus, one of the Twelve, Jerome also found an appropriate place for him in the hierarchy of the first Christians. The sources of James' authority were thus defined better, and his subordination to Peter was well established. Jerome's not very rigorous demonstrations were enough to convince those who had no need to be convinced. For centuries and centuries, James has vegetated in a semi-obscurity which is slowly beginning to dissipate.

Notes

Introduction

1. Flavius Josephus, *Jewish Antiquities* 18, 63–64.
2. Ibid. 20, 198–203.
3. For this question see Louis H. Feldman, *Josephus and Modern Scholarship (1937–1980)*, Berlin: De Gruyter 1984, 704–7. A notable exception is the historian Tessa Rajak in *Josephus*, London: Duckworth 1983, 131.
4. John Dominic Crossan, *Jesus. A Revolutionary Biography*, San Francisco: HarperSanFrancisco 1994, 133–6.
5. Origen, *Against Celsus*, 1.47, translated by Henry Chadwick, Cambridge: Cambridge University Press 1956. Origen takes up the same idea in 2.13 and in his *Commentary on Matthew*.
6. Eusebius, *Church History* 2, 23, 19–20.
7. Jerome, *De viris illustribus*, notice on James the brother of the Lord.
8. It is generally accepted that the author of the Acts of the Apostles is the author of the Gospel of Luke. I shall call the authors of the Gospels Matthew, Mark, Luke and John, with no prejudice to their real identity.
9. The traditions relating to James in the early church have been described and analysed in Scott Kent Brown, *James: A Religio-Historical Study of the Relations between Jewish, Gnostic and Catholic Christianity in the Early Period through an Investigation of the Traditions about James, the Lord's Brother*, PhD thesis, Brown University 1967; Martin I. Webber, *Iakobos Ho Dikaios: Origins, Literary Expression and Development of Traditions about the Brother of the Lord in Early Christianity*, PhD thesis, Fuller Theological Seminary 1985; Roy Bowen Ward, 'James of Jerusalem in the First Two Centuries', *Aufstieg und Niedergang des Römischen Welt (ANRW)*, 2.26.1, Berlin: De Gruyter; and Wilhelm Pratscher, *Der Herrenbruder Jakobus und die Jakobustradition*, Göttingen: Vandenhoeck & Ruprecht 1987.
10. See Jean Daniélou, *The Theology of Jewish Christianity*, London: Darton, Longman and Todd 1964.
11. See Marcel Simon, *Verus Israel. A Study of the Relations between Christians and Jews in the Roman Empire (AD 135–425)*, Oxford:

Clarendon Press 1986; also 'Problèmes du judéo-christianisme' in *Aspects du judéo-christianisme*, Paris 1965, and 'Réflexions sur le judéo-christianisme', in *Christianity, Judaism and Other Greco-Roman Cults*, Leiden: Brill 1975, Vol.2. See similarly Simon C. Mimouni, 'Pour une définition nouvelle du judéo-christianisme ancien', *New Testament Studies* 38, 1992, 161–86. For the problems posed by Jewish Christianity see also A. F. J. Klijn, 'The Study of Jewish Christianity', *New Testament Studies* 20, 1973–1974, 419–31 and Jean-Daneil Kaestli, 'Où en est le débat sur le Judéo-christianisme', in Daniel Marguerat (ed.), *Le déchirement*, Geneva: Labor et Fides 1996, 243–72.

12. The apocryphal Gospels are ancient texts relating actions and sayings of Jesus which are not considered canonical. Experts usually identify three apocryphal Gospels as Jewish-Christian: those of the Hebrews, Ebionites and Nazarenes. However, this is a complex and highly controversial question. See A. F. J. Klijn, *Jewish-Christian Gospel Tradition*, Leiden: Brill 1992, and Ray A. Pritz, *Nazarene Jewish Christianity*, Leiden: Brill 1988.

13. For this complex literature see Oscar Cullmann, *Le Problème littéraire et historique du roman pseudo-clémentin*, Paris: Félix Alcan 1930; F.Stanley Jones, 'The Pseudo-Clementines: A History of Research', *The Second Century* 2, 1982, 1–33, 63–96.

14. Hegesippus, whose orthodoxy is acknowledged by Eusebius, may have been one of the Jewish Christians who joined the mainstream church.

15. Book 5 of the *Hypomnemata*, quoted in Eusebius of Caesarea, *Church History* 2, 23, 4.

16. Quoted in Eusebius of Caesarea, *Church History* 2,1, 3–4. For these quotations see Brown, *James* (n.9), 242–3.

17. The main references can be found in *Against Celsus* and the *Commentary on Matthew*.

18. Eusebius mentions James several times in his *Church History*.

19. Epiphanius, *Panarion*, 29.3–4.

20. In the treatise against Helvidius (*Liber adversus Helvidium de perpetua virginitate B.Mariae*).

21. This is a collection of manuscripts written in Coptic and discovered at the end of 1945 at Nag Hammadi in Upper Egypt. These texts reveal more or less consolidated and developed Gnostic tendencies. A complete English translation is available in James M. Robinson, *The Nag Hammadi Library*, revised edition Leiden: Brill 1988.

22. See ibid., 29–36.

23. The two Apocalypses of James can be found in ibid., 260–76.

24. B. H. Streeter, *The Primitive Church*, London: Macmillan 1929, 39.

25. Jean Daniélou., *L'Église des premiers temps*, Paris: Seuil 1985, 15.

1. Brother of Jesus?

1. Philippe Rolland, *L'Origine et la date des évangiles,* Paris: Saint-Paul 1994, 37.

2. Maurice Goguel, *The Life of Jesus*, London: George Allen and Unwin 1933, 260.

3. The books by J.-C. Barreau (*Biographie de Jésus*, Paris: Plon 1994) and Jacques Duquesne (*Jésus*, Flammarion/Desclée 1994).

4. See Gervais Dumeige, *La Foi catholique*, Paris: Editions de l'Orante 1975, 194, 195, 201, 225–28.

5. I hope readers will excuse me for usually speaking more of the brothers of Jesus. I have not forgotten the existence of sisters, but after all it was the brothers, above all James and perhaps Jude, who, unlike the sisters, played an important role in the early church.

6. The three Synoptic Gospels are very similar in both narrative structure and the redaction of numerous passages. They can be put in parallel columns and surveyed at a glance, hence their name.

7. The problem of the brothers of Jesus has often been discussed. The *locus classicus* remains the discussion by J. B. Lightfoot in his famous commentary, *Saint Paul's Epistle to the Galatians*, London: Macmillan [10]1890. Cf. more recently the excellent studies by John P. Meier (*A Marginal Jew*, New York: Doubleday, Vol. 1, 1991, 316–32, and 'The Brothers and Sisters of Jesus in Ecumenical Perspective', *Catholic Biblical Quarterly* 54, 1992, 1–28) and François Refoulé (*Les Frères et soeurs de Jésus*, Paris: Desclée de Brouwer 1995). The discussion by Jean Gilles (*Les 'Frères et soeurs' de Jesus*, Paris: Aubier 1979) concentrates above all on the linguistic aspects of the question. Finally, it is worth noting the interesting but sometimes controversial ideas of Richard Bauckham (*Jude and the Relatives of Jesus in the Early Church*, Edinburgh: T.&T. Clark 1990, 5–44) and John McHugh (*The Mother of Jesus in the New Testament*, London: Darton, Longman and Todd 1975, 200–54).

8. The testimony of Hegesippus, known only through the quotations of Eusebius in his *Church History*, is ambiguous and has sometimes been used to support Epiphanius's theory. However, Meier (*Marginal Jew* [n.7], 329, 330, 361) and Refoulé ('*Frères et soeurs*' [n.7], 72–9) are doubtless right in arguing that he is defending the Helvidian theory.

9. The testimony of Tertullian is particularly significant. Despite his own asceticism, he always affirmed that James and his brothers were the children of Joseph and Mary. He was convinced that he was defending the true apostolic tradition against innovations.

10. Meier (*Marginal Jew* [n.7], 330–1) thinks that Irenaeus (around 130–200) could have defended this view, but that remains very speculative.

11. R. Pesch, *Das Markusevangelium* 2, 1, Freiburg: Herder 1976, 322–5.

12. Meier, *A Marginal Jew* (n.7), 332.

13. Refoulé, *'Frères et soeurs'* (n.7), 89.
14. Richard Bauckham. 'The Brothers and Sisters of Jesus: An Epiphanian Response to John P. Meier', *Catholic Biblical Quarterly* 56, 1994, 686–700.
15. For all these questions see Gilles, *Les 'Frères et soeurs' de Jesus* (n.7).
16. See especially the story of the marriage feast at Cana (John 2.1–11).
17. For these interpretations see Raymond E. Brown, Karl E. Donfried, Joseph A. Fitzmyer, John Reumann (eds.), *Mary in the New Testament*, London: Geoffrey Chapman 1978, 206–18.
18. See especially Simon Légasse, *Le Procès de Jesus II, La Passion dans les quatre Évangiles*, Paris: Cerf 1995, 546–7.
19. Brown et al. (eds.), *Mary in the New Testament* (n.17), 289.
20. Ibid., 72. Raymond Brown, the great Catholic exegete, accepts that the question of the perpetual virginity of Mary belongs to post-biblical theology (*The Birth of the Messiah*, London: Geoffrey Chapman 1993, 132).
21. *Jerusalem Bible*, note on Matt. 1.25.
22. For the expression *prototokos* (firstborn) see Gilles, *Les 'Frères et soeurs' de Jesus* (n.7), 95–100.
23. See Ben Witherington III, *Women in the Ministry of Jesus*, Cambridge: Cambridge University Press 1984, 90–2.
24. According to Origen, this theory also appeared in the Gospel of Peter, an apocryphal text probably dating from the middle of the second century. We have only extracts from this Gospel, and they contain no references to the brothers of Jesus.
25. For the Protevangelium of James and this question see Edouard Cothenet, 'Le Protévangile de Jacques: origine, genre et signification d'un premier midrash chrétien sur la Nativité de Marie', *ANRW* 2.25.2, Berlin: De Gruyter, 4252–69.
26. 'Protevangelium of James', in *New Testament Apocrypha* 1, ed. W. Schneemelcher and R. McL. Wilson, Louisville: Westminster John Knox Press and Cambridge: James Clarke 1991, 430.
27. The work was probably composed in response to the attacks of Jewish Christians who did not believe in the virgin birth of Jesus, and pagans or Jews who claimed that Jesus was an illegitimate child.
28. *Commentary on Matthew*, 13.55.
29. Luke 23.49 does not give the name of the women present at the crucifixion. Matthew 27.56 mentions Mary Magdalene, Mary (the mother) of James and Joseph, and the mother of the sons of Zebedee.
30. *Commentary on the Epistle to the Galatians* (1.19), quoted by Lightfoot, *Saint Paul's Epistle to the Galatians* (n.7), 260.
31. Jean Cantinat, *Les Epîtres de saint Jacques et de saint Jude*, Paris: Gabalda 1973, 47.
32. For this question see Antoine Malvy, 'Saint Jacques de Jérusalem était-il un des Douze?', *Recherches de science religieuse* 9, 1918.

33. *Jerusalem Bible*, note on Acts 1.13.
34. Joseph Fitzmyer, *The Gospel According to Luke*, New York: Doubleday 1981, Vol.1, 619.
35. Robert H. Gundry, *Mark, A Commentary on His Apology for the Cross*, Grand Rapids, Mich.: Eerdmans 1993, 976–7.
36. For these variants see ibid., 976–8.
37. Légasse, *Le Procès de Jesus II* (n.18), 96, 97, 134, 271.
38. Quoted in Eusebius, *Church History* 4, 22, 4.
39. McHugh, *The Mother of Jesus in the New Testament* (n.7), 234–54.
40. Lightfoot, *Saint Paul's Epistle to the Galatians* (n.7), 261.
41. Even supposing that the evangelists had Aramaic or Hebrew sources at their disposal, they must have been sufficiently informed about the family of Jesus to have used the word *anepsios* (cousin) had Jesus been the cousin of his 'brothers'.
42. Several Catholic exegetes, criticizing the book by Jacques Duquesne, who defends the Helvidian theory, have again used this argument, citing the book of Tobit, which was written around 200 BCE. But it must be said once again that this argument proves absolutely nothing.
43. The word *anepsios* also appears in the letter to the Colossians (4.10), but the authenticity of the letter is disputed. Gilles, *Les 'Frères et soeurs' de Jesus* (n.7), discusses these questions in detail.
44. Meier, *A Marginal Jew* (n.7), 328.

2. *A Galilean Family*

1. The birth of Jesus is usually put in 7 or 6 BCE (John P. Meier, *A Marginal Jew*, New York: Doubleday, Vol.1, 1991, 407).
2. For the infancy narratives in Matthew and Luke see e.g. Raymond E. Brown, *The Birth of the Messiah*, Geoffrey Chapman 1993.
3. For many exegetes Nazarene is linked to the word *nazir*, which denotes a person devoted to God. Other scholars think that the term suggests Isaiah 11.1 ('There shall come forth a shoot from the stump of Jesse, and a branch shall grow out of his roots').
4. On this point see the comments by Fergus Millar, a distinguished Roman historian, 'Reflections on the Trial of Jesus', in P. R. Davies and R. White (eds.), *A Tribute to Geza Vermes*, Sheffield: Sheffield Academic Press 1990, 357–9.
5. See 'The Census of Quirinius', in Emil Schürer, *The History of the Jewish People in the Age of Jesus Christ*, revised edition by G. Vermes and F. Millar, Vol. 1, Edinburgh: T.&T. Clark 1973, 399–427.
6. This is also the conclusion of Meier, *A Marginal Jew* (n.1), 229.
7. For Galilee see Sean Freyne, *Galilee, Jesus and the Gospels*, Philadelphia: Fortress Press 1988; H. Hoehner, *Herod Antipas*, Cambridge: Cambridge University Press 1972; Richard A. Horsley, *Galilee*, Valley Forge, Pa: Trinity Press International 1995.
8. For the population of the towns of Galilee see J. L. Reed, 'Population

Numbers, Urbanization and Economics: Galilean Archeology and the Historical Jesus', in *Society of Biblical Literature 1994 Seminar Papers*, Atlanta, Ga: Scholars Press, 203–19.

9. The population of Nazareth is often put at 1,500 or 2,000 inhabitants on the basis of former erroneous estimates. James F. Strange, who accepted the previous estimate, now considers that the population of Nazareth was lower than 500 ('Nazareth', in *The Anchor Bible Dictionary*).

10. For a traditional history of Israel up to the Persian period see J. Maxwell Miller and John H. Hayes, *A History of Ancient Israel and Judaism*, London: SCM Press 1986. For a critical history see n.17. The period beginning with the Persian or Hellenistic era is covered in Christiane Saulnier, *Histoire d'Israël* III, Paris: Cerf 1985; Peter Schäfer, *Histoire des Juifs dans l'Antiquité*, Paris: Cerf 1989; Schürer, *The History of the Jewish People in the Age of Jesus Christ* (n.5). The Roman period is described in detail in E. Mary Smallwood, *The Jews under Roman Rule*, Leiden: Brill 1981.

11. E. Renan, *Life of Jesus*, London: Walter Scott nd, 43, 95.

12. Geza Vermes, *Jesus the Jew*, London: SCM Press 1983, 46.

13. For recent archaeological research and its implications see the survey by J. Andrew Overman in *Currents in Research: Biblical Studies*, Sheffield: Sheffield Academic Press, Vol.1, 1993, 35–57. See also the contributions by Douglas Edwards, Sean Freyne, Eric M. Meyers and James F. Strange in Lee I. Levine (ed.), *The Galilee in Late Antiquity*, New York: Jewish Theological Seminary of America 1992.

14. Magen Broshi, 'The Role of the Temple in the Herodian Economy', *Journal of Jewish Study* 38.1, 1987, 31–7.

15. See especially Sylvie Honigman, 'The Birth of a Diaspora: The Emergence of a Jewish Self Definition in Ptolemaic Egypt in the Light of Onomastics', in S. J. D. Cohen and E. S. Frerichs (eds.), *Diasporas in Antiquity*, Atlanta: Scholars Press 1993; and M. H. Williams, 'Palestinian Jewish Personal Names in Acts', in *The Book of Acts in its First Century Setting*, Vol. 4, Grand Rapids, Mich: Eerdmans 1995.

16. *Church History* 3.20.1–6.

17. Historians of Israel such as N. P. Lemche, T. L. Thompson and P. R. Davies think that David and Solomon had no more historical reality than the Homeric heroes or King Arthur, see: P. R. Davies, *In Search of Ancient Israel*, Sheffield: Sheffield Academic Press 1992; T. L. Thompson, *The Early History of the Israelite People: The Literary and Archaeological Evidence*, Leiden: Brill 1992. The discovery of the stele of Tel Dan has reopened the discussions without being decisively in favour of the historicity of David. At all events David, and above all Solomon, certainly did not have the importance and power that the Bible attributes to them.

18. We should not forget that in the sixteenth century several European rulers claimed to be descended from Aeneas and the royal family of

Troy (see Mary Tanner, *The Last Descendant of Aeneas*, Yale University Press 1994).

19. Experts are far from unanimous on the question whether Jesus regarded himself as the Messiah.

20. Brown, *The Birth of the Messiah* (n.2), 505–12; Meier, *A Marginal Jew* (n.2), 238–9.

21. For the genealogies of Jesus see e.g. Marshall D.Johnson, *The Purpose of the Biblical Genealogies*, Cambridge: Cambridge University Press 1969; Brown, *The Birth of the Messiah* (n.2); Richard Bauckham, *Jude and the Relatives of Jesus in the Early Church*, Edinburgh: T.&T. Clark 1990, 315–73.

22. Joachim Jeremias, *Jerusalem in the Time of Jesus*, London: SCM Press and Philadelphia: Fortress Press 1969.

23. Johnson, *The Purpose of the Biblical Genealogies* (n.21), 99–108.

24. Ibid., 140–5.

25. Bauckham, *Jude and the Relatives of Jesus* (n.21).

26. Letter to Aristides, quoted in *Church History* 1. 7.

27. *Dialogue*, no.88.

28. Vermes, *Jesus the Jew* (n.12), 21–2.

29. David Flusser, *Jésus,* Paris: Seuil 1970, 28–9.

30. Luke 2.7 may evoke Isa. 1.3 (LXX) or Jer. 14.8. See Brown, *The Birth of the Messiah* (n.21), 418–20.

31. Eusebius, *Church History* 3, 20, 2–3.

32. Richard A. Batey, 'Is Not This the Carpenter?', *New Testament Studies* 30, 1984, 249–58.

33. G.W.Buchanan, 'Jesus and the Upper Class', *Novum Testamentum* 7, 1964–65, 195–209.

34. In a village as small as Nazareth, the lessons may have been read by the *hazan,* the person responsible for operating the synagogue.

35. At all events, that is the hypothesis underlying the description of the educational system in first-century Palestine given in S. Safrai and M. Stern (eds.), *The Jewish People in the First Century,* Assen: Van Gorcum, Vol. 2, 1976. The rabbinic literature is presented in G. Stemberger, *Introduction to the Talmud and Midrash,* Edinburgh: T.&T. Clark ²1996, and S. Safrai (ed.), *The Literature of the Sages,* Assen: Van Gorcum (two vols), 1987. See also Maurice-Ruben Hayoun, *La Littérature rabbinique,* Paris: Presses Universitaires de France 1990.

36. Kethubot 8, 11, 32c.

37. Baba Bathra 21 a.

38. Shaye J. D. Cohen, *From the Maccabees to the Mishnah,* Philadelphia: Westminster Press 1987, 120–3. Meier (*A Marginal Jew* [n.1], 271–8) shares his scepticism.

39. William V. Harris, *Ancient Literacy,* Cambridge, Mass.: Harvard University Press 1989.

40. John 7.15; Luke 4.16–20. The authenticity of John 8.6 is doubtful.

41. The talents of Jesus in this area have been assessed differently. Brad Young (*Jesus, the Jewish Theologian*, Peabody, Mass.: Hendrickson 1995) praises them, whereas D. M. Cohn-Sherbok ('An Analysis of Jesus' Arguments concerning the Plucking of Grain on the Sabbath', *Journal for the Study of the New Testament* 2, 1979, 31–41), thinks them mediocre in comparison to the great rabbis.

42. The complexity of the speech attributed to James is often underestimated by exegetes. See Richard Bauckham, 'James and the Gentiles (Acts 15.13–21)', in Ben Witherington III (ed.), *History, Literature and Society in the Book of Acts*, Cambridge: Cambridge University Press 1996, 154–84.

43. Robert Eisenman (*James the Brother of Jesus,* London: Faber 1997) even considers that James was the famous Essene Teacher of Righteousness. This theory is hard to accept.

3. *What is a Jew?*

1. Francis Schmidt, *La Pensée du Temple. De Jérusalem à Qoumrân*, Paris: Seuil 1994, 57–8.

2. The Cynics tended to reject wealth, honours, power, constraints and traditional family values: Burton L. Mack, *A Myth of Innocence: Mark and Christian Origins*, Philadelphia: Fortress Press 1988, and *The Lost Gospel: The Book of Q and Christian Origins*, San Francisco: HarperSanFrancisco 1993; J. D. Crossan, *The Historical Jesus*, San Francisco: HarperSanFrancisco 1991.

3. George Foot Moore, *Judaism in the First Centuries of the Christian Era: The Age of the Tannaim*, Cambridge, Mass.: Harvard University Press 1927–1930.

4. Joseph Bonsirven, *Le Judaïsme palestinien au temps de Jésus-Christ*, Paris: Beauchesne 1935.

5. Joachim Jeremias, *Jerusalem in the Time of Jesus*, London: SCM Press and Philadelphia: Fortress Press 1969.

6. S. Safrai and M. Stern (eds.), *The Jewish People in the First Century*, Assen: Van Gorcum, Vol.2, 1976.

7. Morton Smith, 'Palestinian Judaism in the First Century', in M. Davis (ed.), *Israel, Its Role in Civilization*, New York: Israel Institute of the Jewish Theological Seminary 1956.

8. In a large number of works, see e.g. *From Politics to Piety: The Emergence of Pharisaic Judaism*, Englewood Cliffs, NJ: Prentice-Hall 1973; 'Josephus' Pharisees: A Complete Repertoire', in L. H. Feldman and G. Hata (eds.), *Josephus, Judaism and Christianity*, Leiden: Brill 1987; *The Rabbinic Traditions about the Pharisees before 70*, Leiden: Brill 1971.

9. From a vast literature see above all S. J. D. Cohen, *From the Maccabees to the Mishnah*, Philadelphia: Westminster Press 1987; Lester L. Grabbe, *Judaism from Cyrus to Hadrian*, Minneapolis:

Fortress Press 1992 and London: SCM Press 1993, Vol. 2; Robert A. Kraft and George W. E. Nickelsburg (eds.), *Early Judaism and Its Modern Interpreters*, Atlanta: Scholars Press 1986; Jacob Neusner (ed.), *Judaism in Late Antiquity*, Leiden: Brill 1995; E. P. Sanders, *Judaism: Practice and Belief, 63 BCE–66 CE*, London: SCM Press and Philadelphia: Trinity Press International 1992; *Paul and Palestinian Judaism*, London: SCM Press and Philadelphia: Fortress Press 1977; E. Schürer, *The History of the Jewish People in the Age of Jesus Christ*, revised edition by G. Vermes and F. Millar, Vol.1, Edinburgh: T.&T. Clark 1973; Schmidt, *La Pensée du Temple* (n.1); Alan F. Segal, *Rebecca's Children*, Cambridge, Mass.: Harvard University Press 1986; N. T. Wright, *The New Testament and the People of God*, London: SPCK 1992.

10. M. Smith, J. Neusner and to a lesser degree E. P. Sanders have certainly underestimated the influence of Pharisaic conceptions, as has been shown by Steve Mason in an important work (*Flavius Josephus on the Pharisees*, Leiden: Brill 1991); see also his article 'Pharisaic Dominance before 70 CE and the Gospels' Hypocrisy Charge (Matthew 23.2–3)', *Harvard Theological Review* 83–84, 1990, 363–81. Mason's position is strengthened by the recent publication of the document 4QMMT from Qumran Cave 4. In this legal text, the Qumran Teacher of Righteousness defends certain conceptions of the Law and opposes them to current practices. These last are very similar to the practices attributed to the Pharisees in rabbinic literature (Elisha Qimron and John Strugnell, *Qumran Cave 4.V*, Oxford: Clarendon Press 1994). That would tend to show that a significant part of the common *halakhah* in the last two centuries of the Second Temple was of Pharisaic inspiration. Some scholars like Daniel R.Schwartz ('MMT, Josephus and the Pharisees', in John Kampen and Moshe J.Bernstein [eds], *Reading 4 QMMT*, Atlanta: Scholars Press 1996, 67–80 adopt a more prudent position.

11. Martin Hengel, *Judaism and Hellenism*, London: SCM Press and Philadelphia: Fortress Press 1974; id., *The 'Hellenization' of Judaea in the First Century after Christ*, London: SCM Press 1989. See also Elias J. Bickerman, *The Jews in the Greek Age*, Cambridge, Mass.: Harvard University Press 1988.

12. See the articles by A. T. Kraabel collected in J. A. Overman and R. S. MacLennan (eds.), *Diaspora Jews and Judaism*, Atlanta: Scholars Press 1992. See also the very recent synthesis by John M. G. Barclay, *Jews in the Mediterranean Diaspora*, Edinburgh: T.&T. Clark 1996.

13. On this point see Wright, *The New Testament and the People of God* (n.9); E. P. Sanders, *Jewish Law from Jesus to the Mishnah*, London: SCM Press and Philadelphia: Trinity Press International 1990, 255–6.

14. For the notion of the Jew see Shaye J. D. Cohen, 'Religion, Ethnicity and "Hellenism" in the Emergence of Jewish Identity in Maccabean Palestine', in Per Bilde (ed.), *Religion and Religious Practice in the*

Seleucid Kingdom, Aarhus: Aarhus University Press 1990.

15. For these elements and their evolution see the excellent study 'Jewish Background of Christianity', in D. R. Schwartz, *Studies in the Jewish Background of Christianity*, Tübingen: J. C. B. Mohr 1992.

16. See E.-M. Laperrousaz (ed.), *La Palestine à l'époque perse*, Paris: Cerf 1994, and especially the contribution by Hedwige Rouillard-Bonraisin. For the development of Judaism during the Persian period see also Jan L. Berquist, *Judaism in Persia's Shadow*, Minneapolis: Fortress Press 1995; Grabbe, *Judaism from Cyrus to Hadrian* (n.9), Vol. 1; Kenneth G. Hoglund, *Achaemenid Imperial Administration in Syria-Palestine and the Missions of Ezra and Nehemiah*, Atlanta: Scholars Press 1992.

17. Bickerman, *The Jews in the Greek Age* (n.11).

18. The development of Judaism from the Maccabean revolt has been particularly well presented in Cohen, *From the Maccabees to the Mishnah* (n.9).

19. In Matthew 5.17; 7.12; 11.13; 22.40; Luke 16.29–31; Acts 13.15; 24.14; 28.23; Rom. 3.21. Luke is the only one to mention 'the law of Moses, the propehts and the psalms'.

20. The *Shema* is made up of three biblical passages, Deuteronomy 6.4–9; 11.13–21 and Numbers 15.37–41. For the *Shema* and the Jewish liturgy see Maurice-Ruben Hayoun, *La Liturgie juive*, Paris: Presses Universitaires de France 1994.

21. There were certainly exceptions in the case of Hellenized Jews taking part in the political life of their city or in social and cultural activities like the theatre, the gymnasium or the public baths. The most significant cases are recalled by Tessa Rajak, 'Jews and Christians as Groups', in Jacob Neusner and Ernest S.Frerichs (eds.), *To See Ourselves as Others See Us*, Chico, Ca: Scholars Press 1985.

22. Philip S. Alexander, 'Jewish Law in the Time of Jesus: Towards a Clarification of the Problem', in B. Lindars (ed.), *Law and Religion*, Cambridge: James Clarke 1988, 51.

23. For the Pharisees, in addition to the works by J. Neusner already mentioned see A. J. Saldarini, *Pharisees, Scribes and Sadducees*, Edinburgh: T.&T. Clark 1989; Sanders, *Jewish Law from Jesus to the Mishnah* (n.13); Günter Stemberger, *Jewish Contemporaries of Jesus*, Minneapolis: Fortress Press 1995. Saldarini and Stemberger remain sceptical about the historical value of most of the facts about the Pharisees at our disposal.

24. The relationship between the inhabitants of the ruins of Qumran, the manuscripts found from 1947 onwards in the caves around, and the Essenes described by Josephus, Philo and Pliny the Elder, is becoming increasingly a matter of controversy. However, the majority of scholars assume that the inhabitants of Qumran were Essenes and that most of the non-biblical texts discovered in the caves express their views. They nevertheless think that Qumran was only one of the many

Essene communities. The others were probably organized in a different way. From a very full bibliography see: James C. Vanderkam, *The Dead Sea Scrolls Today*, Grand Rapids: Eerdmans 1994; Geza Vermes, *The Dead Sea Scrolls. Qumran in Perspective*, London: SCM Press ³1994; H. Shanks (ed.), *Understanding the Dead Sea Scrolls*, New York: Random House 1992. The recent work by Lawrence H. Schiffmann, *Reclaiming the Dead Sea Scrolls*, Philadelphia: Jewish Publication Society 1994, is more complete but also more controversial. For a critique of traditional views see Norman Golb, *Who Wrote the Dead Sea Scrolls?*, New York: Scribner 1995.

25. For the Sadducees, the classical work is J. Le Moyne, *Les Sadducéens*, Paris: Gabalda 1972. Saldarini, *Pharisees, Scribes and Sadducees* (n.23); Stemberger, *Jewish Contemporaries of Jesus* (n.23) and G. Porton ('Sadducees', in *The Anchor Bible Dictionary*) are more critical.

26. This type of remark must certainly be qualified in so far as the Sadducees must necessarily have had their own traditions to be able to interpret and complete the Hebrew Bible, as Stemberger, *Jewish Contemporaries of Jesus* (n.23), has pointed out.

27. On the *'ammē hā-ārets*, the basic work is that of Aharon Oppenheimer, *The 'Am Ha-aretz*, Leiden: Brill 1977.

28. Sanders, *Judaism: Practice and Belief, 63 BCE – 66 CE* (n.9).

29. See especially V. Tcherikover and A. Fuks, *Corpus Papyrorum Judaicorum*, Jerusalem: Magnes Press 1959, Vol. 1, and V. Tcherikover, *Hellenistic Civilization and the Jews*, New York: Jewish Publication Society of America 1959. See also Joseph Mélèze-Modrzejewki, *Les Juifs d'Egypte de Ramsès à Hadrien*, Paris: Armand Colin 1991.

30. See the analyses by Hannah Cotton, 'A Cancelled Marriage Contract from the Judean Desert', *Journal of Roman Studies* 1994.

31. For circumcision see the article by Robert G. Hall in *The Anchor Bible Dictionary*.

32. See especially the *Epigrams* of Martial (7.35; 7.82).

33. E. C. Kreuls, *The Reign of the Phallus: Sexual Politics in Ancient Athens*, New York 1985.

34. I Macc. 1.60–61; II Macc. 6.10–11.

35. Scholars have sometimes argued that at the end of the Second Temple period circumcision was not always considered an indispensable element in becoming a Jew (see N. J. McEleney, 'Conversion, Circumcision and the Law', *New Testament Studies* 20, 1974, 319–41). The arguments in support of this thesis have been refuted by J. Nolland, 'Uncircumcised Proselytes', *Journal for the Study of Judaism* 12, 1981, 173–94. For circumcision and proselytism see John J. Collins, 'A Symbol of Otherness', in Neusner and Frerichs (eds.), *To See Ourselves as Others See Us* (n.21), 170–9.

36. Jer. 4.4; 9.24–25 and Lev. 26.41; Deut. 10.16; 30.6. It is also a matter of circumcision of the lips (Ex. 6.12,30) and the ears (Jer. 6.10).

37. Philo, *De specialibus legibus* 1.1–11.
38. Some contented themselves with a barely visible circumcision.
39. See especially I Macc. 1.14–15; *Antiquities* 12, 241; I Cor. 7.18.
40. Philo, *De migratione Abrahami* 89–94.
41. Mishnah Pesahim 6.1. See Etienne Nodet, 'Galilée juive de Jésus à la Mishna', in François Blanchetière and Moshe David Herr (eds.), *Aux origines du christianisme*, Jerusalem 1993, 28.
42. For these differences see Sanders, *Jewish Law from Jesus to the Mishnah* (n.13), 6–23.
43. Tacitus, *Histories* 5.4.
44. Josephus mentions and quotes certain decrees granting Jews the right to observe the sabbath (*Antiquities* 14, 185–267).
45. For the dietary laws see Sanders, *Judaism: Practice and Belief* (n.9), 214–27 and *Jewish Law from Jesus to the Mishnah* (n.13), 23–8, 272–83.
46. Josephus, *Antiquities* 14, 226, 245, 261.
47. That is notably the case with the ban on abortion. In his *Contra Apionem*, Josephus quotes several commandments which it is difficult to derive from the Bible. See the article 'Law' by E. P. Sanders in *The Anchor Bible Dictionary*.
48. The works of Philo and Josephus contain numerous summaries or syntheses of the moral principles of the law. See also the Testaments of the Twelve Patriarchs, the *Sentences* of Pseudo-Phocylides and the Letter of Aristeas.
49. For the temple, its festivals and rites, see Sanders, *Judaism: Practice and Belief* (n.9); Schmidt, *La Pensée du Temple* (n.1).
50. For the importance of the economic activity of the temple, see the article by Magen Broshi, 'The Role of the Temple in the Herodian Economy', *Journal of Jewish Study* 38.1, 1987, 31–7.
51. Josephus, *Against Apion*, II, 102–4, Loeb Classical Library, London: Heinemann and Cambridge, Mass.: Harvard University Press 1926.
52. The systems of impurity among the sectarians of Qumran and the first rabbis and their biblical foundations have been analysed by Hannah K. Harrington, *The Impurity Systems of Qumran and the Rabbis*, Atlanta: Scholars Press 1995. See also the works of Neusner and Sanders mentioned above.
53. See Sanders, *Jewish Law from Jesus to the Mishnah* (n.13). The debate between Sanders and Neusner has been clarified in Harrington, *The Impurity Systems of Qumran* (n.52), 267–82.
54. The role, the nature, indeed the existence of synagogues as specific buildings are the subject of numerous controversies in academic circles. For these questions see Dan Urman and Paul V. M. Flesher (eds.), *Ancient Synagogues*, Leiden: Brill, Vol.1, 1995; J. Gutmann (ed.), *Ancient Synagogues: The State of Research*, Missoula: Scholars Press 1981 and Lee I. Levine, 'The Nature and Origins of the Palestinian Synagogue', *Journal of Biblical Literature* 115, 1996, 425–48.

55. Lester Grabbe, 'Synagogues in Pre-70 Palestine: A Reassessment', *Journal of Theological Studies* 39, 1988, 401–10.

56. Sanders, *Judaism: Practice and Belief* (n.9).

57. The eschatological conceptions of the Hebrew Bible and the literature from the end of the Second Temple period have been analysed in detail in Emile Puech, *La Croyance des esséniens en la vie future: immortalité, résurrection, vie éternelle?*, Paris: Gabalda 1993. There is a more accessible synthesis in P.-A. Bernheim and G. Stavridès, *Paradis, Paradis*, Paris: Plon 1991.

58. See e.g. Robert Martin-Achard, *De la mort à la résurrection d'après l'Ancien Testament*, Neuchâtel and Paris 1957, and *La mort en face*, Geneva: Labor et Fides 1988.

59. The messianic era is discussed in detail in Joseph Klausner, *The Messianic Idea in Israel: From the Beginning to the Completion of the Mishnah*, London: George Allen and Unwin 1956.

60. We should remember that the book of Isaiah is not a homogeneous work. It contains at least three parts written at different periods by different authors. Only chs. 1–39 (with some exceptions) could be attributed to the prophet Isaiah, who lived towards the end of the eighth century BCE.

61. For conceptions of the Messiah current at the time see John J. Collins, *The Scepter and the Star*, New York: Doubleday 1995; also E.-M. Laperrousaz, *L'Attente du Messie en Palestine à la veille et au début de l'ère chrétienne*, Paris: Picard 1982. Two collections are particularly useful: J. Neusner, W. S. Green and E. S. Frerichs (eds.), *Judaisms and their Messiahs*, Cambridge: Cambridge University Press 1987; James H. Charlesworth, *The Messiah*, Minneapolis: Fortress Press 1992.

62. See pp.33–4 and note 13 of Chapter 2.

63. In particular this is the case with in E. Mary Smallwood, *The Jews under Roman Rule*, Leiden: Brill 1981. The same conception can be found in the works of H. Graetz, E. Schürer and J. Klausner.

64. Sean Freyne, *Galilee from Alexander the Great to Hadrian: A Study of Second Temple Judaism*, Wilmington: Glazier 1980.

65. Uriel Rappaport, 'How Anti-Roman was the Galilee?', in Lee I. Levine (ed.), *The Galilee in Late Antiquity*, New York: Jewish Theological Seminary of America 1992, 95–102.

66. See especially Geza Vermes, *Jesus the Jew*, London: SCM Press 1983.

67. Oppenheimer, *The 'Am Ha-aretz* (n.27), 200–29.

68. *Antiquities* 2, 36–38.

69. S. Safrai, 'The Jewish Cultural Nature of Galilee in the First Century', *Immanuel* 24/25, 1990, 147–86.

70. Lawrence H. Schiffman, 'Was there a Galilean Halakha?' in Levine (ed.), *The Galilee in Late Antiquity* (n.65), 143–56.

71. Nodet, 'Galilèe juive de Jésus à la Mishna', in *Aux origines du christianisme* (n.41).

4. Jesus, James and the Brothers

1. These passages have been analysed at length in Martin I. Webber, *Iakobos Ho Dikaios. Origins, Literary Expression and Development of Traditions about the Brother of the Lord in Early Christianity*, PhD thesis, Fuller Theological Seminary 1985, 183–221. Webber emphasizes the differences between the Gospels. See also, in a more traditionalist perspective, G. D. Kilpatrick, 'Jesus, His Family and His Disciples', *Journal for the Study of the New Testament* 15, 1982, 3–19.

2. J.-M. Lagrange, *L'Évangile selon saint Marc*, Paris: Gabalda ⁶1942, 70.

3. M.-E. Boismard, *L'Evangile de Marc, sa préhistoire*, Paris: Gabalda 1994. Here Boismard has modified his position from his earlier writings.

4. See especially John Dominic Crossan, 'Mark and the Relatives of Jesus', *Novum Testamentum* 15, 1973, 81–113; Étienne Trocmé, *La Formation de l'Evangile de Marc*, Paris: Presses Universitaires de France 1963, 104–9; Michael Goulder, 'Those Outside (Mark 4,10–12)', *Novum Testamentum* 33.4, 1991, 289–302; Werner Kelber, *The Kingdom in Mark: A New Place and a New Time*, Philadelphia: Fortress Press 1971.

5. According to Crossan, 'Mark had redacted the tradition in 3.21–35 and 6.1–6 . . . so that there is a severe opposition between Jesus and his relatives: they have blasphemed against the Holy Spirit; they have dishonoured Jesus and are without faith in him' ('Mark and the Relatives of Jesus' [n.4], 113.

6. For this point see above all Trocmé, *La Formation de l'Evangile de Marc* (n.4), 108.

7. M.-E. Boismard and A. Lamouille, *L'Evangile de Jean*, Paris: Cerf 1987, 100–8. This is the third volume of their *Synopse des quatre Evangiles*.

8. Ibid., and Robert T. Fortna, *The Fourth Gospel and its Predecessors*, Edinburgh: T.&T. Clark 1989, 49–61.

9. Boismard and Lamouille, *L'Evangile de Jean* (n.7), 212.

10. R. E. Brown, 'Other Sheep not of this Fold, the Johannine Perspective on Christian Diversity in the Late First Century', *Journal of Biblical Literature* 97, 1978, 13.

11. Ibid., and J. L. Martyn, *History and Theology in the Fourth Gospel*, Nashville: Abingdon Press 1979.

12. For these sayings see C. Coulot, *Jésus et le Disciple*, Paris: Gabalda 1987; Stephen C. Barton, *Discipleship and Family Ties in Mark and Matthew*, Cambridge: Cambridge University Press 1994.

13. This criterion, which is now widely criticized, presupposes the realization of three hypotheses: a good knowledge of the Jewish world at the time of Jesus; a good knowledge of the primitive church; a lack of

creativity on the part of the disciples of Jesus. Since these three hypotheses cannot be regarded as having been confirmed, the criterion must be used with great caution. Excessive use of it generally tends to accentuate the 'original' and atypical features of the teaching of Jesus.

14. Coulot, *Jésus et le Disciple* (n.12), 35–36.

15. For the subversive conception of the family see A. D. Jacobson, 'Divided Families and Christian Origins', in Ronald A. Piper (ed.), *The Gospel Behind the Gospels: Current Studies in Q*, Leiden: Brill 1995.

16. David Cooper, *Death of the Family*, Harmondsworth: Penguin Books 1972.

17. See Robert Funk, Roy Hoover and the Jesus Seminar, *The Five Gospels*, Sonoma, Ca: Polebridge Press and Macmillan 1993.

18. Martin Hengel, *The Charismatic Leader and his Followers*, Edinburgh: T.&T. Clark 1981.

19. Luke, immediately after Luke 9.59–60, includes an episode which evokes the call of Elisha very clearly.

20. Matthew inserts a similar saying, not in his eschatological discourse in ch.24, but in his discourse on the mission of the apostles (10.21).

21. E.g. Ezek. 38.21; Zech.14.13.

22. E.g. Jubilees 23.16; I Enoch 99.5; 100.1–2; IV Ezra 5.9; 6.24.

23. Translation from James H. Charlesworth (ed.), *The Old Testament Pseudepigrapha*, Vol. 1, New York: Doubleday and London: Darton, Longman and Todd 1983, 81.

24. Geza Vermes, in *Jesus and the World of Judaism*, London: SCM Press 1983, 53, emphasizes the rhetorical exaggeration of these sayings. S. C. Barton connects them more with commonplaces of Cynic tradition and for this reason doubts their historical character.

25. In addition to Trocmé, Crossan and the other authors mentioned above, see also Roy Bowen Ward (James of Jerusalem in the First Two Centuries', *ANRW* 2.26.1, Berlin: De Gruyter, 790); Richard Bauckham (*Jude and the Relatives of Jesus in the Early Church*, Edinburgh: T.&T. Clark 1990, 56–7); and J. K. Elliott (*Questioning Christian Origins*, London: SCM Press 1982, 41–6).

26. For the appearances of the risen Christ see Gerd Lüdemann, *The Resurrection of Jesus*, London: SCM Press 1994.

27. For a synthesis on this difficult question see Gordon D. Fee, *The First Epistle to the Corinthians*, Grand Rapids: Eerdmans 1987, 721–34.

28. See especially Peter J. Kearney, 'He appeared to 500 Brothers (I Cor XV,6)', *Novum Testamentum* 22, 1980, 264–84.

29. Jerome Murphy-O'Connor, 'Tradition and Redaction in I Cor 15, 3–7', *Catholic Biblical Quarterly* 43, 1981, 582–9.

30. Paul Winter, 'I Corinthians XV, 3b-7', *Novum Testamentum* 2, 1957–58, 142–50.

31. Ward, *James of Jerusalem* (n.25), 782.

32. Bauckham defends this position in *Jude and the Relatives of Jesus in*

the Early Church (n.25), 56–7; see also Elliott, *Questioning Christian Origins* (n.25), 41–2.

33. See John P. Meier, *A Marginal Jew*, New York: Doubleday, Vol.1, 1991, 112–41.

34. J. D. Crossan, *The Historical Jesus*, San Francisco: Harper-SanFrancisco 1991; Helmut Koester, *Ancient Christian Gospels*, London: SCM Press 1990.

35. Crossan, *The Historical Jesus* (n.34), 427–34.

36. 'Hebrews, Gospel of the', *The Anchor Bible Dictionary*, Vol.3, 105–6.

37. The Gospel of the Hebrews, in Jerome, *De viris illustribus* . . . , translation from W. Schneemelcher and R. McL. Wilson, *New Testament Apocrypha 1*, Louisville: Westminster John Knox Press and Cambridge: James Clarke 1991, 7.

38. Gospel of Thomas, Logion 12, in *The Nag Hammadi Library*, ed. J. M. Robinson, Leiden: Brill ²1984, 127.

39. For a review of the academic debates see F. T. Fallon and R. Cameron, 'The Gospel of Thomas: A Forschungsbericht and Analysis', *ANRW* 1988, 2.25.6, 4195–251; G. J. Riley, 'The Gospel of Thomas in Recent Scholarship', in *Currents in Research: Biblical Studies*, Sheffield: Sheffield Academic Press, Vol. 2, 1994, 227–52.

40. For an argued defence of this theory see Koester, *Ancient Christian Gospels* (n.34), 84–124; S. Patterson, *The Gospel of Thomas and Jesus*, Sonoma: Polebridge Press 1993.

41. For this complex question, in addition to Henri-Charles Puech, *En quête de la Gnose*, Vol. 2, Paris: Gallimard 1978, 87–91, see Patterson, *Gospel of Thomas* (n.40), 113–20.

5. A Famous Brother

1. The historicity of many of the episodes in the Gospel of John has been defended by C. H. Dodd *(Historical Tradition in the Fourth Gospel*, Cambridge: Cambridge University Press 1963), and above all J. A. T. Robinson *(The Priority of John*, London: SCM Press 1985). See also M. Hengel, *The Johannine Question*, London: SCM Press 1989.

2. For relations between the Gospels see, from a vast literature: David L. Dungan (ed.), *The Interrelations of the Gospels*, Louvain: Presses Universitaires de Louvain 1990; Philippe Rolland, *Les Premiers Evangiles*, Paris: Cerf 1984.

3. John S. Kloppenborg, *The Formation of Q: Trajectories in Ancient Wisdom Collections*, Philadelphia: Fortress Press 1987. It should be mentioned that Kloppenborg's theory has been criticized by a number of exegetes including D. Catchpole, R. A. Horsley, M. Q. Sato and C. M. Tuckett.

4. Notably B. L. Mack, *The Lost Gospel: The Book of Q and Christian Origins*, San Francisco: HarperSanFrancisco 1993.

5. J. D. Crossan, *The Historical Jesus*, San Francisco: HarperSan-Francisco 1991.

6. The great defender of this view is W. R. Farmer, see especially *The Synoptic Problem. A Critical Analysis*, New York: Macmillan 1964; and *Jesus and the Gospel*, Philadelphia: Fortress Press 1982.

7. See especially the contribution by M.-E. Boismard in Dungan (ed.), *The Interrelations of the Gospels* (n.2), 231–43.

8. All these criteria are analysed in detail in John P. Meier, *A Marginal Jew*, New York: Doubleday, Vol.1, 1991, 167–95.

9. See Robert Funk, Roy Hoover and the Jesus Seminar, *The Five Gospels*, Sonoma, Ca: Polebridge Press and Macmillan 1993.

10. Albert Schweitzer, *The Quest of the Historical Jesus*, reissued London: SCM Press 1981 (the first German edition dates from 1906).

11. The current state of research into Jesus is presented in: Marcus J. Borg, *Jesus in Contemporary Scholarship*, Valley Forge: Trinity Press International 1994; Bruce Chilton and Craig A. Evans (eds.), *Studying the Historical Jesus*, Leiden: Brill 1994; Ben Witherington III, *The Jesus Quest*, Downers Grove, Ill.: InterVarsity Press 1996.

12. S. G. F. Brandon, *Jesus and the Zealots*, Manchester: Manchester University Press 1967. See also G. W. Buchanan, *Jesus: The King and His Kingdom*, Macon, Ga.: Mercer University Press 1983.

13. Morton Smith, *Jesus the Magician*, San Francisco: Harper & Row 1978.

14. Graham H. Twelftree, *Jesus the Exorcist*, Tübingen: J. C. B. Mohr 1993.

15. Geza Vermes, *Jesus the Jew*, London: SCM Press ²1983 and *The Religion of Jesus the Jew*, London: SCM Press 1993.

16. Bruce Chilton, *A Galilean Rabbi and His Bible*, London: SPCK 1984. For a proto-rabbi of a slightly different kind see Philip Sigal, *The Halakhah of Jesus of Nazareth According to the Gospel of Matthew*, Lanham: University Press of America 1986.

17. Harvey Falk, *Jesus the Pharisee*, Mahwah, NJ: Paulist Press 1985.

18. Burton L. Mack, *A Myth of Innocence: Mark and Christian Origins*, Philadelphia: Fortress Press 1988, and *The Lost Gospel* (n.4). See also the works of Gerald Downing.

19. Crossan, *The Historical Jesus* (n.5).

20. Markus J. Borg, *Conflict, Holiness and Politics in the Teachings of Jesus*, New York and Toronto: Edwin Mellen Press 1984.

21. Robert A. Horsley, *Jesus and the Spiral of Violence*, San Francisco: Harper and Row 1987.

22. E. P. Sanders, *Jesus and Judaism*, London: SCM Press and Philadelphia: Fortress Press 1985, and *The Historical Figure of Jesus*, London: Allen Lane 1993.

23. Graham Stanton, *Gospel Truth*, London: HarperCollins 1995.

24. Marcus Bockmuehl, *This Jesus*, Edinburgh: T.&T. Clark 1994.

25. Tacitus, *Annals* 15,44.

26. For Gamaliel's speech and its importance see Jeffrey A. Trumbower, 'The Historical Jesus and the Speech of Gamaliel', *New Testament Studies* 39, 1993, 510–17.

27. For Judas the Galilean, Theudas and similar figures see Martin Hengel, *The Zealots*, Edinburgh: T.&T. Clark 1989; R. A. Horsley and J. S. Hanson, *Bandits, Prophets and Messiahs: Popular Movements at the Time of Jesus*, San Francisco: Harper & Row 1988; P. W. Barnett, 'The Jewish Sign Prophets – A.D. 40–70. Their Intentions and Origin', *New Testament Studies* 27, 1981, 679–97; Rebecca Gray, *Prophetic Figures in Late Second Temple Jewish Palestine*, New York and Oxford: Oxford University Press 1993.

28. Josephus, *Antiquities* 18.4–10; *Jewish War* 2, 118.

29. *Antiquities* 20, 97–98.

30. *Antiquities* 20, 169–172; *Jewish War* 2, 261–3.

31. *Antiquities* 20, 167–8; *Jewish War* 2, 258–60.

32. *Antiquities* 18, 116–19. For John the Baptist see Laurent Guyénot, *Le Roi sans Prophète*, Pierre d'Angle 1996; Robert L. Webb, *John the Baptizer and Prophet*, Sheffield: Sheffield Academic Press 1991; W. Wink, *John the Baptist in the Gospel Tradition*, Cambridge: Cambridge University Press 1968.

33. Translation by G. A. Williamson revised E. Mary Smallwood, from Josephus, *The Jewish War*, Harmondsworth: Penguin Books 1981.

34. E. Mary Smallwood, for example, expresses the same scorn as Josephus for the 'pseudo-prophets' (*The Jews under Roman Rule*, Leiden: Brill 1981, 257–75).

35. Sanders, *The Historical Figure of Jesus* (n.22), 254. Sanders tends to regard the event as historical.

36. However, the historicity of the incident in the temple is questioned by several exegetes: R. J. Miller, 'The (A) Historicity of Jesus' Temple Demonstration: A Test Case in Methodology', *Society of Biblical Literature 1991 Seminar Papers*, Atlanta: Scholars Press 1991, 234–62; David Seeley, 'Jesus' Temple Act', *Catholic Biblical Quarterly* 55, 1993, 263–83.

37. See also the comparable passages in Matt. 21.12–13 and Luke 19.45–46. John contains a similar episode (2.14–16), but it is put at the beginning of the ministry of Jesus.

38. Craig A. Evans offers other examples in his *Jesus and his Contemporaries*, Leiden: Brill 1995, 367–80.

39. Brandon, *Jesus and the Zealots* (n.12).

40. J. D. Crossan, *Who Killed Jesus?*, San Francisco: HarperSanFrancisco 1995, 39–65.

41. See especially *Jesus and Judaism* (n.22), 61–76, and *The Historical Figure of Jesus* (n.22), 249–64.

42. C. A. Evans, 'Jesus' Action in the Temple: Cleansing or Portent of Destruction?', *Catholic Biblical Quarterly* 51, 1989, 237–70; Boeckmuehl, *This Jesus* (n.24), 60–76.

43. Evans, *Jesus and his Contemporaries* (n.34), 319–44.

44. Kerithoth 1.7. On this point see Bruce Chilton, *The Temple of Jesus*, University Park: Pennsylvania State University Press 1992, 102–3.

45. V. Eppstein, 'The Historicity of the Gospel Account of the Cleansing of the Temple', *Zeitschrift für die neutestamentliche Wissenschaft* 55, 1964, 42–58.

46. Chilton, *The Temple of Jesus* (n.44).

47. Peter Richardson, 'Why Turn the Tables? Jesus' Protest in the Temple Precincts', in *Society of Biblical Literature, 1992 Seminar Papers*, Atlanta: Scholars Press 1992, 507–23.

48. For a detailed discussion of the kingdom of God in the preaching of Jesus see John P. Meier, *A Marginal Jew*, Vol. 2, New York: Doubleday 1994, 237–506; Jacques Schlosser, *La Règne de Dieu dans les dits de Jésus*, Paris: Gabalda 1980. See also the works of Bruce Chilton, especially *Pure Kingdom: Jesus' Vision of God*, Grand Rapids: Eerdmans and London: SPCK 1996.

49. For the notion of the kingdom of God in the Hebrew Bible and the Jewish literature of the end of the Second Temple period see Meier, *A Marginal Jew* (n.48), 237–88 and 'Kingdom of God, Kingdom of Heaven', in *The Anchor Bible Dictionary*.

50. Translation from James H. Charlesworth (ed.), *The Old Testament Pseudepigrapha*, Vol. 1, New York: Doubleday and London: Darton, Longman and Todd 1983, 931f.

51. For these views see Albert Schweitzer, *The Quest of the Historical Jesus* (n.10).

52. J. D. Crossan, *Who Killed Jesus?* (n.40), 49.

53. For the conceptions of the Messiah at Qumran see John J. Collins, *The Scepter and the Star*, New York: Doubleday 1995; Emile Puech, *La Croyance des esséniens en la vie future: immortalité, résurrection, vie éternelle?*, Paris: Gabalda 1993; and the contributions by J. J. Collins, J. VanderKam and E. Puech to Eugène Ulrich and James VanderKam (eds.), *The Community of the Renewed Covenant*, Notre Dame: University of Notre Dame Press 1994.

54. For this important text see Puech, *La Croyance des esséniens en la vie future* (n.53), Vol.2, 626–92.

55. Ibid. and James VanderKam, 'Messianism in the Scrolls', in Ulrich and VanderKam (eds.), *The Community of the Renewed Covenant* (n.53), 215–16.

56. John J. Collins, 'The Works of the Messiah', in *Dead Sea Discoveries*, Vol.1, 1994, 98–112.

57. There is a vast literature on this question. See above all R. Banks, *Jesus and the Law in the Synoptic Tradition*, Cambridge: Cambridge University Press 1975; R. P. Booth, *Jesus and the Laws of Purity*, Sheffield: Sheffield University Press 1986; E. P. Sanders, *Jewish Law from Jesus to the Mishnah*, London: SCM Press and Philadelphia:

Trinity Press International 1990; Geza Vermes, *Jesus the Jew*, London: SCM Press 1983.

58. Jewish scholars who have written on Jesus like Joseph Klausner, Geza Vermes, David Flusser and Shalom Ben Chorin have generally accepted that Jesus was a Jew who observed the law. Among the more distinguished Christian scholars who have adopted this position mention might be made of E. P. Sanders (*Jesus and Judaism* [n.22] and *The Historical Figure of Jesus* [n.22]) and James D. G. Dunn (*The Partings of the Ways*, London: SCM Press 1993).

59. See the Damascus Document (4.12–5.11) and the Temple Scroll (57.17–19) for divorce and the *Jewish War* (2.135) for oaths. We should not forget that according to Malachi (2.16), YHWH hates divorce. It should also be emphasized that divorce and oaths are not biblical commandments. They are simply tolerated.

60. W. D. Davies and D. C. Allison, *The Gospel According to Saint Matthew*, Edinburgh: T.&T. Clark 1988, Vol.1, 566. H. D. Betz puts forward a similar idea in his massive commentary on the 'Sermon on the Mount' (*The Sermon on the Mount*, Hermeneia, Minneapolis: Fortress Press 1995, 214). '. . . Jesus did not proclaim a "new law" (*nova lex*) or a particularly Christian ethic juxtaposed respectively to the Old Law (Jewish Torah) or rabbinic ethics; rather, he expounded what the will of God as revealed in the Torah had originally intended.'

61. In another episode relating to the sabbath the disciples of Jesus pluck ears of corn and eat them on the sabbath (Mark 2.23–27/Matt. 12.1–8/Luke 6.1–5). We should note that this action is attributed to the disciples and not to Jesus. One saying of Jesus is thought to be particularly radical by many exegetes: 'The sabbath was made for man and not man for the sabbath' (Mark 2.27). But rabbinic literature contains similar reflections (Mekilta of Rabbi Ishmael on Exodus 31.13–14; Babylonian Talmud, Yoma 85b).

62. Sanders, *Jewish Law from Jesus to the Mishnah* (n.57), 6–23; cf. also Herold Weiss, 'The Sabbath in the Synoptic Gospels', *Journal for the Study of the New Testament* 38, 1990, 13–27.

63. For a general discussion of the question see David A. Neale, *None but the Sinners*, Sheffield: Sheffield Academic Press 1991.

64. See James D. G. Dunn, 'Echoes of Intra-Jewish Polemic in Paul's Letter to the Galatians', *Journal of Biblical Literature* 112, 1993, 459–77; 'Pharisees, Sinners and Jesus', in *Jesus, Paul and the Law*, London: SPCK 1990.

65. See especially Heikki Räisänen, 'Jesus and the Food Laws: Reflections on Mark 7,15', in *Jesus, Paul and Torah*, Sheffield: Sheffield Academic Press 1992, 127–48.

66. Dunn, *The Partings of the Ways* (n.58), 118.

67. Such reflection is attributed to Yohanan ben Zakkai (Numbers Rabba 19.18).

68. See William Horbury, 'The Temple Tax', in E. Bammel and

C. F. D. Moule (eds.), *Jesus and the Politics of His Day*, Cambridge: Cambridge University Press 1984, 265–86.

6. An Uncertain History

1. Not much trustworthy evidence about the primitive church can be derived from other writings, inside or outside the New Testament. Some exegetes make wide use of the canonical Gospels (above all Matthew and John), Q and the Gospel of Thomas to reconstruct the history of the primitive church. Such works are often highly speculative. The historical information to be found in Eusebius's *Church History* must be used with caution.

2. Questions and problems relating to the letters and life of Paul are discussed in all the books on Paul. The best work on Paul remains that of Johannes C. Beker, *Paul the Apostle: The Triumph of God in Life and Thought*, Philadelphia: Fortress Press 1980; see also J. Murphy-O'Connor, *Paul: A Critical Life*, Oxford: Clarendon Press 1996.

3. Detail additional to this summary can be found in any commentary on the Acts of the Apostles. See, for example, E. Haenchen, Oxford: Blackwell 1974; H. Conzelmann, Hermeneia, Philadelphia: Fortress Press 1987; T. L. Johnson, Sacra Pagina, Collegeville, Minn.: The Liturgical Press 1994; and C. K. Barrett, International Critical Commentary, Edinburgh: T.&T. Clark (Vol. 1 only), 1994. See also the important composite work edited by F. J. Foakes-Jackson and K. Lake, *The Beginnings of Christianity, Part I: The Acts of the Apostles* (5 vols), London: Macmillan 1920–1933.

4. The Pauline aspect of Peter's speech is analysed in François Refoulé, 'Le discours de Pierre à l'Assemblée de Jérusalem', *Revue Biblique* 100, 1993, 239–51.

5. For the Nazirite vow see G. Buchanan Gray, 'The Nazirite', *Journal of Theological Studies* 1, 1900, 201–11.

6. Mark Allan Powell, *What are they saying about Acts?*, Mahwah, NJ: Paulist Press 1991, offers a good summary of the main questions about the Acts of the Apostles. In *Luc le théologien*, Geneva: Labor et Fides 1988, François Bovon surveys works between 1950 and 1982. The books by Jacques Dupont (*Études sur les Actes des Apôtres*, Paris: Cerf 1967, and *Nouvelles Études sur les Actes des Apôtres*, Paris: Cerf 1984) are also very useful. Ward Gasque, *A History of the Criticism of the Acts of the Apostles*, Tübingen: J. C. B. Mohr 1975, offers a history of the interpretation of Acts. Some books are more specifically concerned with the historicity of Acts. Colin H. Hemer (*The Book of Acts in the Setting of Hellenistic History*, Tübingen: J. C. B. Mohr 1989) and Martin Hengel (*Acts and the History of Earliest Christianity*, London: SCM Press 1979) think that Acts is relatively trustworthy. Étienne Trocmé (*Le 'Livre des Actes' et l'histoire*, Paris:

Presses Universitaires de France 1953) is far more sceptical.

7. This approach can still be found in Vol.1 of *L'Histoire de l'Église*, edited by A. Fliche and V. Martin, Paris: Bloud & Gay 1934. Despite the progress in research over two centuries, this history hardly differs from that of Abbé Fleury, which dates from the eighteenth century.

8. Jacques Dupont, *Les Sources du livre des Actes*, Bruges and Paris 1960, reflects the almost universal scepticism. However, M.-E. Boismard and A. Lamouille *(Les Actes des deux Apôtres*, Paris: Gabalda 1990, 3 vols.), have recently made an impressive reconstruction of the sources of Acts. The imperfect homogenization of these sources would explain the sometimes contradictory theological conceptions to be found in Acts. The authors also try to explain the formation of the two principal versions of the text of Acts (Eastern and Western).

9. This is the opinion of Boismard and Lamouille, *Les Actes des deux Apôtres* (n.8).

10. 'On the "Paulinism" of Acts', in L. Keck and J. L. Martyn (eds.), *Studies in Luke-Acts*, Nashville: Abingdon Press 1966.

11. From a considerable literature see Dupont, *Les Sources du livre des Actes* (n.8); Jerome Murphy-O'Connor, 'Pauline Missions before the Jerusalem Conference', *Revue biblique* 89, 1982, 71–91; Paul J. Achtemeier, *The Quest for Unity in the New Testament Church*, Philadelphia: Fortress Press 1987; David R. Catchpole, 'Paul, James and the Apostolic Decree', *New Testament Studies* 23, 1977, 428–44; C. H. Talbert, 'Again: Paul's Visits to Jerusalem', *Novum Testamentum* 9, 1967, 26–40.

12. The chronology of Paul's life is an extremely complex and controversial question. See in particular Robert Jewett, *Dating Paul's Life*, Philadelphia: Fortress Press and London: SCM Press 1979; S. Légasse, *Paul apôtre*, Paris: Cerf/Fides 1994; Gerd Lüdemann, *Paul, Apostle to the Gentiles: Studies in Chronology*, Philadelphia: Fortress Press and London: SCM Press 1984.

13. See the works mentioned in n.11.

14. That is particularly the case with the commentaries on the Letter to the Galatians by F. F. Bruce (Exeter: Paternoster Press 1982) and R. N. Longenecker (Dallas: Word Books 1990).

15. Légasse, *Paul apôtre* (n.12), 83–93 and 153–60.

16. Lüdemann, *Paul, Apostle to the Gentiles* (n.12), 141–57.

17. Henry J. Cadbury, 'The Speeches in Acts', in Foakes-Jackson and Lake, *The Beginnings of Christianity* (n.3), Vol.5, 402–27.

18. Martin Dibelius, *Studies in the Acts of the Apostles*, London: SCM Press 1956.

19. The vision of the primitive church which Luke seeks to impose is linked to two much-discussed elements: the motives behind the redaction of the Acts of the Apostles and the identity of its intended readers. Luke probably wanted to resolve serious problems of identity

affecting his community. One might suppose that this community included both Jewish Christians who were faithful to the law and pagan Christians who respected the Apostolic Decree. However, this community was rejected by the Jewish synagogue and by the Jewish-Christian churches, which required the conversion of the Gentiles to Judaism. These groups would have criticized Luke's community for breaking the law and would have considered Paul, one of its founding fathers, to be an apostate. The criticisms would have led members of this community to ask questions about their situation *vis-à-vis* the tradition of Israel. To reassure them, Luke wanted to show them that Paul had been a pious Jew and that the chief founders of their community were accepted by James and Peter, Jews with an impeccable pedigree.

20. This conception, which can be found in the classical commentaries of Haenchen and Conzelmann (n.3), has been defended more recently by Robert L. Maddox *(The Purpose of Luke-Acts*, Edinburgh: T.&T. Clark 1982) and Stephen G. Wilson *(The Gentiles and the Gentile Mission in Luke-Acts*, Cambridge: Cambridge University Press 1973).

21. Jacob Jervell, *Luke and the People of God*, Minneapolis: Fortress Press 1972, and 'Retrospect and Prospects in Luke-Acts Interpretation', in *Society of Biblical Literature, 1991 Seminar Papers*, Atlanta: Scholars Press 1991, 383–404. See also Robert Brawley, *Luke-Acts and the Jews: Conflict, Apology, and Conciliation*, Atlanta: Scholars Press 1987.

22. We may recall that the other Jameses are the apostle James, son of Alphaeus (Luke 6.15; Acts 1.13), the father of the apostle Jude (Luke 6.16) and the son or the father of the Mary who was present at the crucifixion.

23. Jacob Jervell, 'James the Defender of Paul', in *Luke and the People of God* (n.21), 185–9.

24. S. G. F. Brandon, *Jesus and the Zealots*, Manchester: Manchester University Press 1967, 185–6.

25. Trocmé, *Le 'Livre des Actes' et l'histoire* (n.6), 67–8.

7. *How Can One Be Christian?*

1. For relations between Jews and Gentiles see above all the survey by Louis Feldman, *Jew and Gentile in the Ancient World*, Princeton: Princeton University Press 1993. See also Martin Goodman, *Mission and Conversion*, Oxford: Clarendon Press 1994; P. R. Trebilco, *Jewish Communities in Asia Minor*, Cambridge: Cambridge University Press 1991. The new Schürer (Emil Schürer, *The History of the Jewish People in the Age of Jesus Christ*, revised edition by G. Vermes and F. Millar, Vol. 2, Edinburgh: T.&T. Clark 1979) and the composite work S. Safrai and M. Stern (eds.), *The Jewish People in the First Century*, Assen: Van Gorcum, Vol. 2, 1976, contain much useful

information. The classic work by Jean Juster, *Les Juifs dans l'Empire romain*, Paris 1914, is still indispensable.

2. For this question see the remarks by Martin Goodman in *Mission and Conversion* (n.1), 38–59.

3. See especially Isa. 40.5; 56.6–8; 60.11–14; Micah 4.2–4; Zech. 8.20–23; 14. 16. Joel 4.17 presents an opposite position: foreigners will no longer get to Jerusalem.

4. This is the view defended by Scot McKnight, *A Light among the Gentiles: Jewish Missionary Activity in the Second Temple Period*, Minneapolis: Fortress Press 1991, 47–8.

5. Paula Fredriksen supports this interpretation in 'Judaism, the Circumcision of Gentiles and Apocalyptic Hope: Another Look at Galatians 1 and 2', *Journal of Theological Studies* 42, 1991, 532–64.

6. See esp. Lev. 20.22–26.

7. See e.g. Lev. 17–18; Num. 15.14–16. For these questions see C. Van Houten, *The Alien in Israelite Law*, Sheffield: Sheffield Academic Press 1991.

8. This typology is inspired by Gabriele Boccaccini, *Middle Judaism*, Minneapolis: Fortress Press 1991. See also John J. Collins, 'A Symbol of Otherness: Circumcision and Salvation in the First Century', in J. Neusner and E. S. Frerichs (ed.), *To See Ourselves as Others see Us*, Chico, Ca: Scholars Press 1985, 163–86.

9. James H. Charlesworth (ed.), *The Old Testament Pseudepigrapha*, Vol. 2, New York: Doubleday and London: Darton, Longman and Todd 1985, 98f.

10. See esp. I Enoch 48.4–5; 90.33; Testament of Benjamin 10. 5–10; Testament of Levi 18.2–9; II Baruch 68.5.

11. Charlesworth, *The Old Testament Pseudepigrapha* (n.9), 813.

12. This view, which appears in the classic works of G. F. Moore, J. Jeremias, E. Schürer and many others, went largely unchallenged up to the beginning of the 1980s. Louis Feldman is still the most ardent and convincing defender of the position (see *Jew and Gentile* [n.1]). James Carleton Paget presents a more balanced view in 'Jewish Proselytism at the Time of Christian Origins: Chimera or Reality?', *Journal for the Study of the New Testament* 62, 1996, 65–103.

13. McKnight, *A Light among the Gentiles* (n.4).

14. E. Will and C. Orrieux, *Prosélytisme juif? Histoire d'une erreur*, Paris: Les Belles Lettres 1992.

15. Goodman, *Mission and Conversion* (n.1).

16. There is a vast literature on the godfearers. Cf. e.g. Trebilco, *Jewish Communities in Asia Minor* (n.1),145–66; Shaye J. D. Cohen, 'Crossing the Boundary and Becoming a Jew', *Harvard Theological Review* 82.1, 1989, 13–33; and Irina Levinskaya, *The Book of Acts in its First Century Setting*, Vol. 5, Grand Rapids: Eerdmans 1996. The view of A. T. Kraabel (see his articles collected in J. A. Overman and R. S. MacLennan [eds.], *Diaspora Jews and Judaism*, Atlanta: Scholars

Press 1992), that the notion of the godfearer is a literary and theological invention, has largely been rejected, particularly after the discovery of an inscription at Aphrodisias mentioning godfearers (J. Reynolds and R. Tannenbaum, *Jews and God-Fearers at Aphrodisias*, Cambridge Philological Society, supplement to Vol. 12, 1987).

17. For the adoption of certain Jewish customs by the pagans see Philo (*Life of Moses* 2, 17; 2, 20–24) and Josephus (*Antiquities* 3, 217; *Jewish War* 2, 463; 7,45; *Against Apion* 2, 123; 2, 280–4).

18. According to Cohen ('Crossing the Boundary' [n.16]), those sympathizing with Judaism could adopt any of seven attitudes: admire certain aspects of Judaism; recognize the power of YHWH and integrate him into their pantheon; favour the Jews or be well disposed towards them; practise Jewish rites as a whole or in part; worship YHWH and reject or ignore the pagan gods; rejoin the Jewish community (e.g. by marriage); become proselytes through conversion.

19. According to Donald Juel, 'the Torah forbids social intercourse with non-Jews' (*Luke-Acts*, Atlanta: John Knox Press and London: SCM Press 1983, 106). For Charles Perrot, 'for Jews and pagans to sit together at table was strictly forbidden' ('Les décisions de l'Assemblée de Jérusalem', *Recherches de science religieuse* 69, 1981, 195–208). See Christian Grappe, *D'un Temple à l'autre*, Paris: Presses Universitaires de France 1992, 256–8, and above all Philip F. Esler, *Community and Gospel in Luke-Acts*, Cambridge: Cambridge University Press 1987, 73–86, who presents arguments in favour of this view.

20. Esler, *Community and Gospel in Luke-Acts* (n.19), expounds most of these texts.

21. The classic, but complex, treatment remains that of G. Alon, 'The Levitical Uncleanness of Gentiles', in *Jews, Judaism and the Classical World*, Jerusalem: Magnes Press 1977. See also Francis Schmidt, *La Pensée du Temple. De Jérusalem à Qumrân*, Paris: Seuil 1994; the important article by E. P. Sanders, 'Jewish Association with Gentiles and Galatians 2, 11–14', in R. T. Fortna and B. R. Gaventa (eds.), *The Conversation Continues, Studies in Paul and John*, Nashville: Abingdon Press 1990; Gary R. Porton, *Goyim: Gentiles and Israelites in Mishnah-Tosefta*, Atlanta: Scholars Press 1988, 269–83; Peter J. Tomson, *Paul and the Jewish Law*, Assen and Maastricht: Van Gorcum 1990, 222–36.

22. Sanders, 'Jewish Association with Gentiles and Galatians 2, 11–14' (n.21), 176.

23. For the position of the Pharisaic sages, in addition to the study by Alon (n.21), see Tomson, *Paul and the Jewish Law* (n.21).

24. See e.g. Babylonian Talmud Aboda Zara 8a and Avot de Rabbi Nathan A 26. The 'decree of eighteen things' adopted in the second half of the first century reflects such a tendency. These measures were inspired by the school of Shammai, which was stricter than the rival school of Hillel.

25. See e.g Mishnah (Aboda Zara 5.5), Pesiqta de Rab Kahana 6.
26. See the works by Tomson and Porton mentioned above (n.21). This posiiton is developed in the study by Y.Cohen, *The Attitude towards the Non-Jew in Halakhah and Reality in the Period of the Tannaim* (in Hebrew).
27. See especially Trebilco, *Jewish Communities in Asia Minor* (n.1), and Feldman, *Jew and Gentile in the Ancient World* (n.1).
28. The integration of the Jews of Sardes has been discussed by A. T. Kraabel in various articles.
29. In Peter's vision, God makes it clear that there are no longer any unclean animals, and so all food is acceptable (Acts 10.11–16; 11.5–10). This is evidently the abrogation of the Jewish dietary laws. This vision is difficult to reconcile with what follows in Acts, where the Jewish Christians are always presented as being very faithful to the law.
30. Etienne Nodet, review of *The Impurity Systems of Qumran and the Rabbis, Revue biblique,* January 1995, 123–6.
31. The idea of the conversion of the Gentiles without circumcision has often been attributed to Stephen and the Hellenists, which would explain the persecutions they suffered. Such a theory has very little basis.
32. George Howard (*Paul: Crisis in Galatia*, Cambridge: Cambridge University Press ²1990) thinks that this view was very widespread in the primitive church.
33. To accept the veracity of Peter's vision would make Galatians 1 and 2 and Acts 15 even more incomprehensible.
34. Howard, *Paul: Crisis in Galatia* (n.32), 37–9.
35. Fredriksen, 'Judaism, the Circumcision of Gentiles and Apocalyptic Hope' (n.5).
36. M.-E. Boismard and A. Lamouille, *Les Actes des deux Apôtres*, Paris: Gabalda 1990, Vol. 2, 279–85.
37. However, it is not certain that the Hebrew version of the Bible that we have (the so-called Massoretic text) corresponds to the Hebrew text used by James. In fact in a certain number of cases the Hebrew text of extracts of the Bible found at Qumran is closer to the Septuagint than to the Massoretic text. So we cannot exclude the possibility that James used a Hebrew text the sense of which was close to that of the Septuagint.
38. This text is as follows: '"In that day I will raise up the booth of David that is fallen and repair its breaches, and raise up its ruins, and rebuild it as in the days of old; that they may possess the remnant of Edom, and all the nations who are called by my name," says the Lord who does this' (Amos 9.11–12).
39. For the Apostolic Decree see Marcel Simon, 'De l'observance rituelle à l'ascèse, recherches sur le Décret apostolioque', *Revue de l'histoire des religions* 193, 1978, 27–104; E. Molland, 'La circoncision, le baptême

et l'autorité du Décret apostolique dans les milieux judéo-chrétiens des Pseudo-Clémentines', *Studia Theologica* 9, 1995, 1–39; A. F. Segal, *Paul the Convert*, New Haven: Yale University Press 1990; Terrance Callan, 'The Background of the Apostolic Decree (Acts 15:20, 29; 21:25)', *Catholic Biblical Quarterly* 55, 1993, 284–97; Markus Boeckmuehl, 'The Noachide Commandments and New Testament Ethics', *Revue biblique* 102, 1995, 72–101.

40. Marcel Simon has often emphasized this point. In addition to the article cited in the previous note see Marcel Simon and André Benoît, *Le Judaïsme et le christianisme antique*, Paris: Presses Universitaires de France ⁴1994, 76, 102. Although we have no proof, the possibility cannot be excluded that some synagogues imposed such obligations on the godfearers who attended them. However, the fluctuating and ill-defined character of the notion of the godfearer from a legal point of view makes any generalization very improbable.

41. Boeckmuehl, 'The Noachide Commandments and New Testament Ethics' (n.39), 93–5.

42. Perrot, 'Les décisions de l'Assemblée de Jérusalem' (n.19), 195–208.

43. For the Noachide commandments, in addition to Boeckmuehl, 'The Noachide Commandments and New Testament Ethics' (n.39), and Segal, *Paul the Convert* (n.39), see above all David Novak, *The Image of the Non Jew in Judaism: An Historical Constructive Study of the Noachide Laws*, New York: E. Mellen Press 1983.

44. Boeckmuehl, 'The Noachide Commandments and New Testament Ethics' (n.39), 90.

45. Callan, 'The Background of the Apostolic Decree' (n.39).

46. Perrot, 'Les decisions de l'Assemblée de Jérusalem' (n.19), 199.

47. Christian Grappe (*D'un Temple à l'autre* [n.19], 268–78) thinks that the sole object of the Decree was to allow pagan Christians 'to take part in meetings of their Jewish-Christian brothers without putting their necesary purity in danger'. It is probable that the Decree encouraged contacts, but doubtful that this was its objective.

48. That was certainly easier outside the land of Israel, since there was no obligation to pay the tithes, and the rules of purity, which did not have either the same meaning or the same importance, were largely impracticable in the absence of the temple and its system of purification.

49. The argument that Paul would never have allowed the imposition of constraints derived from the law on pagan Christians is often thought to be decisive. In fact, I Cor. 5–10 suggests the opposite. As Boeckmuehl ('The Noachide Commandments' [n.39], 96–100) and Tomson (*Paul and the Jewish Law* [n.22]) have emphasized, one must not underestimate the influence – even implicit – of the Torah in the ethics applicable, in Paul's view, to the Gentiles.

50. Boeckmuehl, 'The Noachide Commandments and New Testament Ethics' (n.39), 96–100.

51. Some exegetes, including Gerd Lüdemann (*Paul, Apostle to the Gentiles: Studies in Chronology*, Philadelphia: Fortress Press and London: SCM Press 1984, 44–80), think that the incident at Antioch took place before the Jerusalem conference of Acts 15 and Gal. 2.1–10. So this meeting would have served to resolve the conflict at Antioch. This hypothesis is very improbable. It would make the argument of the letter to the Galatians extremely clumsy.

52. For this view see H.-D. Betz, *Galatians*, Hermeneia, Philadelphia: Fortress Press 1979, 112.

53. For this view see J. D. G. Dunn, 'The Incident at Antioch (Galatians 2.11–18)', *Journal for the Study of the New Testament* 18, 1983, 3–57. This article has been reprinted with additional notes in J. D. G. Dunn, *Jesus, Paul and the Law*, London: SPCK 1990, 129–82.

54. Marcel Simon and André Benoît, *Le Judaïsme et le christianisme antique* (n.40), 101. In the same spirit, Marie-Françoise Baslez (*Saint Paul*, Paris: Fayard 1991, 177, 185) thinks that Peter would no longer have eaten kosher. Similarly, Simon Légasse thinks that the Jews converted at Antioch 'no longer took any account of the dietary prohibitions of the Mosaic law' (*Paul apôtre*, Paris: Cerf/Fides 1994, 162). See also Betz, *Galatians* (n.52), 112.

55. Dunn, 'The Incident at Antioch' (n.53), and *The Epistle to the Galatians*, London: A.&C.Black 1993, 115–31.

56. Sanders, 'Jewish Association with Gentiles and Galatians 2, 11–14' (n.21), 185–7.

57. In addition to Dunn, his pupil Nicholas Taylor (*Paul, Antioch and Jerusalem*, Sheffield: Sheffield Academic Press 1992, 123–39) and Craig C. Hill (*Hellenists and Hebrews*, Minneapolis: Fortress Press 1992) defend this type of interpretation.

58. For this sectarian language see J. D. G. Dunn, 'Echoes of Intra-Jewish Polemics in Paul's Letter to the Galatians', *Journal of Biblical Literature* 112, 1993, 459–77.

59. The probable parallelism between the situation at Antioch and that in Galatia is often ignored by exegetes, as Philip Esler has emphasized (*Community and Gospel in Luke-Acts* [n.19], 87–9, and above all *The First Christians in their Social Worlds*, London: Routledge 1994, 52–69).

60. David R. Catchpole, 'Paul, James and the Apostolic Decree', *New Testament Studies* 23, 1977, 428–44. See also P. J. Achtemeier, *The Quest for Unity in the New Testament Church,* Philadelphia: Fortress Press 1987, 58, and Roland Minnerath, *De Jérusalem à Rome. Pierre et l'unité de l'Église apostolique*, Paris: Beauchesne 1994, 216–17.

61. This is the position supported, among others, in the commentaries by F. F. Bruce, H. -D. Betz and R. Longenecker. P. F. Esler (*Community and Gospel in Luke-Acts* [n.19]), Bengt Holmberg (*Paul and Power*, Lund: CWK Gleerup 1978, 32–4), Christian Grappe (*D'un Temple à l'autre* [n.19]) and Francis Watson (*Paul, Judaism and the Gentiles*,

Cambridge: Cambridge University Press 1986) also defend this position.

62. F. F. Bruce, *Commentary on Galatians*, Exeter: Paternoster Press 1982, 130.

63. Robert Jewett ('The Agitators and the Galatians Congregation', *New Testament Studies* 17, 1971, 198–212) has developed the idea that the Jerusalem church progressively hardened its attitude towards the Gentiles under the pressure of zealots who became increasingly aggressive and intolerant. This idea has been taken up in the commentaries by Longenecker and Dunn. Even if Paul in fact criticized Peter for acting out of fear of the zealots, that does not prove that this accusation was justified.

64. Hill (*Hellenists and Hebrews* [n.57], 129–31) has shown just how speculative such an argument is.

65. We may recall that table relations were doubtless easier in Antioch than in the land of Israel.

66. Tomson (*Paul and the Jewish Law* [n.22], 222–36) defends this interpretation convincingly.

67. Bruce Chilton *(A Feast of Meanings*, Leiden: Brill 1994, 93–108) thinks that James had forbidden the participation of pagan Christians in the eucharistic meal because he likened it to a Passover meal. According to the Mosaic law the Gentiles were not authorized to participate in the Passover meal.

68. Scholars generally suppose that James sent emissaries to Antioch to transmit this type of message. However, there is nothing to indicate that this was the object of their visit to Antioch. Perhaps they only became aware of the practice of sharing tables after they had arrived in the city.

69. Watson (*Paul, Judaism and the Gentiles* [n.61], 53–6) and Esler (*Community and Gospel in Luke-Acts* [n.19], 87–9, and *The First Christians in their Social Worlds* [n.59], 52–69) are among the few scholars who think that at Antioch Peter and James closed entry into the Christian community and the way of salvation to Gentiles who had not been circumcised. Francis Watson thinks that the agreement was not abrogated, in that he denies its existence.

70. In the first century the disciples of Jesus did not generally call themselves Christians. The New Testament mentions this nomenclature only three times (Acts 11.26; 26.28; I Peter 4.16). The word is used above all by individuals outside the community of Jesus' disciples. The Roman authorities in Antioch probably coined the term to denote members of the Jewish sect who recognized Jesus as Messiah. The earliest Christian text in which Christians use the term to denote themselves is the Didache, which dates from the last decades of the first century. For this question see Justin Taylor, 'Why Were the Disciples First Called "Christians" at Antioch? (Acts 11.26)', *Revue biblique* 101, 1994, 75–94.

71. The word *ekklesia* did not originally have the connotations generally associated with the church, its usual tradition. *Ekklesia* means, rather, 'assembly', and is a synonym of synagogue.

72. It should be pointed out that Paul does not put this question in precisely these terms, since he never uses the word 'Christian'.

73. This harmonizing interpretation, which can often be found in Catholic exegetes, has recently been put forward by two young Protestant scholars, Hill (*Hellenists and Hebrews* [n.57]) and Taylor *(Paul, Antioch and Jerusalem* [n.57]).

74. W. W. Gasque, *A History of the Criticism of the Acts of the Apostles*, Tübingen: J. C. B. Mohr 1975, traces the history of this interpretation and the controversies that it has provoked. See also G. Lüdemann, *Opposition to Paul in Jewish Christianity*, Philadelphia: Fortress Press 1989, 1–32.

75. Michael Goulder has recently tried to revive the ideas of F. C. Baur in *A Tale of Two Missions*: London: SCM Press 1994. A less extreme position can be found in Lüdemann, *Opposition to Paul in Jewish Christianity* [n.74], and C. K. Barrett (*Paul*, London: Geoffrey Chapman 1994). See Chapter 8, n.75 (p.329).

76. The question of Paul's opponents has given rise to a considerable literature. For a synthesis which is already old see John J. Gunther, *St Paul's Opponents and their Background*, Leiden: Brill 1973. For more recent views see Barrett, *Paul* (n.75), Taylor *(Paul, Antioch and Jerusalem* [n.57]), and J. L. Sumney, *Identifying Paul's Opponents*, Sheffield: Sheffield Academic Press 1990.

77. I employ this term in its incorrect but customary usage, denoting missionaries who incite or force the Gentiles to live as Jews.

78. Paul's opponents seem to have indicated that the apostle himself preached circumcision (Gal. 5.11). They were perhaps referring to the circumcision of Timothy (Acts 16.1–3). According to some exegetes, they were perhaps thinking less of destroying Paul's work than of completing it.

79. Most exegetes accept that the Jewish-Christian missionaries were linked with the church in one way or another (see the commentaries by Bruce, Dunn and Longenecker).

80. Esler and Watson apart, few scholars are ready to accept that the missionaries to Galatia represented the views of James and Peter. Barrett thinks that it is difficult to pronounce on this question.

81. According to the majority of scholars, the Jewish-Christian missionaries of Galatia affirmed that the pagan Christians could gain salvation only by becoming Jewish proselytes. However, we might think that their position was rather that while in theory the salvation of pagan Christians was perhaps possible, in practice it was uncertain. By becoming Jews they would improve their chances.

82. For this see John Barclay, *Obeying the Truth*, Edinburgh: T.&T. Clark 1988, 36–74.

83. For a more detailed and slightly different reconstruction see J. L. Martyn, 'A Law-Observant Mission to Gentiles: The Background of Galatians', *Scottish Journal of Theology* 38, 1984, 307–24. Martyn presupposes a Jewish-Christian mission to the Gentiles independent of that of Paul.

84. In his commentary on the Letter to the Galatians, Richard Longenecker emphasizes the notion of perfection.

85. In basing themselves on Genesis, Paul's opponents were adopting a perfectly logical position.

86. See above all the articles by C. K. Barrett collected in *Essays on Paul*, London: SPCK 1982, and his commentary on *II Corinthians* (London: A.&C. Black 1973). See also Lüdemann, *Opposition to Paul in Jewish Christianity* (n.74); P. W. Barnett, 'Opposition in Corinth', *Journal for the Study of the New Testament* 22, 1984, 3–17.

87. See above all D. Georgi, *The Opponents of Paul in Second Corinthians*, Edinburgh: T.&T. Clark 1987.

88. Although Paul attributes another Jesus and another gospel to his opponents, Nicholas Taylor thinks that he did not have major doctrinal disputes with them (*Paul, Antioch and Jerusalem* [n.57], 210). This is a curious way of interpreting Paul's writings. Jerome Murphy-O'Connor (*The Theology of the Second Letter to the Corinthians*, Cambridge: Cambridge University Press 1991) shows that the differences were far from being trivial.

89. *Clementine Homilies* 17.19.

90. See R. Joseph Hoffmann, *Marcion: On the Restitution of Christianity*, Chico: Scholars Press 1984.

91. Etienne Trocmé, 'Paul-la-Colère: éloge d'un schismatique', *Revue d'histoire et de philosophie religieuse* 61, 1981, 341–50.

92. See especially Hill, *Hellenists and Hebrews* (n.57), 173–8.

93. Paul's thought on the law is particularly difficult to grasp, hence the numerous arguments between experts. H. Hübner thinks that the difficulties relate largely to the fact that Paul's views developed (*Law in Paul's Thought*, Edinburgh: T.&T. Clark 1982). For H. Räisänen, the problems of interpretation are difficult to solve because Paul's letters contain many internal contradictions (*Paul and the Law*, Tübingen: J. C. B. Mohr [2]1987). For a wide range of opinions on Paul's ideas see also Barrett, *Paul* (n.75); Hendrikus Boers, *The Justification of the Gentiles*, Peabody: Hendrickson 1994; W. D. Davies, *Paul and Rabbinic Judaism*, London: SPCK 1948; Dunn, *Jesus, Paul and the Law* (n.53) and his commentaries on Galatians and Romans; L. Gaston, *Paul and the Torah*, Vancouver: University of British Columbia 1987; E. P. Sanders, *Paul and Palestinian Judaism*, London: SCM Press and Philadelphia: Fortress Press 1977 and *Paul, The Law and the Jewish People*, Philadelphia: Fortress Press and London: SCM Press 1983; H. J. Schoeps, *Paul*, Philadelphia: Westminster Press 1961; Segal, *Paul the Convert* (n.39); S. Westerholm, *Israel's Law and the*

Church's Faith, Grand Rapids: Eerdmans 1988.

94. However, by basing themselves largely on Gal. 5.3 ('I testify again to every man who receives circumcision that he is bound to keep the whole law'), some scholars think that according to Paul the Jewish Christians had certainly to continue to observe the law: observance was at least a necessary, if not a sufficient, condition for their salvation. It is nevertheless doubtful whether such a position, which reflects more the ideas of James, could be attributed to Paul.

95. In the realm of ethics Paul was certainly very influenced by the Torah (see Tomson, *Paul and the Jewish Law* [n.21]). In the ritual and ceremonial sphere there is hardly any doubt that Paul, when living with Gentiles, did not observe the law rigorously. But the nature and extent of his 'infringements' remain difficult to determine.

96. Segal, *Paul the Convert* (n.39, above all chs.VI, VII and VIII), shows how Paul's theological positions and his interpretation of the Hebrew Bible could shock his Jewish contemporaries, whether they believed in Jesus or not.

8. James, the First Pope?

1. O. Cullmann, *Peter: Disciple – Apostle – Martyr*, London: SCM Press 1953.

2. As is shown by the impartial book of the Catholic exegete Pheme Perkins *(Peter, Apostle for the Whole Church,* Columbia: University of South Carolina Press 1994).

3. These schemes are inspired by Raymond E. Brown, Karl P. Donfried and John Reumann (eds.), *Peter in the New Testament*, Minneapolis: Augsburg Publishing House 1973, 48–9.

4. This interpretation is to be found in most Catholic church historians and exegetes. See e.g. Roland Minnerath, *De Jérusalem à Rome.Pierre et l'unité de l'Église apostolique,* 1994; Emmanuel Testa, *The Faith of the Mother Church,* Jerusalem: Franciscan Printing Press 1992.

5. Cullmann, *Peter* (n.1).

6. Maurice Goguel, *The Birth of Christianity*, London: George Allen and Unwin 1953.

7. Etienne Trocmé, 'Le christianisme des origines au Concile de Nicée', in Henri-Charles Puech (ed.), *Histoire des religions*, Paris: Gallimard 1972, Vol.2, and *L'Enfance du Christianisme*, Paris: Noesis 1997.

8. Martin Hengel, *Acts and the History of Earliest Christianity,* London: SCM Press 1979.

9. Christian Grappe, *D'un Temple à l'autre*, Paris: Presses Universitaires de France 1992.

10. Authors who develop this type of interpretation are largely inspired by the approach of J. M. Robinson and H. Koester, *Trajectories through Early Christianity,* Philadelphia: Fortress Press 1971.

11. See especially Robert W. Wall, 'Successors to the "Twelve" according

to Acts 12: 1–17', *Catholic Biblical Quarterly* 53, 1991, 628–43.

12. Jacques Dupont, *Nouvelles Etudes sur les Actes des Apôtres*, Paris: Cerf 1984, 159–60.

13. Etienne Trocmé (*Le 'Livre des Actes' et l'Histoire*, Paris: Presses Universitaires de France 1953, 61) thinks that the author of Acts wanted to present 'a Paul independent of James and the Jerusalem church'. If this was the case, he was not sufficiently clear.

14. Richard Bauckham, 'James and the Jerusalem Church', in *The Book of Acts in its First Century Setting*, Grand Rapids: Eerdmans 1995, Vol.4, 427–41.

15. R. Alastair Campbell, *The Elders*, Edinburgh: T.&T. Clark 1994.

16. J. Weiss, *Earliest Christianity*, reissued New York: Harper 1959, Vol.1, 24.

17. Cullmann, *Peter* (n.1), 39.

18. Ibid., 39f.

19. Nicholas Taylor suggests that things got worse after the interview with James (*Paul, Antioch and Jerusalem*, Sheffield: Sheffield Academic Press 1992, 75–83). But perhaps they got worse because of this discussion.

20. Bengt Holmberg, *Paul and Power*, Lund: CWK Gleerup 1978, 14–57.

21. For this difficult question see Hans Dieter Betz, 'Apostle', in *Anchor Bible Dictionary*, and David L. Bartlett, *Ministry in the New Testament*, Minneapolis: Fortress Press 1993, 27–31.

22. James D. G. Dunn, *The Epistle to the Galatians*, London: A.&C. Black 1993, 77.

23. Brown, Donfried and Reumann (eds.), *Peter in the New Testament* (n.3), 31.

24. The position and image of Peter which emerge from the Gospels pose a complex question. There is an in-depth study in Perkins, *Peter, Apostle for the Whole Church* (n.2).

25. Among recent authors defending the authenticity of Matt. 16.17–29 see G. Claudel, *La Confession de Pierre*, Paris: Gabalda 1988.

26. For Matt. 16.17–19, in addition to the book by Perkins and the collective work *Peter in the New Testament*, see: W. D. Davies and D. Allison, *Matthew*, ICC, Edinburgh 1988, Vol.2, 602–52; Grappe, *D'un Temple à l'autre* (n.9), 87–115; B. P. Robinson, 'Peter and His Successors: Tradition and Redaction in Matthew 16.17–19', *Journal for the Study of the New Testament* 21, 1984, 85–104. Arlo J. Nau (*Peter in Matthew*, Collegeville: Matthew Glazier 1992) shows how ambiguous is the image of Peter in the Gospel of Matthew.

27. This pre-eminence has been well shown in Taylor, *Paul, Antioch and Jerusalem* (n.18), 95–122. See also Dunn, *Galatians* (n.22).

28. For this question see Grappe, *D'un Temple à l'autre* (n.9), 87–93. He mentions the parallels with the Qumran writings.

29. Bauckham supposes that the church was governed by seven pillars, of whom only three were present at the Council of Jerusalem ('James and

the Jerusalem Church' [n.14], 447–8). Before the death of the son of Zebedee the pillars will have been Peter, James the son of Zebedee, John and the four brothers of Jesus).

30. Quoted in Eusebius, *Church History*, 2, 23, 7.

31. For the explanations proposed see D. H. Little, *The Death of James, the Brother of Jesus*, Rice University PhD 1971, 16–22.

32. Bauckham, 'James and the Jerusalem Church' (n.14), 448–9.

33. For example Thomas Aquinas, in his commentary on Gal. 2.2, writes that James is named first as bishop of Jerusalem, where the meeting took place. One still finds similar arguments in the very recent book by Minnerath, *De Jérusalem à Rome* (n.4).

34. This pre-eminence has been accepted by Goguel, Trocmé, Brandon, Hengel, Grappe, Hill, Taylor and many other scholars.

35. Hengel, *Acts and the History of Earliest Christianity* (n.8), 119.

36. René Kieffer, *Foi et justification à Antioche*, Paris: Cerf 1982, 81–132, has outlined the history of interpretations of this conflict.

37. Bauckham, 'James and the Jerusalem Church' (n.14), 439–41.

38. Hengel, *Acts and the History of Earliest Christianity* (n.8), 92–3.

39. Cf. especially Martin Hengel, *Between Jesus and Paul*, London: SCM Press 1983.

40. Hengel, *Acts and the History of Earliest Christianity* (n.8), 92–8.

41. In Les *Premiers Chrétiens*, Montreal and Paris: Bellarmin/Cerf 1983, 88.

42. Grappe, *D'un Temple à l'autre* (n.9).

43. Ernest Renan, *Saint Paul*, London: Mathieson 1888, 47f.

44. For the persecutions of the primitive church by the Jewish authorities see especially Paul Fredriksen, 'Judaism, the Circumcision of Gentiles and Apocalyptic Hope: Another Look at Galatians 1 and 2', *Journal of Theological Studies* 42, 1991; Douglas R. A. Hare, *The Theme of Jewish Persecution of Christians in the Gospel According to St Matthew*, Cambridge: Cambridge University Press 1967; Arland J. Hultgren, 'Paul's Pre-Christian Persecutions of the Church, their Purpose, Locale and Nature', *Journal of Biblical Literature* 95, 1976, 97–111; Jack T. Sanders, *Schismatics, Sectarians, Dissidents, Deviants*, London: SCM Press 1993.

45. Sanders, *Schismatics, Sectarians, Dissidents, Deviants* (n.44), 1–30.

46. The traditional interpretation is defended in Marcel Simon, *St Stephen and the Hellenists*, London: Longmans Green 1958. For a criticism of this interpretation see: Craig C. Hill, *Hellenists and Hebrews*, Minneapolis: Fortress Press 1992, 69–82; Edvin Larsson, 'Temple Criticism and the Jewish Heritage: Some Reflexion on Acts 6–7', *New Testament Studies* 39, 1993, 379–95; Dennis D. Sylva, 'The Meaning and Function of Acts 7.46–50', *Journal of Biblical Literature* 106, 1987, 261–75.

47. For this see Hill, *Hellenists and Hebrews* (n.46), 28–31; Hare, *The Theme of Jewish Persecution of Christians in the Gospel According to*

St Matthew (n.44), 20–4; Simon Légasse, *Stephanos*, Paris: Cerf 1992, 205–12.

48. Hill, *Hellenists and Hebrews* (n.46), 101.

49. Oscar Cullmann, 'Courants multiples dans la communauté primitive', *Recherches de science religieuse* 60, 1972, 55–68.

50. Daniel R. Schwartz, *Agrippa* I, Tübingen: J.C.B. Mohr 1990, 119–24.

51. According to Suetonius *(Lives of the Caesars*, Book 5), the Jews were expelled from Rome after troubles fomented by a certain Chrestus. Historians think that Suetonius is referring to troubles due to Christian propaganda. The extent of this expulsion (all Jews or only those adhering to the Christian movement?) and its date (41 or 49?) are the object of disputes among scholars. Schwartz thinks that it took place in 41 and involved only Christians.

52. According to the Byzantine chronicler Malalas, there were serious troubles involving the Jews in Antioch around 39 or 40. Some scholars think that these disorders were perhaps provoked by Christian propaganda (G. Downey, *A History of Antioch in Syria from Seleucus to the Arab Conquest*, Princeton: Princeton University Press 1961, 192–5; Justin Taylor, 'Why Were the Disciples First Called "Christians" at Antioch? (Acts 11.26)', *Revue Biblique* 101, 1994, 75–94).

53. A letter from Claudius to the Alexandrians might suggest the existence of Christian missionary activity in Alexandria at the beginning of the 40s. This activity would have caused trouble. This interpretation, which is often rejected, is thought plausible by Taylor, 'Why Were the Disciples First Called "Christians" at Antioch?' (n.52).

54. From a vast literature see above all the composite work *The Scrolls and the New Testament*, New York: Harper 1957, and Joseph A. Fitzmyer, 'Jewish Christianity in Acts in the Light of the Qumran Scrolls', in L. E. Keck and J. L. Martyn (ed.), *Studies in Luke-Acts*, Nashville: Abingdon Press 1966, 233–57. See also Grappe, *D'un Temple à l'autre* (n.9), 52–69; W. L. LaSor, *The Dead Sea Scrolls and the New Testament*, Grand Rapids: Eerdmans 1972; Matthew Black, *The Scrolls and Christian Origins*, Chico: Scholars Press 1983.

55. The Community Rule and the Damascus Document specify how goods are to be shared. The Damascus Document and to a lesser degree the Community Rule suggest that some members can keep some of their possessions. Many scholars think that the Community Rule regulated the Qumran community, while the Damascus Document laid down the organization of other Essene communities.

56. See the *Lives of Pythagoras* by Iamblichus and Porphyry and Plato's *Republic*. See also D. L. Mealand, 'Community of Goods and Utopian Allusions in Acts II-IV', *Journal of Theological Studies* 28, 1977, 96–7.

57. Brian Capper, 'The Palestinian Cultural Context of Earliest Christian Community of Goods', in *The Book of Acts in its First Century Setting* (n.14), Vol.4, 323–56.

58. Grappe, *D'un Temple à l'autre* (n.9), 56.
59. See Rainer Riesner, 'Jesus, the Primitive Community and the Essene Quarter of Jerusalem', in James H. Charlesworth (ed.), *Jesus and the Dead Sea Scrolls*, New York: Doubleday 1992, 198–234.
60. In the 1950s, Jacob L. Teicher put forward the hypothesis that the Qumran writings had been produced by Jewish Christians with an Ebionite tendency. This hypothesis, generally abandoned by scholars, has been revived by Robert Eisenman, who identifies James with the Teacher of Righteousness.
61. François Blanchetière, 'La "secte des nazaréens" ou les débuts du christianisme', in id. and M. D. Herr (ed.), *Aux origines du christianisme*, Jerusalem 1993, 83–4.
62. Raymond E. Brown and John P. Meier (*Rome and Antioch*, New York: Paulist Press 1983), have tried to classify the first Christians by their attitudes towards the law. They define four categories which are largely determined by questions relating to the Gentiles.
63. Quoted by Eusebius, *Church History* 2, 23, 5–7.
64. Paul in Gal. 1.15 considers that he has been set apart and called by God 'from his mother's womb'.
65. See for example the oppression of the just in Wisdom 2.10. Note also the analogy with James 5.5 ('You have condemned, you have killed the righteous man'), whether this was intended or not.
66. H. D. Betz, *The Sermon on the Mount*, Hermeneia, Minneapolis: Philadelphia 1995.
67. This sort of criticism is typical of the disputes between sectarian movements within Judaism at the end of the Second Temple period. We should not conclude from it that the Pharisees were generally inflexible legalists, with no deep piety or compassion for their neighbours. Nor must we conclude either that this type of individual did not exist. In fact we meet such criticism in rabbinic literature (Babylonian Talmud, Baba Metzia 29b): 'Rabbi Yohanan . . . said: "If Jerusalem has been destroyed, it is solely because people strictly applied the law of the Torah." What else were they to do? Should they have engaged in untried judgments? Certainly not. But they kept strictly to the Torah instead of being concerned to deepen their judgments.'
68. Matthew 23.23, which seems to reflect the same tradition as the 'Sermon on the Mount', suggests that the Jewish Christians scrupulously paid tithes on the most insignificant plants. Contrary to the scribes and Pharisees, they boasted that they observed the most important points of the law without neglecting aspects like tithes on certain plants which they considered secondary.
69. Eusebius, *Church History* 3, 11. Hegesippus is probably the source of his account.
70. Ibid., 3, 20,1–6.
71. Goguel, *The Birth of Christianity* (n.6), 113. For examples illustrating

dynastic Christianity see Grappe, *D'un Temple à l'autre* (n.9), 286–98.

72. Logion 13 of the Gospel of Thomas, which affirms the primacy of Thomas, corresponds more to Matt. 16.17–19, to which it could be a response. Thus Logion 12, certainly older than Logion 13, could precede Matt. 16.17–19.

73. G. Lüdemann, *Opposition to Paul in Jewish Christianity*, Philadelphia: Fortress Press 1989, 158–64.

74. *Panarion* 78.8. For the treatment of James in the *Panarion* see Aline Pourquier, *L'Hérésiologie chez Epiphane de Salamine*, Paris: Beauchesne 1992, 432–8.

75. Scott Kent Brown, *James: A Religio-Historical Study of the Relations between Jewish, Gnostic and Catholic Christianity in the Early Period through an Investigation of the Traditions about James, the Lord's Brother*, PhD thesis, Brown University 1967, 243.

76. Epiphanius, *Panarion* 29.3.

77. *Clementine Recognitions* 1.43.4. *Clementine Recognitions* 1.27–71, which probably dates from the second century, is sometimes – perhaps wrongly – likened to the *Anabathmoi Iakobou* (Ascents of James) mentioned by Epiphanius in his *Panarion* 30.16.

78. According to F. Manns, the fact that Peter does not appear as first bishop of Jerusalem shows that the authority of the bishop was limited ('Liste des premier évêques du christianisme', 155). This is an uncritical way of approaching the history of primitive Christianity.

79. For James as 'pope' see Martin Hengel, 'Jakobus der Herrenbruder – der erste "Papst"', in *Glaube und Eschatologie. FS W. G. Kümmel*, ed. E. Grässer and O. Merk, Tübingen: J. C. B. Mohr 1985, 71–104.

9. *A Strawy Epistle*

1. In the Septuagint, 'servant' (*doulos*) denotes heroes as considerable as Abraham, Moses, Joshua or David.

2. With the exception of some famous exegetes, including Martin Luther, for whom the author of the epistle would be James son of Zebedee. This identification is rarely defended in our day, since the son of Zebedee died too early to be the author.

3. In his commentary published in 1982 (*The Epistle of James*, Exeter: Paternoster 1982, 2–5), Peter H. Davids reported the views expressed in 55 works since the end of the last century: 7 authors think that it is a lightly Christianized Jewish text; 23 in effect attribute it to James; for the 25 others, the letter will have been written after the death of James; however, 7 of these consider that the anonymous author will have composed the letter on the basis of authentic writings of James.

4. This is the view defended in the commentaries by M. Dibelius (*James*, Hermeneia, Philadelphia: Fortress Press 1976), S. Laws, *A Commentary on the Epistle of James* (London: A.&C. Black 1980) and

Jean Cantinat (*Les Epîtres de saint Jacques et de saint Jude*, Paris: Gabalda 1973).

5. R. P. Martin defends this point of view in his recent commentary (*James*, Waco: Word Books 1988).

6. See the commentary by Davids (*The Epistle of James* [n.3]) and the book by J. B. Adamson, *James: The Man and his Message*, Grand Rapids: Eerdmans 1989.

7. The history of the Letter of James is detailed in Adamson, *James: The Man and his Message* (n.6), 147–66.

8. For the dependence of these two writings see the recent commentary by L. T. Johnson (*The Letter of James*, New York: Doubleday 1995, 72–9). Sophie Laws, who thinks it very probable that the Letter of James has influenced the Shepherd of Hermas, judges that the letter will have been composed at Rome at the end of the first century (*A Commentary on the Epistle of James* [n.4], 21–6). However, Laws' conclusions are far from being shared by other scholars, who ask why the letter should have fallen into oblivion in the Latin churches up to the middle of the fourth century.

9. Patrick J. Hartin, *James and the Q Sayings of Jesus*, Sheffield: Sheffield Academic Press 1991.

10. See especially Ben Witherington III, *Jesus the Sage*, Edinburgh: T.&T. Clark 1994, 236–47.

11. J. N. Sevenster, *Do You Know Greek?*, Leiden: Brill 1968.

12. We may note that Sevenster does not believe in the use of a secretary.

13. The profoundly eschatological character of the letter has been emphasized and analysed in Todd C. Penner, *The Epistle of James and Eschatology*, Sheffield: Sheffield Academic Press 1996.

14. Etienne Trocmé, 'Les Eglises pauliniennes vues du dehors, *Jacques* 2, 1 à 3, 13', *Studia Evangelica* 2, 1964, 666–7.

15. See particularly the commentaries by Davids (*The Epistle of James* [n.3]) and R. P. Martin (*James* [n.5]), and Adamson, *James: The Man and his Message* (n.6), 228–58.

16. Josephus, *Antiquities* 20, 180–1.

17. Adamson, *James: The Man and his Message* (n.6), 257.

18. The allusion to 'the early and the late rain' (James 5.7) applies to the climate of Palestine. But it is also compatible with that of Syria.

19. Adamson, *James: The Man and his Message* (n.6), 3–52, 195–227; Davids, *The Epistle of James* (n.3), 19–21

20. Dibelius, *James* [n.4], 116–17.

21. *Pirqe Avot* 6.2.

22. Babylonian Talmud Shabbath 31a, ed. H. Freedman, London: Soncino Press 1938, 140.

23. Translation from James H. Charlesworth (ed.), *The Old Testament Pseudepigrapha*, Vol. 1, New York: Doubleday and London: Darton, Longman and Todd 1983, 817.

24. For the use of Lev.19 in the letter of James see Luke T. Johnson, 'The

Use of Leviticus 19 in The Letter of James', *Journal of Biblical Literature* 101, 1982, 391–401.

25. Such a position is defended in the commentaries by Douglas J. Moo (*James*, Leicester: Inter Varsity Press) and Davids (*The Epistle of James* [n.3]), and in Adamson, *James: The Man and his Message* (n.6).

26. 'The Theology of James', in A. Chester and R. P. Martin, *The Theology of the Letters of James, Peter and Jude*, Cambridge: Cambridge University Press 1994, 37. Stephen G. Wilson defends the same position in *Related Strangers, Jews and Christians 70–170 CE*, Minneapolis: Fortress Press 1995, 154. See also Dunn, *Unity and Diversity in the New Testament*, London: SCM Press ²1990, 251–2; Penner, *The Epistle of James and Eschatology* (n.13), 86–7.

27. Christians must not only listen but act. This theme recurs constantly, as has been noted by Timothy B. Cargal, *Restoring the Diaspora. Discursive Structure and Purpose in the Epistle of James*, Atlanta: Scholars Press 1993.

28. The traditional biblical conception of faith is detailed in numerous works, including H. J. Schoeps, *Paul: The Theology of the Apostle in the Light of Jewish Religious History*, Philadelphia: Westminster Press 1961; E. Urbach, *The Sages*, Cambridge, Mass.: Harvard University Press 1979, 31–6.

29. See especially E. P. Sanders, *Paul and Palestinian Judaism*, London: SCM Press and Philadelphia: Fortress Press 1977, and *Paul, The Law and the Jewish People*, Philadelphia: Fortress Press and London: SCM Press 1983.

30. See J. D. G. Dunn, *Jesus, Paul and the Law*, London: SPCK 1990, and his commentaries on the letters to the Galatians and the Romans.

31. G. Lüdemann, *Opposition to Paul in Jewish Christianity*, Philadelphia: Fortress Press 1989, 140–9.

10. *The Death of a Just Man*

1. The main events of this period are related in Book 2 of Josephus, *Jewish War*, and Book 20 of the *Jewish Antiquities*. See also E. Mary Smallwood, *The Jews under Roman Rule*, Leiden: Brill 1981; Emil Schürer, *The History of the Jewish People in the Age of Jesus Christ*, revised edition by G. Vermes and F. Millar, Vol. 1, Edinburgh: T.&T. Clark 1973; Martin Goodman, *The Ruling Class of Judaea*, Cambridge: Cambridge University Press 1987.

2. The procuratorship of Cumanus was characterized by three serious incidents which could have degenerated into a national revolt. First, a Roman soldier, posted on the portico of the temple during a religious festival, deliberately exposed his private parts in public, which set off a revolt claiming numerous victims. Soon afterwards, an imperial slave was stolen near Jerusalem. As a reprisal, Cumanus had several

villages near to the place of the crime pillaged. During the pillaging a soldier desecrated and destroyed a Torah scroll, which caused a considerable stir. Moreover very violent incidents broke out between the Jews of Galilee and the Samaritans.

3. According to Josephus, Felix himself ordered this crime to rid himself of a troublesome critic *(Antiquities* 20, 162–5). There is no evidence that this is more than rumour.

4. This widely-accepted position is substantiated in A. I. Baumgarten, 'The Name of the Pharisees', *Journal of Biblical Literature* 102, 1983, 411–28. See also Steve Mason, *Josephus and the New Testament*, Peabody: Hendrickson 1992, 176–7. For a contrary view see James S. McLaren, *Power and Politics in Palestine*, Sheffield: Sheffield Academic Press 1991, 151–2.

5. Among the defenders of this thesis see: Craig C. Hill, *Hellenists and Hebrews*, Minneapolis: Fortress Press 1992; D. H. Little, *The Death of James, the Brother of Jesus*, Rice University PhD 1971; Smallwood, *The Jews under Roman Rule* (n.1), 279–80.

6. This position has been defended in particular by: F. F. Bruce, *New Testament History*, New York: Doubleday-Galilee 1980, 372–3; Maurice Goguel, *The Birth of Christianity*, London: George Allen and Unwin 1953; Gerd Lüdemann, *Heretics*, London: SCM Press and Louisville: Westminster John Knox Press 1996, 49–52; Mason, *Josephus and the New Testament* (n.4), 175–81; Etienne Trocmé, 'Le christianisme des origines au Concile de Nicée', in Henri-Charles Puech (ed.), *Histoire des religions*, Paris: Gallimard 1972, Vol.2, 219–20. See also the books by S. G. F. Brandon cited in n.12.

7. The precise nature of this irregularity is disputed. It is also associated with the capacity of the Sanhedrin to pronounce the death sentence. See Douglas R. A. Hare, *The Theme of Jewish Persecution of Christians in the Gospel According to St Matthew*, Cambridge: Cambridge University Press 1967, 19–36; McLaren, *Power and Politics in Palestine* (n.4).

8. Smallwood, *The Jews under Roman Rule* (n.1), 279–80.

9. For the Sadducees and their severity see Jean Le Moyne, *Les Sadducéens*, Paris: Gabalda 1972, 223–43.

10. Origen, *Against Celsus* 1, 47, translated by Henry Chadwick, Cambridge: Cambridge University Press 1953, 43.

11. For this question see Frances Yates, *The Art of Memory*, London: Routledge 1966.

12. For this see S. G. F. Brandon, 'The Death of James the Just: A New Interpretation', *in Studies in Mysticism and Religion presented to Gershom G. Scholem*, Jerusalem: Magnes Press 1967, 57–69. See also his *Jesus and the Zealots*, Manchester: Manchester University Press 1967.

13. Ibid.

14. *Antiquities* 20, 180–1.

15. It is hard to understand why Agrippa II, who was well disposed towards the priestly aristocracy, should have reacted so unfavourably.

16. Especially Luke (7.36; 11.37; 13.31; 14.1) and Acts (5.34–39; 15.5; 21.20).

17. The death of James in Christian tradition is analysed in detail in Little, *The Death of James, the Brother of Jesus* (n.5). See also G. Lüdemann, *Opposition to Paul in Jewish Christianity*, Philadelphia: Fortress Press 1989, 171–81; Wilhelm Pratscher, *Der Herrenbruder Jakobus und die Jakobustradition*, Göttingen: Vandenhoeck & Ruprecht 1987, 229–60; F. Stanley Jones, 'The Martyrdom of James in Hegesippus, Clement of Alexandria and Christian Apocrypha, Including Nag Hammadi: A Study of the Textual Relations', in *Society of Biblical Literature, 1990 Seminar Papers*, Atlanta: Scholars Press, 322–35.

18. *Church History* 2,1,5.

19. Death by blows from staves evokes the punishment reserved for priests officiating despite certain impurities (Mishnah Sanhedrin 18b). For this point see Martin I. Webber, *Origins, Literary Expression and Development of Traditions about the Brother of the Lord in Early Christianity*, PhD thesis, Fuller Theological Seminary 1985.

20. *Church History* 2, 23, 10–18.

21. At all events this is the hypothesis of Lüdemann, *Opposition to Paul in Jewish Christianity* (n.17), 171–7.

22. This is the Second Apocalypse of James, a Gnostic writing found at Nag Hammadi (see Scott Kent Brown, *James: A Religio-Historical Study of the Relations between Jewish, Gnostic and Catholic Christianity in the Early Period through an Investigation of the Traditions about James, the Lord's Brother*, PhD thesis, Brown University 1967), and a passage from the Clementine Recognitions (see F. A. Stanley Jones, *An Ancient Jewish Christian Source on the History of Christianity: Pseudo-Clementine Recognitions 1, 27–71*, Atlanta, Scholars Press 1995, and Rober E. Van Voorst, *The Ascents of James: History and Theology of a Jewish-Christian community*, Atlanta, Scholars Press 1989).

23. Etienne Trocmé, 'Le christianisme des origines au Concile de Nicée', in Henri-Charles Puech (ed.), *Histoire des religions*, Paris: Gallimard 1972, Vol.2.

24. Goguel, *Birth of Christianity* (n.6), 127.

25. Ibid., 131. Goguel writes that Josephus explains the death of James by the jealousy of the high priest. He deduces from Josephus' account the existence of rivalry between Hanan and James. But in speaking of jealousy Goguel does more than interpret Josephus' text.

Conclusion: The Legacy of James

1. The migration of the Jewish Christians of Jerusalem to Pella, one of the cities of the Decapolis situated east of the Jordan, is related in Eusebius, *Church History* (3,5,3). Its historicity has been challenged by several scholars including S. G. F. Brandon (*The Fall of Jerusalem and the Christian Church*, London: SPCK 1951), and G. Lüdemann ('The Successors of Pre-70 Jerusalem Christianity: A Critical Evaluation of the Pella Tradition', in E. P. Sanders [ed.], *Jewish and Christian Self Definition* 1, London: SCM Press and Philadelphia: Fortress Press 1980). It has been defended by M. Simon ('La migration à Pella – Légende ou réalite'?', *Recherches de sciences religieuses* 60, 37–54), C. Koester ('The Origin and Significance of the Flight to Pella Tradition', *Catholic Biblical Quarterly* 51, 1989, 90–106), and F. Blanchetière and Ray Pritz ('La migration des "nazaréens" à Pella', in F. Blanchetière and M. D. Herr (ed.), *Aux origines du christianisme*, Jerusalem 1993, 93–110).

2. Jean Daniélou, *Theology of Jewish Christianity*, London: Darton, Longman and Todd 1964.

3. Maurice Goguel, *The Birth of Christianity*, London: George Allen and Unwin 1953, 137.

4. The twelfth of the eighteen benedictions of the Amidah, a prayer recited three times a day. It will have been adopted in 80/90 by the rabbis meeting at Jabneh. The nature, extent and development of this benediction have been a matter of controversy. Were the Jewish Christians the only ones to be included in it or did it also embrace pagan Christians? Was it initially addressed to Christians? To what degree was it generalized? For these and other questions see R. Kimelman, 'Birkat Ha-Minim and the Lack of Evidence of an Anti-Christian Prayer in Late Antiquity', in E. P. Sanders (ed.), *Jewish and Christian Self Definition* 2, London: SCM Press and Philadelphia: Fortress Press 1981; and, with different conclusions, William Horbury, 'The Benediction of the Minim and Early Jewish Christian Controversy', *Journal of Theological Studies* 33, 1982, 19–61.

5. Jacob Jervell, 'The Mighty Minority', in *The Unknown Paul*, Minneapolis: Augsburg Press 1984, 26–51.

6. For these new views see J. Andrew Overman, *Matthew's Gospel and Formative Judaism: A Study of the Social World of the Matthean Community*, Philadelphia: Fortress Press 1990; Anthony J. Saldarini, *Matthew's Christian Jewish Community*, Chicago: University of Chicago Press 1994; Alan F. Segal, 'Matthew's Jewish Voice', in David L. Balch (ed.), *Social History of the Matthean Community*, Minneapolis: Fortress Press 1992. The commentaries by Ulrich Luz and Davies and Allison to some degree reflect this view.

7. This opinion is represented in S. G. Wilson, *Luke and the Law*, Cambridge: Cambridge University Press 1985.

8. See especially Jacob Jervell, *Luke and the People of God*, Minneapolis: Fortress Press 1972, and id., 'The Mighty Minority' (n.5); also 'Retrospect and Prospect in Luke-Acts Interpretation', in *Society of Biblical Literature, 1991 Seminar Papers*, Atlanta: Scholars Press 1991, 383–404; M. Klinghardt, *Gesetz und Volk Gottes*, Tübingen 1989.

9. Didache 6.3.

10. For the primitive church of Alexandria see Brandon, *The Fall of Jerusalem and the Christian Church* (n.1); Joseph Mélèze-Modrejewski, *Les Juifs d'Egypte de Ramsès II à Hadrien*, 183–6; Colin H. Roberts, *Manuscript, Society and Belief in Early Egypt*, London: Oxford University Press 1977; and the contributions by Birger A. Pearson and A. F. J. Klijn to B. A. Pearson and J. E. Goehring (eds.), *The Roots of Egyptian Christianity*, Philadelphia: Fortress Press 1986.

11. Justin, *First Apology* 31, translation based on Ante-Nicene Fathers, Vol. I, ed. A. Cleveland Coxe, 1885, reprinted Grand Rapids: Eerdmans nd.

12. Justin, *Dialogue* 47.

13. On this text see Luigi Cirillo and Michel Frémaux, *Évangile de Barnabé*, Paris: Beauchesne 1977. See especially the preface by Henry Corbin.

14. Shlomo Pines, *The Jewish Christians of the Early Centuries of Christianity According to a New Source*, Jerusalem 1966. However, S. M. Stern ("Abd Al-Jabbàr's Account of how Christ's Religion was Falsified by the Adoption of Roman Customs', *Journal of Theological Studies* 19, 1968, 128–85) thinks that Pines' theory is simply 'an act of folly which is regrettable on the part of a distinguished scholar'.

15. For the beliefs of the Jewish Christians see: A. F. J. Klijn and G. J. Reinink, *Patristic Evidence for Jewish-Christian Sects*, Leiden: Brill 1973; Ray A. Pritz, *Nazarene Jewish Christianity*, Leiden: Brill 1988; Marcel Simon, *Verus Israel. A Study of the Relations between Christians and Jews in the Roman Empire (AD 135–425)*, Oxford: Clarendon Press 1986; Daniélou, *Theology of Jewish Christianity* (n.2); and Aline Pourkier, *L'Hérésiologie chez Epiphane de Salamine*, Paris: Beauchesne 1992. Apart from Justin, the main Christian authors to mention the Jewish Christian sects are: Irenaeus (*Against the Heresies*), Hippolytus of Rome (*Refutations of All the Heresies*), Origen (*Against Celsus*), Eusebius (*Church History*), Epiphanius (*Panarion*) and Jerome. This evidence has been collected by Klijn and Reinink, *Patristic Evidence*.

16. Epiphanius, *Panarion* 29, and Jerome, *Letter* 112 to Augustine and *Commentary on Isaiah* 8.20–21; 9.1–4; 29.20–21; 31.6–9. It must be noted that Epiphanius expresses doubts about the orthodoxy of the christology of the Nazarenes.

17. Origen, *Against Celsus* 2.1, translated by Henry Chadwick,

Cambridge: Cambridge University Press 1953, 66; Simon emphasizes the importance of this passage in Origen (*Verus Israel* [n.15]).

18. J. D. G. Dunn, *Unity and Diversity in the New Testament*, London: SCM Press ²1990, 237–45.

19. Hans-Joachim Schoeps, *Theologie und Geschichte des Judenchristentums*, Tübingen 1949, and 'Ebionite Christianity', *Journal of Theological Studies* 4, 1953, 219–24. Schoeps has tried to reconstruct the doctrine of the primitive church from the Pseudo-Clementine literature, which is supposed to be inspired by Ebionites. However, the Pseudo-Clementine romance rejects the sacrificial system of the temple, whereas its rejection by James and the primitive church seems improbable. This rejection could have been provoked by the destruction of the temple.

20. Which means that Jesus has attained a superior status not by his birth but by his later election by God.

21. Pritz, *Nazarene Jewish Christianity* (n.15).

22. Jerome, *Letter 112* to Augustine.

23. Epiphanius, *Panarion* 29.7.

24. See Philip S. Alexander, 'The Parting of the Ways from the Perspective of Rabbinic Judaism', in James D. G. Dunn, *Jews and Christians*, Tübingen: J. C. B. Mohr 1992.

25. Schoeps, *Theologie und Geschichte des Judenchristentums* (n.19), 342.

26. See Henry Corbin's preface to *L'Évangile de Barnabé* (n.13), and Pines, *The Jewish Christians of the Early Centuries of Christianity* (n.14). It is worth adding that the influence of the Jewish Christians on Muhammad is a very controversial topic. According to Michael Cook, it is 'the real joker in the pack' (*Muhammad*, Oxford and New York: Oxford University Press 1983, 79).

27. See the letter from Peter to James in the *Clementine Homilies*. In the 'Letter of Clement to James', Clement describes James as 'lord and bishop of bishops'.

28. Letter from Peter to James in *Clementine Homilies*.

29. *Clementine Homilies*, 11.35. See also *Clementine Recognitions* 4.35.

30. *Clementine Recognitions* 1.43.

31. Arnold Ehrhardt, *The Apostolic Succession*, London: Lutterworth Press 1953, 107–8.

Index of Biblical References

Old Testament

Index of Names